D0758046

THEORY, SPORT & SOCIETY

Research in the Sociology of Sport

Series Editors: Joseph Maguire and Kevin Young

Research in the Sociology of Sport reflects current themes in the sociology of sport and also captures innovative trends as they emerge in the work of scholars across the globe. The series brings together research from experts on established topics whilst also directing attention to themes that are at the 'cutting-edge' of this subdiscipline.

This new and exciting series examines the relationships between sport, culture and society. The function, meaning and significance of sport in contemporary societies are critically appraised. Attention is given to both small-scale micro levels of interaction in sport subcultures and also to how these sport subcultures exist within the macro processes reflected in the historical and structural features of societies.

Each volume of *Research in the Sociology of Sport* will have specially commissioned experts examining a common theme. The existing body of knowledge on specific topics will be reviewed, specific aspects will be focussed on and new material highlighted.

Related titles of interest:

Current Perspectives in Social Theory
Studies in Symbolic Interaction
Studies in Qualitative Methodology

For further details visit the Elsevier Science Catalogue at *http://www.elsevier.com*

THEORY, SPORT & SOCIETY

EDITED BY

JOSEPH MAGUIRE

Loughborough University, Leicestershire, UK

KEVIN YOUNG

Loughborough University, Leicestershire, UK

2002

JAI
An Imprint of Elsevier

Amsterdam – Boston – London – New York – Oxford – Paris
San Diego – San Francisco – Singapore – Sydney – Tokyo

ELSEVIER B.V.
Radarweg 29
P.O Box 211, 1000 AE
Amsterdam, The Netherlands

ELSEVIER Inc.
525 B Street
Suite 1900, San Diego
CA 92101-4495, USA

ELSEVIER Ltd
The Boulevard
Langford Lane, Kidlington,
Oxford OX5 1GB, UK

ELSEVIER Ltd
84 Theobalds Road
London WC1X 8RR
UK

First edition 2002
2nd impression 2005

Library of Congress Cataloging in Publication Data
A catalog record is available from the Library of Congress.

British Library Cataloguing in Publication Data
A catalogue record is available from the British Library.

ISBN: 0-7623-0742-0
ISSN: 1476-2854 (Series)

Working together to grow
libraries in developing countries

www.elsevier.com | www.bookaid.org | www.sabre.org

ELSEVIER   BOOK AID
             International   Sabre Foundation

♾ The paper used in this publication meets the requirements of ANSI/NISO Z39.48-1992 (Permanence of Paper).

Transferred to Digital Printing 2005

*For **Eric Dunning** –*
sociologist, supportive critic, colleague, friend

Contents

Preface

If the promise of sociology is the ability to explain and predict social events and patterns, as well as to broaden our understanding of social issues and realities (Ritzer, 1992), then the promise of the sociology of sport must likewise be to do these things with respect to sports-related behaviours, processes, structures, systems, and experiences. This can only be achieved by moving beyond the descriptive level to the theoretical level. At this point in its subdisciplinary life, the sheer range of sociological theories utilised in the sociology of sport is expansive, and our understanding of sports-related phenomena, though by no means complete, is improving at an impressive rate.

In juxtaposition to Alan Klein's 'insider' view on the "moribund" state of affairs in another sports-related subdiscipline — anthropology (see Chapter 6) — the sociology of sport appears to be in good health. Some excellent journals, a surprisingly large number of regional, national and international organisations, and many recognised professional meetings, are some of the fruits of labours committed by, at this point, several generations of scholars interested in studying sport sociologically. While the often empiricist early phases of sociology of sport (where sport *per se* often tended to take priority over the sociological tools for examining it) have not gone unnoticed, it is fair to say that the subdiscipline has come a long way in the last four decades, and that much of this success is due to the innovative ventures of scholars working out of a growing number of theoretical camps.

The sociology of sport may still be viewed with some justification as a subfield in its infancy (Ingham & Donnelly, 1997), but it is clear that the sweep of theoretical approaches brought to bear on sports-related behaviours, processes and structures is no less impressive here than in other subdisciplinary fields often attributed greater maturity and sophistication. This is not to suggest strong homogeneity or parity between and among the approaches adopted in the subdiscipline, nor to suggest that all approaches have been used at the same rate, at the same time, or indeed that they have attracted the same appeal. For example: some theories are simply more pronounced in their use than others (e.g., since the 1980s, variants of post-structuralism and cultural studies have been widely adopted on both sides of the Atlantic (see Chapters 7, 15 and 16), while the use of structural functionalist approaches has waned noticeably (see Chapter 2)); some have been more pronounced than others at different stages of the development of the subfield (e.g., the ascendancy of feminist approaches has echoed the mainstream shift to gender-sensitive perspectives since the 1970s — see Chapters 5 and 13); some have had more of a lasting impact than others (e.g., arguably, varieties of Marxism and branches of 'interpretive' sociology stemming originally from the work of Weber and Mead have left what Beamish calls "enduring legacies" in the subdiscipline — see Chapters 1, 3, 4, 7, 12, 15, and 16); some perspectives appear to be coming into their own and increasing in popularity (e.g., changes perceived to have occurred in an increasingly "fragmented" and "global" world have persuaded some scholars of the merits of a turn to postmodernism — see Chapter 8); and other perspectives, despite great promise, have been curiously under-utilised, in our view to the detriment of the subfield as a whole (e.g., though becoming more widely used in a number of international settings including Asian countries, figurational sociology has until recently been largely ignored by North American scholars — see Chapters 9 and 13).

The already difficult issue of measuring relative contribution and proportional representation in the subfield is made none the easier by the fact that few, if any, of the approaches discussed in *Theory, Sport & Society* are monolithic, but rather are internally varied, even contradictory. This can be seen in the more orthodox versions of Marxism emphasising economic matters as opposed to the more contemporary Marxist concern with the effects of ideology and culture, in the often dissonant strands of feminist thought, and in the miscellaneous adaptations of structural functionalism. There are further complications. As Ritzer (1992, p.508) has noted: "It is abundantly clear that many sociological theories are now borrowing from one another and cutting across multiple levels of social analysis, with the result that the traditionally clear borders between theories are growing increasingly blurred and porous." However, what seems important to emphasise, as numerous scholars (e.g., Coakley, 2001) before us have done, is that no theory 'has all the answers', and that every theory contains strengths and weaknesses, albeit to a greater or lesser extent.

When we initially solicited chapters for this anthology, we asked contributors to keep student readers in mind and to write as clearly and accessibly as possible, while of course maintaining attention to detail and rigour. We asked this because, in our experience, it is impossible to teach sociology and not know that students tend to view theory as complex, dry and intimidating (Hadden, 1997, p.11). Theory is something that almost all students seem to anticipate with trepidation. We have found that it is this sense of dread that makes students go out of their way to postpone their theory classes until the last possible moment, ironically depriving themselves of the opportunity to better understand the subject matter of the 'easier' courses they select in the interim (as a university-taught subject, statistics tends to suffer the same fate). To be sure, sociological theory can be complex and, regrettably, certain theorists are well known for a writing style that obfuscates as much as it clarifies. Add to this an admittedly jargon–laden discipline, the possibility of unimaginative and abstract pedagogies, and one can begin to appreciate the problems and fears theory elicits in students. But theory need not be so inaccessible or menacing. For instance, using Booth and Loy's notion of the 'classic thinkers as exemplary colleagues', so much of modern sport can be readily understood by students.

Whether it is examining performance-enhancing drugs in sport using Weber's notion of 'instrumental rationality' (see Chapter 3), exploring sport systems as state and political tools, or the injured or exploited athletic body as a source of alienation (see Chapter 1), or understanding sports-based identities and careers as outcomes of complex interaction rituals (see Chapter 4), we believe that 'classical' sociological thinking is possible for all students, including introductory students. Similarly, more contemporary theoretical options provide incisive and student-friendly tools for understanding such things as football-related disorders and globalising trends (see Chapter 9), the ways that some social class groups and cultural settings seem more 'naturally' predisposed to certain sport and recreational endeavours than others (see Chapters 6, 7 and 10), ways in which body shape and exercise practices are 'controlled' by social images, norms and obligations (see Chapter 12), the complex ways in which sports and sport experiences reflect clusters of people 'networked' together (see Chapter 11), and the ways in which new sports stadia's location and construction interface with the desires of local power elites (see Chapter 14). In brief, students otherwise intimidated by the task may become engaged in theoretical sociological pursuits through the judicious use of illustrations and issues that gel with concrete and meaningful parts of the world they observe around them. After all, to borrow from Marx, what resonates most with people is their 'practical life-activity'. None of the aforementioned examples is complicated or unpredictable, but these sorts of straightforward connections are imperative if more considered engagement is to follow. Again, the chapters in this volume are replete with such connections.

Theory, Sport & Society is the opening volume in a new series entitled *Research in the Sociology of Sport*. With both students and colleagues in mind, we wanted to kick-start the series with a review of some of the principle theoretical perspectives that have been used to throw light upon the sports process. Inevitably, as editors and researchers, we bring to the constellation of sociological perspectives discussed here our own theoretical tastes. For one of us (e.g., Maguire, 1999), this has meant exploring the assets of a figurational approach while, for the other (e.g., Young, 1993), neo–Marxist and cultural studies approaches have been preferred. However, we undertook this project from the position that seeing sociological theories as mutually exclusive or as exhaustive entities unto themselves was neither a helpful nor, indeed, particularly sociological point of view. Working once more with the nuts and bolts of the varied perspectives represented in this anthology, and especially in comparing and contrasting between them, has only strengthened our resolve on this matter.

The process of editing is conventionally understood in terms of a number of tasks — collating, sifting, ordering, smoothing. Editing certainly involves these things, but it is also a process of re-evaluation, re-consideration, and reflection. As such, the journey on which this anthology has taken us has been revealing, and we would like to thank each of the contributors for providing us with the opportunity to re-consider our own work, past and present, in light of the perspectives before us. Specifically, while we have been aware that we were, at times, blending aspects of figurational sociology and cultural studies with, for example, symbolic interactionism or elements of feminist thinking (Maguire, 1992; Maguire *et al.*, 2002; Young and White, 1995), the full richness and potential of each of these and other perspectives had, in truth, eluded us. On the other hand, this process has also provided us with the opportunity to reassess theoretical approaches we find less compelling, less fruitful, indeed less sociological. We return to this matter in the Introduction.

Taken together, the chapters in *Theory, Sport & Society* provide a comprehensive, though by no means exhaustive, review of some of the main theoretical perspectives that have been used to date in the sociological study of sport. Both classical and contemporary approaches are represented, as are a number of cross-theoretical endeavours that take seriously the aforementioned notion that no single theory can claim to 'have all the answers'. It is our hope that in considering the various perspectives students and researchers of sport will not only receive an impression of the richness and breadth of explanatory thinking the subdiscipline has to offer, but be better able to apply such thinking to the sports processes and social relationships that concern them the most.

References

Coakley, J. (2001). *Sport in Society: Issues and Controversies*. London: McGraw Hill (7th edition).

Hadden, R. (1997). *Sociological Theory: An Introduction to the Classical Tradition*. Peterborough, Ontario: Broadview.

Ingham, A. G., & Donnelly, P. (1997). A sociology of North American sociology of sport: Disunity in unity, 1965–1996. *Sociology of Sport Journal, 14*(4), 362–419.

Maguire, J. (1992). Towards a sociological theory of sport and the emotions: A process–sociological perspective. In: E. Dunning and C. Rojek (eds), *Sport and Leisure in the Civilising Process: Critique and Counter–Critique* (pp. 96–120). London: Macmillan.

Maguire, J. (1999). *Global Sport: Identities, Societies, Civilizations*. Cambridge: Polity Press

Maguire, J., Jarvie, G., Mansfield, L., & Bradley, J. (2002). *Sport Worlds: A Sociological Perspective*. Champaign, IL: Human Kinetics.

Ritzer, G. (1992). *Contemporary Sociological Theory*. London: McGraw Hill (3rd edition).

Young, K. (1993). Violence, risk, and liability in male sports culture. *Sociology of Sport Journal, 10*(4), 373–396.

Young, K., & White, P. (1995). Sport, physical danger, and injury: The experiences of elite women athletes. *Journal of Sport and Social Issues, 19*(1), 45–61.

Acknowledgements

As with any endeavour of this kind, this book would not have been possible without the assistance of a number of people. We would like to thank the contributors to *Theory, Sport & Society* for their patience and flexibility while we waited for final chapters to arrive and editorial suggestions to be incorporated. For their guidance and support at various stages of the project, we are indebted to Ann Marie Davenport and Lesley Roberts at Elsevier Press. Suzanne Whyman and Michelle Berry assisted with the preparation of portions of the manuscript; many thanks to both. We are particularly indebted to the students we have taught whose sociological curiosities have led them to prod and challenge on theoretical matters. Their comments and queries over the years have not only reminded us of our own uncertainties where theory and indeed sociology are concerned, but have proven to be priceless in forcing us to work through tough but fair challenges on the perspectives to which we ourselves are inclined. Last but not least, we would like to take this opportunity to thank Eric Dunning. While we have been influenced by many people over the course of our careers, neither of us is aware of any other sociologist, nor indeed colleague, with a deeper commitment to his/ her craft. If, over the twenty plus years we have known Eric, just a small portion of his immense knowledge of the field and understanding of the import of theory has rubbed off, our sociological imaginations will be all the richer.

Introduction

'Back to the Future':
Thinking Sociologically about Sport

Joseph Maguire and Kevin Young

At first glance, the rationale underpinning this book is to bring together, for the first time, experts examining sport from a wide range of sociological perspectives. In doing so, this collection provides an overview of the vibrant theoretical debates contained within and between different perspectives when applied to sport (see also Jarvie & Maguire, 1994). As such, we believe this collection will be of benefit to students and teachers alike. Within the book's structure and these introductory remarks, however, lies our second programme. This book is an invitation to those involved in the sociology of sport to restructure their imaginations, to reconsider the ways in which they think and speak about sport, culture and society.

If the contributions to this collection are any indication, the sociology of sport is a buoyant and lively subdiscipline, where rich and insightful research is taking place. However, our invitation to re-thinking and re-envisioning stems from what we see as two main dangers to the sociological study of sport. Navigating through these dangers requires us to reconsider what constitutes the craft of 'good' sociological practice. We must return from whence sociological theory came, we must go 'back to the future', revisit the roots of sociological enquiry and, in so doing, examine our craft, and aspirations.

What, then, are the dangers we detect? The first is the threat of being tied too closely to the 'here and now' and providing solutions to short-term problems. We must resist the siren voices that promote the 'applied knowledge' perspectives of sport management, sport policy, and the pedagogy-sport science industrial complex more broadly. These modes of enquiry typically focus attention on short-term 'social problems', and specific 'interest groups', in an often unreflective and atheoretical manner. They 'steal our clothes' — and, arguably, the academic positions of the next generation of our students. The critical and sceptical character of sociology of sport is lost. Questions of power become neglected. In not challenging this trend in our departments, universities

Theory, Sport & Society
Copyright © 2002 by Elsevier Science Ltd.
All rights of reproduction in any form reserved.
ISBN: 0-7623-0742-0

and associations, we under-estimate the danger that lies therein. As a subdiscipline, sociology of sport could wither in the academy and follow the academic trend towards becoming the mouthpiece of the sports industry and the status quo.

A second threat to a *sociological* study of sport, we believe, arises from the relativism associated with elements of post-modern thinking and speaking, which leads to the denial of the possibility of verifiable, cumulative, reliable social knowledge (Tilly, 1997). This, as Tilly notes, narrows the mission of the social sciences to advocacy and social criticism. In addition:

> It undercuts all interpersonal procedures for assessing the relative validity of competing propositions about social life in general or in particular. It attacks any claim of superior knowledge and thereby removes all justification for the existence of social science as a distinctive enterprise (Tilly, 1997: 29).

The generation of fundamental knowledge that is of potential benefit to humanity as a whole is neglected, and the grounds on which social scientists can critique the sporting status quo are reduced to a question of ideological soundness.

The practice of sociology of sport has not been unaffected by these twin dangers. Both need to be confronted. If not, as Tilly argues, "social science runs the risk of squandering the brains of a talented generation" (Tilly, 1997: 29). With this in mind, both this collection and Introduction should be viewed as attempts to address these dangers, and a move towards new possibilities and syntheses for the sociology of sport enterprise. Let us expand our argument to consider, first, the need for sociological theory. Second, we will examine the qualities involved in thinking with theory. Third, we will explore the characteristics of good sociological craft. Finally, we will briefly highlight the structure of the book and the many lines of argument it contains.

Why do we need Sociological Theory?

The study of sport is embedded in sociological theory. Indeed, we are making the case that to study sport without theory is to simply describe and reproduce the status quo. We see theorising as a process involving several interdependent and mutually reinforcing features. Theory can be understood, variously, as a 'resource of hope', a guide and compass, a friend and colleague, a data set and companion, a craft, and a life-long apprenticeship. Let us examine each of these in turn.

In their chapter on Weber, Hart Cantelon and Alan Ingham refer to the concepts of rationalisation and 'iron-cage'. As Cantelon and Ingham highlight, Weber's work provides us with a rich set of insights into how students of the sociology of sport can "make sense of the techno–bureaucratic world in which we live". By providing us with the tools of interpretation, theory can help us to understand the limits and possibilities in our lives, placing biography in the context of larger historical processes and social structures. Indeed, theory can be understood as a form of scaffolding by which we build explanations about the social world we inhabit. This enables us to understand that our everyday ways of life are not natural and inescapable, but are socially constructed. To paraphrase Karl Marx, people make their own history but in situations not of their own choosing. Theory helps us understand how, in the remaking of history, the present has emerged out of the past.

In reviewing the current state of play in sport we can use theory to help us see that humanity does not have to remain locked into the prevailing performance efficiency model forever (Maguire, 2001). Rather, theory can form what Cantelon and Ingham call the "resources of hope for the next generation", enabling us to think of new models of sport and body cultures. If theory is a resource of hope, it is also a companion and a guide. John Loy and Douglas Booth, in their chapter on Durkheim, highlight how theory can act as a form of data, allowing the reader to learn by restating systematically what specific theorists have argued. This process involves a dialogue between the past and the present, and allows a re-imagining of the future. As colleagues and role models, theorists allow us to recapture a sense of discovery, to see their work, in Weber's sense, as a 'vocation', and to understand both their vision and their craft. In making the case for reading the classics, Loy and Booth cite Sherman who argues that students should "give each paradigm a fair hearing". Sherman (1974: 180) justifies this by concluding, "to know fully what I am doing, I need to know what I am not doing that I could be doing; in other words, I must know the opportunity costs. And for that, I must read the Masters".

Yet, as noted, it is not only a question of reading the 'classics'. Sociological theory as a 'structured whole' demands attention. This is not simply a question of broadening one's knowledge and expanding the data available. Theory needs to be read with a view to grasping its underlying sociological structures, to capturing the continuities and differences between theorists and within theories. Thinking and engaging with a structured account of theory allows the student to see how the sociological enterprise has emerged and developed. In addition, this approach allows students to examine the craft of different sociological practices. Reading theory as a collective whole has distinct advantages.

Jarvie and Maguire (1994) make this point with respect to the work of Pierre Bourdieu. His work is both 'good to think with' itself, and that in thinking with and in opposition to his work, the sociological study of sport is enhanced. The same argument applies to reading sociological theory more generally. Theories need to be read not just as isolated perspectives, but as elements in an ongoing conversation. Bourdieu, in addressing this very point, observed:

> If, for example, you take the relations between Weber and Marx ... you can view them in another way and ask how and why one thinker enables you to see the truth of the other and vice versa. The opposition between Marx, Weber and Durkheim, as is ritually invoked in lectures and papers, conceals the fact that the unity of sociology is perhaps to be found in that space of possible positions whose antagonism, apprehended as such, suggests the possibility of its own transcendence. It is evident, for instance, that Weber could see what Marx hadn't because Marx has seen what he had ... Every sociologist would do well to listen to his/her adversaries as it is in their interest to see what he/she cannot see, to observe the limits of his vision, which by definition, are invisible to him (Bourdieu, in Jarvie & Maguire, 1994: 184).

Note that Bourdieu is referring here to the unity of sociology that can be only grasped when a 'rounded' approach to the study of sociological theory is adopted. Considered in this way, theories need to be read in clusters or groupings — with the underlying aim of seeing linkages as well as differences. Sociological theory can, in this sense, act as a compass, as a guide. It cannot, and should not, provide 'the answers'. That is, answers are not ready-made, but are the products of the interplay between theory and evidence, one of the hallmarks of good practice we will discuss later. Theory does, however, allow us to know which questions have to be asked and which questions are worthwhile asking. It also enables us to put such questions in the right order or sequence — thus allowing us to conduct 'good' sociological craft and practice.

Reference to sociological theory can therefore allow us to know what the discipline already has asked, thought about and reflected on. In making sense of the present, we have to know what we, as a sociological community, already know — we need to have a finely tuned time-space sensitivity. That is, students would be well advised to avoid what Norbert Elias described as the 'retreat of sociologists to the present'. Elias was referring to the tendency of sociologists to view their subject matter as concerning the 'here and now' — without reference to how it has emerged out of the past. Likewise, without a knowledge of how the subject of sociology, and the sociology of sport has emerged, sociologists overlook how we all stand on the shoulders of others (Elias, 1971: 165). From fellow theorists and colleagues we can learn an already acquired fund of knowledge which can thus be extended by the collective endeavour of groups of social scientific communities (Elias, 1971). These issues raise a complex set of questions concerning sociology of knowledge and the development of a fund of sociological knowledge about sport.

These observations may sound deceptively simple but go to the heart of the debate concerning theory and knowledge. We acknowledge the important contribution of Thomas Kuhn (1970) to our understanding of 'scientific revolutions' and paradigm shifts. In particular, his work skilfully situates knowledge development in its social context. What we dispute is his over-emphasis on 'discontinuities'. In contrast, stress is placed here on the need to trace the historical development, and sociological conditions, under which sociology and its subdisciplines, such as the sociology of sport, emerged; that is, how it developed, and accumulates, a measure of 'reality-congruent', relatively adequate knowledge about sport worlds. Reality-congruent knowledge refers to how what we produce is not the 'truth', but an approximation of how the social world really is.

Any given body of knowledge (including the sociology of sport) is then derived from, and is a continuation of, a very long process of knowledge acquisition of the past and can only be explained as part of the wider development of the societies where knowledge develops (Elias, 1971: 158–159). In making this argument, we believe that this tends to reinforce our view about the need to read theory, and to read theories in the manner to which Bourdieu and Sherman direct our attention. Theory is not only a guide and compass, it is an 'exemplary colleague'.

Here is not the occasion to detail the full significance of the perspective outlined of the sociology of sport knowledge base. Yet, in making the case for the need to read sociological theory 'in the round', one crucial addition to the argument must be made. No one specific piece of research, or particular perspective, produces 'the truth' — including this work. This should not, however, lead the reader to conclude that all theories or specific research is of equal value. It is appropriate to point to the ideological components of sociological theories — such baggage is, to a degree, unavoidable. Yet, it is also necessary to highlight the growth of non-ideological knowledge and how such knowledge is built upon, and advances or degrades previous generations' attempts to comprehend sport, culture and society. We would rather not rehearse, once again, the debate between the truth and falsity of knowledge — that is the false dichotomy evident in the absolutist and relativist positions.

A way out of this quandary is to view the contents of this book, for example, as reflecting the existing and potential fund of relatively adequate knowledge available within and between perspectives. Rather than think that 'everything's equal', we believe that social scientists have produced knowledge that is, in specific respects, superior to other accounts of sport worlds. For example, the knowledge gained by social scientists about football hooliganism is far superior to that provided by government agencies or the media. Indeed, the pioneering work of the 1970s and 1980s, by a range of sociologists from different sociological traditions, represents a 'breakthrough' in our collective understanding of the roots of violent confrontations of this kind.

We will have more to say in the next section on how relatively adequate knowledge of this kind reflects and reinforces an overall structure of sociological theory. For now, let us reinforce the case being made with reference to what Elias argued in this connection:

> What practising scientists test if they examine the results of their enquiries, both on the empirical and the theoretical level, is not whether these results are the ultimate and final truth, but whether they are an advance in relation to the existing fund of knowledge in their field. In scientific, though not in moral matters, the concept of 'truth' is an anachronism; criteria of advance, though not yet highly conceptualized, are widely used in the practice of the sciences. They form a central issue in any non-relativistic sociological study and theory of knowledge (Elias, 1971: 158).

From such insights it is possible to make the case for the production of relatively adequate knowledge. That is, while in specific respects the knowledge produced by social scientists is superior to that of others, and indeed that some social scientific accounts are more or less adequate compared to each other, we do not believe that we are producing the 'truth' in some simple sense. As noted, the goal is to produce an approximation of the truth — in doing so we have to better develop criteria by which we judge how adequately research captures how things really are. In the pursuit of producing 'reality-congruent' and relatively adequate knowledge, a host of related questions arise, concerning involvement and detachment, praxis, stand-point epistemology, and ideological commitment. The contributors to this collection, to put it mildly, deal with these issues in different ways. Close examination of the chapters reveals that colleagues cover the range of positions associated with the absolutist and relativist continuum. Not all will share our approach. Yet, one problem faces all of them in their practice as sociologists of sport — the marginality of the subdiscipline. That is, sociologists experience what has been termed 'double-jeopardy' or, indeed, 'triple-jeopardy' (Bourdieu, 1988; Maguire, 1990).

For Bourdieu, several obstacles to a scientific study of sport stem from the fact that sociologists of sport are 'doubly-dominated', both within the field of sociologists and in the arena of sports people. As Maguire (1990) noted, 'fellow sociologists seem to treat the subject with disdain and sports people despise us'. It is safe to assume that over the past decade, despite some exceptions, sociologists have failed to emancipate themselves from the discipline's dominant value system in which primacy is given to work and the other so-called 'serious' aspects of society. Leisure is confined to the 'non-serious' sphere. Rarely, if ever, is discussion of sport provided in introductory sociology texts. Equally, a deep suspicion exists among the sport community towards sociological research in general. Critics of what happens on and off the sports field are seldom welcomed. Thus, the dangers to which we referred earlier are compounded by this double jeopardy. The process of doing sociology of sport is not an easy one! Yet, as noted, a third jeopardy exists. If students adopt a sociological approach that is currently unfashionable, that has not kept pace with the discourse in vogue, and/or focuses less on short-term social problems, and more on sociological problems, then they will suffer a sense of triple-jeopardy. They will be pushed to the margins of the subdiscipline. Has this not been the fate of the classics? Will it also be the fate of sociological theory *per se*?

Thinking with Theory

One of the problems that students encounter with sociological theory and its application to sport is how to make sense of the competing claims of different perspectives. How are they to navigate a route through a veritable maze of concepts, discourse and evidence? In our teaching and involvement in the area we have become convinced that sociology, and by implication, sociology of sport, needs to provide itself with some criteria by which to make sense of the structure and organisation of theory. In addition, there is a need to develop guidelines on how to connect the insights of theory to the empirical in order to make knowledge claims about the real world. What follows, then, is an attempt to outline some of the obstacles that make the task of developing such criteria and guidelines more difficult. On this basis, we will also seek to identify some of the signposts that can be used to map out sociological theory. That is, we are concerned to trace the conditions of fragmentation and *unity* (Johnson *et al.*, 1984: 1).

In attending conferences, reading journals and teaching classes, we have been struck by how advocates of different perspectives compete for academic space and appear to talk past each other. No doubt, we too have contributed to this noise! Yet, despite one of us drawing primarily on a figurational/process sociological perspective, and the other on a neo–Marxist, cultural studies position, we have, over time, become aware of some of the assumptions about sociological theory that we hold in common. One of these assumptions concerns the basis on which students can engage with sociological theory. Let us explain what this entails.

In outlining the terms on which a more fruitful rendezvous with sociological theory can occur, a number of 'fallacies' (Baert, 1998) and 'enemies' (Stones, 1996) prevent this engagement from fully developing. The first fallacy is that of 'perspectivism' — that is, no yardstick exists that would enable us to judge and compare between theories. Taken to its extreme, a similar logic could apply to research conducted within a perspective. Neither is satisfactory. Differences between social theories cannot be reduced to mere differences in emphasis or subject-matter. The main yardsticks by which theories can be judged and compared are intellectual depth, originality, analytical clarity and internal consistency (Baert, 1998: 7). While these are useful pointers, and indeed would serve the student well in appraising the contributions to this book, they do not exhaust the possible benchmarks by which the research acumen and sociological quality can be judged. Others include the link between theory and evidence, the roles of involvement and detachment, adequacy of evidence, and styles of writing and communication. This issue will be dealt with more fully when we consider some of the hallmarks of 'good' sociological practice.

A second fallacy that is also an obstacle to a fruitful engagement with theory is that of 'externalism'. That is, reviewers present external criticisms of the author's work. Competing sociologists are sometimes prone to review books, and/or submissions to journals on the basis of what has *not* been accomplished — even though the researcher sought to do something else. It is sometimes more appropriate to evaluate theories from within — to consider their internal consistency. Too often critiques construct 'straw men'. Yet, 'internal' critique is a necessary, but not sufficient step. We suggest that external critique is possible and desirable. Johnson *et al.* (1984) point to the possibility of detecting the underlining structure of social theory — it is this structure that allows theory to be compared and contrasted.

Some commentators commit what is termed the 'political fallacy' — that is, they criticise theories for their potential or actual effects on socio–political matters. For Baert (1998: 8), "the identification of possible or actual consequences of a theory should not normally interfere with the intellectual appreciation of the theory". Such an observation goes directly to the debate concerning the purpose and social worth of sociological knowledge. Should we judge the worth of a theory, or a particular piece of research, simply by its contribution to a cause whose side we are on (Gouldner, 1970)? Alternatively, should not the accumulation of sociological knowledge be concerned with the production of research for the benefit of humanity as a whole? In making sense of the contributions to this book, the reader would be advised to also bring these questions to the fore.

In seeking to more fruitfully engage with theory, several opponents can be identified that prevent the development of guidelines by which to structure sociological theory. Two alternative responses to the present state of theory can be seen as inadequate and misguided. One is the 'complacency of sociological modernism', the other is the 'defeatism of elements of post-modernism' (Stones, 1996). We wish to steer a path between these two positions. Sociological modernism, with its excessive belief in positivism and the generalisability of natural science methods, both underestimates the rich complexity and diversity of the social world, and correspondingly overestimates the ability of sociologists to obtain accurate and truthful knowledge about that world. Sociologists are cast as the 'experts' who can 'know the truth'. Such thinking deserves to be treated with the scepticism it receives (Tilly, 1997). Following the tradition of C. Wright Mills (1959) and others, the postmodern turn has rightly questioned 'conventional wisdom' on social scientific accomplishments. Equally, the debunking motif contained within postmodern writing correctly highlights the taken-for-granted assumptions concerning sport, culture and society. And, such writing continues the long-standing sociological tradition of stressing the role that theory can play in acting as a spur and a guide to social action and intervention (Tilly, 1997: 26). There is much in the postmodern critique that rightly builds on the traditional stock of sociological knowledge.

Notwithstanding this, there are also dangers in the current discourse, and similar sentiments are sometimes expressed in the sociology of the sport arena. In expressing legitimate concerns regarding both the existence of coherent social processes, and the accessibility of social processes to systematic knowledge (and thereby raising questions of ontology and epistemology), we appear to have ended up in a situation where there are several potential drawbacks. These unduly restrict students' engagement with theory, and include, according to Tilly:

> [the] failure to erect criteria and procedures for the falsification of arguments; unclear criteria for priority among competing analyses; uneasy statement of ontological and epistemological premises; and, hence, abandonment of cumulation as a goal and an actual outcome of social inquiry (Tilly, 1997: 26).

Are we to conclude, therefore, that all knowledge claims are equally as good, as far as accuracy and truth are concerned? For example, is the account provided by the marketing and media departments of Nike with regard to their operations in Southeast Asia as valid as that provided by sociologists such as George Sage (1999) and others? Furthermore, as a sociological community, have we not learned, can we not now learn, build on, develop and accumulate more relatively adequate knowledge about sport worlds? Whilst modernist knowledge claims must be treated with the scepticism that Tilly highlights, and which each generation and approach brings to bear, it is also possible, however, that knowledge accumulation can 'go into reverse'. We may end up not knowing what we once did. We may end up not standing on the shoulders of giants after all!

How do we therefore work our way out of these conceptual snares and the false dichotomy between positivism and relativism? The first step is to develop some basic concepts about the world and how to find out about it. In making this case we will, in the thinking of some, have succumbed to 'foundationalism' (Stones, 1996: 3). Yet, the case we make here does not claim to be the truth, beyond all doubt or criticism. Indeed, it could also be rejected as inadequate. In one sense, we would be happy if alternative scaffolding is developed, which is relatively more adequate than that which we can suggest here. Our goal is more modest. We suggest that in thinking with theory, and using it in the study of sport, such scaffolding is a necessary feature of the research process. If others arrange such scaffolding in a different, more coherent pattern, and this pattern addresses some of the key issues highlighted, then we would be content. The research process is akin to building a house — such scaffolding allows you to collect, assemble and connect the parts. Some designs are less stable than others, and some types of projects require different configurations. Such tasks require a careful adherence to the craft skills involved. Whatever the specific design, for us, the need for scaffolding of some kind has become self-evident.

So far, the case has been made for theory. It has been suggested how theory or theorising enters into any sociological analysis of sport. Thus, by implication, it is being argued that in thinking with theory, the student must be aware of a range of theories, noting connections and differences and how their work builds on a tradition of sociological knowledge. This now brings us to the larger question of the structure of sociological theory.

The Structure of Sociological Theory

It is possible to argue that there is a structure to sociological theory that must be discerned and understood by all students. In doing so, students' understanding and deployment of theory to grasp the real world will be far better grounded. Given this, we share with Johnson *et al.* (1984: 5–6) the view that:

> The proliferation of theoretical schools or 'paradigms' in sociology is, and has been, an *orderly* one; there are crucial questions and issues to which all competing theories attend, and thus pre-suppose. This underlying unity in the sociological enterprise can be reconstructed, and, as a result, competing theoretical traditions can be compared with each other systematically.

If such observations have substance, as we will attempt to show that they do, then it is possible to indicate the "directions theoretical sociology ought to pursue as a corrective to the sources of fragmentation" (Johnson *et al.*, 1984: 6). This will be attempted in the following section, but such sentiments also find expression in the way this book is constructed. The reader should also see how theories within and between sections of this collection link to and build on other theories.

From what has so far been argued, it is clear that any sociological analysis of sport cannot but bring into play a whole body of theorising about the nature of society, and social action, and the generation of knowledge. This collection seeks to capture the diversity of theorising evident in the sociology of sport. Yet, we are also keen to emphasise that such theorising has a structure. This patterned process of knowledge generation derives from the fact that all sociologists pose certain fundamental questions, the answers to which are pre-conditions for sociological enquiry. At bottom, these questions seek to discover the nature of social reality and how it is possible to obtain knowledge. As Johnson *et al.* (1984: 12–13) observe:

> We are suggesting that whenever and wherever sociological analysis is carried out, some kind of answer to both questions is implied: the investigation of social relations logically entails such 'theorising', whether it is recognised by the investigators or not. If it is the case, then, that sociology cannot be carried out except in terms of certain arguments, beliefs, or assumptions about what it *is* that is being studied, and how it is we can obtain valid knowledge about it, then it follows that these questions and the answers to them provide us with a basis or framework, in terms of which we can understand or 'make sense of' any particular sociological enterprise.

It is to this framework, or scaffolding, that we wish to direct the attention of students. Answers to the basic questions posed by Johnson *et al.* (1984) revolve around two polar alternatives. Is the nature of social reality material or ideal? Is it possible to know this reality through the means of nominalism or realism? These issues are dealt with in greater depth by writers such as Severyn Bruyn (1966). The concern here, however, is to note that Johnson *et al.* (1984: 16) propose a four-fold classification that "provides a basis for analysing the structure of theoretical sociology". We concur. In order to trace the structure of sociological theory, it is necessary to detect the general forms in which answers to these questions have been formulated. As Johnson *et al.* (1984: 18) go on to argue:

> The various combinations of solutions to the questions generate four broad strategies of sociological theorising. These strategies and their inter-relationships provide the basis for understanding different and competing theoretical projects in the social sciences.

The four broad strategies are empiricism, substantialism, subjectivism and rationalism. How each relates to the core questions already identified can be illustrated with reference to Figure 1. Empiricism combines the strategies of materialist and nominalist solutions. Empiricists purport to view the social world

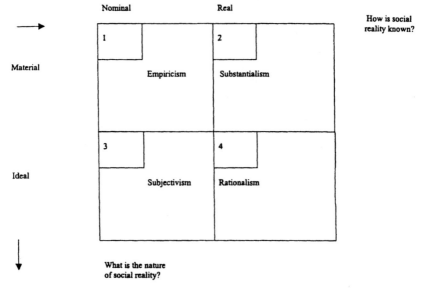

Figure 1: The Structure of Sociological Theory–Johnson *et al.* (1984: 19).

as directly reflected in the senses of the observer. Subjectivism combines the idealist and nominalist solutions and includes those views that understand the social world as an outcome of the interpretative acts of individuals. Substantialism is a strategy that combines materialist and realist solutions, viewing the social world as an objective material structure of relations. Finally, rationalism arises out of a combination of the idealist and realist solutions and understands society as an objective and constraining structure of ideas.

There is much merit in this analysis of the structure of sociological theory and we recommend that students use such an approach in engaging with theory. Although we will not attempt here to 'assign' the different contributions contained in this collection to these strategies, we recommend such a task to the reader. Each perspective arguably reflects these core questions, solutions and answers. Yet, some qualifications need to be made, both to what has been proposed, and how it can be applied to the structure of sociological theorising evident in the sociology of sport.

There is a danger of over-simplification in outlining the structure of sociological theory in this general overview (see Figure 1). We are aware that all theory does not fit neatly into such positions. As Johnson *et al.* (1984: 22) observe:

> We have chosen the term 'strategy' carefully in order to refer to an active, constructive process of theorising in which the alternative resolutions constitute a *field of tensions* rather than established unmoving positions. Thus, theorising in sociology tends not to be the sole product of one or another of the boxes — empiricism, subjectivism, substantialism, or rationalism — but the product of the field of tensions that operates across the axes.

Reviewing the work in sociology of sport in general, and the arguments contained within this collection in particular, it is clear that while theorists may favour one of the strategic resolutions outlined, they do so in conjunction with, or in opposition to, the issues posed by alternative positions. There are, then, both 'pulls' and 'pushes' in the interrelations between the strategies, which result in particular theorists drifting from one to another. This process is not only an ongoing feature of theorising, but it is also desirable. To repeat, as we noted earlier with reference to Bourdieu, "every sociologist would do well to listen to his/her adversaries as it is in their interests to see what he/she cannot see, to observe the limits of his vision" (Bourdieu, in Jarvie & Maguire, 1994: 184).

The strategies identified do not reflect individuals' unique solutions to complex questions of theory. Viewing these strategies as the isolated resolutions of the fundamental problems of sociological theorising misses the point. Such strategies are systematically related to one another and are part of the ongoing accumulation of knowledge by entire communities of individuals (Elias, 1971). It is these interdependent processes of sociological theorising that give rise to its complexity. This network of theorising leads to diversity and unity. In seeking to capture this structure of theorising, Johnson *et al.* are to be complimented. Such an endeavour is both worthwhile and fruitful. In this collection we have not sought to privilege any one strategy or perspective. We wish each approach to speak and think for itself.

It is our view, however, that students will gain more from the collection if these contributions are read, as noted earlier, 'in clusters', as 'a whole', and with reference to the common problems that all sociologists confront. In this way, students will be in a better position to identify the common structure of choices. As well, their own subsequent solutions can build on what is already known and do so in relation to other alternatives — within the field of tensions outlined. It is also our view that such common problems require an approach that seeks a 'synthesis' beyond the confines of one strategy. Hence, the final section of this collection provides a range of possible syntheses. There are other possibilities. If we have avoided the temptation to privilege any one synthesis, let us now be bolder and suggest some hallmarks of what we see as the craft of good sociological practice.

The Craft of Good Sociological Practice

Research within the sociology of sport shares with other branches of sociology a preoccupation with several kinds of analysis. These include the need to describe events, search for patterned recurrences and principles of variation, and identify causality (Tilly, 1997: 25). Clearly, the way sociologists go about this search, and the emphasis they give to these kinds of analyses does vary across strategies and perspectives. Yet, students should keep the debate about these kinds of analyses at the fore of their research design. Following the lead of Johan Goudsblom (1977), we would also suggest that the concepts of precision, systematics, scope and relevance should also be used as 'sensitising concepts' in developing a rationale for a sociological craft. This is what Goudsblom (1977: 198) had to say on the issue:

> The concepts of precision, systematics, scope and relevance . . .
> refer to real problems experienced by real people: problems of
> acquiring precise information; of finding clear and consistent

principles of classification and explanation; of grasping the wider implications of events; of knowing how to make their knowledge of some avail in arranging their lives. They refer, in other words, to problems of orientation in the social world.

That is, sociologists of sport would do well to accumulate knowledge that was precise in its factual references, systematic in its manner of classification and explanation, far-reaching in scope, and relevant to a variety of purposes.

Examination of the production of sociological knowledge of the kind to which Goudsblom refers is therefore necessary. Following the insights provided by C. Wright Mills, among others, Robert Alford's (1998) work highlights how the process and craft of enquiry should begin with an understanding of the position of the researcher relative to the matter at hand. The student/researcher must begin the enquiry by probing how research questions arise as much from elements of their own history, biography and social life, as from their interactions with theory. For Alford (1998: 133) "sociology is a craft, a set of skilled practices that occur in a social context". The craft of sociological enquiry involves, then, a set of tools for the production of knowledge. Several key issues involved in this craft can be identified.

Theory and Evidence

Both in the formulation and execution of research, the sociologist is confronted with the relationship between theory and evidence. Following on from what has already been argued, we would suggest that the craft of sociology necessitates steering between the imposition of 'grand theory' onto evidence, and abstracted empiricism, seemingly uninformed by theoretical insight. For us, the processes of theory formation and empirical enquiry are interwoven and indivisible. A constant interplay between the mental operations directed at theoretical synthesis and at empirical particulars is part of the ongoing craft of the sociologist. This is in no small part due to the recognition of the mutual contamination of theory and evidence. As such, it commits researchers to a rather agile life in which they must work on the empirical without dominating it with theory and, at the same time, develop insights firmly informed by evidence (Abrams, 1982). An uninterrupted two-way traffic takes place in such a skilled practice (Elias, 1983).

Involvement and Detachment

In conducting an enquiry in which the theoretical and empirical modes are indivisible, it is essential to come to terms with the fact that the research craft is also dependent upon processes of involvement and detachment. Students will more usually encounter the debate that follows in terms of the perceived dichotomy between objectivity and subjectivity. Here we want to take a different tack. Involvement and detachment are complementary indicators of the direction of knowledge processes (Elias, 1987: xxi–xxii). Let us address this issue in greater detail.

In setting out to explore the patterns they form together and the character of the networks that bind them to each other, sociologists must recognise that they are also part of this social world. They cannot escape it. Indeed, they must not try to do so. Their very participation and involvement is itself one of the qualities implicated in the craft of comprehending the world they seek to study. That is, sociologists must develop the skills by which they probe how their fellow human beings experience their worlds. At one and the same time, the sociologist-as-participant must be able to stand back and become the sociologist-as-observer-and-interpreter. In performing these tasks, what guidelines can be offered?

First, the researcher must maintain the two-way traffic between theory and evidence to which we have already referred. Second, the sociologist should keep in mind that her/his skills involve being a hunter or destroyer of myths — disrupting the non-reality congruent knowledge (such as racist stereotypes) that informs aspects of people's understanding of social worlds (Elias, 1978: 52). Third, the adoption of a long-term and comparative perspective allows sociologists a greater capacity for distancing themselves, for a while, from the situation at hand (Elias, 1987). This is the part of the craft that counters the tendency to 'retreat to the present' and the adoption of today-centred thinking (Goudsblom, 1977). Fourth, in seeking to avoid perceiving today's world as either timeless and immutable, or as radically different in some postmodern sense, sociologists must think about, and express, their research findings in processual terms (Abrams, 1982; Elias, 1983; Smith, 1991). In reviewing Elias's work, Johann Arnason neatly captured what we have in mind:

> [Elias's] line of reasoning is as opposed to the mainstream theory of modernization as it is to the current diagnoses of a post-modern condition. Elias's challenge to the idea of modernity is not an attempt to show that it has run its course, exhausted its potential and/or discredited itself. Rather, he tries to destroy it from behind

by reducing it to the temporary surface effect of a long-term process (Arnason, 1987: 438).

In following such a strategy, and in refining the skilled practice that this entails, the sociologist must avoid static, non-relational concepts and words. Instead, the use of a personal pronoun model (I–We–Us–Them) can be employed to better represent the set of co-ordinates in terms of which human groupings and societies can be plotted (Goudsblom, 1977). In stressing this need for relative involvement/detachment, both the individual sociologist and the sociological community must make the effort to develop the human/group capacity for observing, for its own sake, social worlds as structured processes. We are reminded of how Cantelon and Ingham highlight in Weber's work the need to see 'sociology as a vocation'. The craft of self-distancing also entails, arguably, the use of particular types of questions and the adoption of specific styles of writing. This is something that will be returned to shortly. At this stage, attention must be given to another facet of the research craft — namely, the issue of the adequacy of evidence.

The Adequacy of Evidence

Several possible problems lead to inadequate research. Inadequacies in research may stem from not only a distorted conception of the making of social structured processes, but may also be a function of the sources utilised, or the interpretation of this evidence. Evidence can, of course, be gleaned by a variety of methods. Irrespective of which approach is adopted, there is always a need to question its status and the ability of researchers to capture 'how it really was, or is'. In archival work, for example, there is no such thing as an innocent text. Texts are produced and survive in a social context. Nor do the facts simply speak for themselves. Whereas, by necessity, analyses have to view the past through the 'narrow' and 'misty lens' of what particular writers thought, felt, and wrote, the researcher is still required and, as argued earlier, *able* to assess how blurred the image actually is. In some respects, the task is to subvert or escape from the ways of thinking and feeling in which the documents were conceived. The aim is to provide an account that is more adequate and more consistent, both internally and in relation to other areas of knowledge, than previous accounts.

The assessment of the relative adequacy of evidence is therefore dependent on establishing the precise pattern of interdependency between classes and other groups. Central in this regard is the balance of power between them. Hence, the analysis should focus on both the level of participation by the observers of the particular events in question, and on the pattern of tension and conflict evident in the relationship between observers and observed. The forms of distortion that permeate evidence are dependent on particular circumstances. The insider's account will provide, sometimes inadvertently, the minutiae and emotional resonance of what is being examined. The outsider's account is likely to provide a more detached view but may be distorted as a result of bias, such as class or gender bias, or lack of detailed knowledge. An analysis, therefore, ideally needs both, but when it is not possible, *verstehen* analysis based on the relative positions of groups can be used (see Chapter 3). Identification with the 'we' perspective of different groups is necessary in order that the researcher understands something of the sense in which certain actions are 'meaningful'. At the same time, it is necessary to grasp that no matter how sincere, these interpretations can be misleading. Comparison of different 'we' perspectives will help, but the employment of 'they' perspectives, which show the situation from a greater distance, offers a different vista on how the actions and intentions of the various groups are interlocked.

Explaining and Going Public

The task of sociology, as argued earlier, is not only to generate substantive research, but also to explain the status, selection and interpretation of such 'facts' as part of a more general endeavour of enlarging our understanding of the various ways in which people are interconnected. This strategy reflects the structure of sociological theory outlined and involves an "interpretative arranging of the facts" (Abrams, 1982: 310). To argue this is not to impose some over-arching theory onto the evidence, but rather involves researchers in an attempt to come to terms with the mutual contamination of theory and evidence and to continually probe the adequacy of their findings. In this regard, consideration must be given to several interrelated issues.

In 'going public' with their findings, researchers must conduct a dialogue between what Abrams (1982: 10–11) sees as the interwoven styles of *narrative* and *theoretical* writings. The power of research springs from the synthesis achieved in these types of explanations. But the actual method employed to communicate one's findings, making it public, is dependent on the manner in which the research has been conducted. In attempting to explore structured processes, it is necessary to employ different sets of questions. 'How it happened' questions allow for the probing of the manifold, sequential and cumulative nature of structuring and the capturing of how 'it really was'. But, on their own, they are not enough. Questions are needed which enable the sociologist to assess the significance of events and to consider their relation to a course or chain of other events. The emphasis is on the craft of the sociologist to judge, interpret, explain and make sense of research in a detailed, substantive manner. Exemplars of such work in the sociology of sport include Dunning and Sheard (1979), Fine (1987), Klein (1991), Gruneau (1983), and Hargreaves (1994). This does not exhaust the possible list! The use of questions that reflect the interweaving of theory and evidence enables the researcher to consider the processes that gave or denied people their opportunity for achievement and fulfilment.

Explaining how the event happened is necessary but not sufficient. It is also necessary to make clear what sort of event it was at that moment in time. The skilled sociologist does this at three levels: the short-term day-to-day phenomena (events); the patterning of action within the flow of such events; and the points at which such patterning reinforces and reflects the ongoing structural features of time-space relations. At each of these levels, the researcher must probe the prevailing balance of power between and within groups, and the pressure and constraints felt and exercised by these groups. But these levels must be viewed as being interwoven. Explanation turns in equal measure on identifying and describing the actions of, and relationships between, participants and providing a coherent theorising of the structured processes at work.

The Structure of the Book

We have divided *Theory, Sport & Society* into four parts. Part I covers what we have termed 'Classical Questions'. Here, classic sociological theorists such as Karl Marx, Emile Durkheim, Max Weber and George Herbert Mead are reviewed. Each of the chapters brings alive the contribution of these sociological 'masters'. While approaching their respective theorists in quite specific ways, all are concerned to emphasise the importance for students to read these theorists, for they pose classical questions that still have resonance today. Part II shifts attention to what we term 'Contemporary Concerns'. Here, the contributions of several more recent approaches are evaluated. These include feminism, anthropology, cultural studies and postmodernism. Each contributor is keen to highlight how their respective approach helps make sense of contemporary concerns that face us all in our increasingly globalised world. In doing so, they also raise important questions regarding the nature and purpose of sociological enquiry.

In Part III, we have drawn together several contributions that offer what we regard as 'Potential Syntheses' of basic questions in sociological theory such as the individual and society. The approaches selected do not exhaust the range of possible theoretical syntheses. We selected contributions derived from the work of Norbert Elias, Pierre Bourdieu, Michel Foucault and Social Network Theory because they reflect the range of possible perspectives available, and because they have been applied quite extensively to the study of sport. Each of the writers provides a robust case for the merits of the kind of synthesis they see as representing a different vision of theorising and future sociological development. Part IV sets out to look to this future. We were conscious that we wanted scholars who would examine possible future directions that sociology of sport could, or would, take. These contributors sometimes blend or draw on two or more sociological approaches. They pull together the structure of sociological theory and engage in theorising in the manner we wish to promote. In Part IV, then, we see contributions that combine feminism and figurational sociology, the work of urban and sport studies, symbolic interactionism and cultural studies, and finally, research derived from subcultural theory and the sociology of the body. By structuring the collection in these ways, we have sought to capture the diversity of theorising within the sociology of sport. Given the quality and richness of the work produced, we feel that this aim has been achieved. Our additional goal was, as noted at the outset, to offer an invitation to those involved in the sociological of sport to restructure their imaginations, to reconsider the ways in which they think and speak about sport, culture and society. We think that the contributions provided within each part assist in this process. We urge students to read such work in clusters and to make the connections within and between them.

Conclusion

That sport is sociologically worthy of study seems, to us, beyond dispute. We write this neither to praise, nor blame, the present state of sport worlds. Our observation that sociologists of sport experience a sense of 'double-jeopardy' should not dishearten newcomers to the field. As a phenomenon, for better and for worse, sport cannot be avoided. Large numbers of people across the globe enjoy it, revel in its positive dimensions, or are exploited by the power elite and set of social practices that underpin and characterise it. Sport worlds have major cultural, economic, social and political significance.

In seeking to comprehend this significance, we have made the case for theorising, for *thinking* with sociological theory. *Theory, Sport & Society* contains broad and varied theoretical insights and visions. In bringing this collection of scholars together, our goal has been to capture the lively nature of the sociology of sport and to highlight the need to think and speak sociologically about sport. This involves, for researchers and sport performers alike, a craft, a skilled practice of what we, as a community already know, and what we can know through the work of others and by our own research endeavours. We hope that the knowledge generated through such practices is of benefit not simply to specific groups, but also to humanity as a whole. To echo the words of Cantelon and Ingham, we also wish that in this way the sociology of sport community can serve as a 'resource of hope for the next generation'. With such a goal in mind, we offer this book as a contribution to the fund of relatively adequate knowledge. Now, to paraphrase Mills, (1959: 123): Theorists, 'get to work'!

References

Abrams, P. (1982). *Historical Sociology*. Shepton Mallet, Somerset: Open Books.

Alford, R. (1998). *The Craft of Inquiry*. New York: Oxford University Press.

Arnason, J. (1987). Figurational sociology as a counter–paradigm. *Theory, Culture & Society, 4*, 429–456.

Baert, P. (1998). *Social Theory in the Twentieth Century*. Cambridge: Polity Press.

Bruyn, S. (1966). *The Human Perspective in Sociology*. Englewood Cliffs, NJ: Prentice-Hall.

Bourdieu, P. (1988). *In Other Words: Essays Towards a Reflexive Sociology*. Cambridge: Polity Press.

Dunning, E., & Sheard, K. (1979). *Barbarians, Gentlemen and Players: A Sociological Study of the Development of Rugby Union*. Oxford: Marten Robertson.

Elias, N. (1971). Sociology of knowledge: New perspectives. *Sociology, 5*(2), 149–168 and *5*(3), 355–370.

Elias, N. (1978). *What is Sociology?* London: Hutchinson.

Elias, N. (1983). *The Court Society*. Oxford: Blackwell.

Elias, N. (1987). *Involvement and Detachment*. Oxford: Blackwell.

Fine, G. A. (1987). *With the Boys: Little League Baseball and Preadolescent Culture*. Chicago: University of Chicago Press.

Goudsblom, J. (1977). *Sociology in the Balance*. Oxford: Blackwell.

Gouldner, A. (1970). *The Coming Crisis of Western Sociology*. New York: Basic Books.

Gruneau, R. (1983). *Class, Sports, and Social Development*. Amherst: University of Massachusetts Press.

Hargreaves, J. (1994). *Sporting Females: Critical issues in the History and Sociology of Women's Sport*. London: Routledge.

Jarvie, G., & Maguire, J. (1994). *Sport and Leisure in Social Thought*. London: Routledge.

Johnson, T., Dandeker, C., & Ashworth, C. (1984). *The Structure of Social Theory*. London: Macmillan.

Klein, A. (1991). *Sugarball: The American Game, the Dominican Dream*. New Haven: Yale University Press.

Kuhn, T. S. (1970). *The Structure of Scientific Revolutions*. Chicago: University of Chicago Press.

Maguire, J. (1990). Triple–jeopardy: A career in the Sociology of Sport in Britain. Paper presented at the North American Society for the Sociology of Sport Conference. Denver, Colorado, November.

Maguire, J. (2001). Body (sport) cultures: Diversity, sustainability, globalisation. Paper presented at the First World Congress for the Sociology of Sport. Seoul, Korea, July.

Mills, Wright, C. (1959). *The Sociological Imagination*. New York: Oxford University Press.

Sage, G. (1999). Justice do it! The Nike transnational advocacy network: Organization, collective actions, and outcomes. *Sociology of Sport Journal, 16*(3), 206–236.

Sherman, L. W. (1974). Uses of the Masters. *The American Sociologist, 9*(4), 176–181.

Smith, D. (1991). *The Rise of Historical Sociology*. Cambridge: Polity Press.

Stones, R. (1996). *Sociological Reasoning: Towards a Past-Modern Sociology*. London: Macmillan.

Tilly, C. (1997). *Roads from Past to Future*. Lanham, MD: Rowman & Littlefield.

Part I

Classical Questions

Chapter 1

Karl Marx's Enduring Legacy for the Sociology of Sport

Rob Beamish

This chapter begins with an overview of some of the central ideas contained in the work of Karl Marx. It was Marx's broad critique of capitalist society that formed the basis for a growing number of sociologists of sport in the late 1960s and 1970s to develop a Marx-inspired critique of sport in modern society. The chapter reviews six of those studies to indicate how early sociologists of sport had drawn specifically from Marx, but also introduced themes found among other Marxists of the same period.

The review of these early neo–Marxist studies of sport is followed by a return to some central themes in the work of Marx himself. The main focal point is Marx's combination of the insights of English political economy with the idealist philosophy of Georg Hegel to produce a new, dynamically materialist study of the creativity of humans, and the forces which keep such creativity in check. It is this fundamental departure point for Marx's critique of capitalist society, the chapter demonstrates, which is Marx's enduring legacy for the sociological study of sport.

Karl Marx (1818–1883), the second son among eight children, grew up in a moderately liberal, professional family in Trier (in, at that time, Prussia). After graduating from the Friedrich–Wilhelm Gymnasium (high school), Marx began to follow his father into law by studying at the University of Bonn in 1835, and then at the University of Berlin. But as Marx became embroiled in student debates of the time, his interests shifted from law, to the philosophy of law, and finally to philosophy where he found a common cause with the radical 'Left-Hegelians' in the 'Doctors Club' in Berlin. Marx completed a doctorate in the Faculty of Philosophy at the University of Jena in 1841, but then lost a university teaching opportunity when his friend and mentor, Bruno Bauer, was forced to leave the University of Bonn for proposing a Left-Hegelian toast at a banquet in honour of a liberal deputy of the Prussian National Assembly. Marx

Theory, Sport & Society
ISBN: 0-7623-0742-0

turned to writing and journalism and began a 42-year odyssey in critical study, social critique, and political activism (see Draper, 1985).

As the editor of the *Neue Rheinische Zeitung*, Marx quickly realised the significance that the economy played in shaping the social landscape and thus, soon moved away from his early Left-Hegelian perspective. As early as 1845, armed with a newly emerging materialistic philosophy, Marx felt that he had assimilated enough information to publish a two-volume work to be entitled *A Critique of Politics and Political Economy*, but the work was never completed. After a dozen years of voracious reading and conceptual refinement, Marx (1973: 108) saw his comprehensive critique of politics and political economy in the following cryptic terms:

> The order obviously has to be (1) the general, abstract deter-minants which obtain in more or less all forms of society, but in the above-explained sense. (2) The categories which make up the inner structure of bourgeois society and on which the fundamental classes rest. Capital, wage-labour, landed property. Their interrelation. Town and country. The three great social classes. Exchange between them. Circulation. Credit system (private). (3) Concentration of bourgeois society in the form of the state. Viewed in relation to itself. The unproductive classes. Taxes. State debt. Public credit. The population. The colonies. Emigration. (4) The international relation of production. Inter-national division of labour. International exchange. Export and import. Rate of exchange. (5) The world market and crisis.

Two years later, Marx (1970: 19) wrote that his critique would "examine the system of bourgeois economy in the following order: *capital, landed property, wage-labour, the State, foreign trade, world market*". He noted that the "economic conditions of the three great classes into which bourgeois society is divided are analysed under the first three headings", while the interconnection of the other three was "self-evident". At the end of the preface, Marx (1970: 20) summarised "the guiding principle of [his] studies" as follows:

> In the social production of their existence, men inevitably enter into definite relations, which are independent of their will, namely relations of production appropriate to a given stage in the development of their material forces of production. The totality of these relations of production constitutes the economic structure of society, the real foundation on which arises a legal

and political superstructure and to which correspond definite
forms of social consciousness.

What would not have been self-evident to Marx in 1859, and he would certainly
not have anticipated as emergent from the guiding thread of his studies, was that
his critique of capitalism would one day be applied to the study of sport. But, for
a variety of reasons, Marx's ideas, and subsequent theoretical perspectives that
were largely inspired by Marx, were turned to the analysis of sport in the late
1960s, and early 1970s, and continue in various forms today.

There is not enough space in a chapter to review all the Marxist or, more
accurately, Marx-inspired studies of sport, but a highly selective overview can be
very helpful.[1] In this overview, I have two objectives. I want to emphasise that
Marx's impact upon the critical study of sport has not been monolithic. Frequently
it has been indirect, and it has not completely followed the "guiding principle of
[his] studies". Marx's critique of capitalist society has almost always been filtered
by later writers' perspectives and the changes to capitalist society over the last
150 years. Because much of the work that has come after Marx has attempted to
emphasise *selected* aspects of his critical work, and turned his legacy in a new
direction, it has been termed 'neo–Marxist' to indicate the newly conceived
departure from Marx's ideas. There have been a number of neo–Marxist positions
in sociology in general and in the sociology of sport in particular. If there are, as
I would argue, good reasons to have revised Marx's critique of capitalist society,
my second objective in this chapter is to emphasise that some of Marx's specific
ideas should still play a significant role in the critical study of contemporary sport.

Neo–Marxist Studies of Sport

Marx's 1857 and 1859 sketches of the critique of capitalist society provided
sociologists of sport with wide scope for their analyses and a number of key
issues to address. And, although many analysts have tried to be comprehensive
in their critical studies of sport, none has tried to look at sport under all of the
different headings that Marx established in 1859. Most have focused upon sport
under one of the capital and wage-labour, the state, or the world market headings,
although the history of the twentieth century has forced neo–Marxist sociologists
of sport to also wrestle with problems of ideology, social integration, and the
relative stability of current social relationships.

[1]More extensive reviews of neo–Marxist studies of sport can be found in Ingham and Donnelly
(1997), and McKay (1986a, 1986b).

Six of the earliest neo–Marxist studies of sport are Bero Rigauer's *Sport und Arbeit (Sport and Work)* (1981), Gerhard Vinnai's *Fußballsport als Ideologie* (translated as *Football Mania*) (1970), Jac–Olaf Böhme, Jürgen Gadow, Sven Güldenpfenning, Jörn Jensen and Renate Pfister's *Sport im Spätkapitalismus (Sport in Late Capitalism)* (1971), Jörg Richter's collection *Die vertrimmte Nation oder Sport in rechter Gesellschaft (The Trim Nation or Sport in a Right Society)* (1972) and Paul Hoch's *Rip Off the Big Game* (1972). At about the same time, Jean–Marie Brohm (1978) published a series of essays spanning from 1964 to 1975 under the title *Critiques du Sport*. All of these books shared the following common themes. Each author argued that sport was not separate from society as a whole, and that a critique of sport in capitalist (and, in some cases state socialist) societies was long overdue. The critique of sport should begin with Marx's general critique of capitalist society because the processes of domination uncovered by Marx applied as much to sport as they did to other areas of life. Sport, the authors also argued, was rife with differing forms of economic and personal exploitation. Finally, these books pointed out that a genuine resolution to the problems of modern sport resided in the transformation of the dominant, bourgeois (or, where appropriate, state socialist) society.

Although these authors shared fundamental ideas, there were also significant differences among them. The differences are important because they demonstrate how later authors, faced with different historical circumstances than Marx, filtered his fundamental concepts, and thus changed the nature of the Marxist critique of capitalist society in general, and sport in particular. While these changes were necessary and important, they also took sport critics further and further away from Marx's most significant contributions to critical sociology.

Rigauer is often identified as one of the first *Marxist* critics of sport, but this is actually misleading. While certainly a neo–Marxist project, Rigauer's *Sport and Work* was influenced far more by the 'critical theory' of Max Horkheimer, Theodor Adorno, Herbert Marcuse, and Jürgen Habermas of the Frankfurt Institute for Social Research than it was directly by Marx. This sets Rigauer quite apart from Vinnai, Böhme, Gadow, Güldenpfenning, Jensen, Pfister, Richter, Hoch, and Brohm. In *Sport and Work*, Rigauer drew a striking parallel between the practices found in high performance sport, and those characterising twentieth century mechanised production. But Rigauer's analysis of the labour process in sport, or in modern production, drew far less from Marx's discussion in *Capital* of how workers were directly exploited by the pursuit of profit and the constant rhythms of assembly line production, than it did from the Frankfurt School's conceptions of how the application of scientific analysis to production now exploited workers and athletes (Marx, 1976a: 283–306, 455–491,

492–574). Scientific and technological efficiency, Rigauer and the Frankfurt School authors argued, had become *the* forces of domination and oppression in modern societies and their influence extended well beyond the capitalist mode of production.[2] Rigauer persuasively illustrated how the drive among physiologists, biomechanicians and coaches to use science to maximise training output and increase performance produced a dehumanised world of athletic-production where systems and performance ideologies dominated athletes' working lives. Using the most current scientific training data, well planned, highly structured training regimes were aimed at pushing the boundaries of human performance at almost any cost to the athlete. The application of science and technology to win contests and set world records has become *the* oppressive and exploitative feature of sport today.

In addition, following the lead of *Negative Dialectics* (Adorno, 1973), Rigauer wanted to expose sport *philosophically* and force readers to re-conceptualise sport so that their practice of sport would be changed. In his famous "Eleventh Thesis" on Ludwig Feuerbach, Marx (1976b) noted that, "The philosophers have only *interpreted* the world in various ways; the point, however, is to change it." Adorno, Horkheimer, Marcuse, Habermas and Rigauer now believed that change could only occur through a *return to philosophy*; through a return to a critical interpretation of the world. Thus, if Marx had found the idealist philosopher Georg Hegel "standing on his head" and figuratively returned him to his feet when presenting his materialist critique of capitalist society, the Frankfurt School in general, and Rigauer in his specific critique of sport, had decided to turn Marx from his materialistic feet to his philosophical head to combat the power of twentieth century ideology.[3]

Vinnai's *Football Mania* (1973) began with the material practice of football (soccer) on the field, where he introduced the concept of 'alienated production', and off, where, with respect to who owns and controls the game, Vinnai critically examined the capitalist relations of production which shape contemporary football like all other businesses. Vinnai's main concern, however, was the ideological consequences of modern day football which he examined in chapters dealing with narcissism, aggression, militarism and then a broader discussion

---

[2]See, for example, Horkheimer (1972, 1974), Marcuse (1971, 1998a, 1998b), or Habermas (1970a, 1970b).

[3]Marx (1976a: 102–3) wrote in the Preface to the first edition of *Capital*:

> I criticized the mystificatory side of the Hegelian dialectic nearly thirty years ago, at a time when it was still the fashion. ... The mystification which the dialectic suffers in Hegel's hands by no means prevents him from being the first to present its general forms of motion in a comprehensive manner. With him it is standing on its head. It must be inverted, in order to discover the rational kernel within the mystical shell.

of sport, ideology and cultural domination. Like Rigauer, Vinnai's treatment was academically inspired, though not without its political objectives and consequences. While superficial in many ways, *Football Mania* indicated the potential that a detailed and thorough neo–Marxist critique of sport might bring to a fuller understanding of sport in the modern period.

Böhme *et al.*'s *Sport in Late Capitalism* (1971) was a more orthodox Marxist critique than Rigauer's, but still showed significant differences from Marx's own work. *Sport in Late Capitalism* was strongly influenced by the work of Ernest Mandel (1975) and others in the 'Fourth International' who had taken Marx's draft ideas about how a developing and expanding world market would influence the economic contradictions of capitalism, and created a Marx-inspired theory of capitalist society in the post-war period of 'late capitalism'.

As neo–Marxists concerned with the late capitalism, Böhme *et al.* focused predominantly on the role sport played in maintaining the stability of the current social order, and the force sport played in integrating the Third World into the capitalist world order. Theorists of late capitalism had argued that the long periods of economic prosperity in the West following World War II had led to materially improved living and working conditions for workers in Europe and North America. Rather than remaining a potentially revolutionary force, Western workers were increasingly integrated as consumers and as political supporters of capitalist democracy. Sport, Böhme *et al.* argued, was a significant, though frequently overlooked, means of integrating workers into the capitalist world system. The results of local, national, and international football matches were of more importance to workers than the exploitation of Third World workers producing consumer goods for Europe and North America. At the same time, the sports industries, like so many other trans-national industries, aided in the flow of capital and profit from the Third World into the First World, thus contributing to the stability of the capitalist world system. Placing a critical analysis of sport into this theoretical framework was a unique undertaking, even though much of the analysis remained more suggestive than unequivocally demonstrative.

Jörg Richter's edited collection, *Die vertrimmte Nation oder Sport in rechter Gesellschaft (The Trim Nation or Sport in a Right Society)* (1972), is a thoughtfully coordinated, moderately polemical, critique of sport that emerged from the Marxism of the New Left of the 1960s. The book, consistent with the objectives of the New Left, was aimed at a popular audience. The title is also atypical of how the German New Left liked to play with words. *Die vertrimmte Nation* was a direct reference to the nationally sponsored German fitness movement's slogan, *"Trimm Dich"* — get yourself fit, make yourself trim, prepare yourself to be ready. *Sport in rechter Gesellschaft* carried the play on words further by simultaneously suggesting 'sport in a prepared society', 'sport in a regular society', 'sport in a proper society', as well as 'sport in a politically right-wing society'. Finally, the title inverted traditional terms. Traditionally one might write about *Die rechte Nation or Sport in vertrimmter Gesellschaft*, but by using *recht* and *vertrimmt* as adjectives in an unusual context, Richter wanted to accentuate the political nature of sport as well as the powerful, and manipulated use of the sport metaphor in social life.

The first part of *Die vertrimmte Nation* is also consistent with New Left concerns. The essays demonstrate that sport is anything but a free-time activity, separate from the social constraints of a productivity-oriented, capitalist society. Sport is not all fun, games, and recreation; it is serious. Sport, the authors emphasise, is a high performance activity that is shaped by the social structures in which it is found. Sport is not autonomous from society and sport tends to support the status quo more than it resists or changes it.

The second part of *Die vertrimmte Nation* concentrates on sport in a divided Germany and illustrates with striking clarity that sport is anything but an apolitical activity. The essays show the extent to which the Federal Republic of Germany put social resources into Olympic sport to compete with the 'Miracle Machine' of the German Democratic Republic. The integration of high performance athletes from the Federal Republic as essentially state workers in pursuit of the immediate political goals of the national government as well as the long-term interests of the capitalist system are elaborated in clear terms. The overt political use of Olympic sport by the German Democratic Republic was already well recognised, so *Die vertrimmte Nation* simply turned the analysis on the Federal Republic.

Again, however, the critique in Richter's collection was closer to the Frankfurt School, and Rigauer (who contributes to the book) than it is to Marx's critique of political economy. Richter's overall objective was to break down the dominant ideological *mis*understanding of sport so that significant change could be introduced into both sport and the social system as a whole. The contradictions that became the focal point of analysis were not economic contradictions; the focus was upon the contradictions existing between sport's mythology and sport's material reality. Implicitly, *Die vertrimmte Nation* admitted that the material contradictions of the sport experience, for both athletes and consumers, did not appear to be enough to lead to significant social reform within sport, let alone in the broader society of West Germany or the Western World. Change required a raising of consciousness.

Although Hoch wrote that *Rip Off the Big Game* (1972) was deeply indebted to Antonio Gramsci's insights into the structure of mass culture, the book was one of the most orthodox Marxist–Leninist treatments of sport that was produced in this period. In it, Hoch examined the power of professional sport team owners and the extent to which athletes were exploited economically. Hoch demonstrated how the sport spectacle had become a new form of 'Bread and Circuses' for the masses and was manipulated by monopoly capitalists to create artificial scarcities, and dupe people into becoming unreflective consumers of mass culture. But Hoch's major arguments linked sport to America's imperialist conquest of the Third World and the militarism of the United States in the Vietnam War era. "In the last analysis", Hoch (1972: 212) wrote, "in the sports world, as in the world as a whole, it will be socialism or fascism, global human liberation or barbarism".

Brohm's *Sport: A Prison of Measured Time* (1978) addressed many of the same themes as the authors above but his focus of analysis was clearly drawn from the French Left in general and the particular interpretation of Marx set forth by Louis Althusser (see Althusser, 1972, 1977, Althusser & Balibar, 1970). Brohm employed and developed two of Althusser's major revisions of Marx. First, Brohm, like Althusser, saw individuals as limited in their ability to change the world because the underlying structures of capitalist society overly determine men's and women's options, and their understanding of the world around them. Second, and following directly from the first point, individual action is constrained because there are a number of key institutions (or, employing Althusser's terminology, 'Ideological State Apparatuses') that structurally serve to maintain the stability of the current social order. Sport, Brohm illustrated with examples of high performance sport in France, in the German Democratic Republic, and in analyses of the Olympic Movement and the Games, should be recognised as one of the more powerful systems for supporting the values, beliefs (in short, ideology) of the dominant groups in power. As a 'prison of measured time', sport does more than dehumanise and constrain athletes. "Sport is an Ideological State Apparatus which fulfills a triple role":

> [Sport] ideologically reproduces bourgeois social relations such as selection, hierarchy, subservience, obedience, etc.; secondly, it spreads an organisational ideology specific to the institution of sport, involving competition, records and output; thirdly, it transmits on a huge scale the general themes of ruling bourgeois ideology like the myth of the superman, individualism, social achievement, success, efficiency, etc. (1978: 77).

Finally, Brohm noted, "sport is the *ideology of the body/machine* — the body turned into a robot, alienated by capitalist labour. Sport is based on *the fantasy of the 'fit', productive body*" (1978: 77).

As one moves through the critical studies of sport that have been published during the decades after 1970, there are obvious attempts to progressively refine the different critical perspectives that have been applied to sport. Neo–Marxist analysis has been integrated into, and drawn insights from, cultural studies, social history, feminism, post-modernism to some extent, as well as the work of Michel Foucault, Pierre Bourdieu and Anthony Giddens. With these movements away from Marx's own writings, the collapse of Soviet-style Communism and the fall of the Berlin Wall, it seems that Marx can finally be relegated to the dustbin of history. But is Marx no longer relevant to the critical, sociological study of sport?

What is Enduring in Marx's Work for Sociologists of Sport

While works like *The Manifesto of the Communist Party* and *Capital* are standard sources for understanding Marx's ideas, it is his copious study notebooks and draft manuscripts that provide the most vital insight into his enduring contribution to sociology. Among the key manuscripts are the early draft notebooks for the proposed *Critique of Politics and Political Economy*. The so-called "Economic and Philosophic Manuscripts of 1844" reveal the processes that enabled Marx (1975) to produce a new basis for understanding human history by uniquely combining the insights of political economy with a radical reformulation of Hegel's philosophy. Because this is a key element in Marx's legacy, it should be looked at carefully.

Hegel firmly embraced the powerful 'Enlightenment' proposition that philosophically discovered reason could lead to the end of abusive, arbitrary political rule and usher in an age of progress, human freedom, and greater social equality (see Kaufmann, 1965). Unable to accept either the narrow empiricist limits David Hume had put on human knowledge, or Immanuel Kant's conclusion that we could never definitively look beyond the "world of appearances", Hegel's philosophy painstakingly refuted the limits that previous philosophers had placed on human reason.[4]

[4]It is ironic today to reflect for a moment on Hegel's quest, because most people would dismiss his philosophical struggles as hopelessly idealistic, excessively obscure, and completely misguided. Yet, those same individuals would argue that science, through continuing research which pushes back the frontiers of knowledge, will continue to discover laws and basic principles of the natural world which will solve many of today's most pressing problems in areas such as disease, nutrition, renewable energy, production of sustainable building materials,

For Hegel, the key to the discovery and implementation of 'Reason' in human affairs lay in the detailed study of *how* the human mind (*Geist*) and, simultaneously, the intellectual spirit (*Geist*) of an age, developed and operated. Hegel's *Phenomenology* (1977) and his *Logic* (1969) began, like Hume and Kant, with the fact that humans are faced with an external world upon which we are dependent for survival, yet do not fully know. At first glance, the external world seems foreign to the mind and separated (or alienated) from it. But, Hegel perceptively argued, to live, humans have to interact with the external world and, to do so successfully, the human mind develops categories of understanding about the external world. But after creating ways of knowing the external world, the mind must necessarily reflect upon the adequacy of the categories it creates and adjusts them, thereby changing how the external world is grasped or understood. This unavoidable, internally critical, self-reflective interaction between the mind and the external world is, according to Hegel, the fundamental dynamic to human history. The *dialectical*, as Hegel termed the process, interaction between mind, and matter, continually forces the mind to supersede (or, to use Hegel's term, *transcend*) limited forms of knowledge and replace them with more comprehensive ones that expand humans' capacity to reason more fully, more comprehensively and thus, more accurately.[5] In addition to demonstrating how the human mind developed, Hegel maintained that the growth of reason and the growth of the use of reason in all human affairs was an intrinsic constituent to our 'Being' as a species. The dialectical development of the mind was fundamental to our 'species-character'.

From 1842 to 1844, as he became increasingly aware of the impact that the economic relations of society have on its political and social dynamics, Marx concentrated upon the works of Adam Smith, James Mill, Jean Baptiste Say

and environmental protection. What would be most ironic of such a dismissal is that Hegel focused his quest on how humans come to know, and come to know in ever increasingly sophisticated terms, the world around us. What modern science accomplishes is but one small part of Hegel's concern about human development and human enlightenment. Hegel wanted the sophistication of human knowledge to improve all aspects of human life, especially the social and political world in which people lived. This concern was also taken over by Marx and became the guiding thread to his life's work as well.

[5]The verb *aufheben* (to transcend) and its noun form *Aufhebung* (transcendence), are important concepts for understanding Hegel. Transcendence is the process where humans discover with one form (or stage) of knowledge, *on the very basis of that form of knowledge*, discrepancies (or contradictions) in what is known. These discrepancies or contradictions can only be resolved by reformulating the existing understanding into a newer one. This reformulation draws upon the older theory or form of knowledge while adding to it — thus *preserving* some of the earlier form of knowledge but also *moving beyond* it. Developments such as the Copernican revolution in astronomy, Einstein's theory of relativity in physics, or Watson and Crick's discovery of DNA in biology are legion.

and Frederick Skarbek. Marx also recognised that for his *Critique of Politics and Political Economy* to have a significant impact in Germany, it would have to lay bare, once and for all, the fundamental weaknesses in Hegel's approach to history and social change, while also addressing the shortcomings of English, French and German political economists. Fresh from reading the political economists' views of production, labour, the division of labour, and the productive capacity of labour, Marx's 1844 critique of Hegel and political economy was a crucial watershed in the development of his ideas.

Whereas Hegel (1969: 31) had always maintained that "we cannot be too often reminded that it is *thinking* which distinguishes men from beasts", political economists had focused upon labour as the defining measure of humankind. The similarity, but at the same time, the significant difference between the two positions had revolutionary implications.

The critique of Hegel that Marx (1975: 326–32) planned for his *Critique of Politics and Political Economy* began with a relatively conventional demonstration of the various weaknesses in Hegel's analysis of the process through which the mind built, and superseded intellectual categories, as it advanced its capacity for 'Reason'. But Marx followed this with a reading of Hegel from the perspective of political economy. Marx (1975: 332–33) noted that, "The outstanding achievement of Hegel's *Phenomenology* and its final outcome, the dialectic of negativity as the moving and generating principle, is thus first that Hegel conceives the self-creation of man as a process". But, Marx then indicated, 'self-creation', for political economists, involves labour — not thought. Read through the prism of political economy, "the self-creation of man as a process" would involve material interaction between humans and nature, a process that produces objects (or objectification). If the inspiration for Hegel's insights into the development of humankind had come less from philosophy, and its fixation on the operation of the mind, and drawn more from political economy, his philosophy would have centred on the process where humans *materially* interacted with the external world. This process of interaction would appear as both the creation of an object (i.e., objectification) and also "as loss of the object, as alienation and as transcendence of this alienation". In this way, Hegel would have grasped "the essence of *labour* and comprehend[ed] objective man — true, because real man — as the outcome of man's *own labour*" (1975: 326–32).

Hegel, of course, had only written about objectification in philosophical terms, but in 1844, Marx saw, in a materialist reading of Hegel, that the type of interaction which genuinely mattered to human history was the *material interaction* between humankind and the external world — the material production of objects through the labour process. Through material production,

Marx now argued, humankind creatively produced and interacted with the world. The creative capacities of humans lay in the labour process where there was a process of production (or objectification — *Vergegenständlichung*), the externalisation of that object (*Entgegenständlichung*) — that is, the physical completion, outside of the worker, of an idea that she or he had held in her head — and then the overcoming of that separation as the producer recognised the product as his or her own and employed it for her or his own use and/or development.

Twenty-three years later, Marx (1976: 283) would describe the process in less philosophically laden terms, although the key ideas had not changed:

> Labour is, first of all, a process between man and nature, a process by which man, through his own actions, mediates, regulates and controls the metabolism between himself and nature. He confronts the materials of nature as a force of nature. He sets in motion the natural forces which belong to his own body, his arms, legs, head and hands, in order to appropriate the materials of nature in a form adapted to his own needs. Through this movement, he acts upon external nature and changes it, and in this way, he simultaneously changes his own nature.

For those who practice or study sport, the fundamental role that physical action plays in the development of individual humans as well as groups, teams and much larger collectivities is readily apparent. Whether it is children learning and refining a skill as recreational as 'skipping rope' or as complex as 'quarterbacking' a power play in ice-hockey, the entire process is one in which ideas are externalised through action and the results of that action monitored, adjusted and refined so that the desired outcome is achieved. The externalisation of ideas and goals through physical action is the central moment in learning to jump rope, just as it is in establishing, in a symbolic form, world supremacy in an Olympic ice-hockey game, or financial security from the spin-offs that accrue from scoring the winning power play goal in front of a world-wide audience using a particular brand of stick, gloves or skates. Thus a major part of Marx's legacy, and his continued relevance today, is the emphasis he placed upon a dialectically understood labour process which combined the creative insights Hegel had attributed to the phenomenological development of the human mind, and spirit, with the immediate and larger productive results of the material labour process discussed in political economy.

In the manuscripts of 1844, Marx did more than establish a new ontological position for understanding human history. Marx used that ontology to critically assess the labour process under the conditions of capitalist society. In his critique of political economy, Marx argued that the generically creative labour process was, in fact, alienated in three ways other than the positive alienation that generically existed in the production process. Marx indicated that in material production within capitalist society, the worker was separated from his or her product; he or she was separated from the way things are made (the production process), and he or she was separated from his or her human potential (his or her species-being). On alienation from the product of labour, Marx (1975: 272) wrote:

> The fact expresses merely that the object (*Gegenstand*) which labour produces — labour's product — confronts it as *something alien*, as a *power independent* of the producer. The product of labour is labour which has been embodied in an object, which has become material: it is the *objectification* of labour. Labour's realization *(Verwirklichung)* is its objectification *(Vergegenständlichung)*. Under these economic conditions this realization of labour appears as *loss of realization (Entwircklichung)* for the workers; objectification *as loss of the object and bondage to it*; appropriation as *estrangement, as alienation*.

This insight is so central to the study of sport and physical activity because — if sporting activity is so rich with creative potential — so robust with opportunities for individuals to explore their own limits and the limitations of human physical performance — the loss of control of the product can have devastating consequences for the creative potential of physical activity. Rather than the athlete primarily pursuing sport as a means of self-expression or self-exploration, sporting activity shaped by the market place (for example, Olympic or professional, recreational or representational) is the production of a product/object (*Gegenstand*) that stands before and against (*steht gegen*) the producer; rather than realising the full productive potential of the athlete, sport stands against the athlete and builds the power of the market's influence over sport while restricting the expressive potential of the athletes themselves. Once again, this central dynamic of sport, which is still so crucial for any critical study of sport, has its legacy in Marx's critical sociology.

Concluding Remarks

From the initiation of neo–Marxist analyses of sport in the late 1960s and early 1970s through to the present time, critical sociologists of sport have drawn from Marx's ideas and blended them with theories and insights from other perspectives. This is, of course, to be expected because the material conditions of contemporary society are different from those of Marx's time. But the refining of the neo–Marxist critique of sport has had the ironic impact of leading critical sociologists of sport further and further away from Marx's work and, in the process, left the fundamental core of his critical insights in a state of neglect, or to the gnawing critique of the 'mice in an out-of-sight place'. Critical sociology of sport is the poorer for that neglect; there is a genuinely powerful legacy to Marx's work upon which we can all still draw. Rather than belonging in 'the dustbin of history', along with Marxism–Leninism, Stalinism, and 'Real Existing Socialism', Marx's fundamental critique of Hegel, and political economy, still holds a vibrant, untapped potential for critical, sociological study today. And nowhere does that critique hold more potential than it does for a radical study of sport in the twenty-first century.

References

Adorno, T. (1973). *Negative Dialectics* (Trans. Ashton, E.) New York: Seabury Press.
Althusser, L., & Balibar, E. (1970). *Reading Capital* (Trans. Brewster, B.) London: New Left Books.
Althusser, L. (1972). *Politics and History* (Trans. Brewster, B.) London: New Left Books.
Althusser, L. (1977). *For Marx* (Trans. Brewster, B.) London: New Left Books.
Böhme, J.-O., Gadow, J., Güldenpfenning, S., Jensen, J., & Pfister, R. (1971). *Sport im Spätkapitalismus*. Frankfurt: Limpert.
Brohm, J.-M. (1978). *Sport: A Prison of Measured Time* (Trans. Fraser, I.) London: Ink Links.
Draper, H. (1985). *The Marx–Engels Chronicle* (Vol. 1 of *The Marx–Engels Cyclopedia*). New York: Schocken Books.
Habermas, J. (1970a). Technical progress and the social life-world. In: *Toward a Rational Society,* (pp. 50–61). (Trans. Shapiro, H.) Boston: Beacon Press.
Habermas, J. (1970b). Technology and science as 'ideology'. In: *Toward a Rational Society,* 81–122. (Trans. Shapiro, H.) Boston: Beacon Press.
Hegel, G. W. F. (1969). *Hegel's Science of Logic* (Trans. Miller, A.) New York: Humanities Press.
Hegel, G. W. F. (1975). *Logic: Being Part One of the Encyclopedia of the Philosophical Sciences* (Trans. Walace, W.) Oxford: The Clarendon Press.

Hegel, G. W. F. (1977). *Phenomenology of Mind* (Trans. Miller, A.) New York: Oxford University Press.

Hoch, P. (1972). *Rip Off the Big Game*. New York: Doubleday Anchor Books.

Horkheimer, M. (1972). Traditional and critical theory. In: *Critical Theory Today* (pp. 188–243). New York: Herder & Herder.

Horkheimer, M. (1974). *Eclipse of Reason*. New York: The Seabury Press.

Kaufmann, W. (1965). *Hegel: A Reinterpretation*. New York: Doubleday and Company.

Ingham, A., & Donnelly, P. (1997). A sociology of North American sociology of sport: Disunity in unity, 1965 to 1996. *Sociology of Sport Journal, 14*, 362–418.

Mandel, E. (1975). *Late Capitalism* (Trans. De Bres, J.) London: New Left Books.

Marcuse, H. (1971). Industrialization and capitalism. In: O. Stammer (ed.), *Max Weber and Sociology Today* (pp. 133–51). New York: Harper & Row.

Marcuse, H. (1998a). Some implications of modern technology. In: H. Marcuse, *Technology, War and Fascism* (ed. Kellner, D.) (pp. 39–66). New York: Routledge.

Marcuse, H. (1998b). 33 Theses. In: H. Marcuse, *Technology, War and Fascism* (ed. Kellner, D.) (pp. 215–28). New York: Routledge.

Marx, K. (1970). *A Contribution to the Critique of Political Economy* (Trans. Ryazanskaya, S.) New York: International Publishers.

Marx, K. (1973). *Grundrisse: Foundations of the Critique of Political Economy (Rough Draft)* (Trans. Nicolaus, M.) New York: Penguin Books.

Marx, K. (1975). Economic and philosophic manuscripts of 1844. In: *Karl Marx, Frederick Engels Collected Works* (Vol. 3, pp. 229–376). New York: International Publishers.

Marx, K. (1976a). *Capital* (Trans. Fowkes, B.) New York: Penguin Books.

Marx, K. (1976b). Theses on Feuerbach. In: *Karl Marx, Frederick Engels Collected Works* (Vol. 5, p. 8). New York: International Publishers.

McKay, J. (1986a). Marxism as a way of seeing: Beyond the limits of current 'critical' approaches to sport. *Sociology of Sport Journal, 3*, 261–72.

McKay, J. (1986b). Some unresolved issues of class, hegemony, and the state in recent Marxist approaches to the Sociology of Sport. In: W. Dowdy (ed.), *Marxist Policies in Today's World*. St. Lucia: University of Queensland Press.

Richter, J. (ed.) (1972). *Die vertrimmte Nation oder Sport in rechter Gesellschaft*. Reinbek: Rowholt Pocket Books.

Rigauer, B. (1981). *Sport and Work* (Trans. Guttmann, A.) New York: Columbia University Press.

Vinnai, G. (1973). *Football Mania* (Trans. Fernbach, D. and Gilard, M.) London: Ocean Books.

Chapter 2

Emile Durkheim, Structural Functionalism and the Sociology of Sport

John Loy and Douglas Booth

Emile Durkheim, Karl Marx and Max Weber form a triumvirate of major classical sociologists. Yet, unlike the key ideas of Marx and Weber which continue to permeate scholarship in the sociology of sport, Durkheim's influence is largely indirect through the structural–functionalism paradigm (cf. Loy and Booth, 2000) of which he laid many of the foundations. Born into an orthodox Jewish family on 15 April 1858 in Epinal, France, Durkheim initially planned to become a *rabbi* like his father. In later youth, he declared himself agnostic and pursued an academic career that led him to become the first person in France to hold an academic appointment in sociology.

Durkheim's Academic Career

After graduating from the prestigious École Normale Supérieure de Paris in 1882, Durkheim began his academic career teaching philosophy in provincial preparatory schools. In 1885–86, he took academic study leave, spending six months each in Paris and Germany. Durkheim studied ethics and morality in Germany and was particularly impressed by Wilhelm Wundt's sociological study of morality and his "experimental work in psychology, with its concentration on 'precise and restricted' problems and its avoidance of 'vague generalisations and metaphysical possibilities'" (Lukes, 1973: 90). Returning home, Durkheim published reports about German social thought. These helped him obtain an appointment in social science and education in the Faculty of Letters at the University of Bordeaux in 1887.

Although "passionately involved in the affairs of French society at large", academia "dominated" Durkheim's life (Coser, 1971: 143). At Bordeaux, he was a role model of scholarship. Durkheim's fifteen years there

Theory, Sport & Society
ISBN: 0-7623-0742-0

were filled with unremitting and productive effort: a heavy teaching load, with new courses every year in sociology and the theory of education; the completion of the required Latin and French doctoral dissertations in 1893 (the first on Montesquieu, the second on *The Division of Labour in Society*); the writing of two other sociological classics, *The Rules of Sociological Method* [1895] and *Suicide* [1897], and scores of articles and reviews; and the organisation and editing of the journal, *L'Année Sociologique* (Smelser & Warner, 1976: 71).

In 1896, Durkheim received the first full professorship in social science in France. Six years later, however, he accepted a lower level appointment as a *charge de cours* at the Sorbonne in Paris in education rather than sociology. Both Bordeaux and the Sorbonne demanded that Durkheim devote most of his time to teaching educational courses. At the time, sociology was a minor discipline and faced "formidable opposition" in the universities where "it had to be smuggled in by the back door" (Thompson, 1982: 41). In 1906, Durkheim gained a Chair in Education (i.e., promoted to Full Professor), but "it was not until 1913, by means of a special ministerial decree, that his Chair was titled 'Science of Education and Sociology'" (Coser, 1971: 41).

Durkheim published the last of his four major works, *The Elementary Forms of Religious Life*, in 1912. During World War I, he wrote pamphlets supporting the French war effort. Durkheim's health deteriorated following the death of his only son from war wounds in 1915, and he died aged 59 on 15 November 1917.

Durkheim's Doctrine

Durkheim's life and work "mark[s] the acceptance of sociology as an autonomous academic discipline" (Campbell, 1981: 139). Although several European sociologists contributed to establishing sociology as a distinct discipline with academic status,[1] "Durkheim was the first to open up a new vista for sociology, namely, the possibility of establishing sociology as a theoretical science with a special subject matter and a special approach" (Abel, 1970: 15). Briefly, Durkheim considered sociology to involve the study of special subject matter that he called

[1]These included the marginal but imaginative German sociologist Georg Simmel (1858–1917), the noted Italian sociologist Vilfred Pareto (1848–1923), and the famous German sociologist Max Weber (1864–1920). See Aron (1967) for a detailed discussion of the similarities and differences among Durkheim, Pareto and Weber.

'social facts', and he believed that social facts were best studied from the approach he called 'scientific rationalism'.[2]

Durkheim regarded social facts as 'things' rather than abstract ideas or speculative concepts. Jary and Jary (1991: 177) offer a succinct explanation of Durkheim's notion of 'things', describing them as general, collective and objective social phenomena, external to individuals, and operating by their constraining or coercive influences on individuals. Durkheim held "that with the possible exception of mathematical units, every object of science is a thing" (Durkheim, 1895/1964: xliv). Thus social facts must "be researched in the real, empirical world just as we investigate other 'things'" (Ritzer, 1975: 38).

Durkheim rejected the prevailing intellectual climate that emphasised atomism and methodological individualism (the philosophical position that properties of individuals determine the properties of societies). He focused on the social milieu as the primary unit of analysis that he held could not be reduced to the individual. "The determining cause of a social fact," he said, "should be sought among the social facts preceding it and not among the states of the individual consciousness" (Durkheim (1895/1964: 110). For example, rather than explaining the social phenomenon of suicide in terms of psychological facts such as anxiety and depression, its cause should be sought in other social facts such as marital status, ethnicity, religious affiliation and nationality.

In summary, Coser (1971: 129) identifies the "main thrust" of Durkheim's doctrine as "his insistence that the study of society must eschew reductionism and consider social phenomena *sui generis* [in its own right]. Rather than biologistic or psychologistic interpretations, Durkheim focused attention on the social–structural determinants of mankind's social problems". Campbell (1981: 144) agrees, noting that "the characteristic feature of Durkheim's positivism is . . . [a] single-minded attempt to approach society as an independent organic reality with its own laws, its own development and its own life". The following section elaborates on Durkheim's doctrine as the foundation for a new scientific sociology.

---

[2]Durkheim's methodology is usually referred to as 'positivism' to denote the doctrine of using the methods of the natural sciences to study human behaviour in the social sciences. However, Durkheim preferred the term "scientific rationalism" to connote that positivism was only one aspect of this rationalism and in order to distinguish his methodological stance from the positivistic metaphysics of Auguste Comte and Herbert Spencer (cf. Durkheim, 1895/1964: xl, especially footnote 2).

Scientific Sociology

In their history of the emergence of sociological theory, Turner and Beeghley (1981: 368) identify six distinctive, but interrelated, features of Durkheim's broad work in sociological theory: a search for scientific laws, "structuralism", evolutionism, causal analysis, "functionalism", and social pathology. We discuss each of these features in turn before examining his broad intellectual influence and his impact on the sociology of sport.

The Search for Scientific Laws

According to Thompson (1982: 164–65), Durkheim's "mission" was that sociology "should become a scientific discipline". Durkheim assumed that an underlying order, or a system of laws, determined human organisation; he "seemed to have a vision that the fundamental properties of the social world could be stated as laws similar to those in the physics of Newton or the biology of Darwin" (Turner & Beeghley, 1981: 368). Indeed, Durkheim (1895/1964: xiv) insisted that a sociologist must:

> put himself in the same state of mind as the physicist, chemist, or physiologist when he probes into a still unexplored region of the scientific domain. When he penetrates the social world, he must be aware that he is penetrating the unknown; he must feel himself in the presence of facts whose laws are as unsuspected as were those of life before the era of biology; he must be prepared for discoveries which will surprise and disturb him.

Although Durkheim rarely stated his abstract principles in propositional, law-like form, many of his theoretical statements can be readily formalised (Clark, 1987; Turner, 1981; Turner, 1990; Turner & Beeghley, 1981). Durkheim's most prominent sociological proposition is his "law of suicide" which states that "suicide varies inversely with the degree of integration of the social groups of which the individual is a part" (Abel, 1970: 16).

Structuralism

Broadly construed, structuralism refers to any form of sociological analysis that emphasises social structures over human agents, although today the term 'structuralism' typically connotes the structural analysis of language.[3] But all forms of structuralism, past or present, abide by the basic principle "that the observable is meaningful only in so far as it can be related to an underlying structure or order" (Swingewood, 1984: 277).

Durkheim's conception of society as having an objective existence independent of individuals, and his notion of an underlying social order, places him firmly within the structuralist paradigm (Alexander, 1982: 75). Indeed, Peter Blau (1998: 268) calls Durkheim "the classic symbol of the structural perspective in sociology".[4] A clear example of Durkheim's structural perspective appears in his discussion of the crowd:

> The great movements of enthusiasm, indignation, and pity in a crowd do not originate in any one of the particular individual consciousness. They come to each one of us from without and can carry us away in spite of ourselves. Of course, it may happen that, in abandoning myself to them unreservedly, I do not feel the pressure they exert upon me. But it is revealed as soon as I try to resist them. Let an individual attempt to oppose one of these collective manifestations, and the emotions that he denies will turn against him. Now, if this power of external coercion asserts itself so clearly in cases of resistance, it must exist also in the first-mentioned cases, although we are unconscious of it (Durkheim, 1895/1964: 4–5).

Similarly, the structural perspective emerges in Durkheim's concept of society as a moral phenomenon: "as a moral system its typical manifestations are the obligations which the individual, however willing, must perform in accordance with the language, laws and customs of his society, all of which are social facts he did not create and to which he must conform or suffer the consequences of social disapproval and punishment" (Campbell, 1981: 143). In his discussion of the coercive aspects of Durkheimian notions of moral obligation, Bierstedt (1966: 79) offers some pertinent contemporary examples: those who disobey the law

---

[3]The founder of modern structuralism, Ferdinand de Saussure (1857–1913), a Swiss linguist, was a Durkheim contemporary and much influenced by his thought. According to Swingewood (1984: 277), Saussure "followed Durkheim in regarding language as an example of a social fact" and "accepted Durkheim's methodological collectivism" in preference to Tarde's methodological individualism.

[4]While noting that societies consist of people who are individuals, who are studied by psychologists, Blau (1998: 272), like Durkheim, argues that "defining sociology in structural terms requires . . . [studying] the attributes of a population that are not attributes of its individual members".

face imprisonment, those who ignore the norms of their profession jeopardise promotion, those who wear alternative clothing encounter ridicule, and those who violate moral codes meet ostracism.

Evolutionism

Given his interest in the historical development of societies from simple to more complex forms, Durkheim's work, not surprisingly, contains a strong evolutionary element. While the social consequences of the transition from feudalism to capitalism occupied the minds of many nineteenth century social theorists, Durkheim analysed several "primitive" and ancient societies in an attempt to explain the relationship between the individual and society. In the process he classified "societies along a developmental continuum, from simple to complex forms" determined by the level of social solidarity (Thompson, 1982: 74). In simple societies, solidarity emanates from a similarity between individuals. Durkheim called this "mechanical" solidarity. By contrast, solidarity in complex advanced societies rests on "the intermeshing and mutual dependence of differentiated roles" (Coser, 1971: 136). Durkheim labelled this "organic" solidarity. But as Lukes (1973: 140) reminds us, Durkheim did not subscribe to "simple unilinear evolutionism". On the contrary, like the British social theorist Herbert Spencer (1820–1903), he used the analogy of a tree to symbolise evolution:

> In saying of one social type that it is more advanced than another, we do not mean that the different social types are ranged in a single ascending linear series, more or less elevated at different moments in history . . . if the genealogical table of social types could be completely drawn up, it would rather take the form of a tufted tree, with a single trunk, to be sure, but with divergent branches (Durkheim cited in Lukes,1973: 149–50).

Causal Analysis

Turner and Beeghley (1981: 371) consider Durkheim a "pioneer in causal modelling". While he maintained that social facts — such as the division of labour, religion, suicide, incest taboos, and cognitive categories — are autonomous and independent, Durkheim looked for the causal and reciprocal relationships between social facts. These relationships formed the foundations of his casual models. For example, organic solidarity results, in the first instance, from migration, population growth and ecological concentration. In turn, these cause increases in social contact and interaction, which are further heightened by new forms of communication and transportation. Within a confined ecological space, however, increased interaction causes increases in competition and differentiation of labour, which in turn, leads to organic solidarity.

Another of Durkheim's causal models explains early religions. When primitive peoples migrate and concentrate in temporary gatherings, increased interaction generates collective emotions that produce a sense that there is "something" external to individuals that constrains them. The essence of this constraint is a sacred force called "mana". In more permanent groups "mana is given more concrete expression as a sacred totem. The creation of totems, and beliefs about as well as rituals towards the totem, promotes clan solidarity" (Turner & Beeghley, 1981: 377–8).

Functionalism

Although both Auguste Comte (1798–1857) — who coined the term "sociology" — and Spencer espoused functional tenets in their organic conceptions of society, Turner and Maryanski (1979: 96–97) credit Durkheim with being "the first to advocate an explicitly functional set of assumptions". Among these assumptions were the following:

> (1) A social system must reveal some degree of internal integration among its constituent parts. (2) The important theoretical task is to determine the consequences, or functions, of a constituent part for the integration of the systemic whole. (3) The "causes" of a part must be analyzed separately from its "functions" for social integration. (4) The need for social integration operates as a selective mechanism for the persistence of those parts that promote integration of the social whole.

In short, Durkheim argued that social institutions exist for the express purpose of fulfilling specific societal needs, principally the maintenance of society as an organic whole. For example, according to Durkheim (1912/1995), religion functions as a symbolic representation of society in which sacred beliefs and practices (those set apart from everyday life and deemed forbidden) strengthen social bonds and integrate individuals into society.

Social Pathology

Durkheim believed that, in general, social systems evolved towards states of equilibrium, 'normality' and 'goodness'. Yet, he stressed that the parts of the system never achieved perfect integration. On the contrary, various forms of mal-integration, such as anomie, egoism and the compulsory division of labour, undermine social cohesion and contribute to instability in advanced societies. Notwithstanding the presence of social pathologies, Durkheim viewed the world as a teleological whole: everything has its place and serves a purpose in the long run. While a forced division of labour may be pathological at some stage in the "evolution" of a society, as a necessary period of transition along the path to reaching a spontaneous division of labour, it is historically normal.

Most significantly, Durkheim made the case for an "ethical science" of society. He contended that:

> for societies as for individuals, health is good and desirable; disease, on the contrary, is bad and to be avoided. If then, we can find an objective criterion, inherent in the facts themselves, which enables us to distinguish scientifically between health and morbidity in the various orders of social phenomena, science will be in a position to throw light on practical problems and still remain faithful to its own method (Durkheim, 1895/1964: 49).

However, by equating a 'healthy' society with a 'normal' society, Durkheim weakened his case for an ethical and scientific sociology. Such an equation meant that he could never reconcile certain facts. In the case of crime, for example, on the one hand it is typically considered pathological while, on the other, it is 'normal' in that it exists in all societies, past and present.

Intellectual Influence

Many contemporary social theorists acknowledge Durkheim's enormous intellectual influence. Anthony Giddens unequivocally states that "the writings of Emile Durkheim have exerted an extra-ordinary influence over the development of modern social thought" (1978: 9). His great influence is particularly remarkable given that he had published most of his major works by age forty. Here we highlight Durkheim's influence in his own time, outline his impact upon the social sciences during the last century, and then, by means of selected case studies, illustrate the influence of aspects of his theory and method for the study of sport-related social phenomena.

A Legend in His Own Time

First and foremost, Durkheim had a major impact on French social thought in his own lifetime. This impact "arose not only from his research and publication but very largely from his teaching and from his exceptional ability to guide and co-ordinate the research of others" (Benoit–Smullyan, 1966: 226). He achieved his main influence as a proselytiser, as distinct from an intellectual leader *per se*, through the founding of the journal *L'Année Sociologique* in 1898, and service as its editor until 1910. "It was around this periodical", writes Bierstedt (1966: 21), that Durkheim "figuratively gathered his friends and disciples and it was through the journal that he was able to exercise so large an influence not only on the development of French sociology but on French intellectual history in general". It is in these contexts — "as teacher, as editor of a distinguished periodical, and a leader of a highly talented and creative group of research scholars" — that Talcott Parsons (1974: lxiii) refers to Durkheim as a "highly effective entrepreneur of sociology". However, for Parsons (1974: lxiii), Durkheim's greatest contribution was his formulation of a theoretical framework that was "precise and clear in its logical structures and imaginative in opening up new ways of considering social phenomena, defining problems, and developing patterns of interpretation".

Influence in the Social Sciences

The fact that so many of Durkheim's works have been published posthumously (cf., Bierstedt, 1966: 28–29; Thompson, 1982: 145–166) lends support to the claim by Rex (1969: 133) that "Durkheim's influence both as a general theoretician and as a contributor to specific fields of empirical study has been lasting". More specifically, Durkheim continues to exert an influence on the sociological study of *scientific knowledge and methodology* (e.g., Giddens, 1976; Gieryn, 1982; Mestrovic, 1989; Turner, 1983, 1984), *religion* (e.g., Bergesen, 1984; Swanson, 1966), *social organisation* (e.g., Clarke, 1987; Turner, 1981, 1990), *suicide* (e.g., Breault and Barkey, 1982; Day, 1987; Douglas, 1967; Masumura, 1977; Pearce, 1987; Pescosolido, 1990), and *anomie* (e.g., Clinard, 1964; Merton, 1957; Marks, 1974).

To illustrate the intellectual influence of Durkheim upon the social sciences in general, we point out that he was the forerunner, if not the forefather, of French structuralism, British social anthropology, and structural–functionalism in North American sociology.

1. *French Structuralism*. Elements of what has become known as structural anthropology, structuralism, or French structuralism, can be found in Durkheim's general works. But his influence on this movement was largely indirect through his influence on his nephew, good friend, and loyal disciple, Marcel Mauss, with whom he co-authored *Primitive Classification* (1903/ 1963). Mauss, in turn, directly influenced the structuralism of Claude Lévi– Strauss (1908–). Lévi–Strauss was a student of Mauss and he acknowledges his debt in the preface to *Introduction to the Work of Marcel Mauss* (1950/ 1987). By reading Mauss' book, *The Gift* (1925/1967), Lévi–Strauss "found the key" to kinship systems and "how they work" (Wiseman & Groves, 1997: 19). His initial theories of kinship systems launched an involvement with the movement now known as structuralism which has had an enormous impact on French social thought in particular, and on a wide range of disciplines world-wide in general. "As one of the leading figures of the structuralist movement, his methods and ideas" influenced many of his "most prominent contemporaries" including Jacques Lacan, Roland Barthes, Louis Althusser, and Michel Foucault (Wiseman & Groves, 1997: 171).
2. *British Social Anthropology*. Outside France, Durkheim's initial influence was on British anthropology, especially the social anthropology of Alfred R. Radcliffe–Brown (1881–1955). According to Leach (1982: 31), Radcliffe–Brown's functionalism followed "the tradition established by Durkheim's *The Division of Labour in Society* (1893) and most of his ideas can be seen to derive from a wide, if somewhat insensitive, reading of contributions to Durkheim's journal, *L'Année Sociologique*". Notable second generation British social anthropologists influenced by Radcliffe– Brown include, Evans–Pritchard, Forde, Fortes, and Gluckman.
3. *North American Sociology*. Radcliffe–Brown also helped spread Durkheim's ideas to North America through the lectures he gave at the University of Chicago in the 1930s. In large measure, however, Durkheim's key ideas were transmitted through the works of Talcott Parsons and Robert K. Merton, the two leading exponents of structural–functionalism in American Sociology. Parsons (1937), for example, devotes four chapters to the work of Durkheim in the first volume of his major work, *The Structure of Social Action*. And Merton (1957) is "responsible for giving new impetus to the sociological application of Durkheim's concept of anomie, particularly with regard to the explanation of deviant behaviour other than suicide"

(Thompson, 1982: 120). Durkheim's influence on Erving Goffman also warrants mention. In his essay "The Nature of Deference and Demeanor", Goffman concludes by suggesting that "Durkheimian notions about primitive religion can be translated into concepts of deference and demeanor, and that these concepts help to grasp some aspects of secular living" (1956: 95).

Influence on the Sociology of Sport

As noted in the introduction, Durkheim's influence on the sociology of sport has been primarily indirect. Nonetheless, two major exceptions, one largely theoretical and one largely empirical in emphasis, stand out.

1. *Man, Play and Games.* Roger Caillois (1913–1978) offers the major theoretical analysis of games and sport from a Durkheimian perspective. A student of Marcel Mauss at the École Normale Supérieure in cultural anthropology, Caillois, like his contemporary Lévi–Strauss, was a direct intellectual descendant of Durkheim. In *Man, Play and Games* (1958/ 1961), Caillois not only proposes a sociology of games, he also "lay[s] the foundations for a sociology derived from games" (1958/1961: 67). In our view, this fully justifies awarding Caillois the title "father of sport sociology".

   Caillois offers a four-fold typology of game forms: *agon* (competition), *alea* (chance), *mimicry* (simulation) and *ilinx* (vertigo). "It is understandable," he argues, "how the choice to which they attest reveals the character, patterns and values of every society" (1958/1961: 66). To illustrate this, Caillois first describes the cultural forms of each game category that exist at the margins of the social order, such as carnival rides, motor-racing, and sky-diving for *ilinx*. He then depicts the institutionalised forms of each game category in everyday life, as, for example, lotteries, slot machines and speculation on the stockmarket for *alea*. Lastly, he details the forms of social corruption that are associated with obsessive addiction to a given game category as, for example, cheating and violence in the case of *agon*, and alienation and split personality in the case of *mimicry*.

   Sociologists of sport have largely ignored Caillois' work. The exceptions include the contributors to the *Encyclopedie De La Pleiade — Jeux Et Sports* (1967) published under the direction of Caillois, Ahokas' (1959) observations on the sociology of games and sports in Finland, and Loy's (1969) analysis of game forms, social structure and anomie in which he juxtaposes Caillois's four-fold typology of games (i.e., *agon, alea, ilinx, mimicry*) with Merton's (1957) five-fold typology of individual modes of adaptation (i.e., conformity, innovation, ritualism, retreatism and rebellion) to institutionalised goals and means.

2. *Suicide and Social Integration*. Durkheim made several explicit and implicit propositions about the relationships between suicide and social integration. Two of his major propositions are that: (1) "suicide varies inversely with the degree of integration of the social group of which the individual forms a part" (1952 [1897]: 209); and (2) the degree of integration is directly related to the degree of participation in collective ceremonies (1995 [1912]: 427). Drawing on Durkheim's propositions, Karnilowicz (1982) hypothesised that the frequency of suicide should be lower on, and around, national religious and civil holidays and major sporting events than on, and around, comparable non-ceremonial days.

To test his hypothesis, Karnilowicz analysed nationwide American data for rates of daily suicide between 1972 and 1978. He sought to ascertain whether rates of suicide were lower on and around (a) two major sporting events, i.e., the last day of the World Series in North American professional baseball and Super Bowl Sunday (the national championship game of American professional football), (b) two national civil holidays, i.e., 4 July and Thanksgiving Day, or (c) two national religious holidays, i.e., Easter Sunday and Christmas Day. He found empirical support for this hypothesis and Durkheim's key propositions that ceremonial occasions simultaneously increase social integration and lessen the incidence of suicides (Curtis, Loy & Karnilowicz, 1986).

Karnilowicz's empirical investigation reinforces Jarvie and Maguire's (1994: 17) theoretical observation that:

> Within a Durkheimian tradition, sport and leisure practices are seen as one of several available "collective representations". Through these, people represent to themselves, in symbolic form, the power of the social groups in which they live. These collective representations symbolise the structures and moral codes of society. By so doing, sport and leisure activities help to create and sustain, yet also be influenced by, existing social relations to which these symbolic structures relate.

Several authors have shown how sport blends the secular with the sacred, especially emphasising how sporting spectacles are functional equivalents of religion (Coles, 1975; Desmonde, 1952; Milton, 1972; Riordan, 1987).

Critical Commentary

Our brief discussion of Durkheim's intellectual influence hopefully confirms Mitchell's assessment of Durkheim that "he endeavoured to distinguish sociology from other sciences, to show that it possesses a distinctive method, and so to indicate it has a unique contribution to make to human knowledge" (1968: 82–3). Yet, notwithstanding his substantial legacy, Durkheim's ideas have been subjected to "unrelenting criticism" (Lukes 1973: 2). Here, we group these criticisms into five themes: "structure versus agency", "causal versus contingent analysis", "social explanation", "empirical adequacy", and "consensus versus conflict".

Structure versus Agency

While contemporary sociologists remain divided between those who stress the external influence of "objective" social structures on human conduct and those who emphasise individuals' "subjective" states and meanings in determining human action, Durkheim certainly erred when he proposed that sociologists should disregard the subjective thoughts and feelings of individual actors. In other words, by failing to develop an adequate theory of the subject (Swingewood, 1984: 119), Durkheim "presents an extraordinarily one-sided portrait of social order and the action which informs it" (Alexander, 1982: 299).

According to Alexander (1982: 75), Durkheim's principal problem is a lack of explanatory precision with respect to structure: "How does structure hold individuals within its limits? Of what are these limits composed? If structure exists, somehow, outside of the individual, can it act only in opposition to freedom?" As Swingewood (1984) illustrates, nowhere is this problem more evident than in understanding the relation between determinism and free action. For example, rather than limiting free action, "structural differentiation in effect allows for greater participation, democratisation and activity within the institutions of civil society: anomie is thus an expression of the increasing autonomy of the human subject struggling against social forces which seek to control and repudiate his/her interests" (1984: 119).

In the 1980s, sociologists of sport debated whether sport constitutes a system of conscious agency or one largely determined by social structure (Gruneau, 1983/1999). The debate largely subsided in the 1990s. Today, sociologists of sport mostly agree that adequate theorising requires sensitivity toward "the dialectical relationships between socially structured possibilities and human agency". In short, there is greater consensus that theories of sport should "avoid one-sided considerations of players as voluntary agents acting in the absence of constraining structures and of structures which do not allow for the creative and transformative capacities of players" (Gruneau, 1983/1999: 27–8).

Causal versus Contingent Analysis

Although Durkheim is credited with being the first sociologist to engage in causal modelling, contemporary critics find his causal models wanting. Turner and Beeghley (1981: 379) point out that Durkheim's models of religion and division of labour are "too abstract, too tied to naïve evolutionism, and too confused by notions of function". In a similar vein, Swingewood (1984: 228) notes that "Durkheim's functional approach to the study of institutions . . . tended to emphasise the synchronic, structural dimensions of society at the expense of the diachronic, the genetic and historical . . . generating abstract, ahistorical social typologies such as mechanical and organic solidarity." Lastly, Ritzer and Bell (1981: 966) point out that "his work is marred by one-way causal attributions, by an overemphasis on the macro-subjective level, by an underdeveloped conception of human nature, and a restricted view of science."

Again, most contemporary sociologists of sport are wary of synchronic explanations of the relationships between sport and, for example, race and gender. They are much more careful to explore the "diachronic connections that explain how and why such patterns are socially generated and how and why, under specific conditions and for specific periods of time, they persist or undergo structured processes of change" (Dunning, Maguire & Pearton, 1993: 7–8).

Social Explanation

Most general criticisms directed at functional explanations also apply to Durkheim (see Campbell, 1981: 163). For example, his causal model of the division of labour "confused causal and functional approaches to explanation" by failing to "specif[y] precisely how the needs met by the division of labour (that is, social solidarity) cause it to emerge". Without such an explanation, Durkheim's model assumes a teleology in which "the end-state (social solidarity) causes the very thing (the division of labour) that brings about this end-state" (Turner & Beeghley, 1981: 371). Similarly, the model is tautological in that it fails to separate cause and effect: "the division of labour causes social solidarity, while the need for social solidarity causes the division of labour" (Turner & Beeghley, 1981: 375–6).

Functionalist explanations in the sociology of sport have also proved susceptible to the problems of teleology and tautology. Some sociologists of sport, for example, attribute what they call the corruption of sport — the mania for winning, widespread cheating, media manipulation and sensationalism, the cult of athletic stardom — to the institutionalisation of an autonomous social practice. According to these explanations, the primary function of sport is to help individuals and groups adapt to stresses induced by industrialisation, or to compensate them for unsatisfying modern lives. But such accounts invariably fail to explain how the needs met by sport — adaptation and compensation — cause sport to emerge. Similarly, they fail to separate cause and effect: institutionalisation corrupts an autonomous practice (sport), while the need to overcome the strains of institutionalisation provided the catalyst for the emergence of sport.

Empirical Adequacy

Theory and explanation aside, Durkheim has received high praise for his focus on empirical inquiry and quantitative methods of investigation and data analysis. Yet, even this "positive" aspect has not escaped criticism. For example, Durkheim's work on *Suicide* (1897) is typically cited as the best demonstration of the application of the principles he outlines in *The Rules of Sociological Method* (1895), but it falls far short of current empirical standards as Smelser and Warner (1976: 82) note:

> Official statistics on suicide rates, on which Durkheim relied, are notoriously subject to error and bias. His use of ecological correlations is problematic, and his refutations bypass the possibility of multiple causation.

They also fault Durkheim's strategy of refuting alternative explanations, suggesting that his attempts to "prove a thesis by refuting alternatives is in principle close to impossible: all alternatives would have to be shown incorrect in order to establish Durkheim's thesis as the only one valid" (Smelser & Warner, 1976: 82–3).

Durkheim's selection and handling of evidence has been roundly condemned. In the former case, commenting on "his enthusiasm to exhibit the comprehensiveness of his purely social explanations of social phenomena," Campbell (1981: 163) criticises Durkheim's "tendency to select just those examples of the phenomena in question which could be fitted in his project". In the latter case, Lukes (1973: 33) refers to Durkheim's alleged "high-handed treatment of evidence": whenever anyone pointed out that the facts were inconsistent with his theories, Durkheim would retort, "the facts are wrong!" Empirical adequacy is, of course, hardly unique to Durkheimian functionalism. Certainly it remains a problem in the sociology of sport where abstract formulations, devoid of concrete historical examples, still find publishers.

Consensus versus Conflict

Perhaps the most valid criticism of Durkheim's work is that conflict is notably absent from his theory of society. This is clearly evident in Durkheim's conception of the State as a phenomenon that reflects *collective consciousness* and, thus, ignores issues associated with the distribution and allocation of power (Jones, 1986: 57). Similarly, in *The Elementary Forms of Religious Life* (1912) Durkheim takes no cognizance of the roles played by dynamic religious leaders, or of "the way religion functions in social conflict and asymmetrical relations of power" (Jones, 1986: 152).

In short, throughout his theoretical writings, Durkheim overemphasises social consensus and integration to the extent that he dismisses those societies in which conflict is the norm as "not really . . . societ[ies] at all" (Rex, 1969: 135). More tellingly, Rex (1969: 135) observes that Durkheim, having correctly contended "that participation in a social and normative order is essential to human happiness, seems to assume wrongly, that any social and normative order, provided it is integrated, will guarantee this happiness". Thompson (1982: 68) attributes at least some of Durkheim's notions of consensus and integration to his concept of evolutionism: "There was an element of wishful-thinking in his belief that contemporary conflicts and social problems were simply part of a transitional crisis before the emergence of a more healthy state."

The consensus versus conflict debate became a major controversy in sociology that spilled over into the study of sport. In *The Joy of Sports* Michael Novak (1976) claims that sports "serve a religious function" (1976: 20) and that the "central rituals" of religion reveal "the unconscious needs of the civilisation" (1976: 29). Brohm (1978), on the other hand, argues that sport meets the ideological functional requirements of the capitalist mode of production by, *inter alia*, mystifying class conflict, justifying and stabilising the established order, depoliticising social life, preparing youth for labour, militarising and regimenting youth, and commodifying people. In so doing, sport strengthens bourgeois rule (1978: 175–182).

Classical Theorists as Exemplary Colleagues

In light of the critiques of his work, much of which is over a century old, the reader is perfectly entitled to ask, "Why read Durkheim?" Indeed, the question might be asked of any of the classical sociologists. By way of concluding our account of Durkheim, we address a critical question for students, "Why read the classics?"

Robert K. Merton contends that "every contemporary sociologist with a claim to sociological literacy has had direct and repeated encounters with the works of the founding fathers" (1967: 29). He suggests that these encounters serve a variety of functions ranging from:

> the direct pleasure of coming upon an aesthetically pleasing and more cogent version of one's own ideas, through the satisfaction of independent confirmation of these ideas by a powerful mind, and the educative function of developing high standards of taste for sociological work, to the interactive effect of developing new ideas by turning to older writings within the context of contemporary knowledge (1967: 29).

C. Wright Mills offers a more succinct version of Merton's explanation: "To the individual social scientist who feels himself a part of the classic tradition, social science is a part of a craft" (1959: 195). With respect to the mastery of sociology as an intellectual craft, Neil J. Smelser and R. Stephen Warner (1976) propose that the classics act both as data and as colleagues.

The Classics as Data

Classical writings in sociology provide a variety of forms of data that serve a number of purposes, including intellectual history, the history of sociology, and comparative sociological analyses. C. Wright Mills is quite specific on this matter: "from some, you learn by restating systematically what the man says on a given point or as a whole; some you accept or refute, giving reasons and arguments; others you use as a source of suggestions for your own elaborations and projects" (1959: 202).

The Classics as Colleagues

Smelser and Warner (1976) recommend treating the classic theorists as colleagues and engaging in what Merton (1967: 35) calls "a dialogue between the dead and the living". They give three major reasons for considering the classics as colleagues. First, the works of the classic social theorists "are replete with . . . sociological ideas — that we can apply to our own understanding of society" (1967: 6). Second, a close reading of their primary materials allows us "to recapture the sense of discovery that they experienced" (1967: 8). Third, the classical social theorists "are or ought to be role models for contemporary sociologists, especially in the breadth of vision of their intellectual efforts" (1967: 9). An implicit fourth reason given by Smelser and Warner (1976) is that the works of classical social theorists should be studied for their moral and ethical implications. For example, in Marx, Weber and Durkheim "there is a strong ethical or normative inclination, a bias toward scholarly issues the resolution of which would significantly enhance the quality of human life" (1967: 10).

Durkheim as an Exemplary Colleague

Sherman (1974) considers Durkheim, Marx and Weber as exemplars of a specific kind of science and a particular kind of Sociology. He traces these to their individual interests and motivations. Max Weber is an exemplar of an interpretive sociology and an historical–hermeneutic form of science "motivated by a practical interest in communication of understanding (Verstehen)" (1974: 176). Karl Marx is an exemplar of a critical sociology and a critical science "motivated by an emancipatory interest in transforming society" (1974: 176). And Emile Durkheim is an exemplar of a nomological sociology and an empirical–analytic form of science, motivated by "an interest in generating nomological (law-like) knowledge" (1974: 176).[5]

Given contemporary concerns about the exploitive nature of sport, and in light of the hermeneutic turn in methodology, it is hardly surprising that Marx and Weber exert a stronger influence on contemporary sociology of sport than Durkheim. But neither these concerns nor interests should make obsolete a reading of Durkheim. Indeed, Sherman (1974: 180) presents a strong case for

[5]Different sociologists apply different classifications to Durkheim as a social theorist. For example, Ritzer (1975) cites Durkheim as the exemplar of "the social facts paradigm"; Stone and Faberman (1967) suggest that Durkheim was moving toward the perspective of "symbolic interaction"; similarly, Coenen (1981) contends that "The opposition between phenomenological sociology and Durkheimian sociology is not as absolute as it has often been presented".

obliging students "to give each paradigm a fair hearing". As he explains, "to know fully what I am doing, I need to know what I am not doing that I could be doing; in other words, I must know the opportunity costs. And for that, I must read the Masters".[6]

References

Abel, T. (1970). *The Foundation of Sociological Theory*. New York: Random House.

Ahokas, J. (1959). The land of competition: Observations on the sociology of games in Finland. *Diogenes, 26*, 97–106.

Alexander, J. (1982). *The Antinomies of Classical Thought: Marx and Durkheim* (Vol. 2, *Theoretical Logic in Sociology*). Berkeley: University of California Press.

Aron, R. (1967). *Main Currents in Sociological Thought II: Durkheim/Pareto/Weber*. New York: Basic Books.

Benoit–Smullyan, E. (1966). The sociologism of Emile Durkheim and his school. In: H. Barnes (ed.), *An Introduction to the History of Sociology (an abridged edition)* (pp. 205–243). Chicago: Phoenix Books.

Bergesen, A. (1984). Swanson's Neo–Durkheimian sociology of religion. *Sociological Analysis, 45*(3), 179–184.

Bierstedt, R. (1966). *Emile Durkheim*. London: Weidenfeld and Nicolson.

Blau, P. (1998). Culture and social structure. In: A. Sica (ed.), *What is Social Theory?: The Philosophical Debates* (pp. 265–275). Oxford: Blackwell.

Breault, K. D., & Barkey, K. (1982). A comparative analysis of Durkheim's theory of egoistic suicide. *Sociological Quarterly, 23*, 321–331.

Brohm, J.-M. (1978). *Sport: A Prison of Measured Time*. London: Ink Links.

Caillois, R. (1958/1961). *Man, Play and Games*. New York: Free Press.

Campbell, T. (1981). *Seven Theories of Human Society*. Oxford: Clarendon Press.

Clarke, C. J. (1987). The Durkheimian relationship between the division of labour and population: Cross-national historical evidence. *Sociological Focus, 20*(1), 13–31.

Clinard, M. B. (ed.) (1964). *Anomie and Deviant Behavior: A Discussion and Critique*. New York: Free Press.

Coenen, H. (1981). Developments in the phenomenological reading of Durkheim's work. *Social Forces, 59*(4), 951–965.

Coles, R. (1975). Football as a surrogate religion? In: M. Hill (ed.), *A Sociological Yearbook of Religion in Britain* (pp. 61–77). London: SCM Press.

Coser, L. A. (1971). *Masters of Sociological Thought*. New York: Harcourt, Brace Jovanovich.

Curtis, J. E., Loy, J. W., & Karnilowicz, W. (1986). A comparison of suicide-dip effects of major sports events and civil holidays. *Sociology of Sport Journal, 3*(1), 1–14.

[6]"Presentists" and "historicists" currently debate the "proper" way to read the masters (cf., Kelly, 1990).

Day, L. H. (1987). Durkheim on religion and suicide — a demographic critique. *Sociology,* *21*(3), 449–461.

Desmonde, W. (1952). The bullfight as a religious festival. *American Imago, 9,* 173–195.

Douglas, J. D. (1967). *The Social Meanings of Suicide.* Princeton, NJ: Princeton University Press.

Dunning, E., Maguire, J., & Pearton, R. (1993). *The Sports Process: A Comparative and Developmental Approach.* Champaign, IL: Human Kinetics.

Durkheim, E. (1893/1933). *The Division of Labor in Society.* Glencoe, IL: Free Press.

Durkheim, E. (1895/1964). *The Rules of Sociological Method* (8th edition). Glencoe, IL: Free Press.

Durkheim, E. (1897/1952). *Suicide.* London: Routledge & Kegan Paul.

Durkheim, E. (1912/1995). *The Elementary Forms of Religious Life.* New York: Free Press.

Durkheim, E., & Mauss, M. (1903/1963). *Primitive Classification.* Chicago: University of Chicago Press.

Encyclopedie de la Pleiade–Jeux et Sports. (1967). Paris: Editions Gallimard.

Giddens, A. (1976). *New Rules of Sociological Method.* New York: Basic Books.

Giddens, A. (1978). *Emile Durkheim.* Harmondsworth: Penguin Books.

Gieryn, T. F. (1982). Durkheim's sociology of scientific knowledge. *Journal of the History of the Behavioral Sciences, 18,* 107–129.

Goffman, E. (1956). The nature of deference and demeanor. *American Anthropologist, 58,* 473–502.

Gruneau, R. (1983/1999). *Class, Sports, and Social Development.* Champaign, IL: Human Kinetics.

Jarvie, G., & Maguire, J. (1994). *Sport and Leisure in Social Thought.* London: Routledge.

Jary, D., & Jary, J. (1991). *Collins Dictionary of Sociology.* London: HarperCollins Publishers.

Jones, R. A. (1986). *Emile Durkheim: An Introduction to Four Major Works.* Beverly Hills, CA: Sage Publications.

Karnilowicz, W. (1982). *An Analysis of the Effects of Ceremonial Occasions on Frequency of Suicides in the United States, 1972–1978.* Unpublished master's thesis, University of Illinois, Urbana, Illinois.

Kelly, C. (1990). Methods of reading and the discipline of sociology: The case of Durkheimian studies. *Canadian Journal of Sociology,* 301–324.

Leach, E. (1982). *Social Anthropology.* Oxford: Oxford University Press.

Levi–Strauss, C. (1950/1987). *Introduction to the Work of Marcel Mauss.* London: Routledge & Kegan Paul.

Loy, J. W. (1969). Game forms, social structure and anomie. In: R. Brown and B. J. Cratty (eds), *New Perspectives of Man in Action* (pp. 181–199). Englewood Cliffs, NJ: Prentice-Hall.

Loy, J., & Booth, D. (2000). Functionalism, sport, and society. In: E. Dunning and J. Coakley (eds), *Handbook of Sports Studies* (pp. 8–28). London: Sage Publications.

Lukes, S. (1973). *Emile Durkheim: His Life and Work.* London: Allen Lane.

Marks, S. R. (1974). Durkheim's theory of anomie. *American Journal of Sociology, 80*(2), 329–363.

Masumura, W. T. (1977). Social integration and suicide: A test of Durkheim's theory. *Behavior Science Research, 12*(4), 251–269.

Mauss, M. (1925/1967). *The Gift: Forms and Functions of Exchange in Archaic Societies.* New York: W. W. Norton.

Merton, R. K. (1957). *Social Theory and Social Structure* (2nd edition). Glencoe, IL: Free Press.

Merton, R. K. (1967). *On Theoretical Sociology.* New York: Free Press.

Mestrovic, S. G. (1989). Searching for the starting points of scientific inquiry: Durkheim's rules of sociological method and Schopenhaur's philosophy. *Sociological Inquiry, 59*(3), 267–286.

Mills, Wright, C. (1959). *The Sociological Imagination.* New York: Grove Press.

Milton, B. (1972). *Sports as a Functional Equivalent of Religion.* Unpublished Master's thesis, University of Wisconsin, Madison.

Mitchell, G. D. (1968). *A Hundred Years of Sociology.* Chicago: Aldine Publishing.

Novak, M. (1976). *The Joy of Sports.* New York: Basic Books.

Parsons, T. (1937/1968). *The Structure of Social Action* (Vol. I). New York: Free Press.

Parsons, T. (1974). The life and work of Emile Durkheim. In: E. Durkheim, *Sociology and Philosophy* (pp. xliii–lxx). New York: Free Press.

Pearce, F. (1987). A reworking of Durkheim's *Suicide. Economy and Society, 16*(4), 526–567.

Pescosolido, B. A. (1990). The social context of religious integration and suicide: Pursuing the network explanation. *Sociological Quarterly, 31*(3), 337–357.

Rex, J. (1969). Emile Durkheim. In: T. Ralson (ed.), *The Founding Fathers of Social Science* (pp. 128–135). Harmondsworth: Penguin Books.

Riordan, J. (1987). Soviet muscular socialism: A Durkheimian analysis. *Sociology of Sport Journal, 4*(4), 376–393.

Ritzer, G. (1975). *Sociology — A Multiple Paradigm Science.* Boston: Allyn & Bacon.

Ritzer, G., & Bell, R. (1981). Emile Durkheim: Exemplar for an integrated sociological paradigm? *Social Forces, 59*(4), 966–995.

Sherman, L. W. (1974). Uses of the masters. *The American Sociologist, 9*(4), 176–181.

Smelser, N. J., & Warner, R. S. (1976). *Sociological Theory: Historical and Formal.* Morristown, NJ: General Learning Press.

Stone, G. P., & Farberman, H. A. (1967). On the edge of rapprochement: Was Durkheim moving toward the perspective of symbolic interaction? *Sociological Quarterly,* 149–164.

Swanson, G. E. (1966). *Birth of the Gods.* Ann Arbor, MI: University of Michigan Press.

Swingewood, A. (1984). *A Short History of Sociological Thought.* New York: St. Martin's Press.

Thompson, K. (1982). *Emile Durkheim.* London: Tavistock Publications.

Turner, J. H. (1981). Emile Durkheim's theory of integration in differentiated social systems. *Pacific Sociological Review, 24*(4), 379–391.

Turner, J. H. (1990). Emile Durkheim's theory of social organization. *Social Forces, 68*(4), 1089–1103.

Turner, J. H., & Beeghley, L. (1981). *The Emergence of Sociological Theory*. Homewood, IL: Dorsey Press.

Turner, J. H., & Maryanski, A. (1979). *Functionalism*. Menlo Park, CA: Benjamin Cummings.

Turner, S. P. (1983). Durkheim as a methodologist–Part I–realism, teleology, and action. *Philosophy of the Social Sciences, 13*, 425–450.

Turner, S. P. (1984). Durkheim as a methodologist–Part II–collective forces, causation, and probability. *Philosophy of the Social Sciences, 14*, 51–71.

Wiseman, B., & Groves, J. (1997). *Lévi–Strauss for Beginners*. St. Leonards, NSW, Australia: Allen & Unwin.

Chapter 3

Max Weber and the Sociology of Sport

Hart Cantelon and Alan G. Ingham

Our objective in this chapter is to introduce some of Max Weber's ideas and how they have been or can be used in the study of sport. It is our contention that much of what was written in the sociology of sport between 1960 and 1980 has a basis in the issues that were part and parcel of the research and methodological concerns of Max Weber (see Ingham & Donnelly, 1997). In an academic career which spanned three decades, Weber's research interests included comparative religion, economic history, German politics and sociological theory. From Weber's multiple writings, we have chosen themes that we believe are most important for those students interested in the sociology of sport.

We begin with a brief introduction of the man and his theoretical work. Then we introduce his 'ideal type' methodology that dictated how Weber performed his historical and comparative research. We introduce the serious reservations that Weber had about the instrumental rationality in, and the rationalisation of, contemporary life (his so-called *iron cage*), and its manifestations in bureaucracy and technologised science. Finally, we look at Weber's analysis of social stratification, paying particular attention to his concept of status and his analysis of open and closed relationships.

Weber: A Brief Biography

Weber was born on April 21, 1864 in Erfurt, Germany. While today we think of Weber primarily as a sociologist, sociology was the last of a succession of disciplines with which he was professionally associated (Hughes, 1958: 292). Weber began his scholarly life in Law, was offered a professorship in Economics at Freiburg and later at Heidelberg. It was only towards the end of his life that he began to lecture in sociology, in Vienna and, finally, Munich (Hughes, 1958: 292). Throughout his scholarly endeavours, Weber practised the historian's craft although he was never formally trained as such.

Theory, Sport & Society
Copyright © 2002 by Elsevier Science Ltd.
All rights of reproduction in any form reserved.
ISBN: 0-7623-0742-0

Weber travelled an intellectual path that encountered the works of notable European scholars like Benedetto Croce, Wilhem Dilthey, Sigmund Freud, Karl Marx, and Heinrich Rickert. He tried to effect a compromise between various theoretical positions: the historical materialism of Marx; French positivism; the German tradition of idealism; and, in his work on charisma, Weber came close to the treatises of Nietzsche on the will to power. As regards the latter, he recognised that both historical and structural determinants impacted upon charismatic leaders. In particular, Weber noted that the ascetic rationalism of charisma inevitably led to patterned behaviour which he called *routinisation* (see Mitzman, 1969: 242).

Weber was a superior thinker. In 1889, upon the submission of his doctoral thesis, *History of Commercial Societies in the Middle Ages*, the noted German historian, Theodor Mommsen stated: "When I have to go into my grave, I would gladly say to no other than the highly esteemed Max Weber: My son, here is my spear; it is becoming too heavy for my arm" (Mitzman, 1969: 140). This was praise indeed coming from an intellectual of Theodor Mommsen's stature; and it was not misguided. Despite suffering from severe mental depression after his father's death, Weber's scholarly productivity was as voluminous as it was diverse. He had what Talcott Parsons called "an encyclopaedic mind" (1937: 500). Much of Weber's work remains in the original German, but the more important writings have been translated into English. They include *Economy and Society* (1968), *The Protestant Ethic and Spirit of Capitalism* (1958a), *General Economic History* (1927), *The Religion of China* (1951), *The Religion of India* (1958b), *Ancient Judaism* (1952) and *The Methodology of the Social Sciences* (1949). Many of his essays have been translated and appear in edited anthologies (e.g., Runciman, 1978; Eisenstadt, 1968; Martindale, 1958; Eldridge, 1980; Andreski, 1983; Hamilton, 1991).

There are countless reasons why one might settle upon a Weberian type of sociology in the study of sport. For one of the authors (Cantelon), the choice was as pragmatic as it was fortuitous. If one was interested in ice hockey in the Soviet Union, one needed to understand the modern bureaucratic state. Thus, the directive from the thesis supervisor to *read Weber;* and in the subsequent reading, it was found that the man, unlike many of his contemporaries, did have things to say about sport, be it the comprehensive apprenticeship of the feudal knight for competition in the tournament (Bendix, 1960: 364) or the peculiarities of sport in American education (Gerth & Mills, 1958: 149). For the other author (Ingham), his advisor, Charles Page, simply considered any student uneducated if s/he had not read Weber. Moreover, for both authors, Weber did provide the theoretical backbone for the doctoral thesis (Ingham, *American Sport in Transition: The Maturation of Industrial Capitalism and its Impact upon Sport,*

1978; Cantelon, *A Weberian Analysis of the Rational Development of Ice Hockey under Scientific Socialism in the Soviet Union*, 1981). Consequently, we firmly believe in the importance of a Weberian Sociology for the serious study of sport.

Weber: The Ideal Type

In order to most fully understand human action, Weber felt it was important to develop an objective definition, an archetype/prototype of the concept under consideration (1949: 49–112). Thus, he developed the "ideal type" methodology. Weber argued that much of the scholarly work in sociology suffered from ambiguity and lack of clarity. The "ideal type" methodology was one means by which Weber believed these shortcomings could be overcome.

It is perhaps expedient to begin a discussion of the methodology with an example from sport, such as Ingham *et al*'s (1987) research on the development of American baseball. How might one make sense of the transformation of a game from the great American pastime into a profitable business enterprise, employing wealthy professional entertainers? This is the underlying question that the ideal type might answer. Through a compilation of the key historical actors and events, and by applying a subjective understanding to interpret the motives of the former (Weber's *verstehen*), Ingham *et al.* were able to suggest a perfectly plausible series of characteristics which would define baseball as a business. Thus, William Hulbert disciplined the market by selling others on the need for one prestigious league with only a select number of the most economically viable clubs able to apply for membership. This is called "cartelisation" and it guaranteed that member firms would have a monopoly in their consumer marketplaces. The introduction of binding contracts and the right to reserve players' services disciplined athletes who were wont to sell their skills to the highest bidder, sometimes in the middle of a season. Further, with Hulbert's interventions, there was no longer the assumption that spectators would be active members of a club. They were considered paying customers who were urged to consume an attractive product; and with this change came the gradual dislocation between the ball club and the community in which it was located. In short, Ingham *et al.* were able to provide a clear understanding of what is meant by the baseball business.

In keeping with Weber's contention that reality remains "infinitely complex" (1949: 78), Ingham *et al.* were able to suggest the long term outcome that Hulbert's actions had upon American sport — his experiment would eventually make cartelisation, monopoly, and monopsony (i.e., control of inputs that restrict the choice of teams to which a player could offer his services) taken-for-granted features of the American sport industry regardless of whether or not the sport league was exempted from anti-trust litigation. Ingham, Howell and Schilperoort (1986) also extrapolated from the American case to the English Football League. They argued, at the time of writing, that the new Premier League under debate would essentially reproduce the American characteristics in the cartelisation/monopoly "game". Were they wrong? We do not think so. The possibility of a new 'Euro League' only confirms their predictions.

Others in sport studies have implicitly used Weber's "ideal type" methodology. Eric Dunning's contrast between folk games and modern sports, and his "bifurcation of football" model found in *Barbarians, Gentlemen and Players: A Sociological Study of the Development of Rugby Football* (Dunning & Sheard, 1979) exemplify Weber's ideal type. Charles Korr, in his in-depth historical study of West Ham United Football Club (1986) and Allen Guttmann (1978) in the widely cited *From Ritual to Record: The Nature of Modern Sports* also show evidence of the methodology. Each developed visions of sport that owe much to what Weber was trying to achieve with the ideal type. In fact, Weber himself, in conceptualising ideal types, anticipated that others would use them, explicitly or implicitly. As he put it: ". . . as soon as [the historian] attempts to go beyond the bare establishment of concrete relationships and to determine the cultural significance of even the simplest individual event in order to 'characterise' it, [he/she] must use concepts which are precisely and unambiguously definable only in the form of ideal types" (Weber, 1949: 92).

In his contrast between folk games and modern sports, Dunning (1975) did not intend that his ideal-typical portrayals would describe the characteristics of *every* folk game or of *every* modern sport. Rather, he selected key features that allowed him to show the effects of social development on the constitution of modern sport. The same can be said of Ingham's (1978) ideal types that contrasted pre-modern with modern sport. With the "ideal type" methodology, he developed hypotheses concerning the determinants of sport's social transformation. Ingham was indebted to Dunning for some of the key elements of the former's ideal types. But if one looks at the two, it is obvious that they are dissimilar. The reason is that they were constructed for different purposes and from varied theoretical orientations.

It should be emphasised that the ideal typical methodology ties in with Weber's underlying principle of *verstehen* (the notion of subjective understanding) in that the ideal type is constructed in terms of one's perception of the world that is to be analysed. *Verstehen*, therefore, allows the scholar to attribute to others those thoughts and feelings one would experience if found in like circumstances (see Weber, 1968: 8–10). At this point, we wish to introduce

Weber's concept of rationalisation since it is this that is at the basis of much of what we have to say about contemporary sport. It is important therefore, that we clarify the term and, in so doing, to outline the four ideal typical constructs by which Weber explained social action.

Modes of Social Action

In developing the concept of rationalisation, Weber was resolved that it was not so much an orientation as it was a *process*; one through which "... explicit, abstract, intellectually calculable rules and procedures are increasingly substituted for sentiment, tradition, and rule of thumb in all spheres of activity" (Wrong, 1970: 26). It is a process of systematisation and standardisation, the result of which is to increase the number of cases to which explicit, abstract, impersonal rules and procedures can be applied. Hence, rationalisation facilitates the trend from particularism to universalism, but it does so at the price of depersonalisation and often, oppressive routine. Weber saw this process as one of *disenchantment, demystification*, and *estrangement* and he called it "the iron cage of rationalisation" (see Mitzman, 1969: 171–175).

Weber's concept of estrangement has overtones of Marx's concept of *alienation*. While the latter was developed in class theory (in terms of the capitalist forces and relations of production), the former was developed from a more liberal republican perspective. Nonetheless, both Marx and Weber, in their different ways, were concerned with human rights and with the forces leading to their denial. The process of rationalisation, Weber thought, had a profound impact upon how life was lived and he characterised social action accordingly.

He classified social action into four ideal types: the instrumentally rational; the value rational; the traditional; and the affectual or emotional. Instrumental rationality involves action in the quest towards a goal that is deliberately selected by the actor from several goals that are available, none of which is absolute. In instrumentally rational action, Talcott Parsons translates: "... the end, the means, and the secondary results are all taken into account and weighed. This involves rational consideration of alternative means to the end, of the relations to the end, to other prospective results of employment of any given means, and finally of the relative importance of different possible ends" (Weber, 1947: 117). In Parsons' definition, the emphasis is on the *calculative* and *conditional* nature of instrumental rationality. In other words, under specific circumstances, one weighs the advantages/disadvantages of pursuing one goal over another, and how best to achieve this objective.

While rationalisation and instrumental rationality are analytically distinct ideal type concepts, in the real world, they are related reciprocally. The instrumentally rational orientation to social action provides the impetus for rationalisation and rationalisation widens the sphere in which instrumental rationality is taken for granted. Through the process of rationalisation, instrumental rationality intrudes into more and more of our personal life circumstances. As Weber put it in his classic study of Protestantism and capitalism, the early captains of industry chose to be rational. We are compelled to be so (see Weber, 1958a: 181).

Consequently, we would argue that it is instrumental rationality which is the dominant form of social action in contemporary society, and that much of our sporting experience relies on such a world-view. Consider the following. Instrumental rationality is widely employed by those who control the careers of athletes — "What is the performance value or gate value of this athlete?" "Should we keep him or her?" Instrumental rationality also is employed by those whose scholarly careers are anchored in the *performance discourse* of elite sports (e.g., exercise scientists, biomechanicians, sport medical personnel, sport psychologists, etc.). They ask: 'How can I construct knowledge which not only enhances the performance of athletes, but which brings me prestige in the globalised scientific community of sport?' (See Ingham & Lawson, 1999). In the Royal Commission testimonies after the infamous Ben Johnson drug scandal, it was telling that by his own admission, Chief Justice Charles Dubin was astounded to learn how matter-of-fact were the calculations of Canadian athletes and coaches, as to whether or not the use of performance-enhancing drugs should be considered (1990) and the relative ease of finding medical doctors willing to prescribe anabolic steroids.

Value-rational action refers to action undertaken with regard to consciously formulated, ultimate or *absolute* values. It involves the unremitting pursuit of such values regardless of the costs entailed. The sought-after goal is fixed and so are the means for its attainment. Value-rationality can be seen in anyone who practices his/her convictions — such as those related to duty, honour, or a religious calling — unmindful of its prospects for success. Weber cited the actions of the sea captain, intent on ensuring that everyone else left the sinking ship before himself (see Gerth & Mills, 1958). Such behaviour is best summed up by the declaration, "I did what I did because, given my beliefs, it was my duty, my obligation. On my honour, I could not have chosen to do otherwise" (Weber, 1968: 25).

Such value-rational action deserves to be considered when examining organisations such as the International Olympic Committee (IOC). While we would agree with many of the conclusions developed by journalists Simpson and Jennings (1992) in their exposé of the IOC, we would also suggest that it is important to acknowledge, as well, the unswerving loyalty (value rationality) an IOC member may have to the spirit of Olympism. The classic example would be Avery Brundage whose commitment to amateurism could only be sustained by his millionaire income.

Under Juan Antonio Samaranch, the value-rational idealism of de Coubertin and Brundage has been commodified. The 1984 Los Angeles Games were the first in the history of the modern Olympics to use an instrumentally rational marketing strategy to privatise the Games and to, "embarrassingly", make a profit (see Gruneau & Cantelon, 1987). All the Games that have followed have taken the L.A. strategy as *the* model for their Olympic bids. The corruption of the value-rational Olympic ideal by capitalism has been evidenced in the revelations concerning the Salt Lake City Organising Committee and its bribing of certain IOC members. This is not a new phenomenon — the instrumental rationality of corporate capitalism and of performance-enhancing technology (ergogenic aids) have been undermining the value-rationality of Olympism for years.

Traditional social action seems less rational because it is like a reflex-action — an automatic response to an habitualised stimulus. Such action is dictated by custom or by beliefs that have become second nature. Thus, the actor need not imagine a goal, or be conscious of a value, or be stirred by immediate emotion: he/she simply obeys "cultural reflexes" that have become entrenched by conditioning, what Weber called a "settled orientation" (see Weber, 1964: 75; Aron, 1970: 221). One does something merely because it has always been done this way. It is important for disadvantaged groups to understand this form of social action. One has a richer and deeper understanding of resistance by those in authority towards the democratisation of sporting opportunities for others (such as in the case of the Title IX debates in the USA — see Chapter 5).

Moreover, as Raymond Williams (1977) and Eric Hobsbawm (1983) have noted, the use of tradition by dominant members of society is always selective — residuals are put to use to serve the interests of the dominant. Thus, authority figures can instrumentally call upon selective tradition or "invent" tradition (Belanger, 1999). Dominant interests frequently use nostalgia to sustain their authority in the present in the form of civic rituals that they portray as being in the interests of the whole (Ingham *et al.*, 1987). Sporting events (such as New Year's Day football bowl games in the USA, Cup Finals and Championships on both sides of the Atlantic) and calendar events (St. Patrick's Day, National State holidays) are crucial here. "Let's have a parade," say those in both the private and public sectors. Just as the value-rational philosophy of the IOC has been pre-empted by instrumentality, so too can traditional rationality be made to serve instrumental rational interests.

Affectual or emotional social action ". . . stands on the borderline of what can be considered 'meaningfully' orientated . . . It may, for instance, consist in an uncontrolled reaction to some exceptional circumstance" (Weber, 1968: 25). In fact, Weber did not develop this ideal-type to the same extent as he did the other forms of rationality. According to Parsons (Weber, 1947), it became a residual dumping ground for behaviour that did not necessarily fit conveniently into the other forms. As an example, one might classify a kick delivered in anger in a soccer game as affectual action. In a civilised society, when asked about this kick, an athlete might say "Well, there is no good reason for what I did, but I couldn't control myself" (e.g., Englishman David Beckham's infamous retaliation to an Argentinian player in the 1998 World Cup in France). Be that as it may, like the other forms of social action, much of what might be considered affectual may be deliberate/calculated, instrumentally rational action to put an opponent off his/her game and to provoke the retaliation penalty. The instrumental creates a condition (a climate of tolerance) for the affectual to occur — in this case, the possibility of further violence.

As already noted, we contend that it is instrumental rationality that characterises most social action in advanced capitalist societies. The modern nation state is organised structurally and ideologically to legitimate the claims to authority of the dominant capitalist classes. To expand upon this observation is beyond the scope of our present discussion but it does lead nicely into what we shall have to say about the parallel administrative structures and the technologies that appear compatible with a particular social action. This compatibility lies in the fact that not all forms of social action are equal. There is a power differential that must be introduced, for as Weber notes:

> Even without any formal power of command, an 'empire state' or more correctly, those individuals who are the decisive ones within it, either through authority or through the market, can exercise a far-reaching and occasionally even a despotic hegemony (Weber, 1968: 945).

One may conceive of administration as the complexity of structures, rules of conduct, norms, ethical beliefs, and appropriate everyday behaviour, which is designed within a particular form of social action. As such, bureaucracy is much more expansive and complex than the "red tape" which is most often associated with the term. It is a complex "structure of domination [which affects] the general habits of the people more by virtue of the 'ethos' which it [establishes] than through the creation of . . . technical means of commerce" (Weber, 1968: 1104). What then is this structured form of domination, and what is its relevance for the sociology of sport?

Rationalisation and Structured Domination

Weber's pure types of *imperative coordination* or structured domination can be viewed as falling into two major historical periods that Giddens (1973) classified as pre-rationalistic and rationalistic. Like his ideal types of social action, Weber distinguished between three types of administrative authority; namely traditional, charismatic and rational-legal. He called a system of imperative control traditional "if legitimacy is claimed for it and believed in on the basis of the sanctity of the order and the attendant powers of control as they have been handed down from the past" (Weber, 1968: 341). "Obedience is owed not to enacted rules but to the person who occupies a position of authority by tradition or who has been chosen for it by the traditional master" (1968: 227). Here the master rules with or without an administrative staff. In general, Weber refers to this form of imperative co-ordination as *patrimonialism*. These conceptual observations are important in the interpretation of sport in a pre-industrial, estate society, where the aristocracy and the gentry relied on their retainers in the pursuit of predatory sport, selective breeding, country house games, and the enforcement of poaching statues (cf., Brailsford, 1969; Longrigg, 1977; Malcolmson, 1973). It could also be argued that it was the traditional authority vested in the squires that maintained the organisation of predatory sports long after commercialised agriculture was impinging upon the open spaces conducive to their pursuit.

Imperative control is charismatic if it rests upon personal devotion "to the exceptional sanctity, heroism, or exemplary character of an individual person, and of the normative patterns or order revealed or ordained by him" (Weber, 1968: 215). While this ideal-type is less evident in sport, its sub-type, "institutional charisma", has considerable significance when one looks at conservative organisations like the IOC. It is a viable means of understanding the motives of various IOC Presidents (cf., Guttmann, 1984; MacAloon, 1981) and parallels what we have already stated about value-rational social action.

The concept of charisma might also apply to sport in its more routinised variant. Once more, it is instrumental rationality that subverts the form. By this, we mean that celebrities are turned into hero/ines and corporate capitalist sign vehicles (see Ingham, Howell, & Swetman, 1993). Few athletes are heroic in the sense of the real political drama of history. However, as celebrities, the media turn their performance accomplishments into quasi-heroic deeds, i.e., media-manufactured fame. This we call "pseudo–charisma". But pseudo–charisma is a form of imperative control in that it is linked with the consumption of goods. And so, manufactured fame contours the consumer demands and buying habits of millions.

Michael Jordan is an excellent example of this process of corporate organisational dynamics. Jordan sells anything from Haynes briefs to sport drinks, to MCI phone services (along with his "Space Jam" buddies). In some cases, the corporations themselves take on a perverse (given their treatment of Asian labour) form of institutional charisma, such as Nike and its "Just do it!" transnational advertising campaign (see Sage, 1999).

It is the final ideal-construct (rational-legal) which is most critical in contemporary sociology of sport. Weber was convinced that it was this imperative coordination which was one of the unique features of Western civilisation, especially in an age of *higher capitalism*. We agree. With the collapse of state communism in the Soviet Union and Eastern Europe, there are no formidable alternatives to its expansion in the former Soviet bloc, or other industrially developing societies. Consequently, in a globalising economic environment, the rational-legal is *the* accepted form of imperative control. The 'under-developed' nations become developed on First-World terms. In this regard, capitalism becomes conflated with democracy and its rational-legal imperatives *per se*.

The purest example of the exercise of rational-legal domination is one that employs a bureaucratic administrative staff. Here, it is generally the case that only the head of the organisation occupies the position of authority by virtue of appropriation, election, or designation. The rest of the administrative staff are salaried and are normally hired on the basis of technical qualifications. Within the administrative structure, offices are hierarchically arranged and the career mobility of the official is one of progression from lower to higher rungs on the administrative ladder — a progression that is determined by credentials, achievement, seniority, or a combination of these. It is the case that the office is treated as the sole, or at least the primary, occupation of its holder; it constitutes a career.

The qualities of this type of bureaucratic organisation are welcomed by capitalism. Indeed, as Giddens has observed, they may even be demanded because the capitalist economy requires that operations be discharged with speed and precision (1971: 159). Capitalism, above all, demands that administration succeed in eliminating irrational elements in the discharge of business. The rational-legal administration operates "without regard for persons" and this is also the "watchword of the market and, in general, of all pursuits of naked economic interests" (Weber, 1947: 215). The development of bureaucratic administration thus becomes the most crucial phenomenon of the modern Western State and corporate capitalism, and has become the prototype for a globalised economic order. It is the most tangible manifestation of rationalisation.

Finally, and critically, because of the technical efficiency of the bureaucracy, its methods and ethos have tended to permeate all facets of social life, including sport. For example, in North America, owners of professional sport franchises act as a collegial council and appoint one of their own to be a league president who, in turn, acts mainly as the spokesperson for the whole (the cartel). But below this rule of "plutocrats", there is an appointed commissioner who heads a bureaucratic staff that oversees day-to-day operations of the league. And within each sport franchise, a form of bureaucratic managerialism, headed by a Chief Executive Officer, prevails in the front office operations. Further, given the media exposure to this type of organisation, it is seen to be the way to organise *real sport*, whether it is that played by highly paid professionals or youngsters entering their first competitive experience. And, as the former state socialist societies demonstrated, the higher the degree of state centralisation in sport, the more bureaucratic the sport agencies become (see Cantelon, 1981).

Much of what has been researched in the areas of the social policy of sport, case study research of organisations like the NCAA or IOC, or the increasing use of technology to improve athletic performance, all have implicitly or explicitly used Weberian concepts of rationalisation to come to some understanding of sports in contemporary society (e.g., Hoberman, 1992). As well, the current debates that surround the place that sport will play in a globalised world can benefit from a study of Weber. We concur with Giddens' assertion that:

> The future expansion of capitalism thus completes the disenchant-
> ment of the world (through a commitment to scientific progress);
> transmutes most forms of social relationships into conduct which
> approximates to the 'Zweckrational' type (rational coordination
> of tasks in bureaucratic organisations); advances the spread of
> norms of an abstract legal type which, principally, as embodied in
> the state, constitutes the main form of modern 'legitimate order'
> (Giddens, 1995: 45).

Earlier, we mentioned how capitalism spurred on the conflation of science with technology. Also, we argued that exercise and sport science in the academy, by virtue of its adherence to the performance principle, has accommodated itself to both the rationalisation of the human body and to the rationalisation of administration (programmes in sport administration).

These combined themes link the rationality of science to the rationality of domination and were taken up theoretically by what is referred to as the Frankfurt School. We urge students to read the writings of Adorno, Habermas, Horkheimer, and Marcuse (see Bernstein, 1994; Jay, 1973 for overviews) so as to understand how important Weber was (as a negative identifier) for much of the theory involved in the "one-dimensional man", "mass society", "mass consumption" hypotheses. Weber, like Marx, was concerned about the effects that institutional reification had upon the individual and the individual's capacity to exercise free will. Students should also read the works of Ellul, Gouldner, and Mumford on the domination of technics, i.e., the instrumental rationality of technique (see Vanderberg, 1981; Gouldner, 1976; Miller, 1986). Their reflections have applicability to issues in the sociology of sport.

In all instances, the salient point to be derived from a reading of these works is that which asks: What is our role as responsible citizens, as intellectuals? Are we (sport scientists) the servants of the corporate capitalist agenda, the state agenda, or are we a new class seeking political power? Weber's essays on "Science as a Vocation" and "Politics as a Vocation" (in Gerth & Mills, 1958) are essays in enlightenment in response to these questions (see also Ingham & Donnelly, 1990 with reference to the sociology of sport). Sport scholarship must move beyond thoughtless cheerleading (Loy, 1969) to a serious and critical examination of sport. But being critical does not mean renouncing a love of play and organised games. One can adopt a critical scholarly stance while continuing to exhibit a genuine love and appreciation of athletic performance. One does not negate the other.

Status and Open and Closed Relations

There have been few more contentious sociological issues than those involving Weber's concept of social status versus that of Marx's concept of social class. In the USA in particular, liberal sociologists have tried to deny the existence of classes in favour of a distributive theory of open mobility. One gains status in society by working diligently and the most diligent are rewarded accordingly. Such liberal sociologists have invented a new Weber — one who has no common understanding with the likes of Marx. This is an Americanised version of Weber, but one that has its counterparts in Canada and Britain.

Weber's analysis of power was historical. In his essay on "Class, Status, and Party" (Gerth & Mills, 1958: 180–195), Weber used his concepts of stratification in a very deliberate way. Status was clearly linked to an estate society, class to a capitalist society, and party to a socialist society. Weber identified ascription in estate or caste societies as the key status criterion that led to social closure and the denial of opportunities in both recruitment and reward. Status played an important role in what games one could pursue and with whom one would play. Obviously, organised sport as we know it could not function with such social constraint. But it does not mean that somehow power differentials were overcome with the advent of capitalist societies.

Under a capitalist regime, the key determinants of power lay in the mode of production, especially the relations of production. Those most responsible for the organisation of the economy (the captains of industry), Weber recognised as displaying an elective affinity between the Protestant *Ethic* and the *Spirit* of Capitalism (see Weber, 1958a). This was an affinity anchored in the achievement principle that the bourgeoisie used ideologically to undermine the ascriptive power of the aristocracy and its estate society. It was encased in the philosophy of utilitarianism through which the bourgeoisie proclaimed that they were the useful class (the producers of wealth) and that the aristocracy were merely its conspicuous consumers (Gouldner, 1970: Ch. 3).

Arguably, where Weber and Marx most differ is in the organisation of society based on principles of democratic socialism. Social cleavages anchored in party were, for Weber, linked to socialist regimes in which membership/non-membership in the political party was instrumentally linked to an access to power. In the former Soviet Union, for example, Weber saw membership in the Communist Party as critical to identifying those with authority (Cantelon, 1981).

Liberal sociologists ignored this historical analysis of social position and power. They chose to interpret Weber's concept of status as ahistorical and identifiable in all forms of societal organisation. Thus, Weber's concept of status became not one of class or estate, but one of a stratificational hierarchy in which the concept of gradation reigned supreme. The key class division between the owners and managers of property (the capital function), and those who merely had their labour power (the labour function) to sell was rendered invisible. Appearances prevailed over essences. Weber's debt to Marx was ignored. Stratification became the moral acclamation of occupational status. Thus, in sociology and the sociology of sport, gradational and distributive analyses took centre stage. Studies of social stratification and social mobility within organised sport were quite prevalent in the late 1960s and early 1970s (e.g., Gruneau, 1972; Loy, 1969, 1972; Luschen, 1969; Pavia, 1973; see Gruneau, 1975; Bend & Petrie, 1978, for overviews). But nowhere in this literature was Weber's analysis of open and closed relationships pursued.

Who and what in capitalist societies determine the access to opportunity and reward? How do those among the dominant classes identify and select those who might serve them and even join their rank? How do the privileged maintain their privileges? Weber spent much of his analytical sociological life trying to answer these questions. The sociology of sport has been relatively silent in addressing these same questions. A notable exception lies in the work of Ed Gross (1979). Gross undertook a theoretical and empirical analysis of organisational stratification using sport and education as his examples. He sought to clarify issues of prestige in organisational sets. Gross revealed how prestige organisations maintained their prestige through knowledge networks and hegemony in the recruitment process. Similarly, Giddens' (in Stanworth & Giddens, 1974) analysis of elite formations and power structures offers important insights for the understanding of coaching mobility in sport (see Keon, 1991).

Sy Goode's *The Celebration of Heroes* (1978) analyses the role that prestige and honorific awards play in the social control over individual performances (mandatory and voluntary). If we can take just one conclusion from Goode, it is that "performity" and conformity are inter-related. One can only gain in prestige by being recognised by those who already possess it. And, from Gross (1979), we can conclude that prestige begets prestige — meaning that once the demanded competency levels have been achieved, mobility is based on whom you know in the prestige networks. This has been described as contest and sponsored mobility (Turner, 1960). Competence in the contest mobility pyramid has to be connected to sponsorship in the prestige mobility pyramid.

Perhaps the most neglected Weberian text by those in the sociology of sport is that of Frank Parkin, *Marxism and Class Theory: a Bourgeois Critique* (1979). Parkin develops Weber's analysis of open and closed relationships with a view to closure and usurpation strategies. This text should be particularly relevant to those who have vested interests in the social differentiation of gender and race. Parkin's key questions are: How do those with privilege and power seek to maintain their privileges, and how do those who are lacking in such privilege seek to gain the advantages of the rich and powerful? How are exclusionary tactics of elite formations combatted by the usurpationary tactics of subordinated groups and classes? While Cantelon and Ingham turn to Weber to seek an answer, these are clearly questions of relevance in sport studies, regardless of one's theoretical position.

Conclusion

A meta-narrative might be thought of as a personal world view, a particular theory of the world in which one lives and one's place within this world. It asks questions like "What are my inimitable responsibilities and rights as a person?" and "What is required of me to be considered a good citizen?" Our contention is that the sociology of sport has lost sight of the meta-narrative of inequality in terms of social justice. Indeed, we could ask, what has happened to the analysis of social class in either Marxian or Weberian terms? For us, the binary of inequality and difference has to be resolved on the side of questions of inequality: that is, difference is subordinate to class; difference operates within the conflicts of class. Here is the *rapprochement* between Weber and Marx.

With Weber, our opportunity as students of the sociology of sport is to make sense of the techno–bureaucratic world in which we live. We have the chance to make a difference and to challenge the *iron cage* of rationality and the process of rationalisation. We have the chance to replace the performance discourse with the developmental discourse and to impede the corporate capitalist process of globalisation. But, as Max Weber would ask us, have we the will?

Sadly, passivity has become the fate of most athletes, particularly the non-unionised amateur and the child/youth athletes engaged in representational forms of organised sport, regardless of the performance level. Upon entering the feeder system of sport, autonomy yields to heteronomy and substantial rationality to the formal or functional rationality of the system; to the bureaucratic managerialism of its authority structures and to the scientised technicism of its coaches. And when things go wrong, it is the legal bureaucracy and the technocrats who are contacted to make things right. If for no other reason than to test out Weber's iron cage pessimism in a rational-legal world, there is good reason to consider his methodology. One must, like Weber, ask if this is our implacable fate? Or can we be the resources of hope for the next generation?

References

Andreski, S. (ed.) (1983). *Max Weber on Capitalism, Bureaucracy and Religion: A Selection of Texts* (Trans. Andreski, S.) London: Allen & Unwin.

Aron, R. (1970). *Main Currents in Sociological Thought II*. Garden City, New York: Anchor Books.

Belanger, A. (1999). *Where Have the Ghosts Gone?: Sport Venues and the Political Economy of Memory in Montreal*. Unpublished doctoral dissertation. School of Communication, Simon Fraser University. Burnaby, B. C., Canada.

Bend, E., & Petrie, B. (1977). Sport participation, scholastic success, and social mobility. *Exercise and Sport Sciences Reviews, 5*, 1–44.

Bendix, R. (1960). *Max Weber: An Intellectual Portrait*. Garden City, New York: Doubleday.

Bernstein, J. (ed.) (1994). *The Frankfurt School: Critical Assessments*. In six volumes. London: Routledge.

Brailsford, D. (1969). *Sport and Society: Elizabeth to Anne*. London: Routledge & Kegan Paul.

Cantelon, H. (1981). *A Weberian Analysis of the Development of Ice Hockey Under*

Scientific Socialism in the Soviet Union. Unpublished doctoral dissertation. Department of Physical Education, University of Birmingham, England.

Dubin, C. (1990). *Commission of Inquiry Into the Use of Drugs and Banned Practices Intended to Increase Athletic Performance*. Ottawa: Canadian Government Publishing Centre.

Dunning, E. (1975). Industrialisation and the incipient modernisation of football. *Stadion, 1*(1), 103–109.

Dunning, E., & Sheard, K. (1979). *Barbarians, Gentlemen and Players: A Sociological Study of the Development of Rugby Football*. Oxford: M. Robertson.

Eisenstadt, S. N. (ed.) (1968). *Max Weber on Charisma and Institution Building*. With an introduction by S. N. Eisenstadt. Chicago: University of Chicago Press.

Eldridge, J. E. I. (ed.) (1980). *Max Weber: The Interpretation of Social Reality*. With an introductory essay by J. E. I. Eldridge. New York: Schochen Books.

Ellul, J. (1964). *The Technological Society*. New York: Knopf.

Gerth, H., & Mills, Wright, C. (eds) (1958). *From Max Weber: Essays in Sociology*. New York: Oxford University Press.

Giddens, A. (1971). *Capitalism and Modern Social Theory: An Analysis of the Writings of Marx, Durkheim and Weber*. Cambridge: University Press.

Giddens, A. (1973). *The Class Structure of the Advanced Societies*. New York: Harper & Row.

Giddens, A. (1974). Elites in the British class structure. In: P. Stanworth and A. Giddens (eds), *Elites and Power in British Society* (pp. 1–21). London: Cambridge University Press.

Giddens, A. (1995). *Politics, Sociology and Social Theory: Encounters With Classical and Contemporary Social Thought*. Cambridge: Polity Press.

Goode, W. (1978). *The Celebration of Heroes: Prestige as a Control System*. Berkeley: University of California Press.

Gouldner, A. (1970). *The Coming Crisis of Western Sociology*. New York: Basic Books.

Gouldner, A. (1976). *The Dialectic of Ideology and Technology: The Origins, Grammar, and the Future of Ideology*. New York: Oxford University Press.

Gross, E. (1979). Sport leagues: A model for the theory of organisational stratification. *International Review for the Sociology of Sport, 14*(2), 103–112.

Gruneau, R. (1972). *A Socio–Economic Analysis of the Competitors of the 1971 Canada Winter Games*. Unpublished M. A. thesis. Department of Sociology, University of Calgary. Calgary, Alberta, Canada.

Gruneau, R. (1975). Sport, social differentiation and social inequality. In: D. Ball and J. Loy (eds), *Sport and Social Order: Contributions to the Sociology of Sport* (pp. 116–184). Reading, MA: Addison–Wesley.

Gruneau, R. & Cantelon, H. (1987). Capitalism, commercialism and the Olympics. In: J. Segrave and D. Chu (eds), *The Olympic Games in Transition* (pp. 345–364). Urbana, IL: Human Kinetics Publishers.

Guttmann, A. (1978). *From Ritual to Record: The Nature of Modern Sports*. New York: Columbia University Press.

Guttmann, A. (1984). *The Games Must Go On: Avery Brundage and the Olympic*

Movement. New York: Columbia University Press.

Habermas, J. (1970). *Toward a Rational Society: Student Protest, Science, and Politics.* Boston: Beacon Press.

Hamilton, P. (ed.) (1991). *Max Weber: Critical Assessments.* In four volumes. London: Routledge.

Hobsbawm, E. & Ranger, T. (eds) (1983). *The Invention of Tradition.* Cambridge: Cambridge University Press.

Hoberman, J. (1992). *Mortal Engines: The Science of Performance and the Dehumanisation of Sport.* New York: Free Press.

Hughes, H. S. (1958). *Consciousness and Society: The Reorientation of European Social Thought, 1890–1930.* New York: Alfred A. Knopf.

Ingham, A. (1978). *American Sport in Transition: The Maturation of Industrial Capitalism and its Impact Upon Sport.* Unpublished doctoral dissertation. Department of Sociology. University of Massachusettes. Amherst, MA, USA.

Ingham, A. & Donnelly, P. (1990). Whose knowledge counts?: The production of knowledge and issues of application in the Sociology of Sport. *Sociology of Sport Journal, 7*(1), 58–65.

Ingham, A. & Donnelly, P. (1997). A sociology of North American sociology of sport: Disunity in unity, 1965 to 1996. *Sociology of Sport Journal, 14*(4), 362–418.

Ingham, A. Howell, J. & Schilperoort, T. (1986). A rickety bridge between abstract and social space: The American sport franchise. *Keynote Address.* VIII Commonwealth and International Conference on Sport, Physical Education, Dance, Recreation, and Health. Glasgow, Scotland.

Ingham, A. Howell, J. & Schilperoort, T. (1987). Professional sports and community: A review and exegesis. *Exercise and Sport Sciences Reviews, 15*, 427–465.

Ingham, A. Howell, J. & Swetman, R. (1993). Evaluating sport hero/ines: Contents, forms, and social relations. *Quest, 45*, 197–210.

Ingham, A. & Lawson, H. (1999). Prolympism and globalisation: Knowledge for whom, by whom? *Keynote Address.* German Association of Sport Science. Heidelberg, Germany.

Jay, M. (1973). *The Dialectical Imagination.* Boston: Little, Brown & Co.

Keon, T. (1991). Elite groups, prestige sets and coaching patterns in NCAA Division one hockey. Unpublished M. A. thesis. Department of Physical Education, Health & Sport Studies. Miami University, Oxford, OH, USA.

Korr, C. P. (1986). *West Ham United: The Making of a Football Club.* Urbana: University of Illinois Press.

Longrigg, R. (1977). *The English Squire and His Sport.* New York: St. Martin's Press.

Loy, J. (1969). The study of sport and social mobility. In: G. Kenyon (ed.), *Aspects of Contemporary Sport Sociology* (pp. 101–119). Chicago: The Athletic Institute.

Loy, J. (1972). Social origins and occupational mobility of a selected sample of American athletes. *International Review of the Sociology of Sport, 7*, 5–23.

Luschen, G. (1969). Social stratification and social mobility among young sportsmen. In: J. Loy and G. Kenyon (eds), *Sport, Culture and Society* (pp. 258–276). New York: Macmillan.

MacAloon, J. (1981). *This Great Symbol: Pierre de Coubertin and the Origins of the Modern Olympic Games*. Chicago: University of Chicago Press.

Malcolmson, W. R. (1973). *Popular Recreations in English Society, 1700–1850*. Cambridge: Cambridge University Press.

Martindale, D. (ed.) (1958). *The Rational and Social Foundations of Music*. (Trans. Martindale, D., Riedel, J. and Newwirth, G.) Carbondale: Southern Illinois University Press.

Miller, D. L. (ed.) (1986). *The Lewis Mumford Reader*. New York: Pantheon Books.

Mitzman, A. (1969). *The Iron Cage: An Historical Interpretation of Max Weber*. New York: Alfred A. Knof.

Mumford, L. (1970). *The Pentagon of Power: The Myth of the Machine*. New York: Harcourt Brace Jovanovich.

Parkin, F. (1979). *Marxism and Class Theory: A Bourgeois Critique*. New York: Columbia University Press.

Parsons, T. (1947). *The Structure of Social Action: A Study in Social Theory with Special Reference to a Group of Recent European Writers*. In two volumes. New York: McGraw-Hill Book Company.

Pavia, G. (1973). An analysis of the social class of the 1972 Australian Olympic team. *The Australian Journal of Physical Education, 61*, 14–19.

Runciman, W. G. (ed.) (1978). *Max Weber: Selections in Translation*. (Trans. Matthews, E.) Cambridge: Cambridge University Press.

Sage, G. (1999). Just do it! The NIKE transnational advocacy network: organisation, collective actions, and outcomes. *Sociology of Sport Journal, 16*(3), 206–235.

Simpson, V. & Jennings, A. (1992). *The Lords of the Rings: Power, Money and Drugs in the Modern Olympic Games*. Toronto: Stoddart.

Stanworth, P. & Giddens, A. (eds) (1974). *Elites and Power In British Society*. London: Cambridge University Press.

Turner, R. (1960). Sponsored and contest mobility in the school system. *American Sociological Review, 25*, 855–867.

Vanderburg, W. H. (ed.) (1981). *Perspectives On Our Age: Jacques Ellul Speaks on His Life and Work*. (Trans. Neugroschel, J.) Toronto: Canadian Broadcasting Corporation.

Weber, M. (1927). *General Economic History*. (Trans. Knight, F. H.) New York: Greenberg.

Weber, M. (1947). *The Theory of Social and Economic Organisation*. (Trans. Henderson, A. M. and Parsons, T.) Edited with an introduction by Talcott Parsons. New York: Free Press.

Weber, M. (1949). *The Methodology of the Social Sciences*. New York: Free Press.

Weber, M. (1951). *The Religion of China: Confucianism and Taoism*. (Trans. Gerth, H. H.) (ed.) Glencoe, IL: Free Press.

Weber, M. (1952). *Ancient Judaism*. (Trans. Gerth, H. H. and Martindale, D.) (eds). Glencoe, IL: Free Press.

Weber, M. (1958a). *Protestant Ethic and Spirit of Capitalism*. (Trans. Parsons, T.) with a forward by R. H. Tawney. New York: Scribner.

Weber, M. (1958b). *The Religion of India: the Sociology of Hinduism and Buddhism*. Glencoe, IL: Free Press.

Weber, M. (1964). *Basic Concepts in Sociology.* (Trans. Sechner, H. P.) New York: Carol Publishing Group.

Weber, M. (1968). *Economy and Society: An Outline of Interpretative Sociology.* New York: Bedminster Press.

Williams, R. (1977). *Marxism and Literature.* Oxford: Oxford University Press.

Wrong, D. (ed.) (1970). *Max Weber.* Englewood Cliffs, NJ: Prentice Hall.

Chapter 4

George Herbert Mead and an Interpretive Sociology of Sport

Peter Donnelly

In the mid-1960s, as a recognisable subdiscipline of sociology devoted to the study of sport and leisure emerged in North America, John Loy conducted a major search of sociological and anthropological literature in an attempt to establish legitimacy and discover precedents for this new field of study. He found that the particular dynamics of 'games' had intrigued such diverse 'fathers' of the field of sociology as Georg Simmel, Max Weber, and George Herbert Mead (Loy & Kenyon, 1969: 2–3). In the case of Mead, games were employed as a major exemplar in his analysis of the discovery of 'self'.

However, while Mead's use of games as an homologue (a form of analogy) is our entrée into his influence on the sociology of sport, it is his indirect influence on subsequent theorists and schools of theory that has been most significant. This chapter will first consider Mead's origins and intellectual background, and then examine his use of games as an homologue — part of his larger theoretical contribution to sociology. The remainder of the chapter is devoted to reviewing Mead's influence on the formation of the schools of theory which constitute 'interpretive sociology', and which, in turn, have had a major influence on the development of an interpretive sociology of sport.

Mead's Origins and Intellectual Background

George Herbert Mead (27 February, 1863–26 April, 1931) was born in South Hadley, Massachusetts.[1] His father was a Congregational church minister, and his mother became President of Mt. Holyoke College (1890–1900). After graduating from Oberlin College, Mead taught grade school for several months,

---

[1] Biographical information about Mead is from Miller (1973).

Theory, Sport & Society
Copyright © 2002 by Elsevier Science Ltd.
All rights of reproduction in any form reserved.
ISBN: 0-7623-0742-0

and then spent three years working with a crew surveying the route for a Wisconsin Central railroad connection with the Canadian Pacific railroad (from Minneapolis, Minnesota to Moose Jaw, Saskatchewan). Mead continued his education, beginning at Harvard University in 1887 where he studied philosophy and psychology while living in William James' home and tutoring James' children. Moving to Germany, Mead became involved in further studies (Leipzig and Berlin, 1888–1891), developing an interest in physiological psychology, and then returned to the United States to teach philosophy and psychology at the University of Michigan. In 1894, Mead moved to the University of Chicago, where he worked in the Philosophy Department until his death in 1931.

It should be noted that Mead came to prominence at a time before the current crystallisation of disciplines and disciplinary boundaries in the social sciences and humanities, when psychology and sociology were both off-shoots of philosophy, and when significant changes were occurring in both the natural sciences and philosophy. Thus, among the major intellectual influences on Mead were Charles Darwin (theory of evolution), Wilhelm Wundt (established the first physiological psychology laboratory at Leipzig), and philosopher John Dewey (particularly his theory of coordination). These influences:

> . . . were the main factors in helping Mead get "meanings" out in the open: that is, in helping Mead develop a biosocial — or a social–behavioristic — account of mind, reflective thinking, and shared meanings (universals) (Miller, 1973: xvi, original parentheses).

However, in many academic circles, Mead is best known as a 'pragmatist' philosopher. Pragmatism is still considered to be the major American school of philosophy. When Mead joined Dewey at the University of Chicago, those two, along with Charles Sanders Peirce and James, formed the core of a school of pragmatist thought in which, "meaning, and ultimately the truth, of a concept or proposition relates merely to its practical effects" (Jary & Jary, 1995: 517). The pragmatists proposed that:

1) The best test of what is commonly referred to as the 'truth' of an idea or concept is to ask whether it 'works' in the sense of solving a specific problem confronted in a particular situation.

2) The appropriate test is an instrumental one which considers the idea's usefulness in pursuing specific enquiries. In fact, according to this view, thinking is best understood as mental

effort directed at finding solutions to the problems which arise when practical activities are frustrated in some way.

3) Concepts acquire meaning in terms of the habits and practices which they bring about in the course of seeking solutions to problems of the kind just mentioned (Smith, 1988: 59).

Although pragmatism is connected in many ways to American liberalism, influences on critical thought are also evident (see below).

In sum, Mead's work has been categorised into three main philosophical themes:

1) the emergence of mind and self from the communication process between organisms (the 'social behaviourism' noted above), discussed in *'Mind, Self and Society'* (Mead, 1934);

2) the psychological genesis of scientific categories in purposeful acts, discussed in *'The Philosophy of the Act'* (Mead, 1938); and

3) the social conception of nature and the location of reality in the present, discussed in *'The Philosophy of the Present'* (Mead, 1932) (Edwards, 1967: 231).[2]

However, it is 'social behaviourism', and the ideas expressed in *'Mind, Self and Society'*, which had the most influence on the development of American sociology, and indirectly on the sociology of sport.

Mead's Use of 'Games' as a Homologue

Mead's encounters with sociology, or perhaps more accurately sociological social psychology,[3] began when he discovered Wundt's work at Leipzig. Wundt's idea of 'the gesture':

. . . is indispensable to all of Mead's later thinking. Involved in the idea of the gesture is the concept of communication as a

---

[2]Mead published little during his lifetime [see Mead (1934) and Miller (1973) for bibliographies]. The works noted here were compiled by his students from his unfinished manuscripts and their lecture notes.
[3]See Strauss (1964) for a more extended statement on Mead's social psychology.

social process. (A gesture is that phase of a social act which evokes a response made by another participant in the act, a response necessary for the completion of the act) (Miller, 1973: xvi, original parentheses).

Additionally, when Mead and Charles Cooley were both at the University of Michigan, it is evident that both were influenced by Adam Smith's notion of 'the looking-glass self'. While Smith was concerned with the relationship between buyers and sellers in the market, Cooley adapted the concept to the 'social self':

> ... in which an individual's sense of self is derived from the perceptions of others. Just like the reflection in a mirror, the self depends on the perceived responses of others [and] has three components: the imagination of our appearance to the other person; the imagination of their judgement of that appearance; and self feelings, such as pride (Marshall, 1994: 296).

In Mead's social psychology, 'the looking-glass self' was adapted to become "taking the role of the other." However, perhaps the most significant, and two-way, sociological influence on Mead was to occur at the University of Chicago where he encountered the emerging and influential 'Chicago School' of Sociology (Smith, 1988).[4]

If the most fundamental question in sociology is, 'how is society possible?' (i.e., how do independent individuals come together to form communities, and refrain from some of their own 'wants' and 'needs' in order to maintain those communities?), then Mead's work certainly advanced our understanding of the process from a micro-sociological perspective (see Vaitkus, 1991). Erving Goffman pointed to the significance for Mead of "the special mutuality of immediate social interaction" (1963: 16).

In focusing on that interaction, Mead noted the significance of symbols[5] to human interaction:

> Without symbols, there would be no human interaction and no human society. Symbolic interaction is necessary since man has

---

[4]Motivated by Robert Park's (1916/1952) paper, 'The City: Suggestions for the Investigation of Human Behaviour in the City Environment', and Thomas and Znaniecki's (1918–19/1927) 'The Polish Peasant in Europe and America', the Chicago school developed an evidence-and field work-based sociology which led to a real distinction between sociology and philosophy.
[5]Symbols, especially language, "are man-made and refer not to the intrinsic nature of objects and events but to the ways in which men perceive them" (Haralambos, 1985, p. 544).

no instincts to direct his behaviour. He is not genetically programmed to react automatically to particular stimuli. In order to survive, he must therefore construct and live within a world of meaning (Haralambos, 1985: 544).

The meanings of symbols must be mutually understood in order for individuals to interact, and then "each person involved must interpret the meanings and intentions of others" (Haralambos, 1985: 544). We accomplish this by 'role-taking' (Mead's development of 'the looking-glass self'), placing ourselves in the position of the person with whom we are interacting. Each of the parties to an interaction is thus continually engaged in a process of role-taking.

It is through this process that individuals achieve a sense of 'self', and Mead distinguishes between "the 'I' (myself as I am) [which] is involved in a continual interaction with the 'Me' (myself as others see me)" (Jary & Jary, 1995: 402–3). Thus, the idea of 'self' is not natural, but develops as a result of human childhood socialisation and interaction. Mead identifies two stages of maturity here — the 'play stage' and the 'game stage'. In the 'play stage', children engage in the type of role playing and role taking described by Mead:

> A child plays at being a mother, at being a teacher, at being a policeman; that is, it is taking different roles. . . . He plays that he is, for instance, offering himself something, and he buys it; he gives a letter to himself and takes it away; he addresses himself as a parent, as a teacher; he arrests himself as a policeman. . . . Such is the simplest form of being another to one's self. . . . The child says something in one character and responds in another character, and then his responding in another character is a stimulus to himself in the first character, and so the conversation goes on (Mead, 1934: 150–151).

Through such play, children learn the difference between themselves and the parts they are playing.

The 'game stage' represents the second step towards maturity as children learn to see themselves as others see them. As Mead notes:

> At the first of these stages, the individual's self is constituted simply by an organisation of the particular attitudes of other individuals toward himself and toward one another in the specific social acts in which he participates with them. But at the second stage in the full development of the individual's self, that self is

constituted not only by an organisation of these particular individual attitudes, but also by an organisation of the social attitudes of the generalised other or the social group as a whole to which he belongs (Mead, 1932: 158).

With evident reference to team ball games, Mead suggests that:

What goes on in the game goes on in the life of the child all the time. He is continually taking the attitudes of those about him, especially the roles of those, who in some sense, control him and on whom he depends. . . . It goes over from the play into the game in a real sense. He has to play the game. The morale of the game takes hold of the child more than the larger morale of the whole community. The child passes into the game and the game expresses a social situation in which he can completely enter; its morale may have a greater hold on him than that of the family to which he belongs or the community in which he lives (Mead, 1932: 160).

Greg Stone[6] (1981) has provided a good description of the way in which Mead used sports, especially team games, as homologues for the analysis of this stage of socialisation:

One plays out positions so arranged that they constitute the organisation of the community in which he lives, and one develops a reflected conception of self as he generalises the organisation of others in the community, addressing his own acts to their organised expectations of his performance. Mead makes the specific analogy to the team player in a game. . . . To play the game he must address his performance to the expectations of the generalised team. On the one hand, there is simply no time in the contest for the player to assess and summate the expectations of his performance held by each separate member of the team. On the other, too great a preoccupation with the expectations of one or two other teammates would distort his own team play and contributes to team (or community) disorganisation. The team, for Mead, is a metaphor useful for the interpretation of the place

[6]Greg Stone was a prominent American sociologist, who worked from an interpretive perspective, and who began to recognise the significance of sport some years before the emergence of the sub-discipline of sociology of sport.

community organisation has in the development of the self (1981: 215; see also Berger, 1963: 99).

Thus, through this process of socialisation — first with 'significant others' (parents, etc.), and then with the 'generalised other' (society in general), children develop their sense of 'self'.[7] And, through this process of communication — symbolic interaction — individuals develop their self-consciousness as human beings, and make society possible.

Mead's Influences on Subsequent Theorists and the Sociology of Sport

Mead's influence on subsequent theorists, and on the sociology of sport, has been extensive, and this section outlines three of these levels of influence. First, there is his rarely recognised influence on the development of critical sociology in North America. Second, there is his widely recognised influence on the development of several of the interpretive sociologies in North America. And third, although the distance from Mead is by now considerable, is his influence on cultural studies, to the extent that the perspective brings together critical and interpretive sociologies.

Critical Sociology

The influence of Mead is particularly evident in the work of C. Wright Mills (cf., Mills, 1966), both in terms of pragmatism, and in his adaptation of Mead's concepts of the 'generalised other' and the 'significant symbol'[8] (Eldridge, 1983). As Hamilton (1983) notes, "Mills considered himself firmly located in that tradition of thought (pragmatism) with its emphases on the union of the practical and the intellectual which is symbolised in his notion of the sociologist as a sort of 'cultural workman' " (1983: 8). And while Mills is widely associated with a critical shift in both American sociology and in the sociology of sport (see Ingham & Donnelly, 1997), there are other indications of Mead's connections with a critical tradition. For example, and remembering Mead's influence on the

---

[7]It should be noted that these ideas have been tested and received empirical support (Miyamoto & Dornbusch, 1956).

[8]Zimmerman and Pollner note that, "Mead's famous definition of the significant symbol — a gesture that calls out the same response in an auditor that it calls out in its producer — is perhaps the archetypical solution for sociologists to the problem of how members manage to understand one another" (1970: 101).

development of this approach to sociology, the sub-title to Smith's (1988) book on the 'Chicago School' is, "A Liberal Critique of Capitalism". In Hansen's (1976) *'An Invitation to Critical Sociology'*, Mead, Marx, and Weber are each considered in terms of their contributions to critical sociology. And Shalin (1991) draws a direct connection between Mead, socialism, and the progressive agenda.

Thus, although the connection to Mead is relatively obscure, it is important to note that the critical shift during the 1970s may be considered to be a key moment in the development of North American sociology of sport (Ingham & Donnelly, 1997). Interestingly, this connection between Mead and critical sociology, and specifically between Mead and Marx, is addressed in two studies of high risk sports (Lyng, 1990; Mitchell, 1983) carried out by sociologists not usually associated with the sociology of sport. Mitchell (1983) draws heavily on Mead in order to examine the production of meaning within the subculture of mountaineers in the United States, but turns to Marx in order to explain their motivation as a response to their perception of alienating social circumstances. Lyng (1990) provides a more sophisticated integration of Marx and Mead in his study of skydivers in the United States. His:

> . . . micro-level analysis is linked to a macro-level speculation on the alienating effects of work in postindustrial capitalism. The result, he posits, is a hyperextension of the individual's experience of the 'me' and an associated compression of the individual's opportunities to experience the 'I' [see p. 8] (Miller, 1991: 1531).

Donnelly (2000b) provided a critique of both of these analyses of risk, noting that any perspective which viewed risk-taking as a response (e.g., to alienating conditions of work) could only be seen as a simplified and partial interpretation which did not do justice to the ethnographic evidence. Most risk taking in sport occurs in the social formations which form around risk-taking activities, and in which risk-taking behaviour is given meaning. It is in groups that identities are reconstructed and reaffirmed — especially when a significant part of that identity involves being seen to take risks. But this is also where the character contests take place, as well as the bonding and affirmation of friendships. It is where the meaning of risk-taking is defined and redefined, and it is the site of cultural production (Donnelly, 2000c).

Interpretive Sociologies

Just as 'pragmatism' is considered to be the principal American School of Philosophy, the 'interpretive sociologies' are generally considered to represent a major American contribution to sociology. And just as Mead was involved in the development of pragmatist philosophy, the interpretive sociologies are also considered to derive in large part from Mead's work. These include: symbolic interactionism, role theory, and dramaturgy.

While the process of 'interpretation' is fundamental to all science, it takes on a particular meaning when referring to sociological processes. The 'system' approach to sociology suggests that social life is a product of the objective cultural and structural characteristics of social systems. The 'action' approach suggests that social life is continually constructed and reconstructed by the participants. The two approaches are not mutually exclusive, and the most comprehensive sociologies view society as something which is constructed by humans, *and* which also constrains human behaviour. American 'interpretive' sociologies are 'action' sociologies, more concerned with the ways in which humans construct and reinvent society than with the ways in which social structures constrain human behaviour.

Symbolic Interactionism Herbert Blumer, who was a student of Mead, synthesised and developed Mead's work from *Mind, Self and Society* into the approach to sociology known as symbolic interactionism. This approach has three basic premises:

- human beings act toward things on the basis of the meanings that the things have for them;
- the meaning of such things is derived from, or arises out of, the social interaction that one has with one's fellows; and
- these meanings are handled in, and modified through, an interpretive process used by the person in dealing with things he encounters (Blumer, 1969: 2).

Through observation, participant observation, or in-depth and open-ended interviews, researchers have conducted a wide variety of studies using this approach. These methods, often associated with anthropology, were indirectly advocated by Mead (1934: 1–8) in his approach to 'social behaviourism'. The strategy, as Denzin noted, "is to work from overt behaviours back to the meanings attached to those behaviours and objects" (1970: 266), an approach that is now completely naturalised in sociological methodology.

Studies of sport which take a symbolic interactionist approach fall into two general overlapping categories: (a) the process of socialisation; and (b) studies of sport subcultures.[9]

[9]Parts of the following section are adapted from Donnelly (2000a). A number of the socialisation studies are collected in Coakley and Donnelly (1999).

(a) Socialisation:

While Mead, as noted previously, has shown the importance of the 'play stage' and the 'game stage' in human childhood socialisation (often referred to as 'socialisation through sport'), sociologists of sport have generally been more interested in how people become involved in sport and physical activity participation ('socialisation into sport'). However, insights from research employing a symbolic interactionist perspective have shown that these two approaches are not mutually exclusive, and that socialisation is an active, two-way process. Individuals "influence those who influence them, they make their own interpretations of what they see and hear, and they accept, revise, or reject the messages they receive about who they are, what the world is all about, and what they should do as they make their way in the world" (Coakley, 1998: 88).

Studies of initial involvements in sport and physical activity have been carried out by Hasbrook (1993, 1995) in inner city school playgrounds, Fine (1987) in little league baseball, Ingham and Dewar (1989) in peewee ice hockey, and Grey (1992) in a high school with a large immigrant population. These studies show not only the processes of becoming involved, but also how sport and physical activity are major sites in which traditional and stereotypical notions of gender and race/ethnicity are reproduced and contested. The two-way process of socialisation is emphasised in Chafetz and Kotarba's (1995) study of male little league baseball players and their parents.

Socialisation is an ongoing process, and several studies have focused on meaning and identity in the process of becoming an athlete — e.g., Donnelly and Young's (1988) study of rock climbers and rugby players, Coakley and White's (1992) study of adolescent decision-making regarding participation, Stevenson's (1990) study of the process of becoming an international athlete, Bryshun and Young's (1999) study of hazing/initiation practices, and Messner's (1992) study of the meanings of success and relationships in the lives of elite male athletes. Thompson (1999) emphasises the two-way process again by examining the impact on the lives of wives and mothers resulting from having children and/or husbands actively involved in sport. Several studies have also examined sport-related identities among non-athletes such as ticket 'scalpers' (Atkinson, 1997) and student athletic therapists (Walk, 1997).

A third aspect of socialisation involves sport career interruptions and retirements. Studies of what retirement means to athletes have been carried out by Swain (1991), Messner (1992), Koukouris (1994), and Rosenberg (1984). More dramatic interruptions have been examined in Coakley's (1992) study of adolescent burnout, and studies of sport injuries by Curry (1993), Young, White and McTeer (1994) and Young and White (1995). It is striking to examine the meanings developed about pain, injury, and burnout in sports outlined in these studies, and to compare them with, for example, the meanings given to the same phenomena in the workplace. While both contexts generate concern about the lack of performance/production resulting from injury, the normalisation of injury, and the expectations that individuals will continue to be involved despite pain and injury, may be far more pronounced in sport.

(b) Subcultures:
The notion of different meanings being constructed in different sectors of social life leads to the idea of subcultures. As noted above, a worker who incurs a minor ankle sprain at his/her workplace may be more likely to take time off and seek treatment than that same person incurring the same injury during sport participation — the person is expressing two different sets of norms and values, each in accord with the culture of the setting (see also Role Theory, below). Passive definitions note that subcultures are 'any system(s) of beliefs, values and norms . . . shared and actively participated in by an appreciable minority of people within a particular culture' (Jary & Jary, 1995: 665). More active definitions emphasise that such subcultures are actively produced (socially constructed) and reproduced by participants in communication (symbolic interaction) with each other.

Studies of sport subcultures overlap with studies of socialisation in that they often use the idea of an individual's 'career' (from initial involvement to retirement) in their analysis of the culture of various sports. Weinberg and Arond's (1952) work on boxers was the first of many such studies. It was followed by Stone's studies of wrestlers (1972; Stone & Oldenbourg, 1967), Scott's (1968) work on the subculture of horse racing, Polsky's (1969) analysis of pool hustlers, Faulkner's (1974a, 1974b) studies of ice hockey players, and Theberge's (1977) work on female professional golfers. The concept of career also permitted some comparative studies of subcultures. Unlikely but interesting comparisons included Faulkner (1975) on ice hockey players and Hollywood musicians, Rosenberg and Turowetz (1975) on physicians and professional wrestlers, and Birrell and Turowetz (1979) on professional wrestlers and female university gymnasts.

By the late 1970s, studies of subcultures began to focus less on careers, and more on the cultural characteristics of particular sports. Thomson's (1977), Young's (1988) and Donnelly and Young's (1985) studies of Canadian rugby players, Pearson's (1979) work on surfers in Australia and New Zealand, Donnelly's (1980) analysis of rock climbers, and Albert's series of studies on racing cyclists (1984, 1990, 1991) all fall into this category. Donnelly (1985) has provided an extensive review of these studies of sport subcultures. During the 1980s, there was further shift, with studies of sport subcultures becoming more political and contextual under the influence of cultural studies (see Chapters 7, 15, 16).

In all of the studies cited under the auspices of symbolic interactionism, Mead's work is rarely cited by the authors, and his influence is perhaps more directly through Blumer (who is also rarely cited). However, Mead's ideas are implicit in the concerns with identity, meaning, communication, and the creation of the self and meaning through communication.

Role Theory Just as symbolic interactionism was developed from the work of Mead, role theory is also derived from Mead's ideas about the development of the self in interaction with others. Different selves are called on in different circumstances — playing with one's friends requires different roles from interacting with one's grandparents. And there is a mutuality of expectations — teachers are expected to behave like (i.e., take the role of) teachers and students are expected to act like students. As Berger notes, a role "may be defined as a typified response to a typified expectation" (1963: 95). Since the language is derived from the theatre, there is sometimes a sense of falsehood about the idea of individuals 'playing parts'. However, in the process of socialisation identified by Mead, such roles become a part of our identities. Thus, in addition to being a 'student', 'daughter', 'friend', 'sister', and 'babysitter', an individual also learns other associated roles, such as racial and sexual roles.

In the sociology of sport, it is in the area of sex roles that role theory has inspired the most research and achieved the most notoriety. In an attempt to explain the relatively low levels of participation by women in sport during the 1960s and 1970s, a number of sociologists and psychologists of sport — the two subdisciplines were much more closely related at that time — proposed the notion of role conflict (or gender role 'deviance'). Comparing the typical characteristics associated with being an athlete with the stereotypical characteristics associated with being female, it was concluded that athletic characteristics were 'masculine', and that women resolved that conflict by dropping out of participation. As female participation began to increase during the 1970s and 1980s, and as women began to participate in what had formerly been men-only sports, concern began to be expressed about the consequences of living with role conflict, or of violating sexual norms (e.g., loss of femininity, the 'masculinisation' of women athletes). Research was carried out using 'sex role inventories' which purported to measure one's level of masculinity or femininity (e.g., Jackson & Marsh, 1986; Matteo, 1986).

The continuing participation of women without any apparent ill-effects on their mental health led to a short 'honeymoon' with the notion of androgyny — the idea that true mental health (for women and, as some feminists and pro-feminists asserted, for men) lay in possessing a combination of both masculine and feminine characteristics, exactly the characteristics that were showing up in sex role measures of women athletes. But the very premise of sex roles and sport participation resulted from a growing misunderstanding of the concept of role, which resulted in an over-simplified explanation of complex human interactions. The misunderstanding took on ideological overtones during a time of increasing political power (and sport participation) of women. Rather than roles being identities that are created and re-created in interaction with others, they came to be thought of as stable, identifiable, and measurable statuses. Thus, roles came to be synonymous with traits, even though their original conception had been much closer to the theatrical notion of role — no two actors will play Hamlet in exactly the same way, and even the same actor may play the part differently on different nights, and certainly in different productions.

The notion of sex roles began to disappear in the sociology of sport in the 1980s, although the concept and related research has lasted much longer in the psychology of sport. As the status of women changed, so did the sex roles of women. Currently, sociologists accept the notion of multiple femininities (and masculinities) — i.e., there is not just one way to be a man or a woman, or indeed to be 'straight' or 'gay', and resisting stereotypical characterisation is a legitimate pursuit (see Hall, 1996: 18–23, for a more substantial critique of role theory and gender in sport).

There are no clear distinctions between symbolic interactionism and role theory. Many of the studies of socialisation and subcultures cited above employ the concept of role. Perhaps the best work in the sociology of sport that is clearly grounded in role theory is a study of American collegiate basketball players (Adler & Adler, 1991). The fans and media created identities for these Division I athletes which the athletes felt constrained to live up to, and the Adlers showed how these students became engulfed in the role of basketball player (and future professional) at the expense of alternatives such as being 'themselves', passing courses and obtaining a degree.

Dramaturgy Dramaturgy, associated primarily with the work of Goffman, is in many ways a logical extension of role theory. Goffman is connected to Mead in that he was a student of Blumer at the University of Chicago. He took the notion of role and developed it to use the stage as a major metaphor for social life. Thus, individuals play their roles, and manage the impression that they give to others in order to appear in as favourable a light as possible. Goffman was aware of the way in which roles could be manipulated for impression management, and in order to deceive others (e.g., Goffman, 1959, 1969). His major contribution, the micro-analysis of face-to-face interaction between humans, has contributed to a number of studies in the sociology of sport. Again, this approach is in the broad family of symbolic interactionism, and a number of the concepts developed by Goffman are evident in many of the sport studies cited above. In fact, Goffman's ideas have become so much a part of the language of sociology that while they may be inferred, they are rarely cited any more.

However, there are a few studies in the sociology of sport which are explicitly derived from Goffman's work. Susan Birrell (1978, 1981) was at the forefront of adapting Goffman's work for the sociology of sport, and her studies of wrestlers and gymnasts (Birrell & Turowetz, 1979), and the process of trying out for (collegiate and professional) sport teams (Turowetz & Birrell, 1982), carefully analysed impression management in stressful situations. Donnelly (1978, 1982, 1994) was more concerned with the way in which individuals had their claims (to be the person they purported to be, to have accomplished what they claim to have accomplished) accepted. His studies of 'credentialing' (a process of establishing one's ability and status — one's credentials) among rock climbers (1978), and verification (1982) and trust (1994) among climbers and birders show how claims are negotiated in face-to-face interaction among actors. Atkinson (1997) has also explored this process of negotiation and trustworthiness among ticket scalpers and their clients. Donnelly has recently begun to incorporate Goffman's (1967) work on 'character' into his analysis of risk taking (Donnelly, 2000c).

As noted, Goffman's ideas are widespread in interpretive studies of sport, but perhaps the only other work to focus specifically on Goffman-like situations are Nixon's (1986) and Stevenson's (1999) studies of the way in which lane order is established in swimming pools, and Muir's (1991) study of skill-status exclusivity in a tennis club (i.e., how weaker players attempt to improve their game by playing with stronger players, and how stronger players collude to avoid having to play with weaker players).

Cultural Studies

A brief mention of cultural studies is warranted here since it has now become perhaps the predominant paradigm in the sociology of sport (see Chapters 7, 15 and 16). With the eclectic blend of interpretive, critical and postmodern theories, the use of multiple methods, and drawing on historical and geographical contexts and concepts, cultural studies are far removed from the work of Mead.

And yet, his direct influence on the interpretive sociologies, and indirect influence on critical sociology, indicate that cultural studies owe a small debt to Mead. In addition, his pragmatism has a distant connection to current concerns in cultural studies about the sufficiency of evidence involved in drawing certain conclusions, and current concerns about relevancy in work relating cultural studies and cultural policy.

Conclusions

The intellectual track from Mead to Blumer to Goffman has been outlined in this chapter. Their influences on sociology, and the sociology of sport, are pervasive, but rarely recognised in citation. Their ideas and sensitising concepts are the currency of broad areas of sociology. Sociology was far behind literature in recognising that, "All the world's a stage, and all the men and women merely players" (Shakespeare, '*As You Like It*', Act II, Scene vii), but the analogy has been crucial in the development of interpretive sociology. Concepts developed by Mead, systematised by Blumer, and taken to their dramaturgical extreme by Goffman, have been key to understanding human development and interaction. In a quotation which is intended to describe Blumerian symbolic interaction, but which includes Mead's concepts of the 'significant other' and the 'generalised other', and terms from the stage such as 'script', Turowetz and Birrell (1981: 10) note that: "Persons acting and interacting, analysing scripts, making sense of their social world and responding meaningfully and in context to messages given off by both significant and generalised others is how the social world operates." Mead is key to understanding how "the social world operates", and his insights have been crucial to our understanding of the social world of sport.

References

Adler, P., & Adler, P. (1991). *Backboards and Blackboards: College Athletes and Role Engulfment*. New York: Columbia University Press.

Albert, E. (1984). Equipment as a feature of social control in the sport of bicycle racing. In: N. Theberge and P. Donnelly (eds), *Sport and the Sociological Imagination* (pp. 318–333). Fort Worth: Texas Christian University Press.

Albert, E. (1990). Constructing the order of finish in the sport of bicycle racing. *Journal of Popular Culture, 23*, 145–154.

Albert, E. (1991). Riding a line: Competition and cooperation in the sport of bicycle racing. *Sociology of Sport Journal, 8*, 341–361.

Atkinson, M. (1997). *Rounders or Robin Hoods?: Questioning the Role of the Ticket Scalper in Urban Marketplace Activity*. Unpublished Master's thesis, McMaster University, Canada.

Berger, P. (1963). *Invitation to Sociology: A Humanistic Perspective*. New York:Anchor.

Birrell, S. (1978). *Sporting Encounters: An Examination of the Work of Erving Goffman and its Application to Sport*. Unpublished doctoral dissertation, University of Massachusetts, Amherst.

Birrell, S. (1981). Sport as ritual: Interpretation from Durkheim to Goffman. *Social Forces, 60*, 354–376.

Birrell, S., & Turowetz, A. (1979). Character work-up and display: Collegiate gymnastics and professional wrestling. *Urban Life, 8*, 219–246.

Blumer, H. (1969). *Symbolic Interactionism: Perspective and Method*. Englewood Cliffs, NJ: Prentice-Hall.

Bryshun, J., & Young, K. (1999). Sport-related hazing: An inquiry into male and female involvement. In: P. White and K. Young (eds), *Sport and Gender in Canada* (pp. 269–292). Toronto: Oxford University Press.

Chafetz, J., & Kotarba, J. (1995). Son worshippers: The role of little league mothers in recreating gender. *Studies in Symbolic Interaction, 18*, 219–243.

Coakley, J. (1992). Burnout among adolescent athletes: A personal failure or a social problem? *Sociology of Sport Journal, 9*, 271–285.

Coakley, J. (1998). *Sport in Society: Issues and Controversies* (6th edition). Boston: Irwin McGraw-Hill.

Coakley, J., & Donnelly, P. (eds) (1999). *Inside Sports*. London: Routledge.

Coakley, J., & White, A. (1992). Making decisions: Gender and sport participation among British adolescents. *Sociology of Sport Journal, 9*, 20–35.

Curry, T. (1993). A little pain never hurt anyone: Athletic career socialisation and the normalisation of sports injury. *Symbolic Interaction, 16*, 273–290.

Denzin, N. (1970). Symbolic interactionism and ethnomethodology. In: J. Douglas (ed.), *Understanding Everyday Life: Toward the Reconstruction of Sociological Knowledge* (pp. 259–284). Chicago: Aldine.

Donnelly, P. (1978). On determining another's skill. Paper presented at the Canadian Sociology and Anthropology Association / Learned Societies Conference, London, ON.

Donnelly, P. (1980). *The Subculture and Public Image of Climbers*. Unpublished doctoral dissertation, University of Massachusetts, Amherst.

Donnelly, P. (1982). On verification: A comparison of climbers and birders. In: A. Ingham and E. Broom (eds), *Career Patterns and Career Contingencies in Sport* (pp. 484–499). Vancouver: University of British Columbia.

Donnelly, P. (1985). Sport subcultures. In: R. Terjung (ed.), *Exercise and Sport Sciences Reviews*, (Vol. 13, pp. 539–578). New York: Macmillan.

Donnelly, P. (1994). Take my word for it: Trust in the context of birding and mountaineering. *Qualitative Sociology, 17*, 215–241.

Donnelly, P. (2000a). Interpretive approaches to the sociology of sport. In: J. Coakley and E. Dunning (eds), *Handbook of Sports Studies* (pp. 77–91). London: Sage.

Donnelly, P. (2000b). Victory at all costs!: Taking risks in 20th century war and sport. Keynote address presented at the Japanese Society for the Sociology of Sport Annual Conference, Tokyo.

Donnelly, P. (2000c). Sticking my neck out: Taking risks in the sociology of sport. Presidential Address presented at the annual meeting of the North American Society for the Sociology of Sport, Colorado Springs, CO, USA.

Donnelly, P., & Young, K. (1985). Reproduction and transformation of cultural forms in sport: A contextual analysis of rugby. *International Review for the Sociology of Sport, 20* (1/2), 19–38.

Donnelly, P., & Young, K. (1988). The construction and confirmation of identity in sport subcultures. *Sociology of Sport Journal, 5*, 223–240.

Edwards, B. (1967). *The Encyclopedia of Philosophy*, (Vol. 5). New York: Macmillan.

Eldridge, J. (1983). *C. Wright Mills*. London: Tavistock.

Faulkner, R. (1974a). Coming of age in organisations: A comparative study of career contingencies and adult socialisation. *Sociology of Work and Occupations, 1*, 131–173.

Faulkner, R. (1974b). Making violence by doing work: Selves, situations, and the world of professional hockey. *Sociology of Work and Occupations, 1*, 288–312.

Faulkner, R. (1975). Coming of age in organisations: A comparative study of the career contingencies of musicians and hockey players. In: D. Ball and J. Loy (eds), *Sport and Social Order* (pp. 521–558). Reading, MA: Addison–Wesley.

Fine, G. (1987). *With the Boys: Little League Baseball and Preadolescent Culture*. Chicago: University of Chicago Press.

Goffman, E. (1959). *The Presentation of Self in Everyday Life*. Garden City, New York: Anchor.

Goffman, E. (1963). *Behavior in Public Places*. New York: Free Press.

Goffman, E. (1967). *Where the Action is: Interaction Ritual* (pp. 149–270). Garden City, New York: Anchor.

Goffman, E. (1969). *Strategic Interaction*. Philadelphia: Univ. of Pennsylvania Press.

Grey, M. (1992). Sports and immigrant, minority and Anglo relations in Garden City (Kansas) High School. *Sociology of Sport Journal, 9*, 255–270.

Hall, A. (1996). *Feminism and Sporting Bodies*. Champaign, IL: Human Kinetics.

Hamilton, P. (1983). Editor's foreword. In: J. Eldridge, *C. Wright Mills* (pp. 7–9). London: Tavistock.

Hansen, D. (1976). *An Invitation to Critical Sociology: Involvement, Criticism, Exploration*. New York: The Free Press.

Haralambos, M. (with R. Heald) (1985). *Sociology: Themes and Perspectives*, (2nd edition). Slough, UK: University Tutorial Press.

Hasbrook, C. (1993). Gendering practices and first graders' bodies: Physicality, sexuality, and body adornment in a minority inner-city school. Paper presented at the North American Society for the Sociology of Sport Annual Conference, Ottawa, Canada.

Hasbrook, C. (1995). Physicality, boyhood, and diverse masculinities. Paper presented at the North American Society for the Sociology of Sport Annual Conference, Sacramento, CA.

Ingham, A., & Dewar, A. (1989). Through the eyes of youth: 'Deep play' in PeeWee ice hockey. Paper presented at the North American Society for the Sociology of Sport Annual Conference, Washington, DC.

Ingham, A., & Donnelly, P. (1997). A sociology of North American sociology of sport: Disunity in unity, 1965 to 1996. *Sociology of Sport Journal, 14*(4), 362–418.

Jackson, S., & Marsh, H. (1986). Athletic or antisocial?: The female sport experience. *Journal of Sport Psychology, 8*, 198–211.

Jary, D., & Jary, J. (1995). *Collins Dictionary of Sociology* (2nd edition). Glasgow: HarperCollins.

Koukouris, K. (1994). Constructed case studies: Athletes' perspectives of disengaging from organised competitive sport. *Sociology of Sport Journal, 11*, 114–139.

Loy, J., & Kenyon, G. (eds) (1969). *Sport, Culture, and Society*. New York: Macmillan.

Lyng, S. (1990). Edgework: A social psychological analysis of voluntary risk taking. *American Journal of Sociology, 95*(4), 851–886.

Marshall, G. (1994). *The Concise Oxford Dictionary of Sociology*. Oxford: Oxford University Press.

Matteo, S. (1986). *The Effect of Sex and Gender-Schematic Processing on Sport Participation. Sex Roles, 15*, 417–432.

Mead, G. H. (1932). *The Philosophy of the Present* (ed. Murphy, A.) Chicago: Open Court.

Mead, G. H. (1934). *Mind, Self and Society: From the Standpoint of a Social Behaviorist* (ed. Morris, C.) Chicago: University of Chicago Press.

Mead, G. H. (1938). *The Philosophy of the Act* (ed. Morris, C. with Brewster, J., Dunham, A., and Miller, D.) Chicago: University of Chicago Press.

Messner, M. (1992). *Power at Play: Sports and the Problem of Masculinity*. Boston: Beacon Press.

Miller, D. (1973). *George Herbert Mead: Self, Language, and the World*. Austin: University of Texas Press.

Miller, E. (1991). Assessing the risk of inattention to class, race / ethnicity, and gender: Comment on Lyng. *American Journal of Sociology, 96*(6), 1530–1534.

Mills, Wright, C. (1966). *Sociology and Pragmatism*. Oxford: Oxford University Press.

Mitchell Jr., R. (1983). *Mountain Experience: The Psychology and Sociology of Adventure*. Chicago: University of Chicago Press.

Miyamoto, F., & Dornbusch, S. (1956). A test of interactionist hypotheses of self-conception. *American Journal of Sociology, 61*, 399–403.

Muir, D. (1991). Club tennis: A case study of taking leisure very seriously. *Sociology of Sport Journal, 8*, 70–78.

Nixon, H. (1986). Social order in a leisure setting: The case of recreational swimmers in a pool. *Sociology of Sport Journal, 3*, 320–332.

Park, R. (1916 / 1952). The City: Suggestions for the investigation of human behaviour in the city environment. In: *Human Communities* (pp. 13–51). Glencoe, IL: Free Press.

Pearson, K. (1979). *The Surfing Subcultures of Australia and New Zealand*. St. Lucia: University of Queensland Press.

Polsky, N. (1969). *Hustlers, Beats and Others*. New York: Anchor.

Rosenberg, E. (1984). Athletic retirement as social death: Concepts and perspectives. In: N. Theberge and M. Donnelly (1984) (eds), *Sport and the Sociological Imagination* (pp. 245–258). Fort Worth: Texas Christian University Press.

Rosenberg, M., & Turowetz, A. (1975). The wrestler and the physician: Identity work-up and organisational arrangements. In: D. Ball and J. Loy (eds), *Sport and Social Order* (pp. 559–574). Reading: Addison–Wesley.

Scott, M. (1968). *The Racing Game*. Chicago: Aldine.

Shalin, D. (1991). *G.H. Mead, Socialism, and the Progressive Agenda*. In: M. Aboulafia (ed.), *Philosophy, Social Theory, and the Thought of George Herbert Mead* (pp. 21–56). Albany, New York: State University of New York Press.

Smith, D. (1988). *The Chicago School: A Liberal Critique of Capitalism*. New York: St. Martin's Press.

Stevenson, C. (1990). The early careers of international athletes. *Sociology of Sport Journal, 7*, 238–253.

Stevenson, C. (1999). Trust and claims of identity: A case study of Masters swimming. *Avante, 5*, 23–38.

Stone, G. (1972). Wrestling: The great American passion play. In: E. Dunning (ed.), *Sport: Readings from a Sociological Perspective* (pp. 301–335). Toronto: University of Toronto Press.

Stone, G. (1981). Sport as community representation. In: G. Luschen and G. Sage (eds), *Handbook of Social Science of Sport* (pp. 214–245). Champaign, IL: Stipes.

Stone, G., & Oldenbourg, R. (1967). Wrestling. In: R. Slovenko and J. Knight (eds), *Motivations in Play, Games and Sports* (pp. 503–532). Springfield, IL: Charles C. Thomas.

Strauss, A. (1964). Introduction. In: A. Strauss (ed.), *George Herbert Mead on Social Psychology* (pp. vii–xxv). Chicago: University of Chicago Press.

Swain, D. (1991). Withdrawal from sport and Schlossberg's model of transitions. *Sociology of Sport Journal, 8*, 152–160.

Theberge, N. (1977). An occupational analysis of women's professional golf. Unpublished doctoral thesis, University of Massachusetts, Amherst.

Thomas, W. I., & Znaniecki, F. (1918/1927). *The Polish Peasant in Europe and America*, two Vols. New York: Knopf.

Thompson, S. (1999). *Mom's Taxi: Sport and Women's Labor*. Albany, New York: State University of New York Press.

Thomson, R. (1977). Sport and deviance: A subcultural analysis. Unpublished doctoral dissertation, University of Alberta.

Turowetz, A., & Birrell, S. (1981). Trying out: Character generating responses to structured uncertainty. Paper presented at the 1st Regional Conference of the International Committee for the Sociology of Sport, Vancouver, BC.

Vaitkus, S. (1991). *How is Society Possible?: Intersubjectivity and the Fiduciary Attitude as Problems of the Social Group in Mead, Gurwitsch, and Schutz*. Boston: Kluwer Academic Publishers.

Walk, S. (1997). Peers in pain: The experience of student athletic trainers. *Sociology of Sport Journal, 14*(1), 22–56.

Weinberg, S., & Arond, H. (1952). The occupational culture of the boxer. *American Journal of Sociology, 57,* 460–469.

Young, K. (1988). Performance, control, and public image of behavior in a deviant subculture: The case of rugby. *Deviant Behavior, 9,* 275–293.

Young, K., White, P., & McTeer, W. (1994). Body talk: Male athletes reflect on sport, injury, and pain. *Sociology of Sport Journal, 11,* 175–194.

Young, K., & White, P. (1995). Sport, physical danger, and injury: The experiences of elite women athletes. *Journal of Sport and Social Issues, 19,* 45–61.

Zimmerman, D., & Pollner, M. (1970). The everyday world as a phenomenon. In: J. Douglas (ed.), *Understanding Everyday Life: Toward the Reconstruction of Sociological Knowledge* (pp. 80–103). Chicago: Aldine.

Part II

Contemporary Concerns

Chapter 5

Sport, Gender, Feminism

Shona M. Thompson

How often have you heard the phrase "I'm not a feminist, but . . .", used in conversations concerning women? Every time it is uttered, it seems to perfectly capture the enormous ambivalence that continues to surround feminism. In making such a statement, the speaker is personally distancing herself from the negative stereotypes surrounding what has been derogatively described as the latest 'f-word' (Richards & Parker, 1995). At the same time, however, she is acknowledging that feminism is recognised as having been responsible for bringing about some major gains for women.

The 'but' in the statement is significant. It is usually followed by a call for some form of change in gender relations; some desire for a better deal for herself or other women expressed in response to a personally experienced or perceived injustice based on gender. Among sportswomen, for example, it may be anything from having her soccer game relegated to a second-rate field, to recognising the enormous disparity in rewards between sportsmen and sportswomen. Such situations illustrate what has long been understood by feminists — that in women's everyday experiences, 'the personal is political'.

Although feminism remains a much misrepresented and often feared term, it is nevertheless recognised for having helped forge major social and political change in the past century, and for revolutionising the way gender and gender relations are now theorised and understood. Here lies a reason for the negative, sometimes hostile, responses to the word. For women to gain greater opportunities and access to public life, it has often required men to give up some of the privileges they have historically enjoyed. When social and political activism highlights inequalities in the way social life is organised, and advocates for changes that require those in privileged positions to give up some of that status, controversy and resistance seem likely (Coakley, 1994).

So, 'What is feminism, anyway?' Chris Beasley's (1999) recent book of that title explains how, after approximately thirty years of what is known as the 'second wave' of feminism, it remains an ill-defined and misunderstood term.

Theory, Sport & Society
Copyright © 2002 by Elsevier Science Ltd.
All rights of reproduction in any form reserved.
ISBN: 0-7623-0742-0

Furthermore, over that time, feminism has developed into a highly complex and sophisticated mode of understanding, which has tended to add to the confusion. While it is now well recognised that there are many forms and applications of feminism, it is nevertheless still possible to identify some of the key principles that underpin its various approaches.

Fundamentally, feminism champions the belief that women have rights to all the benefits and privileges of social life equally with men. For the purposes of those concerned with sport, this means that girls and women have the right to choose to participate in sport and physical activity without constraint, prejudice or coercion, to expect their participation to be respected and taken seriously, and to be as equally valued and rewarded as sportsmen. These do not seem too much to ask.

Nevertheless, feminist attention to sport has revealed a history of women being denied opportunities, of being restricted and excluded from participation, of having our accomplishments ignored or ridiculed, of hearing our efforts being used as male forms of derision, of having our labour and our bodies exploited in the name of sport, and of being divided against each other by endemic misogyny and homophobia. Sport remains one of the most problematically gender-defined and gender-divided aspects of social life, and our understandings of this have come about largely through the deliberate engagement of feminist perspectives to the study of sport as a social institution.

When feminism is used to study any social institution, it is engaged, by definition, at three interconnected levels. First, feminism critiques traditional forms of knowledge to expose how these may be generated from an androcentric perspective, developed traditionally by men, based largely on male subjects and male experiences. Second, it develops its own knowledge and theories, based on the understanding that society is predominantly patriarchal and structured in ways which give men greater power and privilege. Feminist analysis focuses on what this means to the ways women experience their lives. Third, feminism is a form of activism, directed by knowledge about the reality of women's lives that feminist analysis seeks to illuminate. This knowledge provides the motivation and focus for whatever pressure is necessary to bring about social change for women's equal opportunities, enhanced quality of life and greater safety.

In this chapter, I shall focus on the impact of feminist scholarship on the sociological study of sport. I begin with an overview of the early meeting of sociology of sport and feminism, and introduce some of its 'foremothers'. Following that, I discuss feminism as being concerned with political advocacy and social change. Then I identify some of the key areas to which feminist scholarship has, over many years, been applied to the study of sport and give examples of the understandings that have resulted from this scholarship. These include women's experiences of sport, patriarchy and male power in sport, media representations of sportswomen, and issues relating to female sporting bodies.

Sociology of Sport meets Feminism

The application of feminism to studies of sport began in earnest in the late 1970s. While there was a growing academic interest in women's participation in sport prior to this, it was not characterised by an obvious or consistent feminist focus. Susan Birrell's (1988) article, 'Discourses on the Gender/Sport Relationship: From Women in Sport to Gender Relations', concisely documents the transition in the sociology of sport from a focus on women's sport to an understanding of the significance of gender in the analyses of all sport, which was clearly informed by feminist scholarship. Birrell dates Ann Hall's (1978) monograph as the turning point. She described Hall's work as "the first to attempt a definition of feminism, the first to understand the feminist critique of social science, and the first to bring feminist paradigms to bear on sport" (Birrell, 1988: 472). At the time, Birrell correctly predicted that a theoretically-based feminist perspective would inform future sociology of sport.

One of the earliest tasks undertaken by feminist scholars was a critique of the androcentric scientific models that had been previously used to address questions regarding women and sport. It was recognised that scientific research questions are derived from sets of assumptions which, in turn, translate into the sorts of explanations that the answers to those questions bring. Feminist scholars saw it necessary to base their inquiries on a new set of assumptions, and therefore asked different questions from those that had informed traditional male-oriented science. For example, as Birrell (1988) explained, when faced with women's low participation rates in sport, shifting the research question from 'why aren't women more interested in sport?' to 'why are women excluded from sport?', or 'why is the relationship between women and sport problematic?', reflects vastly different assumptions about the 'causes' of women's low participation rates. The feminist scientific agenda was to ask questions that reflected the social world as perceived and experienced by women.

Much of the early feminist sociology of sport of the 1980s drew on the developing feminist critiques of other academic disciplines, particularly the social sciences, challenging the methodological, theoretical and political practices that had prevailed, and exposing the intellectual sexism in the scientific traditions (Birrell, 1984; Hall, 1984; Theberge, 1985). This exercise did not happen without tension. As feminist scholars challenged other theoretical perspectives, there was much debate about the supremacy of various types of analyses, particularly regarding the relative importance of class or gender (e.g., Deem, 1989). Feminists argued, however, that intellectual disciplines that did not adopt a feminist perspective would be left 'gender-blind' and therefore grossly inadequate in theoretical terms (Cole, 1994; Deem, 1988; Hall, 1985a).

While much of this work was being done in North America, the influence of feminism was occurring world-wide, albeit with differing emphases. In the UK, for example, the study of women and sport was contextualised in a broader critique of leisure, posing questions about women's access to leisure time and space. Griffin *et al.* (1982) highlighted how patriarchy, structuring all levels of society, was based on the sexual divisions of labour and control over women's sexuality and fertility, which "allocat(ed) women to a *primarily* reproductive role, through which all their other roles are mediated (1982: 90, original emphasis). This, they argued, had implications for women's leisure in that it both structured women's lives and affected perceptions of what was appropriate behaviour for them. Other feminist scholars identified the constraints and controls on women's leisure as being related to how they were (or were not) engaged in paid work, their primary responsibility for the care of others, and male control of women's activities and leisure spaces (Deem, 1986; Green *et al.*, 1990; Wimbush and Talbot, 1988). Sporting opportunities for women were considered in the context of their access to leisure.

The rapid spread to other parts of the world of feminist concerns about sport and physical activity came about through publications in international journals, such as Hall (1987), and through many, specifically focused conferences where it was common practice for speakers to be deliberately invited to bring a feminist perspective. For example, conferences held in Sydney, Australia (1980) and in Wellington, New Zealand (1981) featured feminists from other countries who 'spread the word', calling for the urgent application of feminist analysis and activism to sport and recreation, to help bring about the necessary changes for women's greater participation opportunities and rewards (Darlison, 1981; Hall, 1985b).

Feminism, Advocacy and Change

As mentioned previously, feminism is multi-dimensional. As well as being a theoretical perspective employed to analyse the social world, it encompasses a commitment to changing aspects of that world which disadvantage women and other marginalised groups. Feminists deliberately strive for that change. There have been, however, vastly differing views about what exactly needs to be changed, and how those changes could or should be brought about. Two of the main views, derived from differing forms of feminism, became known as 'liberal' and 'radical'.

Liberal feminism advocates for women's greater involvement in social life by enhancing their opportunities to join existing institutions and structures, such as government, paid work or sport. The way to achieve this, for example, is through the development and use of legal and social policies, such as Human Rights and Equal Opportunity legislation, to open up social structures for increased opportunities for girls and women.

Advocates of radical change, on the other hand, are more likely to be critical of those social structures, to want to challenge the practices and ideologies surrounding them that are considered fundamentally sexist, exclusionary or harmful. For example, radical feminists would advocate that it is not good enough to simply add more women (or more from ethnic minority groups, or more people with disabilities) to sports organisations in their existing forms, but that the organisations themselves, and sport as it is practised, needs to be 'radically' changed to make it a fairer, safer, more enriching and rewarding possibility for everyone.

In effect, the liberal agenda has been more successful. Hall (1995) compared women's sport advocacy organisations and provided a thorough overview of advocacy efforts for women and sport to that date. In this, she analysed four feminist organisations: the Women's Sport Foundation (USA); the Canadian Association for the Advancement of Women in Sport and Physical Activity; the Women's Sport Foundation (UK); and Womensport Australia. Hall also included a description of the 1994 international conference where The Brighton Declaration on Women and Sport was drawn up and where the organisation, Womensport International, was launched. While women's participation in sport has increased, she concluded that it has been difficult to 'politicise' sportswomen and women's sport. Although there have been "significant gains in bringing more girls and women into sport, . . . sport itself remains as male-dominated and as male-oriented as always. This is not meaningful progress" (Hall, 1995: 245).

Women in sports advocacy organisations have commonly envisaged radical changes to the institution of sport but have had little success (Hall, 1996). Those who have been critical of sporting structures have noticed how difficult it is to accomplish radical change against the strength of the conservative, patriarchal power controlling sport, and hegemonic values that are increasingly 'market' orientated. For example, Jim McKay was funded by the Australian Sports Commission (ASC) to investigate why there were so few women in Australian sports organisations with the understanding that this would help improve the situation (McKay, 1992). When his interviews with sports administrators turned up unsolicited criticism about how the ASC handled gender equity issues, his research was discredited (by both the ASC and the media), his academic integrity attacked, and he was forced to change aspects of the research report before it was approved for release (McKay, 1993).

Another example; in 1987, I described how huge numbers of women in New Zealand had protested against the country's sporting exchanges with what was then Apartheid South Africa, directing that protest at men's rugby in ways that clearly demonstrated existing fury and frustration at how this sport symbolised and perpetuated white supremacist patriarchal power (Thompson, 1988). At the time I noted the general optimism felt in the aftermath of the protests for a resulting change in gender relations, in which men's rugby would no longer dominate New Zealand social life or psyche. Instead, we have witnessed what Jackson (1995) succinctly described as the "transformation, reinvention and reassertion" of rugby as a fully professionalised, commercialised and mediated sport. Its dominance in New Zealand culture has arguably surpassed anything previously known, and young New Zealand women are now numbered large amongst its fans (Thompson, 1999a). Such examples have illustrated how difficult it is to achieve radical feminist visions for change and how change that comes about is not always for the better.

The Standpoint of Women and their Experiences of Sport

From the earliest feminist studies of sport, similar stories emerged from many parts of the world about the dismal, inequitable status of women's sport. It was never suggested that women had not always been active in sport and physical recreation, but that the opportunities for this had been limited, women's involvement made difficult and their achievements hidden. Margaret Talbot (1988) commented that the, by then, well documented constraints mitigating against women's participation in sport made depressing reading. Detailed accounts of women's experiences in sport were rare. Like other areas of human endeavour, sport histories and biographies were mainly written by men, about men, and for men, and thus records of the struggles, joys and richness experienced by sportswomen were conspicuously few (Hargreaves, 1994). Furthermore, there was an emerging preoccupation with issues considered problematic in women's sport, such as the supposed conflict between athleticism and femininity. To counter this, Talbot (1988) drew on personal accounts of sportswomen to explain the importance and meaning of sport in their lives, illustrating the importance of empowerment and "the ability and capacity of women to speak for themselves, to control their own activities, to be taken seriously, and to define elements of their worlds according to their own terms and values" (Talbot, 1988: 88). Knowledge from the standpoint of women was much needed.

Feminist scholars proposed that women's 'standpoint' was the only authentic base from which knowledge about women's lives could be generated and understood. Some argued that, because women were located in a position of subordination, this allowed them to understand the world both through their own experiences of it and from the knowledge of their oppressors, in a form of 'double consciousness' (Smith, 1987). This double vision was not available to the dominant group because they had no experience of the world from marginal positions (Reddock, 1998). It was acknowledged that there was, therefore, a distinctive feminist epistemology (Hall, 1985a; Harding, 1990). In other words, feminism informed the production of knowledge by challenging and addressing questions about what is 'known', how knowledge is validated, and who is a 'knower' (Stanley & Wise, 1990). These questions underpin the principles guiding the ways to 'do' feminist research. While the specific methods vary, feminist research is grounded in recognition of women's standpoints, and is motivated to produce and extend the knowledge about women's lives and realities to assist change (Roberts, 1981; Stanley & Wise, 1983). Such research has contributed much to the literature about women's experiences of sport. Not surprisingly, it has shown how these experiences are culturally framed, particularly by gendered definitions of femininity, sexuality, wifehood and motherhood, and are influenced by specific economic and socio–political structures.

For example, Jay Coakley and Anita White (1992) talked with teenagers in England about what influenced their involvement in sport. They found that decisions about integrating sport into these young people's lives were based on their sense of what was important in their lives, and this had very strong ties with gender. The young women seldom defined themselves as athletes, having a narrow definition of what this meant and not relating readily to that definition, even those who were active in sport. These young women accepted gender-based constraints on their activities, such as limited family funds for their sport, parental constraints that were more rigid for daughters, and the expectation of ceasing their interests to accommodate those of their boyfriends. The research showed how traditional cultural practices related to gender had been incorporated into these young women's lives and identities in ways of which they were mostly unaware and did not generally resist.

Scraton *et al.* (1999) also followed qualitative research procedures to "allow sportswomen to articulate their own feelings about being women who play and enjoy sport" (1999: 101), highlighting the necessity to consider these experiences in historical and cultural contexts. Theirs was a multi-national study, based on interviews with sportswomen in England, Germany, Norway and Spain, done by nationals of those countries. Their report on soccer indicated differences between the countries, such as the extent to which the liberal-feminist agenda had increased women's access to sporting opportunities. These were less developed in England and Spain, where schools are "particularly . . . inscribed by powerful gender ideologies" and do not provide encouragement for young women to play soccer (Scraton *et al.*, 1999: 107). While the researchers acknowledged the need to understand national differences, they considered it important to note similarities in order to recognise the gender regimes experienced by sportswomen across national boundaries. One similarity was the acceptance, encouragement and admiration these soccer players had received as young girls who challenged conventional standards of femininity by being 'tomboys' or 'like boys' in playing soccer. As adult women, however, transgressing such gender boundaries became problematic, as distinctions between masculinity and femininity move into the realm of sexuality: "Adult women face tensions between their active physicality as footballers and what is deemed 'safe' heterosexual femininity" (Scraton *et al.*, 1999: 108). Similar tensions were expressed by women soccer players in New Zealand (Cox & Thompson, 2000).

In Australia, I interviewed women aged over 40 who had long careers as recreational tennis players (Thompson, 1992). These women were passionate about their sport and had spent decades organising their domestic lives in elaborate ways in order to continue playing. Their participation was facilitated by a regular, large-scale tennis competition established under the assumption that women tennis players were not in full-time paid employment but whose sport needed to be confined to times outside those during which husbands and children demanded care. The conditions under which these women played their sport were in stark contrast to those experienced by male tennis players, where a husband's participation could have an immense impact on the lives of his wife and children (Thompson, 1999b).

Furthermore, women's domestic labour actually facilitated and serviced the participation of their husbands. These women's experiences of sport were constructed by the gendered relationship to paid work and domestic labour, and ideologies of wifehood and motherhood, which privileged the sport of men and children while women's remained invisible.

Nancy Theberge's (1999) analysis of women's ice hockey in Canada challenges the notion that women's version of such masculinised sport is somehow different because women are involved, or that women have different expectations of sport. She cited "strong evidence of the enjoyment and sense of accomplishment that women hockey players (and all athletes) derive from the physicality of sport" (1999: 155). Theberge focused on images through sport of women's strength, power and aggression, and engages with the debate about whether women should 'buy into' male models of sport including those that are inherently violent. Through a discussion about the prohibition of body-checking in women's hockey, she raises issues about what are considered 'real' versions of sport, and how women's can be construed as alternative and inferior.

In 1993, Alison Dewar reminded us that, what had to date been universalised as 'women's sporting experiences', were more precisely the experience of white, middle-class, heterosexual, non-disabled women (Dewar, 1993). As feminist researchers, this was a call for us to be explicit about whose experiences we were representing and to recognise that generalisations could not be readily made to other women. Also, we needed to listen to women with backgrounds other than our own and make space for their experiences to be heard. Birrell (1989) had earlier drawn attention to the absence of writing in the sociology of sport by women of colour. These calls highlighted the issue of 'identity politics' within feminist scholarship, "the belief that the most radical politics comes directly out of our own identity (as a woman of colour, as a lesbian, as a woman with disabilities, as an old woman)" (Hall, 1996: 44). This required re-theorising relations among women, to understand how the oppression of women who did not identify with the dominant group is qualitatively different because of the layering of other 'isms', such as racism, heterosexism, able-bodyism and ageism.

Studies conducted from the standpoint of other marginal identities are emerging in the sociology of sport. Arguably, the largest volume is that concerning lesbian identities, such as Birgit Palzkill's (1990) accounts of women athletes in Germany, Gill Clarke's (1997) record of the experiences of lesbian physical education teachers in Britain, and Caroline Fusco's (1998) interviews with lesbian team-sport players in North America. Some are informed by 'queer theory', such as Eng (1997). All document the impact of heterosexism and homophobia in sport and physical education, and its impact of silencing lesbians and discrediting their achievements, such as has also been addressed by Griffin (1998) and Lenskyj (1991).

There are fewer published reports of the experiences of sport written by women of colour. Recently, Deslea Wrathall in New Zealand, speaking for Maori women, reported on the institutionalised racism in sports organisations which, among other oppressive practices, failed to recognise the importance to Maori sportswomen of their whanau (extended family), who are ignored in the everyday decisions made about the experiences of Maori women as elite sport performers (Thompson, Rewi & Wrathall, 2000). Jennifer Hargreaves (1994) argues that the British sports system (from which New Zealand's is derived) reflects traditions based in 'white' culture, and values that include the celebration of individualism and 'free will', which are "inappropriate for a modern multi-racial society". She explains that this "is why the discourse of racism in women's sport has to a large extent been repressed" (Hargreaves, 1994: 260), highlighting research done in the UK about the experiences of Afro Caribbean women and those in British Asian communities (Carrington, Chivers & Williams, 1987; Lovell, 1991). The intersecting relationship between racial identity and gender relations, framed by colonial relations of power, is also explored by Victoria Paraschak (1999) in reference to Canada's First Nation's women.

Examining women with disabilities, Jennifer Hoyle recognised the contribution of feminist theory when she commented, "feminist theory complements disability research in terms of the advances it has made in bringing the voices of oppressed groups to the fore" (Hoyle & White, 1999: 255). She challenges the notion that women with disabilities view their experiences in only negative terms, highlighting how their strengths as women with disabilities also become part of their realities. They challenge the norms of sporting experiences for the way "the boundaries between the disabled and the non-disabled are left undisturbed" (1999: 265), being well aware of the need to constitute themselves in a world that values health and beauty from a non-disabled orientation.

As Hargreaves concludes, "the idea that women in sport are a homogeneous group has been resisted" (1994: 288), just as the myth of women's consensual, shared experience of sport must also be challenged. Feminist concerns for women's standpoint and identity politics have highlighted how "such factors as age, disability, class, ethnicity and sexuality make women different from one another", irrespective of their variable and complex relationships with men (Hargreaves, 1994: 288). Fully recognising and giving voice to such differences remains our challenge.

Sport, Patriarchy and Male Power

A basic assumption of feminist theory is the view that society is patriarchal, in that every avenue of power is male controlled (Millet, 1970) and we live by an ideology of male superiority (Hartman, 1981). In this context, sport is viewed not simply as yet another patriarchal structure, but also one in which patriarchy is symbolised and reconstructed. Feminist-inspired sociology of sport has recognised the power that men hold in and through sport, and how this power is both real and symbolic. Men dominate and control sport structures, and sporting ideologies carry messages that connect masculinity, power and superiority.

Aside from the more obvious, international, patriarchal sports organisations, like the IOC, FIFA, and FINA, research from various parts of the world has shown the persistent male control of sport, and the immense obstacles with respect to change (Cameron, 1996; Fasting & Sisjord, 1986; Hall *et al.*, 1989; McKay, 1997; White & Brackenridge, 1985). These obstacles largely come from male resistance to power-sharing, but are also testament to masculine hegemony in sport. Feminist sociology of sport has recognised the significance of sport as a key site for creating ideologies of male dominance, where images, beliefs and practices of masculine power and superiority are continually replayed and reproduced. The potency of messages about male power relies upon maintaining beliefs in distinct differences between genders, which is assisted by producing images of male physical strength and muscularity, alongside those that denigrate femininity, women and their sporting activities.

In 1973, Kenneth Sheard and Eric Dunning wrote an article titled 'The Rugby Football Club as a Type of 'Male Preserve'', in which they detailed how traditional practices within rugby culture, "(had) as a central theme, the mocking, objectification and defilement of women and homosexuals" (1973: 7). The significance of this article to understanding how oppressive practices towards women are embedded in men's sport was not recognised for many years (Birrell, 1988). Then followed Lois Bryson's (1983) 'Sport and the Oppression of Women', which focused on the rituals surrounding men's sport. Bryson saw these as reinforcing male dominance in two ways: "First, they link maleness with highly valued and visible skills; and second, they link maleness with the positively sanctioned use of aggression/force/violence" (1983: 431). Bryson described how the practises of ignoring and trivialising women's sport serve to devalue women's achievements and therefore maintain the belief in women's inferiority. Alongside the hegemonic form of masculinity associated with men's sport, this supports the concept of male dominance and female subordination because men are therefore seen as 'naturally' more powerful and superior (Bryson, 1987).

Birrell (1988: 483) argued that American sport developed in the late nineteenth century "in a social context dominated by tensions surrounding changed gender relations", which included women's greater demand for and gains in equality. The resulting 'crisis in masculinity' meant that sport was claimed as male territory, producing myths of male dominance to restore masculine hegemony. Her thesis is reflected in the title of Mariah Burton Nelson's (1996) book, *'The Stronger Women Get, The More Men Love Football'*.

In Hall's (1993) review of gender and sport she pointed out, "The reaction of male scholars to feminist theory ranges from ignoring it, to recognising it exists but not reading it, to utilising it in their work, to actively contributing to it" (Hall, 1993: 60). Those who have actively contributed include men whose work has helped expose the relationship between masculinity and gender-power relations in sport. There is now a large body of work which explores the many dimensions of this theme, including the recognition of marginalised and subordinated masculinities, the oppression of Gays and Blacks, violence, and other stated problems of masculinity within sport (Connell, 1995; Kaufman, 1987; McKay, Sabo & Messner, 1999; Messner, 1992; Messner & Sabo, 1994; Pronger,1990). These analyses have been most valuable when they "go beyond merely investigating the male experience in sport and examine how male hegemony reproduces unequal gender relations" (Hall, 1996: 45), such as Tim Curry's (1991) study of male bonding in sport locker rooms, and the sexism and homophobia learned within those settings.

In her recent analysis, Varda Burstyn (1999) argues that the 'hyper-masculine heroic ideal' is gaining in prominence in capitalist culture, and that this is modelled and moulded by sport. While sport culture is highly varied, there is one singular purpose and effect that cuts across class, race, ethnic and national differences: "the culture of sport has supported the greater power of men as a gender-class in the key economic, political, and military power apparatus of civil and state society" (Burstyn, 1999: 252).

Because of how this situates women, it has long been a feminist motive to critique and look for ways to change the associations between sport and male power. As has already been mentioned, bringing about such change is difficult. One area of hope has been the increased involvement of women in sport, but the question remains whether this will, in fact, lead to major shifts in the power base in sport and broader gender relations. Scraton *et al.* (1999) concluded that, despite the recent growth in women's soccer, there is little evidence to suggest that this has presented a serious threat to the gender order. In their study of windsurfing, Wheaton and Tomlinson (1998) hypothesised that more egalitarian practises may have developed in this 'new', non-traditional, non-team sport. Instead, they found that elite women windsurfers "work within, rather than subvert, traditional patterns of gendered domination" (1998: 270), attesting to the persisting patriarchal hegemony.

There are documented examples of cases where women have retained control of their own sporting experiences, sometimes deliberately subverting the ideologies and practices of the dominant male model (Birrell & Richter, 1987; Hargreaves, 1996; Nauright & Broomhall, 1994). The debate has long raged about whether it is better for women's sport to be separate from or integrated within male controlled structures. As dominant sport practises become more globally and commercially driven, however, the opportunities and rewards for women in sport become more tied to and reliant on male dominated structures. Feminists, therefore, struggle to be optimistic about the possibility of achieving significant changes to gender relations either within or through sport.

Women, Sport and the Media

From early on, feminist sociologists of sport were alerted to how negatively the mass media represented women athletes, and how these forms of representation undermined the promotion of women's sporting events or sportswomen as legitimate athletes. Initially, the concern was with the volume of media coverage, noting how little attention was being paid to women's sport in comparison with men's. From a liberal standpoint, feminists lobbied to increase the media profile of sportswomen, to give equal recognition to their achievements. It was argued that this would lead to greater rewards for sportswomen and heighten their visibility as potential role models to promote increased female participation in physical activity.

Media content analysis studies have been done in various countries, investigating numerous media (Brown, 1994; Klein, 1988; McGregor & Fountaine, 1997; McKay & Huber, 1992; Toohey, 1997). All have consistently shown large disparities in the amount of media attention given to women's and men's sport, with women's being considerably smaller. This situation does not appear to be improving with time. On the contrary, there is evidence to suggest that in some regions, the proportion of coverage of women's sport has decreased, as McGregor and Fountaine (1997) have shown of newspapers in New Zealand.

Feminist analysis of the media soon made it obvious, however, that the quantity of media attention given to women's sport was not the only concern. An equally important issue was the form this coverage took, i.e., how were sportswomen being portrayed in the media? This question led to detailed analyses of photographs, texts and media production processes which showed that women athletes were not merely ignored but, when given visibility, were trivialised, denigrated, infantalised and sexualised. Studies of newspapers, television, magazines and calendars have consistently arrived at this conclusion (Creedon, 1994; Davis, 1997; Duncan, 1990; Duncan *et al.*, 1991; Lenskyj, 1998; Rintala & Birrell, 1984).

Mediated sport has become a site where sexual differences are powerfully portrayed and guarded, a process that relies strongly on images and texts that distance sportswomen as far as possible from sportsmen. Duncan and Messner

(1998) summarise how the media's treatment of sport emphasises gender differences and exaggerates the inequalities of male and female athletes. They see these differences being conveyed in many ways. For example, an initial form occurs through media production, such as the disparities in quantity and quality of coverage. This is coupled with the justification that inequalities are merely a reflection of audience-related demand and supply when, they state, "in actuality, television producers are not merely giving audiences what they want to see. Producers, in association with athletic organisations, actively build audiences for major events" (Duncan & Messner, 1998: 173). Second, language describing the play and attributes of athletes is used differently for men and women. This exaggerates gender differences and inequalities by emphasising binaries such as strength/weakness, success/failure. A third difference is what Duncan and Messner (1998) describe as the 'symbolic dominance' of men and men's sport, conveyed in a variety of ways. These include: asymmetrical gender marking, where the language used defines sport generically as male and that played by women labelled as a deviation (e.g., 'basketball'/ 'women's basketball'); hierarchies of naming, such as using titles and descriptions which infantalise sportswomen by referring to them as girls or by their first names, compared to references to sportsmen which accord them adult status; and the sexualisation of women's sport, through emphases on the appearance of sportswomen, overt sexual depictions of them and pre-occupations with sexual identities and family relationships.

Kane and Lenskyj (1998: 188) point out, "Over the last two decades, sociologists of sport have convincingly demonstrated that media representations of women's identities in sport link their athleticism to deeply held values regarding femininity and sexuality." Media images and narratives impose normative expectations of female athletes which include traditional notions of femininity, (hetero)sexual appeal and conformity to roles as wives and mothers. As Pat Griffin (1992) suggested, the insistence that sportswomen conform to traditional notions of femininity is really an insistence that they be, or appear to be, heterosexual. Media portrayals, therefore, are primarily about the 'image problem' that pervades women's sport: "The underlying fear is not that a female athlete or coach will appear too plain or out of style; the real fear is that she will look like a dyke or, even worse, is one" (Griffin, 1992: 254).

Pamela Creedon's work (1994, 1998) has focused on media production. She suggests that even if gender equality in numbers is achieved in news journalism, little would likely change in how news is gathered and defined: "Entry-level employees adapt to work-place norms" and, in the media workplace, those norms "privilege a patriarchal world view" (Creedon, 1998: 93). Creedon cites, for example, the treatment of women sports news reporters within the industry in the USA, including cases of sexual harassment in sportsmen's locker rooms.

Creedon (1998: 99) also discusses the implications for both liberal and radical feminist reforms of the media, concluding that "the ultimate arbiter will be the market place" and "what sells". Currently, she suggests, 'little girls', 'sweethearts' and 'heroines' sell women's sport. Homosexuality does not sell, and there are mixed results regarding heterosexual appeal. For example, despite the increased television exposure of women's beach volleyball, recognised for its sexual display, sponsorship revenue has not increased. On the other hand, "heterosexual sex appeal presented in terms of fitness sells very very well" (Creedon, 1998: 97).

Sporting Bodies

Regularly identified as the earliest critical analysis of women and sport, Paul Willis's 1973 essay (published later in 1982), noted the "colossal social interest" in biological differences between women and men, when there are a myriad of other biologically-based differences between people about which there is little or no interest. Willis argued that this interest in physical gender difference, rather than gender similarities, took on an ideological 'life of its own', and the belief in such differences passed into 'common sense'. Within sport, these beliefs fuelled "popular consciousness with its prejudices about femininity" (Willis, 1982: 134).

Historical studies, such as those by Cahn (1990), Lenskyj (1986), McCrone (1988) and Vertinsky (1990) recorded how medical and scientific rhetoric about women's bodies has been effectively used to discourage women's participation in sport, by emphasising so-called limited physical capabilities and aspects of women's reproductive capacity which was thought to need safe-guarding. Research from Britain showed how these perceptions of women's physicality were translated into education, influencing the physical education curricula and girls' experiences of embodiment (Fletcher, 1984; Scraton, 1992).

A recent focus on sporting bodies by feminist sociologists of sport arose from a new 'corporeal feminism' influenced in large part by the work of Michel Foucault, and feminists who took up his ideas about gendered and sexualised bodies, such as Bordo (1993) and Grosz (1994). This work and its significance to the sociology of sport are discussed in more depth elsewhere in this text (see Chapter 12). The point I wish to make here, however, is that the post-modern/post-structural perspective has been useful in allowing us to see how bodies are socially constructed through a variety of discourses, such as medical, scientific and sports-related. This has enabled us to get beyond debates about biologically determined difference and essentialism, providing a way to understand how the body can be socially constructed sexually "without positing an original sexual difference or fixed biological essence" (McNay, cited in Hall, 1996: 53).

Such work is based on the assumption that women are neither powerless victims of oppressive discourses nor entirely free from structural constraints. Analyses from this perspective have, therefore, been able to recognise the contradictory ways in which the body is lived, and how women's involvement in sport can unsettle and disrupt common sense understandings of female bodies. For example, Pirkko Markula's (1995) ethnographic research with female aerobicisers highlighted how these women experienced pleasure from movement and energy while simultaneously struggling to conform to societal constructions of the ideal body, which is itself contradictorily empowered and sexualised. Obel's (1996) analysis of women bodybuilders discusses how these women transgress the normative ideal of femininity by demonstrating muscularity and strength yet, in competition, are judged according to feminine ideals. Cox and Thompson (2000) focus on the multiplicity of bodily constructions to understand how women soccer players appear to move seamlessly between social situations that have contrasting expectations of female bodily practices, such as presenting strong, competent physicality on the sport field and 'heterosexy' femininity at meetings with sponsors. Analyses, such as Mikosza and Phillips' (1999) of the Australian 'Golden Girls' calendar, and the controversies which surround such publications, highlight the tensions between women's physicality expressed through sport and the sexualisation of women's bodies.

In 1987, Nancy Theberge advocated the liberating potential of sport, allowing women the opportunity to defy restrictive notions of feminine embodiment, to experience creative energy and develop strength, power and physical confidence. Many more women are now experiencing this. Feminist analysis of the ways the athletic female body is socially constructed have contributed to destabilising perceptions of sport that have been "trapped in ideologies" (Willis, 1982), of gendered body differences, helping to undermine the power differentials such ideologies have attempted to maintain. They have also made an important contribution to a growing volume of literature about women's corporeality (e.g., Brackenridge, 1993).

Conclusion

The significance of the sociological study of sport to wider feminist agendas has not been fully appreciated, either in terms of the ways in which sport has subordinated women through its symbolic representation of masculine power, nor in its potential as a site for understanding the social construction of femininity and challenging notions of female weakness. Well recognised now, however, is that sport cannot be theorised without taking gender into account. From this point of view, it would not be overstating the case to say that, over the past twenty years, feminism has had a profound impact on the sociology of sport.

Those of us who have witnessed the progress of feminist scholarship have seen the ways that it has evolved, shifted, changed its focus and approach (Beasley, 1999; Hall, 1996). However, it has not gone away and for many reasons is as important and necessary as ever. There is no evidence to conclude that the agenda of feminism, to make this an equitable and safe world for all women to inhabit, has been completed.

While some women do have opportunities in sport and physical activity that were not readily available several decades ago, there are still huge problems within the institution. For example, recent research has focused on the extent and nature of abuse and sexual harassment in sport (Brackenridge, 1997; Brackenridge & Kirby, 1997; Lenskyj, 1992; MacGregor, 1998). Young, physically active feminists can clearly articulate the experience of struggling to retain a sense of their own empowerment under the hefty weight of commercialism (Valdes, 1995), and the struggles of marginal groups disadvantaged in or oppressed by sport are still rarely heard.

Mary McDonald (2000), who recently analysed the corporate-driven women's sport 'boom' in the US, highlighted how this is both derived from, and in turn creates, strong post-feminist assumptions that women can now 'have it all' through the opportunities made available by enhanced consumerism and vigorous individualism. Aligned with this is the belief that those women who fail to gain it 'all' have only themselves to blame, which "(marginalises) any 'radical' focus on sexual politics and (refuses) to acknowledge the continuing power differentials that remain" (McDonald, 2000: 36). If sport is to be available, liberating and rewarding for all, not just for some, sociological analysis and advocacy still needs a clearly and proudly identified feminist agenda in response to growing post-feminism.

References

Beasley, C. (1999). *What is Feminism, Anyway?* St. Leonards, NSW: Allen & Unwin.

Birrell, S. (1984). 'Studying gender in sport: A feminist perspective'. In: N. Theberge, and P. Donnelly (eds), *Sport and the Sociological Imagination* (pp. 125–135). Fort Worth: Texan Christian University Press.

Birrell, S. (1988). Discourses on the gender/sport relationship: From women in sport to gender relations. *Exercise and Sport Sciences Review, 16*, 459–502.

Birrell, S. (1989). Racial relations theories and sport: Suggestions for a more critical analysis. *Sociology of Sport Journal, 6*, 212–227.

Birrell, S., & Richter, D. (1987). Is a diamond forever?: Feminist transformations of sport. *Women's Studies International Forum, 10*, 295–409.

Bordo, S. (1993). *Unbearable Weight: Feminism, Western Culture and the Body*. Berkley: University of California Press.

Brackenridge, C. (ed.) (1993). *Body Matters: Leisure Images and Lifestyle*. Brighton: University of Brighton, Chelsea School Research Centre.

Brackenridge, C. (1997). "He owned me basically": Women's experiences of sexual abuse in sport. *International Review for the Sociology of Sport, 32*, 115–130.

Brackenridge, C., & Kirby, S. (1997). Playing safe: Assessing the risk of sexual abuse to elite child athletes. *International Review for the Sociology of Sport, 32*, 407–418.

Brown, P. (1994). The 'containment' of women in the Australian sporting press from 1890 to 1990. *ACHPER Journal, 41*, 4–8.

Bryson, L. (1983). Sport and the oppression of women. *Australian and New Zealand Journal of Sociology, 19*, 413–426.

Bryson, L. (1987). Sport and the maintenance of masculine hegemony. *Women's Studies International Forum, 10*, 349–360.

Burstyn, V. (1999). *The Rites of Men. Manhood, Politics and the Culture of Sport*. Toronto: University of Toronto Press.

Cahn, S. K. (1990). *Coming on Strong: Gender and Sexuality in Women's Sport*. New York: Free Press.

Cameron, J. (1996). *Trail Blazers: Women Who Manage New Zealand Sport*. Christchurch: Sports Inclined.

Carrington, B., Chivers, T., & Williams, T. (1987). Gender, leisure and sport: A case study of young people of South Asian descent. *Leisure Studies, 6*, 256–279.

Clarke, G. (1997). Playing a part: The lives of lesbian physical education teachers. In: G. Clarke, and B. Humberstone (eds), *Researching Women and Sport* (pp. 36–49). London: Macmillan.

Coakley, J. (1994). *Sport in Society: Issues and Controversies* (5th edition). St. Louis: Mosby.

Coakley, J., & White, A. (1992). Making decisions: Gender and sport participation among British adolescents. *Sociology of Sport Journal, 9*, 20–25.

Cole, C. (1994). Resisting the canon: Feminist cultural studies, sport and technologies of the body. In: S. Birrell and C. Cole (eds), *Women, Sport and Culture* (pp. 5–29). Champaign, IL: Human Kinetics.

Connell, R. W. (1995). *Masculinities*. Sydney: Allen and Unwin.

Cox, B., & Thompson, S. (2000). Multiple bodies: Sportswomen, soccer and sexuality. *International Review for the Sociology of Sport, 35*, 5–19.

Creedon, P. J. (ed.) (1994). *Women, Sport and Media: Challenging Gender Values*. Thousand Oaks, CA: Sage.

Creedon, P. J. (1998). Women, sport and media institutions: Issues in sports journalism and marketing. In: L. A. Wenner (ed.), *MediaSport* (pp. 88–99). London: Routledge.

Curry, T. (1991). Fraternal bonding in the locker room: A profeminist analysis of talk about competition and women. *Sociology of Sport Journal, 8,* 119–35.

Darlison, L. (1981). The politics of women's sport and recreation: A need to link theory and practice. In: A. Welch (ed.), Papers and Reports from the 1981 Conference on Women and Recreation *Council for Recreation and Sport* (pp. 15–25). Wellington, New Zealand.

Davis, L. (1997). *The Swimsuit Issue and Sport.* Albany, New York: SUNY Press.

Deem, R. (1986). *All Work and No Play: The Sociology of Women and Leisure.* Milton Keynes: Open University Press.

Deem, R. (1989). New way forward in sport and leisure studies — a reply to Robert Sparks. *Sociology of Sport Journal, 6,* 66–69.

Dewer, A. (1993). Would all the generic women in sport please stand up? Challenges facing feminist sport sociology. *Quest, 45,* 211–229.

Duncan, M. C. (1990). Sports photographs and sexual difference: Images of women and men in the 1984 and 1988 Olympics. *Sociology of Sport Journal, 7,* 22–43.

Duncan, M. C., & Messner, M. (1998). The media image of sport and gender. In: L. A. Wenner (ed.), *MediaSport* (pp. 170–185). London: Routledge.

Duncan, M. C., Messner, M. A., & Williams, L. (1991). *Coverage of Women's Sport in Four Daily Newspapers.* Los Angeles: Amateur Athletic Foundations of Los Angeles.

Eng, H. (1997). Queer studies and sport. Paper presented at the ISSA Symposium, Norwegian University of Sport and Physical Education, Oslo, July.

Fasting, K., & Sisjord, M. K. (1986). Gender, verbal behaviour and power in sports organisations. *Scandinavian Journal of Sport Science, 8,* 81–85.

Fletcher, S. (1984). *Women First: The Female Tradition in English Physical Education 1880–1980.* London: Athlone Press.

Fusco, C. (1998). Lesbians and locker rooms: The subjective experiences of lesbians in sport. In: G. Rail (ed.), *Sport and Postmodern Times* (pp. 87–116). Albany, New York: SUNY Press.

Green, E., Hebron, S., & Woodward, D. (1990). *Women's Leisure. What Leisure?* London: Macmillan Education.

Griffin, C., Hobson, D., MacIntosh, S., & McCabe, T. (1982). Women and leisure. In: J. Hargreaves (ed.), *Sport, Culture and Ideology* (pp. 88–116). London: Routledge & Kegan Paul.

Griffin, P. (1992). Changing the game: Homophobia, sexism and lesbians in sport. *Quest, 44,* 251–265.

Griffin, P. (1998). *Strong Women, Deep Closets. Lesbians and Homophobia in Sport.* Champaign, IL: Human Kinetics.

Grosz, E. (1994). *Volatile Bodies: Towards a Corporeal Feminism.* Bloomington: Indiana University Press.

Hall, M. A. (1978). Sport and gender: A feminist perspective on the sociology of sport.

CAHPER Sociology of Sport Monograph Series, Ottawa: Canadian Association for Health, Physical Education and Recreation.

Hall, M. A. (1984). Feminist prospects for Sociology of Sport. *Arena Review, 8,* 1–10.

Hall, M. A. (1985a). Knowledge and gender: Epistemological questions in the social analysis of sport. *Sociology of Sport Journal, 2,* 25–42.

Hall, M. A. (1985b). Women, sport and feminism: Some Canadian and Australian comparisons. In: *Fit to Play. Women, Sport and Recreation* (pp. 25–28). Sydney: NSW Advisory Council to the Premier.

Hall, M. A. (ed.) (1987). The gendering of sport, leisure and physical education. *Women's Studies International Forum, Special Issue, 10,* 333–468.

Hall, M. A. (1993). Gender and sport in the 1990s: Feminism, culture and politics. *Sport Science Review, 2,* 48–68.

Hall, M. A. (1995). Feminist activism in sport: A comparative study of women's sport advocacy organisations. In: A. Tomlinson (ed.), *Gender, Sport and Leisure* (pp. 217–250). Brighton: Chelsea School Research Centre.

Hall, M. A. (1996). *Feminism and Sporting Bodies. Essays on Theory and Practice.* Champaign, IL: Human Kinetics.

Hall, M. A., Cullen, D., & Slack, T. (1989). Organisational elites recreating themselves: The gender structure of national sports organisations. *Quest, 41,* 28–45.

Harding, S. (1990). Feminism, science and the anti-enlightenment critiques. In: L.J. Nicholson (ed.), *Feminism/Post-modernism* (pp. 83–106). London: Routledge.

Hargreaves, J. (1994). *Sporting Females: Critical Issues in the History and Sociology of Women's Sports.* London: Routledge.

Hartman, H. (1981). The unhappy marriage of Marxism and Feminism. In: L. Sargent (ed.), *Women and Revolution.* Montreal: Black Rose Books.

Hoyle, J., & White, P. (1999). Physical activity in the lives of women with disabilities. In: P. White and K. Young (ed.), *Sport and Gender in Canada* (pp. 254–268). Don Mills, ON: Oxford University Press.

Jackson, S. (1995). New Zealand's big game in crisis: Mediated images of the transformation, reinvention and reassertion of rugby. Paper presented at the Annual Meeting for the North American Society for the sociology of sport. Sacramento, November 1–4.

Kane, M. J., & Lenskyj, H. J. (1998). Media treatment of female athletes: Issues of gender and sexualities. In: L. A. Wenner (ed.), *MediaSport* (pp. 186–201). London: Routledge.

Kaufman, M. (ed.) (1987). *Beyond Patriarchy: Essays by Men on Pleasure, Power and Change.* Toronto: Oxford University Press.

Klein, M.-L. (1988). Women in the discourse of sports reports. *International Review for the Sociology of Sport, 23,* 139–152.

Lenskyj, H. (1986). *Out of Bounds: Women, Sport and Sexuality.* Toronto: Women's Press.

Lenskyj, H. (1991). Combating homophobia in sport and physical education. *Sociology of Sport Journal, 8,* 61–69.

Lenskyj, H. (1992). Unsafe at home base: Women's experiences of sexual harassment in university sport and physical education. *Women in Sport and Physical Activity Journal, 1,* 19–34.

Lenskyj, H. (1998). 'Inside sport' or 'on the margins'? Australian women and the sport media. *International Review for the Sociology of Sport, 33,* 19–32.

Lovell, T. (1991). Sport, racism and young women. In: G. Jarvie (ed.), *Sport, Racism and Ethnicity.* London: Falmer Press.

McDonald, M. (2000). The marketing of the Women's National Basketball Association and the making of post-feminism. *International Review for the Sociology of Sport, 35,* 35–47.

McCrone, K. (1988). *Sport and the Physical Emancipation of English Women, 1870–1914.* London: Routledge.

MacGregor, M. (1998). Harassment and abuse in sport and recreation. *CAHPERD Journal de l'ACSEPLD, 64*(2), 4–13.

McGregor, J., & Fountaine, S. (1997). Gender equity in retreat: The declining representation of women's sport in the New Zealand print media. *Metro, 112,* 38–43.

McKay, J. (1992). *Why So Few?: Women Executives in Australian Sport.* Belconnen, Australia: Australian Sports Commission.

McKay, J. (1993). Masculine hegemony, the state and the politics of gender equity policy research. *Culture and Policy, 5,* 223–240.

McKay, J. (1997). *Managing Gender: Affirmative Action and Organisational Power in Australian, Canadian and New Zealand Sport.* Albany, New York: SUNY Press.

McKay, J., & Huber, D. (1992). Anchoring media images of technology and sport. *Women's Studies International Forum, 15,* 205–218.

McKay, J., Sabo, D., & Messner, M. (eds) (1999). Men and sport. *Men and Masculinities, Special Issue, 1,* 243–318.

McNay, J. (1991). The Foucauldian body and the exclusion of experience. *Hypatia, 6,* 125–139.

Markula, P. (1995). Firm but shapely, fit but sexy, strong but thin: The post-modern aerobicizing female bodies. *Sociology of Sport Journal, 12,* 424–453.

Mikosza, J. M., & Phillips, M. G. (1999). Gender, sport and the body politic: Framing femininity in the 'Golden Girls of Sport' calendar and 'The Atlantic Dream'. *International Review for the Sociology of Sport, 34,* 5–16.

Millet, K. (1970). *Sexual politics.* New York: Doubleday.

Messner, M. A. (1992). *Power at Play. Sport and the Problem of Masculinity.* Boston: Beacon Press.

Messner, M. A., & Sabo, D. F. (eds) (1994). *Sex, Violence and Power in Sports: Rethinking Masculinities.* Freedom, CA: The Crossing Press.

Nauright, J., & Broomhall, J. (1994). A woman's game: The development of netball and a female sporting culture in New Zealand 1906–70. *International Journal of History of Sport, 11,* 387–407.

Nelson, M. B. (1996). *The Stronger Women Get the More Men Love Football: Sexism and the Culture of Sport.* London: The Women's Press.

Obel, C. (1996). Collapsing gender in competitive bodybuilding: Researching contradictions and ambiguities in sport. *International Review for the Sociology of Sport, 31*, 185–201.

Palzkill, B. (1990). Between gymshoes and high-heels: The development of a lesbian identity and existence in top class sport. *International Review for the Sociology of Sport, 25*, 221–234.

Paraschak, V. (1999). Doing race, doing gender: First nations, 'sport' and gender relations. In: P. White and K. Young (eds), *Sport and Gender in Canada*. Don Mills, Ontario: Oxford University Press.

Pronger, B. (1990). *The Arena of Masculinity: Sports, Homosexuality and the Meaning of Sex*. Toronto: Summerhill Press.

Reddock, R. (1998). Challenging sociology: Feminist critical reconceptualisations and Caribbean contributions. In: L. Christiansen–Ruffman (ed.), *The Global Feminist Enlightenment: Women and Social Knowledge* (pp. 45–58). Madrid: International Sociological Association.

Richards, A., & Parker, J. (1995). The F-word. *New Internationalist*, (August): 24–25.

Rintala, J., & Birrell, S. (1984). Fair treatment of the active female: A content analysis of 'Young Athlete' magazine. *Sociology of Sport Journal, 1*, 231–250.

Roberts, H. (1981). *Doing Feminist Research*. London: Routledge & Kegan Paul.

Scraton, S. (1992). *Shaping up to Womanhood: Gender and Girls' Physical Education*. Buckingham: Open University Press.

Scraton, S., Fasting, K., Pfister, G., & Bunuel, A. (1999). It's still a Man's Game?: The experiences of top-level European women footballers. *International Review for the Sociology of Sport, 34*, 99–112.

Smith, D. (1987). *The Everyday World as Problematic. A Feminist Sociology*. Toronto: Toronto University Press.

Sheard, K., & Dunning, E. (1973). The rugby club as a type of 'male preserve': Some sociological notes. *International Review of Sport Sociology, 8*(3/4), 5–24.

Stanley, L., & Wise, S. (1983). *Breaking Out: Feminist Consciousness and Feminist Research*. London: Routledge & Kegan Paul.

Stanley, L., & Wise, S. (1990). Method, methodology and epistemology in feminist research process. In: L. Stanley (ed.), *Feminist Praxis* (pp. 20–59). London: Routledge.

Talbot, M. (1988). Beating them at their own game?: Women's sport involvement. In: E. Wimbush and M. Talbot (eds), *Relative Freedoms. Women and Leisure* (pp. 102–114). Milton Keynes: Open University Press.

Theberge, N. (1985). Towards a feminist alternative to sport as a male preserve. *Quest, 10*, 193–202.

Theberge, N. (1987). Sport and women's empowerment. *Women's Studies International Forum, 10*, 387–393.

Theberge, N. (1999). Being physical: Sources of pleasure and satisfaction in women's ice hockey. In: J. Coakley and P. Donnelly (eds), *Inside Sports* (pp. 146–155). London: Routledge.

Thompson, S. M. (1988). Challenging the hegemony: New Zealand women's opposition to rugby and the reproduction of a capitalist patriarchy. *International Review for the Sociology of Sport, 23*, 205–212.

Thompson, S. M. (1992). Mum's tennis day: The gendered definition of older women's leisure. *Loisir et Société/Society and Leisure, 15*, 271–89.

Thompson, S. M. (1999a). Legacy of 'The Tour'. A continued analysis of women's relationship to sport. In: B. Patterson (ed.), *Sport, Society and Culture in New Zealand*. Wellington: Stout Research Centre.

Thompson, S. M. (1999b). Mother's taxi. *Sport and Women's Labor.* Albany, New York: SUNY Press.

Thompson, S., Rewi, P., & Wrathall, D. (2000). Maori experiences of sport and physical activity: Research and initiatives. In: C. Collins (ed.), *Sport in New Zealand Society* (pp. 241–252). Palmerston North: Dunmore Press.

Toohey, K. (1997). Australian television, gender and the Olympic Games. *International Review for the Sociology of Sport, 32*, 19–29.

Valdes, A. L. (1995). Ruminations of a feminist aerobics instructor. In: B. Findlen (ed.), *Listen Up: Voices from the Next Feminist Generation*. Washington: Seal Press.

Vertinsky, P. A. (1990). *The Eternally Wounded Woman: Women, Doctors and Exercise in the Late Nineteenth Century*. Manchester: Manchester University Press.

Wheaton, B., & Tomlinson, A. (1998). The changing gender order in sport? The case of windsurfing subculture. *Journal of Sport and Social Issues, 10*, 252–274.

White, A., & Brackenridge, C. (1985). Who rules sport? Gender divisions in the power structure of British sports organisations from 1960. *International Review for the Sociology of Sport, 20*, 95–107.

Willis, P. (1982). Women in sport in ideology. In: J. Hargreaves (ed.), *Sport, Culture and Ideology* (pp. 117–135). London: Routledge.

Wimbush, E., & Talbot, M. (eds) (1988). *Relative Freedoms. Women and Leisure*, Milton Keynes: Open University Press.

Chapter 6

The Anthropology of Sport: Escaping the Past and Building a Future

Alan Klein

The anthropology of sport should have, by now, been celebrated as the premier diagnostic field for the study of culture and society. Instead, it has languished. The reasons why it has failed to inform modern social science, and the path out of the morass is the focus of this chapter. Differences between the fields of anthropology and sociology figure into this predicament. While the old cliché, 'sociologists study the West while anthropologists study the rest', doesn't hold true as much these days as it did a quarter of a century ago, it continues to serve as a marker of different approaches to sports studies. Sociologists of sport rarely venture outside of North America and Western Europe, thus ignoring most of the world's sporting institutions. The continuation of this division of intellectual interest has kept sport anthropologists mutely living on the periphery. It is not only the study of the more unfamiliar cultures of the world that separates the two disciplines, however. Were this the beginning of the twentieth century, instead of the twenty-first, such a position would not prove troubling. For most of the last century, the spread of sport outside of Europe and North America was only casually mentioned by sports scholars, mostly historians (e.g., Guttmann, 1994; Beezley, 1987; Roden, 1980). With the recent and powerful rise of globalisation processes becoming central in almost every social science, treating sport as a Western notion is now seen as dated.

   A second area of significant difference between the two fields lies in the core foci of each, with sociology concerned mostly with society, while anthropology remains oriented towards culture. The rise of cultural studies in the past few decades has attempted to wrest control of the culture concept from anthropology, but most people who use a cultural studies approach do not really grasp culture as an object of study and a method of studying for two reasons. First, cultural studies rarely use ethnographic field methods in generating data (that is, if any of them even use data!), and secondly, cultural studies students are not trained in cross-cultural analysis, preferring their view that, in a postmodern world, all difference is flattened out, and hence irrelevant (Jameson, 1991). The use of the ethnographic method is, I am pleased to say, a growing practice in sociology, and sociology of sport in particular. On the other hand, however, the use of cross-cultural comparisons outside of anthropology remains rare.[1] In short, anthropologists are trained to work in and with culture(s). They have developed the concept, tested, and refined it for over a century all over the world. In the final analysis, what distinguishes sport anthropology from the sociology of sport is the attempt to understand patterns of similarities and differences between cultures for the purpose of establishing general laws of process.

A third difference is that, by contrast with primary institutions such as politics, economics and religion, sport is often viewed as an ancillary anthropological practice. W. H. Auden could just as easily have described sport when he wrote, "Poetry makes nothing happen . . ." (1968). This same declaration was made by anthropologist Clifford Geertz (1972) writing of the overall impact of cockfighting (and by extension sport) in Bali where the sport is the centre of intense interest. His comments may apply directly to the study of sport in anthropology:

> Cockfighting is 'really real' only to the cocks — it does not kill anyone, castrate anyone, reduce anyone to animal status, alter hierarchical relations among people, or refashion the hierarchy; it does not even redistribute income in any significant way (1972: 443).

By contrast, anthropologists have been working throughout the world under a certain amount of duress, in that they saw themselves rushing to provide a picture of culture before it was substantially impacted by the West. In this context, cultural institutions were often prioritised so that only the most important ones were to be ministered to. Clearly, the role of economics, religion, politics, and social organisation were central, while things like play, recreation, and sport or art were more marginal. Since sport was perceived as "making nothing happen", it remained an after-thought. More importantly, those who focused upon sport as central risked being thought of in the profession as non-serious. Studying wrestling among the Bachama of Nigeria may prove interesting within the overall context of their culture, but it remains a sidebar. It is nothing to build an academic career around, and Phillips Stevens (1975), who produced several pieces on *Bachama*

---

[1]Examples of non-anthropological cross-cultural sport analysis can be found in Arbena's anthology (1988) on sport in Latin America, Sugden's study of Cuban sport (1997), Riordan's work on sport in the USSR (1977, 1981), and the Mandle's work on basketball in Trinidad and Tobago (1988).

sport, understood that. Getting tenure based upon one's identity as a sport anthropologist would have been and remains somewhat risky, further dampening the likelihood of recruiting like-minded young graduates.

I distinguish between anthropologists who have made occasional (at times significant) contributions to the field of the sociology of sport, and those who have thrown caution to the wind by building their careers around the study of sport. The vast majority of works found in Blanchard's (1995) textbook on the Anthropology of Sport fall into the former category. As late as the 1970s, Kendall Blanchard (1974, 1975, 1979) and Alyce Cheska (1975, 1978a, 1978b) were the discipline's only self-identified and full-time sport scholars. Several others existed on the margins of the field. Andrew Miracle (1977, 1980, 1981), for instance, found a home among sociologists rather than anthropologists. The most notable of these peripheral sport anthropologists is John MacAloon (1981, 1984, 1992), whose ethno-historical account of Pierre de Coubertin and the modern Olympic Games placed him, briefly, at the forefront of sport studies. At present, he remains an occasional contributor to debates related to his interests, although he has essentially ceased researching the field, and he never really engaged in ethnography and fieldwork.

It is for this same reason that I do not consider Pierre Bourdieu (1990) a central figure even though anthropologists love to prominently cite his work in their bibliographic essays on the sociology of sport. I agree wholeheartedly with sport anthropologist Noel Dyck (2000) who argues that it is the placement of ethnographic fieldwork and participant–observation at the centre that distinguishes the anthropology of sport from other related methods of inquiry. Ethnographic fieldwork, while highly significant in distinguishing anthropological work from other fields, is not in and of itself capable of elevating the position of sport anthropology, however. Another subtle, but significant, index of the marginality of sport anthropology is found in Geertz's (1972) classic article on Balinese cockfighting. If anything should have directed attention to the serious study of culture and sport, it should have been Geertz's piece, and yet, even with this, sport anthropology failed to take flight.

In this chapter, I will selectively review what I consider to be substantial contributions in the anthropology of sport in an effort to point to ways by which the field may yet break free from constraints, and the prejudicial perceptions held by others toward it. This chapter is not intended to be a complete survey of the field. Considering the moribund state of the anthropology of sport, such surveys need only be done occasionally (see Blanchard, 1995; Sands, 1998). A brief mention of some of the early work is appropriate, however, in order to illustrate the directions we need for future growth.

Brief History of the Field

Anthropologists have been examining sport since at least 1879 when British anthropologist Sir Edward Burnett Tylor published an article showing that the study of games and sport could be used as a means of showing prior contact between people (Blanchard, 1995: 10). Through the next eight decades, some famous anthropologists published pieces dealing with cross-cultural sport. James Mooney (1890), Alexander Lesser (1933), Morris Opler (1944), all luminaries in Native North American ethnology, wrote about sport among the *Cherokee, Pawnee,* and *Apache* respectively. In Britain, Raymond Firth (1931) included pieces on sport in his lifelong work on the *Tikopia* of Polynesia.

Blanchard (1995) argues that the field of sport anthropology finally arrived in the 1960s and early 1970s with the publication of articles by Robin Fox (1961) and Geertz's aforementioned masterpiece. These publications dovetailed with the American Anthropological Association's 1964 Presidential Address in which Leslie White alluded to the possibilities inherent in sport studies. Blanchard would have us believe that the budding field of the anthropology of sport was progressing. Kendall's history is crowned with the creation of TAASP (The Association for the Anthropological Study of Play) in 1974. TAASP hung on for 20 years before quietly being put to sleep. Without a critical mass of anthropologists of sport, TAASP was kept alive by infusions of sport scholars from other fields. During that period, however, other sport organisations in History and Sociology succeeded in establishing a presence within their natal organisations, again prompting the question, why not anthropology?

Most recently, Susan Brownell (2000), whose work on sport in China is reviewed below, has argued that if the anthropology of sport is to attain a more respected position, we need to accumulate contributions in several key theoretical areas, such as national identity and trans–nationalism, gender, and practice theory. This is an important and legitimate call to action. By uniting 'cutting edge' theory with sport ethnography in mainstream cultures, while downplaying other aspects of the anthropological arsenal, I believe we can showcase the best that sport anthropology has to offer. I would like to argue that what is needed is a critical mass of work in targeted areas, for it is clear that isolated contributions, no matter how stellar, tend to be ignored. I have selected what I believe to be some of the most significant contributions to the anthropology of sport to present at some length.

Blood Sport as a Cultural Projection: Cockfighting in Bali

Any discussion of sport anthropology has to begin with Geertz's work on Balinese cockfighting (1972). Geertz is widely considered to be one of the pre-eminent anthropologists of our time. His fieldwork in Bali included ethnographic observations of 57 cockfighting matches, which he compressed into a single article considered to be a minor classic in anthropology. It is one of the most erudite, and widely reprinted pieces ever written on sport, offering abundant insights into the relationship between sport and culture. Cockfighting may be confined to the 'cultural dustbin' in North America and Europe, but in many other parts of the world, it is a locus of cultural practices and beliefs. Geertz, for instance, describes the attention men (for it is certainly a male institution) lavish upon their cocks, noting among other things that these birds are better fed and cared for than many people. The relationship between the sport and masculinity, men and their cocks is amply commented upon as an extension of each other (1972: 416).

In Bali, while some cockfights are legal, most are not. Little can be done to suppress them. As Geertz's landlord pointed out, "We're all cock crazy" (1972: 413). The events involve about ten contests. After the razor-sharp spurs are affixed to the bird's legs and they are placed facing each other at centre ring, they usually commence to fight. The 'round' is roughly 20 seconds long and as the cocks start hacking each other almost from the onset, the match rarely goes on beyond a single round. As one might imagine, these are wildly bloody contests, but what drives the crowd to madness is the wagering that takes place on each fight.

One feature of the gambling struck Geertz as especially odd. The centre or largest bets involved large sums, but always remained 'even money'. This is not rational from a Western economic standpoint, which would have linked large sums to odds of one sort or another. In Bali, the substantial sums and the even money of the bet functioned to highlight the evenness of the two combatants, and the win connoted the symbolic one-upping of victor over loser. Cockfighting contains much more than economic reward; to the Balinese it has everything to do with status and social relations.

Socially deciphering some of the complexity of the cockfight was only the beginning of Geertz's analysis, however. Any observations of cockfighting must also note the intensity of emotions which surrounds the sport, making it something more than chickens hacking away at each other in pursuit of human gain. While it may not alter anything of social-cultural import, sport does carry symbolic and psychological meaning: "Fighting cocks . . . is like playing with fire; only not getting burned . . . in play form you come dangerously and entrancingly close to the expression of open and direct interpersonal and inter-group aggression (something which again, almost never happens in the normal course of life)" (1972: 440).

For Geertz, it is the "sentiments upon which the hierarchy rests . . ." and not simply the social hierarchy that matters. What is central is "the use of emotions for cognitive ends" (1972: 440). Hence, winning and losing status and money are set against the backdrop of exultation and agony. Cockfighting expresses a range of emotions that the Balinese understand as animalistic, dangerous, bloody, something they fear of themselves. The sport is not what Balinese society is, but rather how they imagine it might be. In this blood sport, the Balinese receive a "sentimental education" of what psychologically lurks beneath the placid surface of social relations.

Geertz's analysis simultaneously shows us that sport reflects *and* obscures culture. In that cockfighting is a template for masculinity and status distinctions; it reflects Balinese culture. There are aspects of Balinese culture that are not easily revealed, however. Cockfighting's deeper significance is somewhat shrouded by the more manifest issues just mentioned. The psychological and cultural forms of unbridled aggression are also expressed and dealt with in cockfighting, but neither simply nor directly. Here, Geertz uses ethnographic observations to reveal not only cultural dimensions of Balinese behaviour, but the psychological tensions that intertwine with their lives. The layers of meaning in this sport are so deftly revealed and elegantly handled that, in some respects, it is not surprising that this piece failed to launch sport anthropology. It simply exists on its own plane.

Nationalism and Culture

Brownell's relevance for the anthropology of sport centres upon cultural expressions of nationalism and is powerfully presented in her book, *Training the Body for China: Sport in the Moral Order of the People's Republic* (1995). Three criteria mark her study as significant: it is cross-cultural work in an area that badly needs it; it is ethnographic; and it is theoretically sophisticated. Adding to the mix is the fact that Brownell took participant–observation to new heights by actually competitively running track for Beijing University. While the latter is ethnographically important, it would count for little were not Brownell first and foremost a successful anthropologist.

In China, Brownell studied the interaction between the state and "body culture," which she defines as:

> . . . everything that people do with their bodies (Mauss' body techniques) and the elements of culture that shape their doing. Body culture is a broad term that includes daily practices of health, hygiene, fitness, beauty, dress and decoration, as well as gestures, postures, manners, ways of speaking and eating, and so on (1995: 10).

By using the term 'body culture', Brownell fuses Pierre Bourdieu's notion of 'habitus' (the body as *socially* inscribed by such things as social class) with American anthropological concerns with *culture*. Michel Foucault's notion of 'power relations' — imprinting the body — is also brought into her study of Chinese sport.

Because sport reflects China to the international community, the state seeks to control every component of an athlete's life: "The microtechniques of state power are more carefully applied to the minds and bodies of top athletes than they are to most other groups in the PRC (People's Republic of China)" (1995: 155). Brownell sees it in the way Chinese athletes walk, train, eat, and even in their social relations. The 'National Games', China's major athletic competition taking place every four years, is a case in point. The spectacle is, "portrayed as a showcase for socialist spiritual civilization at its best" (1995: 124). The state is shown to control individuals and groups alike in its extravagant mass calisthenics, marching, sloganeering, and emphasis upon control of self in a heavily autocratic society. In her chapter, "Training the Body for China", Brownell outlines the ways in which the state weaves together practice, morality, and ideology in dealing with athletes. The regimentation of their daily lives is defined and justified in terms of a 'civilizing process' (1995: 156). The traditional Maoist notions of 'criticism and self-criticism' are heavily utilised in the athletic calendar, which along with 'thought education', 'self-evaluations', and endless meetings seek to impose ideological correctness everywhere in the athlete's life. There are gaps in the PRC's ability to completely carry this out, however. Brownell chronicles counter social trends such as the emerging popularity of bodybuilding, and "old people's disco", among other things that people practice in an effort to continue the push away from Communist culture to consumer culture.

Traditional Chinese cultural notions of what comprises an individual are also heavily represented in the relationship between the athlete and his or her body. The Chinese individual is first a social being with very strong kin and class ties. This has implications for ego development, social sense of self, and gender formation. Because Chinese athletes were and remain generally perceived as 'low(er) class', benefits that accrue from sport comprise a route towards upward mobility for the working class and peasants. While the class position of these athletes has strong social and political implications, none is stronger, for Brownell, than gender. She points out that it is women who have had greater international sporting success than men. The women's volleyball champions of 1991, and the 1999 women's soccer team which played against the US for the World Cup have put them in the spotlight as icons around which to build images of modernising China. Nationalism is heavily reflected in women's athletic accomplishments, even eclipsing other gender issues: "the promotion of women's sports came to be more a matter of national pride than of women's liberation" (1995: 237).

Brownell's work is innovative because it really works the cross-cultural comparative material almost at every turn. Whether she is speaking of the gait of the athlete, or conceptions of self, gender, or even civilisation, she is making comparisons between North America and China. We see this, for instance, in her discussion of martial arts. Chinese martial arts emphasise Yin/Yang principles in a way that sees the two as inter-related; that is, Yin is in Yang and Yang is in Yin, hardness is in softness and vice versa. Hence, "because of the alternation of alternatives, martial arts are not perceived as an arena exclusive to virile young men (whose yang, hardness and strength, might be exalted in the Western system)" (1995: 221).

The comparative nature of Brownell's work is absolutely essential to building macro-theories of sport and nationalism. When combined with other large-scale ethnographies, we can build a comparative model that will further our efforts to understand sport and nationalism on a macro-theoretical level.

Inventing a Sporting Tradition: The Modern Olympics

Perhaps no sporting event in the world is as caught up in the cross-fire of nationalism and internationalism as the Olympic Games. The desire to build a sporting spectacle that fosters international understanding, and by extension, peace, is at the heart of the Olympics. MacAloon's ethno-historical account, *This Great Symbol: Pierre de Coubertin and the Origins of the Modern Olympic Games* (1981), constitutes a valuable examination of the Olympic's inherent tensions. Although strongly psychological, this work contains a very compelling assessment of the Olympics using a base of Victor Turner's ritual analysis. By focusing upon de Coubertin, MacAloon weaves together the anthropological study of ritual with the life-history of the man who resurrected the Olympic movement in the modern era. Speaking through de Coubertin, MacAloon highlights the Janus-faced character of the Olympics:

In his conclusions to his 1896 summary of the Olympics, Coubertin
had written: "Should the institution prosper . . . it may be a potent,
if indirect factor in securing universal peace." Coubertin was
eventually forced to recognize, in the aftermath of the first Olympic
Games, that it could also be a potent, if indirect, factor in the
destruction of regional peace" (1981: 260).

These opposing tendencies can co-exist in the Olympics because, as de Coubertin
points out, there is a distinction between 'patriotism,' and 'nationalism'. He
described the former as "the love of one's country and the desire to serve her",
while nationalism was, "the hatred of the other countries and the desire to do
them ill" (1981: 258).

The rituals that so dominate the Olympics are chronicled by MacAloon in a
fullness that details these contrasting notions of nationalism and patriotism. To
this end, MacAloon uses Turner's notions of 'frames of ritual'. Much of this
has to do with the conscious manipulation of images as seen through the lens of
cultural ritual. Hence, the various ceremonies in the Olympics can frame local
holidays and disparate cultural traditions into a seamless spectacle.

While MacAloon was unaware of Eric Hobsbawm's and Terrence Ranger's
(1983) edited collection heralding "invented traditions", at times he paralleled
their thinking. Hobsbawm and Ranger had moved into a cultural realm by
describing a range of customs and rituals that were of recent vintage but had
the look of antiquity. These invented traditions worked to foster, among other
things, a feeling of unity among people who might otherwise have no common
identity or connection. MacAloon's study of the 1896 Olympic Games is a
wonderful case study of how this process is constructed. The Olympics as a
'cultural performance' is more than a set of rituals for MacAloon because,
"cultural performances do not simply express human experience; they constitute
it" (1981: 270). Few can argue that at the turn of the twenty first century, the
Olympics have not come to validate MacAloon's view of them.

Following the Flag: Latin Baseball and National Identity

Alan Klein published two ethnographies that further examine nationalism and
trans–nationalism related to sport. Both works concern baseball in a Latin
American context but in very different countries — the Dominican Republic and
Mexico. *Sugarball: The American Game, The Dominican Dream* (1991) studied
the relationship between US-based major league baseball and Dominican
baseball in cultural–political terms. Two models, often contrasting, were used:

dependency theory and cultural resistance. The former examines the world as divided between core nations (industrial) and periphery (developing) nations. The core needs to systematically appropriate and control the resources of the periphery for it to maintain its position. This results in a continued under-development of Third World nations. With the racial integration of North American baseball in 1946, major league baseball was able to 'move into' Latin America in search of talent. While American baseball offered unprecedented opportunities to Latin players who were Black, the movement of the sport into previously segregated areas resulted in the destruction of unique cultural products. Ironically, the game played by Latin Americans (and North American Blacks) during racial segregation was also a game completely controlled by the Black community both in the US and the Dominican Republic. The game was owned, operated, and played by and for excluded populations. This is an oft-overlooked dimension of segregation that requires us to integrate within the context of introducing power relations into areas where there had been none. How does a community enter into relations with other communities and continue to control its own destiny?

With the expansion of major league baseball into the Dominican Republic and elsewhere in Latin America, control of the game shifted to the US First, in the 1950s, scouts looking to sign Black talent, then in the late 1970s, the creation of US baseball academies in the Dominican Republic, resulted in diverting the flow of talent away from Dominican amateur and pro ranks, and to the academies owned and operated by North American teams. The result was a destruction of the local control of the game and to a large extent, the game itself. This point is lost in the face of the exultation surrounding the handful of Dominicans (relative to those attempting to play the game) who actually make multi-million dollar salaries.

In this regard, the sport operates as do other multinational corporations on the island, making comparisons with other dependency studies inevitable. Dominican baseball was altered. Most notably, this meant changes in terms of the seasons when the game is played, the emotional make-up of the game, dampening the desire of returning heroes who are stars in major league baseball from playing for their countrymen back home, etc. Klein asks the question, "Are these changes taken as a matter of course, or is there some cultural response?" In seeking an answer, he uses a 'cultural resistance' model (see Scott, 1986, 1991).

Dominican response to US control over all sectors of their society has been remarkably mute. Looking at news reports and traveling around the country, Klein saw little evidence of widespread resentment toward Americans. The single, and surprising, exception is within the context of baseball. Using a range of techniques, including surveys, media content analysis, and ethnography, Klein began to uncover a pattern of resistance in Dominican baseball. A small, and simple, survey was designed to determine which cultural product (in this instance, baseball hats) Dominicans would prefer and why. Based on general cultural consumption patterns, Klein hypothesised that Dominicans would prefer American baseball paraphernalia to Dominican products. The survey revealed the opposite, with 79 percent of Dominicans opting for Dominican paraphernalia. Equally surprising were the reasons given. For the first time, Klein was receiving widespread nationalistic responses, nationalism built upon resentment of the 'foreigner'. We see here that building nationalism in the Third World has a very important function, namely to cut into the widespread reverence of foreign culture, and the self-loathing that accompanies modern cultural colonialism.

In looking at a national daily newspaper, Klein noted that there was rarely news dealing with political unrest, or critical appraisals of foreign presence. In the sports pages, however, the tone was different. There was a willingness to express anger and resentment unseen elsewhere. Two kinds of reportage were noted. During the summer, when major league baseball was in session, Dominicans were playing in the US and coverage of them was predictably heavy. There was a different twist, however. Instead of reports of daily games, the Dominican press preferred only to report on Dominican performers in those games, to the point where one had difficulty finding out who had won or lost. When Dominicans were not playing, the reports would focus upon other Latinos; anyone, as it were, but Americans.

During the winter, the game shifted to the Dominican winter leagues where Americans were allowed to play. The major issue during this period (1987–1990) had to do with declining attendance at games. Editorials regularly expressed outrage at North American teams for trying to prevent Dominicans from playing at home. Whereas anger was rarely expressed in other parts of the paper, editorials in the sports pages called for "expulsion of the foreigners". The General Manager of the *Estrellas Orientales* was outraged when the Houston Astros were placing pressure on one of the Dominican players under contract with them to decline playing in his homeland. An outraged General Manager exclaimed, "We can never, under any criterion accept an organisation affecting our national sport in such a way as to impede the people of San Pedro de Macoris from having a title" (1991). By claiming the game of baseball as a "national sport", baseball thus becomes a contested property. Dominicans are shown as willing to make the case of national pride here in a way they do not elsewhere.

There were also behavioural incidents that expressed forms of cultural resistance. Klein documented the intentional loss of a championship series by a team, the refusal of a player to conduct an interview in English (making Klein do it in Spanish), and the pattern of established stars who verbally and publicly express resentment that others among their countrymen cannot. Klein concludes that the reason that baseball is a major source of nationalism has to do with it being the one key area in which Dominicans are not inferior to Americans, and that the nature of that nationalism serves as an antidote to cultural colonialism.

Klein also studied nationalism on the US–Mexican border in his book, *Baseball on the Border: A Tale of Two Laredos* (1997). The Tecos is a team in the Mexican League, which is the only foreign league recognised by Major League Baseball. Unique in the sport world, they were the only binational franchise in existence, with home fields in two different countries (Laredo, Texas and Nuevo Laredo, Mexico), two national anthems played at the games, a Mexican owner and a Texas General Manager, and a combination of Mexican and American players. Klein spent two seasons (1993–1994) conducting an ethnography of the club and the relations between its Mexican and American components. In the course of this investigation, Klein explored new dimensions of nationalism that have allowed him to expand upon the definition of the concept.

His two years of fieldwork with the club required participant-observer status, and in the course of that he observed not one, but three forms of nationalism. What Klein calls 'Autonationalism' is the traditional form of nationalism in which a combination of pride in one's own nation and demonising of others fosters national identity. The strained relations between Mexican and American elements of the Tecos were chronicled in Klein's ethnography as an expression of this kind of nationalism. Were one to observe the players' behaviour on the field, one would take away a sense of harmony and goodwill as they constantly congratulate and support each other. A very different picture emerged when viewed from the 'outside' of the game. American players routinely disrespected Mexican culture and the players. Mexicans, in turn, resented the Americans. The team, then, becomes a microcosm of border relations and the national antagonism that characterises these two countries.

Life on the border, however, requires that despite regular international acrimony, there are times and circumstances during which people must find a way to address common problems, such as in the case of environmental crisis or civil unrest. Klein calls this 'binationalism', the establishment of a set of roles in which certain members of each population are competent in the language and cultural logic of the other, and these parties meet to work out solutions. The General Manager and Manager of the Tecos were excellent examples of these binational figures. Both regularly cross cultural and national lines as they sought to deal with the functioning of a binational enterprise, in the same way that governmental agencies seek to resolve problems arising from, for instance, desperately needed water supplies along the border.

Finally, Klein revealed the existence of a third kind of nationalism, 'transnationalism'. In this, the people living on both sides of the national border have more in common politically, economically, and socially with each other than they do with their respective governments. In this instance, they develop a cross-border culture and institution. The two Laredos did just that in 1849, for example, when parts of Texas (US) and Tamaulipas and Nuevo Leon (Mexico) briefly seceded from their respective countries to form the Republic of the Rio Grande. This transnationalism was also born out in modern day baseball terms. The two Laredos would field teams that would compete against each other for local bragging rights, but when faced with an outside foe, the towns would field a joint team for the greater glory of the 'borderlands' versus outsiders.

These are not the only efforts by anthropologists to examine nationalism and sport. One can look at the anthology by MacClancy (1996), a welcome addition to the cross-cultural literature. Here we have discussions of nationalism and sport among Spanish Basques, Pakistanis in Great Britain, and other sport experiences in Italy, Turkey, Northern Pakistan, Zimbabwe, and Spain. While these studies most definitely add to our corpus of inter-cultural efforts, they remain efforts by scholars who have invested energies elsewhere. Space considerations in this format preclude rich ethnographic detail and the lengthy theoretical building of one's position, but more importantly, none of these British anthropologists have longer works on sport in their past or futures.[2] While I applaud the MacClancy anthology, the position taken here argues for anthropologists forsaking occasional forays into sport in favour of a full-time commitment to the creation of sport monographs. The impact of monographs over articles may be argued, but in making the case for concentrating finite efforts on key issues, we are, I believe, better served by book-length studies which tend to get cited more often in the literature and which offer us more richness in depth.

All of these anthropologists have, in one way or another, furthered our understanding of the relationship between sport and nationalism. Brownell focuses on how the state inscribes its ideology on the body through its control

[2]Were I to include good work done on sport and nationalism by non-anthropologists, I would list Maguire (1999), Arbena (1993), Elias and Dunning (1986), Dunning (1999), Sugden (1997) and Sugden and Bairner (1998). I would also mention that the current essay does not take into account some of the work carried out by anthropologists in Europe except where they have had a noteworthy impact upon general discussion in the field of sport studies and cultural anthropology. The work of British sports scholars has had a profound effect upon the field not only because they have produced so many notable works but also because they have presented it widely.

over sport. MacAloon excavates the contrasting notions of nationalism and internationalism in the modern Olympic Games. Klein looks at the cultural and political consequences of First World and Third World interactions. The way in which nationalism is configured differs radically at times. In China, the state (nationalism) is shown to play a constraining role relative to the individual and athlete. In Mexico nationalism is a tool for building identity around the image of the hated "other", and in the Dominican case nationalism is politically more progressive. In the Olympics, nationalism is juxtaposed against the more encompassing ideology of internationalism. In all of these studies by Brownell, MacAloon, and Klein, as well as the anthology by MacClancy, we glimpse the capabilities of ethnography and cross-cultural comparisons in amplifying the ways in which the study of sport aids our understanding of nationalism.

Building Gender Through Sport

Studying gender in a cross-cultural context has spawned a coalescence of theory and ethnographic contributions by a large number of anthropologists dating back to the 1920s and the work of Margaret Mead. Some seventy-five years later, gender studies continue to define contemporary theory. Returning to her work on China, Brownell's interest in gender sprang from her history as a high level athlete, an interest that became cross cultural almost from the outset. Initially, Brownell ethnocentrically thought of women as tradition-bound, "I had erroneously assumed that Chinese concepts of gender would be more 'traditional' than American . . . and that therefore, I would find strong feeling against women in sports" (1995: 214). Yet, cross-cultural differences were apparent from the start. Whereas, in the West, we tend to distinguish between gender (cultural orientation) and sex (biological), the Chinese merged the two around the area of reproduction. All of this in turn is subordinated to the Chinese view of 'personhood', a fusion of generation, class, and kin relations. Hence, Chinese women who are muscular athletes are not thought of or stigmatised as 'lesbians', but rather as potentially 'having problems finding a mate' (1995: 216).

Cultural ideas around gender were part of the Chinese female athletes' experience, whether it involved training during one's period, competing beyond the age of 25, or enduring hunger. Brownell's analysis linked these gender comparisons to the historical role of sport in China. In search of an answer to her question of why Chinese females were more successful in integrating themselves into sports than their American counterparts, Brownell noted that sport is not seen as an elite male preserve in China. In fact, quite the opposite historically, as sport was identified as lower class and less status-bearing than other pursuits. Because it was not important, women's entrance was not obstructed. By the 1980s, however, China was hungry for international recognition and altered its traditional view of sport. Sport now became emblematic of cultural achievement, and since women's sporting success was greater than men's, women found themselves serving the state as icons of the new nationalism.

The 1980s also ushered in more Western ideas, among them the sport of bodybuilding. Predictably, the Party condemned it originally (1953) as 'bourgeois', but the sport continued to gain popularity. In 1983, the Party rescinded its ban and two years later held the first ever bodybuilding competition in China. The first contests were for men, but women's bodybuilding emerged shortly after (1986). Early competitions featured women in one-piece bathing suits, but bikinis (or two piece suits) were quickly added. Because bikinis are potent icons of the West, and because the Chinese feel that the public 'display' of women is indicative of low order morality, the wearing of bikinis in competitions generated controversy. The state sport commission ultimately allowed it because bodybuilding had established popularity outside of the commission, and it did not want to risk its credibility any further. Brownell noted that women bodybuilders did not think of their 'showdown' with the state apparatus as 'resistance', so much as pursuing something that was intrinsically worthwhile. In short, women's bodybuilding was not so much about 'empowering' women as enabling them another outlet for their talents (since most were from an athletic background).

Like Brownell, Anne Bolin combines anthropology and athletic competition (as a bodybuilder), but centres her analysis on women in the United States. Bolin has been studying bodybuilders (1992a, 1992b, 1996, 1998, 2000a, 2000b) and competing as one for a decade. She is also publishing a collection of readings on women and sport (with Granskog, 2000), which studies various aspects of women's bodybuilding. There is a strong cultural studies component in her work, which interprets women bodybuilders within the larger cultural context of women in Western societies. Hence, Bolin looks at mainstream pressures, including aspects of diet, adornment, and concerns with femininity (mainstream culture), juxtaposed against female bodybuilders who constantly push the limits of acceptable somas.

For Bolin (and in contrast to Brownell's Chinese example), Western culture has separated gender and sex since the 18th century, and further has established gender as a set of quasi-binary oppositions (e.g., 'masculinity' is characterised by hardness, muscularity, toughness, while 'femininity' is represented by softness, lack of muscularity, and docility). Historical trends like this are "inscribed" upon the body; hence, the study of somatypes becomes a catalogue of cultural interpretations of women and men. Female bodybuilders represent a challenge to this cultural system. As Bolin notes, " 'Physical correctness' among women bodybuilders is dramatised and transacted on the competitive stage wherein muscularity and femininity collide and are negotiated" (1998: 187). Bolin's ethnographic work has centred on the ways in which female bodybuilders have struggled to fashion their bodies in accord with their sport but in opposition to their larger culture. Throughout her work, we see how bodybuilding has the potential to empower women by neutralising physiological differences between the sexes. Bolin, for instance, sees "the anti-structural elements of the pre-contest diet preparation as provid(ing) both sexes with opportunities to transcend their gender" and because bodybuilding can ". . . unmark the body with fat as a gender symbol" (1992b: 396). The female bodybuilder is, for Bolin, truly iconoclastic, and is interpreted as existing in the full ambivalence that has come to characterise her position in society.

In another cultural studies-like ethnography, Eduardo Archetti's *Masculinities: Football, Polo, and Tango in Argentina* (1999) attempts to study men and sport in Argentina. Archetti's use of discourse analysis has yielded more insight into Argentinian nationalism than into masculinity, however. In his interviews, he attempts to show that most fans can identify those attributes of Argentinian soccer that distinguish it from other countries, in particular ball control (*criollo*, dribbling) and the cultural view of the spirited, often difficult boy-star (*pibe*). This part of the book is the most convincing. Unfortunately, on the matter of masculinity, there is virtually no ethnography, no sense of his having done anything more than casually interview several (of the millions of) men in the country. Sadly, Archetti 'comes off' as quite distanced from his subject. Where Archetti intended to view soccer as a site of contested culture, "challenging an official and puritanical domain" (1999: 18), he never once shows us how this actually plays itself out, how real people illustrate this through action or interaction, or how the system manifests these points.

Whereas both Brownell and Bolin have submerged themselves into sport subcultures for long periods and published in great detail on their subjects, Douglas Foley authored a single article looking at how gender, race, and class interact through football in a South Texas town. Foley's article represents a solidly worked, if brief, exploration of masculinity and an antidote to the wide ethnographic gaps found in Archetti's work. *The Great American Football Ritual: Reproducing Race, Class, and Gender Inequality* (1990) is thick in ethnographic content and presents the performance perspective of Victor Turner (1974) as believable. The football ritual complex that Foley studied includes a range of agents that begins with the players themselves, and extends to coaches, members of the marching band, cheerleaders, boosters, and other non-athletic males. These agents are observed in a cycle of performances that surround the game such as 'pep rallies', 'homecoming' rituals, and a 'Powder Puff' football game. Foley attempts to show that Texas football faithfully reproduces dominant social and economic relations of gender, class, and race. There remains a place within this complex, however, where resentment and refusal can also occur. Hence, while athletic rituals are shown as the wellspring for conventional male status for team members, as well as a source of denigration of non-sporting males, one finds males (*vatos*) who reject the rituals as irrelevant. Similarly, while cheerleaders are thought of as the play things of athletes and the butt of sexual jokes, Foley points out that these, "highly prized females are dangerous, status confirming creatures that were easier to relate to in rhetorical performance than real life" (1990: 116). Foley's is an analysis of gender and sport that draws on the Birmingham Centre for Contemporary Culture Studies in which Gramscian processes of hegemony and counter-hegemony vie with each other.

Alan Klein's study of masculinity among elite American bodybuilders, *Little Big Men: Bodybuilding Subculture and Gender Construction* (1993) was a six year ethnographic field study that focused upon the social–psychological core of male bodybuilders. In an elite American gym, a core of amateur and professional males were observed, interviewed, and trained with over years, revealing a pattern of low self-esteem, faulty parental relationships, self-perceived flaws, and other psycho–social wounds. These shortcomings demanded a certain form of compensation: the building of as large a physique as possible. By erecting an imposing exterior, these men would, it was hoped, be able to deflect questions of their personal worth, at the same time projecting an image of supreme confidence and control.

Klein also examined infrastructural dimensions of the subculture, including political *moguls* controlling the sport, the formal and informal economy, and general social relations. The neurotic core, however, was the primary element in this book, and here Klein pieces together what he terms "cartoon masculinity" — the bodybuilder's sense of masculinity built around elements of hyper-masculinity, misogyny, homophobia, narcissism, and fascism, an altogether unstable and socially reactionary mix. Throughout his ethnography, Klein sought to use participant-observation in a dynamic tension with the cultural frameworks that address narcissism, fascism, homophobia, and misogyny in which ethnography and theory would seek symbiosis rather than for either one to be causative.

Once again, we see a group of anthropologists using differing methods and theories to focus on the study of sport and gender.[3] Bolin, Klein, and Foley all use more of a conflict perspective (whether it be couched in Foucauldian or Gramscian terms), whereas Brownell and Archetti downplay a critical component. Bolin and Foley direct their conflict analysis at the larger society, while Klein's work critiques the actual sport subculture of bodybuilders, and through the masculine contradictions, he explores the larger culture. Brownell, Bolin, and Foley all rely on a combination of Victor Turner's symbolic anthropological theory and Michel Foucault's power-informed cultural perspective. Klein's critique is a combination of political economy, social psychology, and cultural history borrowing strongly from Geertz. There is, among these anthropologists, a strong core of gender ethnography as it relates to sport in this collective body and, rather than answer questions of culture and gender, these studies open up even greater questions through the cross-cultural nature of their work.

Conclusions

In this chapter, I selected what I feel are the best examples of sport anthropology based upon combining theory and ethnography, with those who have contributed book-length works and/or defined themselves primarily as anthropologists who study sport. Included were two outstanding examples of anthropologists (Geertz and Foley) who conducted single pieces of such high quality that they have been widely received. We can see that the list is small and somewhat selective. Others were excluded because their work lacks a clear theoretical focus, or because they only occasionally study sport. Even if we were to be generous and include every anthropologist who has ever written on sport, our numbers would be modest.

As sport anthropologists, we must avoid defining ourselves primarily by what we do (study culture) and how we do it (ethnography). The use of culture and sport combinations have historically done little but reinforce the idea that sport anthropology is little more than the dessert at the table. Robin Fox's article, *Pueblo Baseball: A New Use for Old Witchcraft* (1961), was an informative piece that cleverly tied witchcraft, the most important institution in Pueblo society, to a sport, thereby illustrating how sport reflects culture. It is illustrative

---

[3]The ethnography of soccer hooligans by Gary Armstrong (1998) should also be mentioned here. This study was both a book-length ethnography and dealt with masculinity, but, arguably, it more readily falls into the literature on gang subculture than sport ethnography. The work contains sections on masculinity that seems to reify the macho bellicosity of this subculture, but neither masculinity, nor sport, is at the centre of this work.

of the point that cultural analyses, in the absence of larger theoretical positions, are doomed to remain sidebars.[4]

Regarding the claim that ethnography should be our calling card, the 1999 North American Society for the Sociology of Sport conference included a session on the anthropology of sport featuring several excellent sport anthropologists. The theme (wrongly, I believe) inflated the virtues of ethnography (as defined by the participants). First, such a presentation in the midst of our sociological colleagues sends a somewhat hostile message by claiming it is only anthropologists that can use ethnography. Secondly, ethnography is neutral, and by itself does nothing of consequence until it is fused with theory. In short, as anthropologists, we must blend culture, rich ethnography, with strong theory, or face the prospect of having no presence in the anthropological field. Further, we must somehow find a way to coordinate our analytical efforts around certain key topics that are currently being debated within the field of anthropology.

The future is not so bleak, however. Sport-related ethnography is beginning to accumulate depth in at least two well-theorised areas — nationalism/ transnationalism and gender — and it is conceivable that at least a few of these intrepid anthropologists might soon enable our group to break out of the intellectual ghettos that we have been forced to inhabit.

References

Arbena, J. (1993). Sport and Nationalism in Latin America, 1880–1970. *History of European Ideas, 16,* 837–844.

Archetti, E. (1999). *Masculinities: Football, Polo, and Tango in Argentina.* Oxford: Berg.

Armstrong, G. (1998). *Football Hooligans: Knowing the Score.* Oxford: Berg.

Beezley, W. (1987). *Judas at the Jockey Club, and Other Episodes of Porfirian Mexico.* Lincoln: University of Nebraska Press.

Blanchard, K. (1995). *The Anthropology of Sport: An Introduction.* Westport, CT: Bergin Garvey.

Bolin, A. (1992a). Vandalized vanity: Feminine physiques betrayed and portrayed. In: F. Mascia-Lees and P. Sharpe (eds), *Tattoo, Torture, Adornment and Disfigurement: The Denaturalization of the Body in Culture and Text* (pp. 179–99). Albany, New York: SUNY Press.

[4]For another example see George Gmelch's *Baseball Magic* (1972), a widely reprinted cultural study, cited for its cross-cultural connections and contemporary use of Malinowski. Despite its success, *Baseball Magic* has had no impact in pushing the sport anthropology agenda forward. Again, the lack of a full-scale study and absence of a powerful and timely theoretical position is, I believe, responsible.

Bolin, A. (1992b). Flex appeal, food, and fat: Competitive bodybuilding, gender and diet. *Play and Culture, 5*(4), 378–400.

Bolin, A. (1996). Bodybuilding. In: D. Levinson and K. Christensen (eds), *Encyclopedia of World Sport* (pp. 125–133). Santa Barbara, CA: ABC–CLIO.

Bolin, A. (1998). Muscularity and femininity: Women bodybuilders and women's bodies in culturo–historical context. In: K. Volkwein (ed.), *Fitness as Cultural Phenomenon*. Munster, Germany: Waxmann.

Bolin, A. (2000). Women Bodybuilders. In: K. Christiansen and A. Guttmann (eds), *Encyclopedia of Women and Sport*. Santa Barbara, CA: ABC–CLIO.

Bolin, A., & Granskog, J. (eds) (2000). *Athletic Intruders: Women, Culture, and Sport*. Albany, New York: SUNY Press.

Brownell, S. (1995). *Training the Body for China: Sport in the Moral Order of the People's Republic*. Chicago: University of Chicago Press.

Brownell, S. (2000). Why should an anthropologist study sports in China? In: N. Dyck (ed.), *Getting into the Game: Anthropological Perspectives on Sport* (pp. 132–160). London: Berg.

Dunning, E. (1999). *Sport Matters*. London: Routledge.

Dyck, N. (2000). Games, bodies, celebrations and boundaries: Anthropological perspectives on sport. In: N. Dyck (ed.), *Games, Sports and Cultures* (pp. 12–41). Oxford: Berg Publishers.

Elias, N., & Dunning, E. (1986). *Quest for Excitement: Sport and Leisure in the Civilizing Process*. Oxford: Blackwell.

Firth, R. (1930). A dart match in Tikopia: A study in the sociology of primitive sport. *Oceania, 1*, 361–368.

Foley, D. (1990). The great American football ritual: Reproducing race, class, and class inequality. *Sociology of Sport Journal, 7*(2), 111–135.

Fox, J. R. (1961). Pueblo baseball: A new use for old witchcraft. *Journal of American Folklore, 74*(1), 9–16.

Geertz, C. (1972). Deep play: Notes on Balinese cockfight. In: C. Geertz, *Interpretation of Cultures* (pp. 412–453). New York: Basic Books.

Gmelch, G. (1972). Magic in professional baseball. In: G. Stone (ed.), *Games, Sports, and Power* (pp. 128–137). New Brunswick, NJ: Dutton.

Guttmann, A. (1994). *Games and Empires: Modern Sports and Cultural Imperialism*. New York: Columbia University Press.

Hobsbawm, E. J., & Ranger, T. (eds) (1983). *The Invention of Tradition*. Cambridge: Cambridge University Press.

Jameson, F. (1991). *Postmodernism or the Cultural Logic of Late Capitalism*.

Klein, A. M. (1991). *Sugarball: The American Game, the Dominican Dream*. New Haven, CT: Yale University Press.

Klein, A. M. (1993). *Little Big Men: Bodybuilding Subculture and Gender Construction*. Albany, New York: SUNY Press.

Klein, A. M. (1997). *Baseball on the Border: A Tale of Two Laredos*. Princeton, NJ: Princeton University Press.

Lesser, A. (1933). *Pawnee Ghost Dance Hand Game: A Study of Cultural Change*. Columbia University Contributions to Anthropology 16, New York: Columbia University Press.

MacClancy, J. (ed.), *Sport, Identity and Ethnicity*. London: Berg.

Maguire, J. (1999). *Global Sport: Identities, Societies, Civilizations*. Cambridge: Polity Press.

Mandle, J., & Mandle, J. (1988). *Grassroots Commitment: Basketball and Society in Trinidad and Tobago*. Iowa: Caribbean Books.

Miracle, A. (1977). Some functions of Aymara games and play. In: P. Stevens (ed.), *Studies in the Anthropology of Games and Play*. Westpoint, New York: Leisure Press: 98–105.

Miracle, A. (1980). School spirit as a ritual by-product. In: H. Schwartzman (ed.), *Play and Culture* (pp. 98–103). Westpoint, New York: Leisure Press.

Miracle, A. (1981). Factors affecting interracial cooperation: A case study of a high school football team. *Human Organization, 40*(2), 150–154.

Mooney, J. (1890). Cherokee ball play. *American Anthropologist, 3*(2), 105–132.

Opler, M. (1944). Jicarilla Apache ceremonial relay race. *American Anthropologist, 46*(1), 75–97.

Riordan, J. (1977). *Sport in the Soviet Union*. London: Cambridge University Press.

Riordan, J. (1981). *Sport Under Communism*. London: C. Hurst & Co.

Roden, D. (1980). Baseball and the quest for national dignity in Meiji Japan. *American Historical Review, 85*(3), 490–530.

Sands, R. (1999). *Sport and Culture: At Play in the Fields of Anthropology*. Needham, MA: Simon & Schuster Custom Publishing.

Scott, J. (1985). *Weapons of the Weak: Everyday forms of Peasant Resistance*. New Haven, CT: Yale University Press.

Scott, J. (1991). *Domination and the Arts of Resistance*. New Haven, CT: Yale University Press.

Stevens, P. (1975). Social and cosmological dimensions of Bachama wrestling. Paper presented at American Anthropological Association Meetings.

Sugden J., & Bairner, A. (1993). National Identity, community relations, and the sporting life in Northern Ireland. In: L. Allison (ed.), *The Changing Politics of Sport* (pp. 171–196). Manchester: Manchester University Press.

Turner, V. (1974). *Dramas, Fields, and Metaphors: Symbolic Action in Human Societies*. Ithaca, New York: Cornell University Press.

Tylor, E. B. (1879). The History of games. *The Fortnightly Review, 25*, 735–747.

Chapter 7

Cultural and Sport Studies: An Interventionist Practice

Jeremy W. Howell, David L. Andrews and
Steven J. Jackson

In their introductory text entitled 'Doing Cultural Studies', du Gay *et al.* refer to
the "massive upsurge of interest in things cultural in many of today's academic
institutions" (du Gay *et al.*, 1997: 1). They contend that this interest stems, in
part, from both the increasing influence of cultural practices and institutions
(e.g., the mass media and global technologies) on our daily lives, and the related
recognition that cultural practices are as constitutive of the *real world* as the
political and economic processes that previously occupied the attention of sociologically focused researchers. Either way, scholarship that attests to these
substantive and epistemological effects of popular cultural practices on the fabric
and experience of our public and private lives now abounds.

This 'cultural turn' is particularly noticeable in the explosion of intellectual
interest in sport as a pivotal social, political, and economic institution within
varied historical and contemporary contexts.[1] Among other things, this growing
body of work has focused on the emergence of institutionalised sport during
the second half of the nineteenth century, and specifically how it related to the
simultaneous maturation of nation state-based capitalism in Western Europe and
North America. Here, institutionalised sport is examined as an emergent site of
'surveillance, spectacle, and profit' (Miller & McHoul, 1998), in the newly
defined and rapidly commercialised realm of 'free' time. Bringing the discussion
up to date, numerous arguments have also been made to the effect that sport
has been subsumed by what Frederic Jameson (1984) famously described as

---

[1]This is well evidenced in journals that focus on sport specifically (e.g., the *Sociology of Sport
Journal*, the *Journal of Sport and Social Issues*, and the *International Review for the Sociology
of Sport*) as well as journals that analyse many cultural popular forms (e.g., *Theory, Culture and
Society*, *Cultural Studies*, and *Cultural Studies: A Research Annual*).

Theory, Sport & Society
Copyright © 2002 by Elsevier Science Ltd.
All rights of reproduction in any form reserved.
ISBN: 0-7623-0742-0

the cultural logics of late capitalism that crystallised in the final decades of the twentieth century. Sport is now increasingly integrated into the media industries, promotional agencies, and transnational corporations that define the global flow of goods, experiences, pleasures, technologies, traditions, and information. In this way, the merger of sport, media, and consumer capitalism speaks to the "culturalisation of economics" (Rowe, 1990: 70) whose correlative is none other than the hyper-commodification of culture.

While many of these sport studies have emanated out of the various fields of critical inquiry, we wish to focus on a particular strain of scholarly work that has its point of institutional origin with Richard Hoggart's founding of the Centre for Contemporary Cultural Studies at the University of Birmingham, England, in 1964. This strain of cultural studies has long had a foothold within the sociology of sport community.[2] In recent times, and perhaps prompted by its global expansion into the broader intellectual community, it has begun to influence a growing number of sport oriented scholars.

However, it is not our intention to provide an in-depth history of British cultural studies. There are excellent resources that cover both its intellectual and institutional history in a detailed manner (see Frow & Morris, 2000; Gilroy, Grossberg, & McRobbie, 2000; Grossberg, 1997a; Grossberg, 1997b; Grossberg, 1997c; Morley & Chen, 1996; Turner, 1990). Neither is it our intention to offer a chronological review of the key theoretical debates that have shaped its impact on the sociology of sport community. This, too, has been extensively covered elsewhere (Hargreaves & McDonald, 2000; Ingham 1997; Andrews & Loy, 1994). Rather, we wish to frame our discussion around some of the key interventionist and strategic principles that we think are deeply at stake as we witness this rapid growth of a cultural and sport studies perspective. While we make no claims to the authority of what we have to say (see Hebdige, 1986), we recognise that as "more and more people jump onto the cultural studies bandwagon", the more "it needs to protect some sense of its own specificity as a way into the field of culture and power" (Grossberg, 1997a: 7). It is to this specificity that we now turn our attention.

[2]In his seminal 1983 book *Class, Sports, and Social Development*, Richard Gruneau addressed the work of the Birmingham school as he began his foray into a neo–Marxist analysis of sporting practices in Canada. Much of the following years in the Sociology of Sport were spent with North American debates that advanced a cultural studies sensibility within the field (see Theberge & Donnelly, 1984; Harvey & Cantelon, 1988; Gruneau, 1988; and Ingham & Loy, 1993). Similar arguments began to arise in the field of Leisure Studies in Great Britain and from within the Centre of Contemporary Cultural Studies directly (see Jennifer Hargreaves, 1982; Clarke & Critcher, 1985; John Hargreaves, 1986; and Deem, 1986).

Theory as Politics, Politics as Practice

Any discussion of British cultural studies must begin by emphasising that its academic institutionalisation is tied to empirical and epistemological shifts that grew, not surprisingly, out of the socio–political cauldron of the 1950s and 1960s Britain. Specifically, this 'British' tradition emerged as an intellectual response to the failure of the Marxist Left to comprehend, in theoretical, strategic, interventionist, and political terms: the effects of consumer capitalism upon the working class and the emergence of seemingly contradictory political alliances; the beginning of late capitalism; the new forms of colonial imperialism; the place of ideology and culture in relations of power; and the existence of racism in the so-called democratic world.

We use the word 'failure' in a particular way here. In a sense, all social theories 'fail' at some level or another. The complexity of social life can never be totally captured by a single theory because "movements provoke theoretical moments. And historical conjunctures insist on theories: they are real moments in the evolution of theory" (Hall, 1996: 270). So, as a society transforms itself, it would only make sense that we may need more appropriate theories by which to comprehend the exact forces enacting those changes, theories that are always partial and never completely definitive. Influential figures such as Hoggart, the social historian E. P. Thompson, and the cultural critic Raymond Williams recognised this in that they were motivated by a need to understand why, among other things, in the wake of the emergence of the welfare state and the affluence of the post World War period, large sections of the working class voted for the Conservative Party, thereby aligning themselves with a political ideology and power bloc historically non-representative of their core interests.

The institutionalisation of cultural studies at the University of Birmingham encouraged the emergence of a critical cultural theorising, which led to the questioning of long held beliefs pertaining to the relationship between the economic base of a society, and the cultural institutions and practice of everyday life. In so doing, a new political and intellectual space was opened up for academic and public intellectuals to *intervene* into the historical context of post-war Britain. We mention this to immediately emphasise that, in its original mani-festation, cultural studies was "firmly anchored in a strategy of political struggle . . . its priorities were those of an elaboration of the cultural problems facing the left" (Davies, 1990: 2).

If the origins of cultural studies are found in the 1950s and 1960s, its growth and legacy in the United States and Britain[3] can be tied to the attempt to

---

[3]We should note that while anchored in Birmingham, such critical cultural sensibilities also

develop new theoretical positions by which to strategically intervene into new contexts associated with: (1) a new wave of women's liberation; (2) the rise of neo-conservative social and political formations; (3) the increasingly complex relationships we have to media representations and new technologies of communication; (4) the growth of marketing forces and the emergence of new forms of consumerism; (5) the relationship between new global forces and local cultures; and, (6) the diaspora associated with the extraordinary degree of national, regional, and global mobility and fluidity.

In this fashion, as Frow and Morris (2000) note, "cultural studies has not only been a response to the political and social movements of the past three decades but has also derived many of its themes, its research priorities, its polemics, and, in some ways, its theoretical emphases and privileged working methods from an *engagement* with those movements" (2000: 332). Such engagement by necessity means understanding and struggling with various formations of power networks working at any particular historical moment. As such, cultural studies must always be seen as both political and contextual. Here we agree with Grossberg (1997c) in saying that the intellectual trajectory of cultural studies — and for us, by implication, a cultural and sport studies — necessitates a process of inquiry that is: *disciplined* (far from wallowing in relativism, it constantly seeks new forms of intellectual authority); *inter-disciplinary* (its focus demands the straddling of traditional disciplinary boundaries); *self-reflective* (never complacent in its intellectual authority, it realises the inadequacies and potential contradictions of the knowledge it produces); *political* (fundamentally concerned with understanding, with a view to transforming, people's lived realities); *theoretical* (while not dogmatically adhering to one theoretical position, it stresses the necessity of theory); and, *radically contextual* (the object, method, theory, and politics of critical inquiry are inextricably tied to the context within which it is embroiled).

To operate within such a cultural studies strategy means recognising that the meaning, politics, and hence identity of sporting practices can only be understood by the way in which they are *articulated* into a particular set of

emerged independently within differing national cultural contexts, thus problematising the "general impression of cultural studies as a UK/US affair" (Frow & Morris, 2000: 319). Suffice it to say that if cultural studies is committed to investigating its objects of analysis contextually, then it is hardly surprising that there are historically grounded cultural studies projects in Australia, East and South East Asia, South Africa and Latin America, each with its own historical connections (e.g., colonialism), themes (e.g., Black, Chicano), and narratives and theoretical conditions (see Frow & Moriss, 2001; Gilroy *et al.* (2000). This, of course, has also had a marked effect on the Sociology of Sport in recent years. For instance, there is a significant body of work on cultural and sport studies that has emerged out of Australia (see Rowe, McKay, & Lawrence, 1997).

complex historical, economic, and political relationships. As Stuart Hall (1981) notes,[4] the meaning and effect of any social practice is "given, in part, by the social field into which it is incorporated, the practices with which it articulates and is made to resonate. What matters is not the intrinsic or historically fixed objects of culture, but the state of play in cultural relations" (1981: 235). Articulation for Hall involves the production of contexts, the ongoing effort by which particular practices are removed from and inserted into different structures of relationships that make up the historical conjuncture. This conjunctural view sees society as a concrete, historically-produced fractured totality made up of different types of social relations, practices and experiences. Each form of social practice has its own relatively autonomous field of effects. But, the meaning and effects of any concrete practice, its conjunctural identity, are always over-determined by the network of relations with which it is articulated (see Hall, 1986a; Hall, 1986b).

Articulation, then, incorporates a methodology that involves the deconstruction and reconstruction of a historical context, in order to produce a contextually specific map of the social formation. Fundamental to this approach is an adherence to E. P. Thompson's (1972) understanding of history as "the discipline of context" (1972: 45). This approach involves "the interrelating, the integrating, the weaving together of strands of evidence that point to change or continuity in human life in the past" (Struna, 1986: 22). Through this fusion of historical sources — the reconstruction of a context — the historical fact becomes meaningful "only in an ensemble of other meanings" (Thompson, 1972: 45).

For us, the strategic, interventionist, and methodological implication of articulation is partly found in the struggle to uncover the way in which particular sporting practices are positioned into specific contexts. It begins by questioning how sporting practices get their meaning and identity through the power structures and relationships to which they are connected. It is an attempt to contextually destabilise connections that appear natural and extremely stable in any given historical context while always recognising that the individual is both responsible for the definition of his/her own socio-cultural reality, and constrained by the socio-cultural context in which he or she is positioned.

Historical Materialism.

---

[4]Stuart Hall is a seminal figure in the development of cultural studies in Britain and across the globe. As former Director of the Centre for Contemporary Cultural Studies at the University of Birmingham, and later as Professor of Sociology at The Open University, Hall has been an enormously influential leader in developing academic and intellectual spaces that have forged new directions in cultural theory, cultural politics, and social intervention (see Gilroy *et al.*, 2000).

Doing Cultural Studies

To emphasise this contextual specificity of cultural and sport studies, we offer three vignettes that address a variety of empirical and political problems ranging from debates over social policy related to lifestyle, health and fitness, to struggles over soccer and social class in suburban America, and finally to issues of local resistance to global capitalism. They are radically different problems and are addressed in very different ways by each of us, but we think they point to how particular "discourses of social involvement" (Frow & Morris, 2000: 327) and interventionist strategies mark our respective pedagogical and research practices.[5]

Lifestyle, Politics and Urban Health Culture

'Commit to Get Fit', 'Just Do It', 'Lean for Life': whether it be over radio airwaves, digital cable lines, the magazine racks of the local grocery store, or the billboard messages of our city thoroughfares, we appear to be continually bombarded with what Barbara Ehrenreich (1992) has called the 'morality of muscle tone'. As a signifier of lifestyle success and mobility, improving the physical body is increasingly promoted and realised in the virtuous terms of success and failure, ambition and achievement, commitment and determination, good and bad behaviour, discipline and effort. For the physically committed, the consequences are reported as increased self-confidence, improved quality of life, personal empowerment, and a sense of control over one's own destiny. For the apathetic, the rewards are disease, misery and a serious dose of personal guilt. Be it through government reports (the 1996 *Surgeon General's Report of Physical Activity; Healthy People*, 2000) or the promotional armatures of the commercial health club, exercising smart lifestyle choices is increasingly articulated to the individual becoming personally responsible for his or her own quality of life. Fitness as self-improvement through personal action is delivered against a backdrop of the virtuous self.

Of course, there is nothing terribly new about a conversation that links

---

[5]While heavily influenced by the ongoing debates within the sociology of sport community, our own appropriation of cultural studies comes largely through its institutionalisation at the University of Illinois in the United States of America. During the late 1980s and early 1990s, Illinois hosted a number of important lectures, conferences and seminar series on British cultural Studies, attracting some of the key practitioners of the day. It was as graduate students at Illinois, particularly under the tutelage of Larry Grossberg who had attended Birmingham as a student of Richard Hoggart and Stuart Hall, that our own relationship to cultural studies as an intellectual and interventionist practice took shape.

physical practices to the moralising narratives of lifestyle. The history of the body is full of discourses extolling the healthy virtues of the active life. In this way, the body always has a historical context from which it finds its meaning. But there is something different about the way in which the word 'lifestyle' is currently articulated to a very contemporary debate that has taken place over the role of the government in daily life, the emergence of new consumer identities, the rise of a populist conservatism and the actual meaning of the healthy individual (see Howell & Ingham, 2001).

Here, to be sure, fitness can be mapped onto a broader social, ideological and affective landscape where public issues of all kinds are increasingly defined as individual problems. Whether it is illness, obesity, disease, homelessness or unemployment, each is redefined as a private issue of character and as a failure in individuals to self-discipline. Both state and civil sectors of society have pushed the idea that self-help is morally preferable to intervention and entitlement. Items of bad luck, it seems, have begun to shift to a lifestyle vice (Bichovsky–Little, 1982). As US Secretary for Health, Louis Sullivan, M. D., declared in the government report *Healthy People 2000*, developing a 'culture of character' was, quite simply, the best route for preventing illness among members of marginalised ('low-socio-economic status', 'disadvantaged', and 'poor') populations:

> If we are to extend the benefits of good health to all of our people, it is crucial that we build in our most vulnerable populations what I have called a "culture of character", which is to say a culture, or a way of thinking and being, that actively promotes responsible behavior and the adoptions of lifestyles that are maximally conducive to good health. This is prevention in the broadest sense (US Department of Health and Human Services, 1992: v).

Of concern to us are the ways in which this 'culture of character' has been inserted into the academic realm of the exercise sciences where the official cry of preventive health and lifestyle choice seems to have taken hold. Of course, this does not mean that the language of lifestyle modification is not beneficial. Neither does it mean that one is deluded if one thinks that some social problems do indeed have solutions associated with personal responsibility. Similarly, we do not want to imply that if one is committed to exercising in commercial health clubs then one has been duped into an act of self-absorption or physical obsession. Having said that, we do think that in the midst of popular cries for personal action and responsibility, we need to be sure that our pedagogical practices are not articulated to political and cultural positions where "pathologies are re-individualised from a 'social' determination into a moral order" (Rose, 1996: 145).[6]

In our push for lifestyle modification and fitness as a health care practice, we need to remember that our science is not value-free. Academic practice, despite intellectual arguments about the objectivity of research and the ideological neutrality of knowledge, is neither innocent nor neutral (Ingham, 1985). The knowledge researchers produce cannot escape having some impact on the context they attempt to describe and explain. That production is always already articulated into larger political and theoretical frameworks. Of course, some might argue that this relationship between academic knowledge and the political economy of culture is beyond the scope of the 'exercise scientist'. This may be so. But we think it is one of the defining features of the 'cultural studies practitioner'. We simply cannot idly stand by as fitness practices are conceptualised as somehow independent of the problems of social milieu, analysed within "object-of-analysis vacuums" (Ingham, 1985: 7). Here, pedagogy (including vigorous faculty debates over curriculum design) itself acts as a mode of cultural criticism.

But the interventionist strategy of cultural studies is not just contained to the classroom and academic institution. Cultural studies also encourages us to strategise and politicise intellectual practice in new and innovative ways. For instance, with regard to what Cole (2000) has referred to as the 'new urban health culture', how might we, as cultural studies practitioners, intervene into the articulation of fitness–themed–entertainment facilities, the rise of the medical fitness industry (the revitalisation of hospitals through practices and products associated with the commercial fitness industry), the privatisation of public parks, and a multitude of health food, new age / high-tech-inspired consumer objects? What opportunities and strategic spaces exist to re-articulate the numerous 'lifestyle' practices of good nutrition, self-development, and fitness to the growing social movements associated with spiritual fulfilment and civic commitment to our community, our ecology and our environment (Howell, 1991)? Can we intervene using workshops and other strategic programmes and make interesting connections between the scientific world of the American College of Sports Medicine (ACSM) and the alternative and transformative

---

[6]The work of Nikolas Rose suggests that very similar processes are at work in Britain. But, we should also point out that the translation of a "theoretical ideology into a populist idiom" (Hall, 1988: 47) is nevertheless not universal in nature. While we recognise certain transatlantic similarities between the USA and Britain in terms of the cultural formation of sport and exercise, any transatlantic translation demands specific and conjunctural analysis (see Howell & Ingham, 2001).

mind-body practices of groups such as the Human Potential Movement?[7] Or, are the latter necessarily to become translated into another personalised lifestyle consumer oriented strategy of the commercial 'self-help' sector?

For instance, since the publication of his best selling book, *Ageless Body Timeless Mind*, Deepak Chopra has been the most visible proponent of the mind/body relationship. In a 1997 '*Newsweek* front cover' story under the lifestyle section, Chopra refers to a 1993 appearance on 'The Oprah Winfrey Show' after which 130,000 copies of his book were sold in one day, as a 'media-generated phenomenon' (see Leland & Power, 1997: 54). Despite the fact that the meaning and effects of lifestyle practices can never be guaranteed ahead of the context from which they emerge, it is hard to ignore the immense promotional forces pushing them in that direction. But even if this may be the case, are there strategic opportunities (e.g., pedagogy, writing, practitioner workshops, social activism, industry advisory work) that might allow us to articulate that commercial strategy to a broader sense of a public and participatory urban health culture (Howell, 1996)? Or, are we to be left with an urban health culture that is simply themed, experienced, and defined by the landscape, language and imagery of consumption (Cole & Howell, 2000)?

Take, for example, the annual California AIDS Ride in the USA. In 1994, 478 cyclists departed San Francisco for a 525-mile, seven-day journey to Los Angeles. Challenged to raise $2,000 in individual sponsorship, each rider raised an average of $3,100, raising a total of $1.6 million for AIDS services at the Jeffrey Goodman Special Care Clinic housed in the Los Angeles, Gay and Lesbian Community Services Center. In 1999, just five years later, 2,950 rode the 560-mile ride from Fort Mason, San Francisco to West Hollywood, Los Angeles. The $11.1 million in pledges raised was the highest since the event began. Along the way, the riders drank 35,000 gallons of water, ate 20,000 bananas and suffered 1,000 flat tires. Each night, a mobile city of 700-member support crews brought tents, hot meals, snacks for five daily stops, medical and mechanical services and camping supplies. The Ride raised money for both the Los Angeles' Gay and Lesbian Center and the San Francisco AIDS Foundation.

The California AIDS Ride model has now been adopted in five USA cities, each lasting between three and seven days, over distances of 265 to 560 miles. Each Ride is a spectacular journey that is marked by the creation of a most

---

[7]Western Athletic Clubs, a San Francisco based health and sports club corporation, requires all of its personal trainers to be ACSM Health/Fitness Instructor certified. In recent years, they have organised coaching sessions and weekend retreat programmes with George Leonard and Michael Murphy, internationally renowned authors and instrumental figures in the burgeoning human potential movement. To further explore the relationship between exercise science and integral human transformative practices, see Leonard and Murphy (1995).

communal and supportive participant environment. This encouragement begins long before the Ride itself. Pledges are sought, training teams and schedules are developed, and the local community support is embraced. As the official AIDS Ride web-site notes:

> The Ride is not easy. You will have to train. And through our training club and your Rider Representative, we'll help you do that. But the fact that the Ride is tough and challenging is where most people find meaning in it. They've got to push themselves into the land of their true potential. The fact that you're not sure you can do this may be the very reason to register. In the challenge of it you may discover a new friend — your true self. And to do something about AIDS that measures up to the 17,000 lives that it took last year alone . . . people who do the AIDS Rides are not athletes. In fact, most have never done anything like this in their lives (http://aidsride.org/learn/training.asp).

To date, the various AIDS races have collectively raised over $65 million. As importantly, though, the AIDS Ride is an event where the individual motive for action is something other than self-interest. This is not to say that people do not participate for personal reasons of physical improvement. Neither is it to say that the commercial sector does not benefit from the selling of goods and the provision of training programmes. Tanqueray is now the official sponsor and members of the Sporting Goods Association and the International Health, Racquet and Sportsclub Association (IHRSA) are actively involved in promoting the event and reaping the reward of increased sales of products (e.g., cycles) and services (e.g., personal training). What the AIDS Ride does show is that it is possible for fitness practices to be connected to civil intervention rather than voluntary adjustments in lifestyle.

To be sure, during the 1980s, a political vocabulary of lifestyle individualism was partly enveloped by a developing conservative formation (e.g., the Moral Majority, the Republican Party, privately funded Think Tanks) to explain inner city poverty, welfare, unemployment, drug use, and AIDS, in ways which deflected attention from, and made it difficult to think about, broader political and economic conditions reconfiguring everyday life (see Cole, 2000; Ingham, 1987; Howell & Ingham, 2001). The AIDS Ride is one example of how private practice is directly fused into definitions of public health, and cultural practices once contextualised as selfish and self-indulgent are redefined as something else. And maybe, in the process, no matter how fleeting, we may have "relocated the seat of virtue" (Ehrenreich, 1992: 65) back onto the public agenda.

We do not provide these scenarios as answers but rather to imply that intervening into the new urban health cultures in this way is not simply political window dressing. It is within these spaces that some serious struggles are taking place that are restructuring the way in which we think of citizen and community, private and public, teacher and practitioner, researcher and activist; struggles in which the cultural studies practitioner can be immersed.

America's Suburban Soccer Phenomenon

Notwithstanding its multi-ethnic manifestations, at the beginning of the twenty-first century, soccer in the United States can be considered "a white, middle-class, suburban sport, just the opposite of the game's demographics in most of the world" (Hersh, 1990: 1). Certainly, the bulk of the 45 million "Soccer Americans" (Steinbrecher, 1996) responsible for the phenomenal growth in soccer participation rates — otherwise referred to as "America's silent sporting revolution" (Anon, 1996: 27) — can be located within the affluent and largely racially exclusive suburban enclaves that characterise American cities.

Contextualising youth soccer within the political economy of suburban American affluence uncovers soccer's role in sublimating the very real social class relations (and indeed gender and race relations) through which a suburban landscape of the powerful (white middle class) is bounded and experienced. However, as with many other suburban practices, participation in youth soccer is commonly viewed as simply a lifestyle choice, thereby effectively obscuring the very real economic barriers that preclude many from involvement. In so doing, the uncomfortable notion of socio-economic classes is erased, and the suburban middle class allowed to bolster its sense of self-righteous achievement and privilege (Duncan & Duncan, 1997).

Contemporary manifestations of suburban existence represent the latest (and by no means the last) phase in the ongoing reformation of metropolitan spaces and populations around the central logic of commodity consumption (see Binford, 1985; Fishman, 1987; Jackson, 1985). Within the post-war context, the nature of "decentralisation of population from the cities" (Savage & Warde, 1993: 76) to suburban peripheries was markedly different from previous enactments, particularly in terms of scale and scope. The suburban American nation was born, and subsequently grew from 41 million in 1950 (27% of total US population) to 76 million in 1970 (37% of total US population), by which time, suburban dwellers outnumbered either their urban or rural counterparts (Holleb, 1975). Continuing this trend, the 1990s has witnessed the ascension of

American suburban dwellers to the absolute majority of the national population (Thomas, 1998).

Despite its cultural, economic, and political significance, it would be remiss to portray the contemporary American suburb as a homogeneous bastion of upper middle class affluence. At the beginning of the twenty first century, the phrase 'American suburb' could legitimately refer to anything from swathes of underclass poverty to districts of middle/upper class affluence, and a multitude of variations in-between (Zwick & Andrews, 1999). By the 1980s, the post-war American suburb constituted a mix of variously sized consumption communities (ranging from collections of houses to vast sub-divisions) whose lifestyle practices exhibit contrasting degrees of affluence.

Nevertheless, despite its inherent variability and fluidity, the vision of the American suburb that pervades the popular imagination continues to be that of the post-war, middle class, European–American utopia: those largely white metropolitan peripheries and populations dominated by an aesthetic and consumer oriented possessive individualism, that underlies a more self-righteously advanced adherence to notions of achievement, morality, and privilege.

During the 1950s, membership of the new suburban class was exhibited through the consumption of particular domestic commodities, the acquisition of which set suburban individuals apart from the urban hordes. By being 'defined and asserted through difference', the post-war suburban landscape became a material statement and mechanism of class based power, prestige, and privilege (Bourdieu, 1984: 172). This advancement of unreserved suburban materialism as the new American way of life, effectively fuelled an epidemic of peer referenced spending:

> By the fifties, the Smiths had to have the Joneses' fully automatic washing machine, vacuum cleaner, and, most of all, the shiny new Chevrolet parked in the driveway. The story of this period was that people looked to their own neighbourhoods for their spending cues, and the neighbours grew more and more alike in what they had. Like compared with like and strove to become even more alike (Schor, 1998: 8).

Toward the end of the 1950s, maturating economies of scale within America's highly regulated economy reduced production costs for mass consumer goods, and resulted in previously restricted commodities such as automobiles, refrigerators, and televisions, becoming accessible to a broader spectrum of the population. Since affluence, and the social status accrued from it, are primarily relational constructs, the appropriation of the working class into America's consumer culture created anxiety among a suburban American populace now challenged to differentiate their lives from lower status groupings. Rejecting the conformist consumption that framed the immediate post-war suburban experience, many suburbanites sought to reaffirm an elevated social standing by engaging in escalating cycles of competitive consumption (Schor, 1998). In simplistic terms, the doctrine of 'Keeping up with the Joneses' was rejected in favour of an obsessive desire to keep at least one step ahead of them. Rather than allaying middle class insecurities, if anything, they were heightened by the advancement of a culture of unremitting competitive upscaling. For, through 'fear of falling' down the American class ladder (Ehrenreich, 1989), suburban consumers were compelled to continually aspire to bigger and better things, and were thus consigned to what Lasch (1979) characterised as feelings of perpetual dissatisfaction and status anxiety: the "new forms of discontent peculiar to the modern age" (1979: 72). Out of this fundamentally competitive cultural context, the American suburban soccer phenomenon was to emerge.

Linking financial (economic capital) and educational resources (cultural capital), the suburban middle class presently derives its sense of self (social capital) from the assemblage of "goods, clothes, practices, experiences, appearance and bodily dispositions they design together into a lifestyle" (Featherstone, 1991: 86). This focus on the aesthetic rendered suburban existence an effect of consumer taste, rather than being in any way linked to the possession of the economic capital necessary for its realisation. Lifestyle became viewed as an effect of individual choice and sophistication, rather than being necessarily over-determined by "the choice of destiny" which, for those less fortunate, are "produced by conditions of existence which rule out all alternatives as mere daydreams and leave no choice but the taste for the necessary" (Bourdieu, 1984: 178). Being steeped in spurious notions of freedom and individuality, the notion of suburban lifestyles as 'tastes of luxury' conveniently obscured the privileged social and economic conditions of which they are a product.

The contemporary American suburb discussed here represents a complex social space, comprising multiple interrelated fields and sub-fields (housing, decor, diet, employment, education, dress, leisure, sport) in which individual agents compete for the various types of capital (economic, cultural, intellectual, physical), with which they seek to constitute their lifestyle practices in accordance to the regulatory codes of suburban taste cultures. Within such settings, sometimes discrete, oftentimes not, acts of consumption coalesce to constitute the lifestyle projects through which suburban subjects become actualised to selves and others. For this reason, the ritualised public forums of suburban display — excessive malls, extravagant country clubs, and indeed, exclusive soccer fields — have become civic promenades for the performance of individuals' carefully managed commodity based lifestyles.

Over the past two decades, youth soccer has become embroiled in the suburban context to the extent that it contributes to the very constitution of this competitive "universe of practices and consumptions" (Bourdieu, 1990: 159). That is not to say soccer occupies a singular position within American culture, since the spatial distribution of the game is evidently divided along socio-economic and ethnic lines (see Hayes–Bautista & Rodriguez, 1994; Malone, 1994). However, this discussion draws upon ethnographic research focused specifically on the game's widespread appropriation by America's suburban elites (cf. Andrews, 1999; Andrews *et al.*, 1997; Zwick & Andrews, 1999). Soccer's socio-spatial distribution is at least partly attributable to its position as "an elective luxury," only afforded by parental possession of not inconsiderable amounts of economic capital (Bourdieu, 1984: 178). As an illustration, participation in competitive youth soccer has been estimated to cost between $3,500 and $4,000 per year — that includes the direct (annual membership fees, uniforms, boots, and soccer balls for practice sessions) and indirect (entrance fees, travelling, accommodation, meals, and entertainment expenses incurred during regular trips to weekend tournaments) costs of participation (Zwick & Andrews, 1999). Without question, the economics of competitive soccer instantiate a degree of social exclusivity, from which the game derives a "distinctive rarity (Bourdieu, 1978: 835). Access to the considerable amounts of spare time demanded by soccer involvement (identified by Bourdieu [1978] as a transformed form of economic capital) is also a telling determinant in the class distribution of suburban soccer participants. Quite simply, the life of affluent youthful suburbanites incorporates an "absence of necessity", meaning there exists no financial compulsion to enrol in the part-time workforce in order to augment their own, or their families', economic capital (see Bourdieu, 1984, 1986).

Although steeped in the economics of suburban privilege, youth soccer represents an important cultural field (Bourdieu, 1993) upon which the differentiating logics of consumption-based suburban lifestyles-cultures are practiced and displayed. Thus, as "a unitary set of distinctive preferences which expresses the same intention in the specific logic of the symbolic sub-spaces, furniture, clothing, language or body hexis" (Bourdieu, 1984: 173), the differentiating taste culture of the suburban middle class has been faithfully transposed to the soccer field. Having been raised within a climate of competitive aestheticism in which self-identity represents a project constituted through consumption based display (the converting of economic capital to cultural capital), the children of the suburban middle class are fully attuned to the processes involved in the consumer stylisation of the self (Lury, 1996). The search for distinction through the aestheticisation of existence is an important part of the soccer experience, especially for children in the older age categories. The increasingly convoluted taste cultures of middle class youth are evidenced within the soccer setting: there is even evidence to suggest that 'soccer style' has informed wider aesthetic trends (see Grish, 1998; Perez, 1997). Thus, merely responding to the fleeting ascendancy of particular fashion statements (be they Adidas, Nike, Umbro, or alternative 'other'; single-coloured or multi-coloured; round-necked or v-necked; cotton or nylon; 'grunge', 'retro' or 'urban') requires considerable financial investment on the part of parents.

Suburban youth soccer is also a particularly interesting site of lifestyle differentiation, since it can be viewed as a sub-field within the larger field of child rearing (among the most outwardly visible, and hence obsessively nurtured, sites of suburban lifestyle consummation):

> The one place where keeping-up behaviour is paramount and conscious is where the kids are concerned. Whatever doubts the average American parents may have about the importance of the Joneses' new kitchen, there's little doubt that they are worried about whether their children are maintaining the pace with the Joneses' offspring (Schor, 1998: 85).

The constitution of a child's education, apparel, footwear, toys, bodies, teeth, and even soccer boots, are points of social distinction and comparison that compel parents to conform to ever escalating norms of stylised existence.

Within the context of America's elite suburban spaces, youth soccer culture is evidence of the extent to which the more mundane aspects of children's leisure time have been engulfed by the normalising competitive lifestyle ethos (see Zwick & Andrews, 1999): no longer seemingly allowed to engage in unstructured or unsupervised play, many young suburbanites are 'encouraged' by their achievement-oriented parents into gruelling after-school schedules of commercially organised "extended education", despite the financial, logistical, and/or emotional problems frequently posed to children and parents alike (Ehrenreich, 1989: 82). Exhibiting the kernel of the suburban habitus, the motivation for such prompting appears to be the conspicuous manufacturing of healthy, cooperative, goal-oriented, and competitive children. This betrays the extent to which suburban soccer has become a "wholly owned subsidiary of competitive adults" (Russakof, 1998: A1), in that they betray and seek to assuage parental anxieties about their own lives.

In summary, soccer in the USA acts as a principal "source, as well as an indicator of social differentiation" for the innately competitive suburban middle class (Schor, 1998: 30). Challenging the taken-for-granted emergence and growth of a sport such as youth soccer can be a pedagogical strategy of intervening into the social context with which it is concerned. Specifically, within American undergraduate classes at institutions populated predominately by middle class suburban students (and there are many such institutions), soccer provides a useful vehicle for interrogating the relations of culture and power associated with contemporary elite suburban existence. Soccer is a cultural practice with which this constituency is intricately familiar, but which most of them have uncritically accepted as a natural and unquestioned part of their everyday lives. Identifying the social, economic, and politically based derivatives and influences of suburban soccer culture brings to light the wider culture of suburban privilege, in a manner that challenges students to truly consider the necessarily unequal social, economic, and political forces at work in the construction of their own lives and those of other — perhaps less privileged — individuals.

But, as we have mentioned previously, the effects of pedagogical and research practices can never be guaranteed in advance. Sometimes our work can be party to a less pre-meditated vein of contextual intervention. In an article that appeared in the popular weekly newspaper *Soccer America*, this articulation between lifestyle, class, the suburbs and soccer was dismissed as irrelevant. Despite the negative tone of the commentary (Gardner, 1997), it is worth noting that the work is being discussed in a public sphere outside of academe, thus creating a space for an ongoing dialogue on sport, contemporary American culture and dominant power relations.

Nike, Globalisation and Local Resistance

Due to its impact on almost every facet of everyday life, the process of globalisation has occupied a central place within cultural studies theorising over the past decade (Appadurai, 1996; Featherstone & Lasch, 1995; King, 1990; Robertson, 1992). New communications technologies, including satellites and computers, have accelerated the rate of social change. Indeed, this has occurred to such a degree that it is redefining our traditional notions of time and space. As never before, distant people and events impact our lives with greater effect and immediacy. Consequently, the emerging global economy has contributed to a seemingly borderless world where the role of the nation state is increasingly being questioned.

Indeed, critics have argued that unrestricted access to global commodities, services and ideas is not only reinforcing an unequal distribution of resources but is also contributing to an erosion of unique cultural identities on a local level. Given the relative dominance of the United States in areas of popular culture, including those related to sport, the perceived threat to local cultural identities has often been characterised as a form of Americanisation. A cursory look at the global impact of the National Basketball Association (N.B.A.), along with stars like Michael Jordan, who are, in turn, used as vehicles in transnational marketing campaigns by companies like Nike, reveals some evidence of America's reach (Andrews, 1997; Andrews *et al.*, 1996). However, it would be naïve to simply assume that the presence of American or even more generally 'global' commodities are having a unilateral, negative effect on local cultures and contributing to the erosion of the nation state. As Rowe (1996) states:

> There is . . . . a role for the nation-state . . . . to act strategically in those spheres of culture where it still retains the power to influence outcomes in the interests of social equity and cultural citizenship. In spite of the trans-border powers of the global media, there remain opportunities for national governments to do more than accede to the decisions of markets made under the rubric of the inexorable progress of globalisation (1996: 581).

Consequently, we must, as we have previously emphasised, consider the context within which the global meets the local. Within the framework of discussions about globalisation, it is important that we account for the complexity and constantly shifting local or national terrain within which the global-local relationship exists. As Murdock (1997) notes:

> unpicking the shifting relations between the global, the state and the market, citizen and consumer, is one of the central tasks for cultural studies . . . Case studies are essential, as a basis for puzzling out the complexities and nuances of current collisions and encounters as an anecdote to facile generalisations and comparisons (1997: 66).

Here, we draw upon the global sporting company Nike and locate it within the context of one of the world's smallest and geographically isolated nations, New Zealand. Nike, the world's most successful sport shoe company, now ranks among the top 1,000 corporations internationally (US News & World Report, 1996). With gross earnings well into the billions, Nike continues to extend its global reach and to amass increasing profits and market shares (Sage, 1999). As a result, Nike has found itself the object of both adulation and resentment, both within and outside of America (Jackson, 1998). Employing high profile, international sporting celebrities along with innovative, and often controversial, advertising campaigns, Nike has developed what could almost be described as a cult following among its consumers and has become the standard by which all other corporate models are compared (Jackson, 1998).

Yet, Nike has also been the subject of criticism on many fronts including: the corruption and monopolisation of youth and high school sport in America, the use of advertising which reinforces sexist (Cole & Hribar, 1995) and racist stereotypes (McKay, 1995) and, perhaps most significantly, its exploitation of "Third World" labour (Enloe, 1995; Sage, 1999). In New Zealand, it is Nike's advertising that has recently been the subject of controversy and resistance. Indeed, a number of its recent commercials have been banned from New Zealand television screens. The banning of Nike's advertisements reveals a form of cultural resistance at work that could be attributed to several factors. For example, the banning of ads. could be interpreted in light of New Zealand's self-purported conservative stance on media violence. Or, it could be read as opposition to global capitalism and in particular those aspects most closely linked with the negative excesses of America, real or imagined. With respect to the latter point, the banning of Nike ads. may serve to reinforce a sense of local identity by using America and American produced violence as a point of difference out of which New Zealand identity can be constructed. Here, we examine a second type of interventionist strategy that, in part, illustrates how global forces are being resisted at one particular cultural site. Yet, as we will also demonstrate, the exclusion of Nike ads. in New Zealand is fraught with contradictions that reveal local contestations of power and politics.

Before presenting a brief description of a banned Nike advertisement, it is important to understand how the New Zealand advertising regulation system operates. In effect, there are two key institutions involved, the Television Commercials Approvals Board (TVCAB) and the Advertising Standards Complaints Board (ASCB). All advertisements that are to be screened on New Zealand televisions must first be examined by the TVCAB. However, even if an advertisement is approved by this agency, any member of the public who can demonstrate that it violates the advertising codes of practice, can still challenge it. Thus, while individuals may have limited power to challenge global capitalism as a whole, they have some sense of agency with which to resist. If, for example, a member of the public feels that a particular advertisement was offensive, he/she is entitled to lodge a protest with the ASCB. The ASCB consists of a Chairperson, four members of the public and four members of the media/advertising industry. Their job is to evaluate public complaints to determine whether there has been a breach of the written codes. Recently, the ASCB had to assess a Nike advertisement that was the subject of public complaint.

In brief, the advertisement, which was produced for an Australasian market, features a rugby football coach in the process of 'psyching up' his team during a pre-game address. He commands his players to "visualise your opponent as your worst enemy. The person you absolutely despise the most." In turn, the audience sees alternating shots of the locker room and the players' visions of their worst enemies which include: a traffic warden, an Australian talk show host, former England cricketer Ian Botham, and a New Zealand 'All Black' rugby player. The commercial ends with the players tackling a final 'enemy' — the coach himself. As the screen fades to black, and the Nike "Just do it" slogan appears, we hear him, in strained tones, telling his players, "You boys are quick learners." In many respects, it seemed like a fairly harmless commercial; indeed, some people might even find it humorous. However, two members of the public complained. In their formal complaint they argued that the ad was ambiguous, in bad taste and was subtly inciting sports people to become violent (ASCB, 1994: 1). Their formal complaint cited Rule #4: Decency, of the Advertising Code of Ethics, which states that: "Advertisements shall not contain statements or visual presentations which clearly offend against prevailing standards of decency or cause undue offence to the community or to a significant section of the community." In its defence, Nike noted that:

> This commercial was produced by our advertising agency in the USA, Weiden and Kennedy, and we are surprised that the commercial has been interpreted as violent. We at Nike believe in fair play and do take a stance against foul play and violence on our sports fields . . . . The commercial has received very positive comments from the public, referees, players and administrators alike. Nike's support for the sport of rugby in New Zealand and globally is significant and will continue. We would not produce a commercial that we believed would jeopardise this profile (ASCB, 1994: 1–2).

What is perhaps most fascinating about this case is the decision of the ASCB. In its written decision, the ASCB, while acknowledging that the ad was intended to be a "spoof", deemed the commercial to be violent. As stated in the formal decision: "the representation of people being tackled in the advertisement was violent and that violence of any form was not a proper subject to 'spoof' " (ASCB, 1994: 1–2).

So, what does this case study tell us about cultural studies, globalisation, and the power of the nation-state? First, although Nike, as previously noted, has gained a reputation for its controversial advertising campaigns and will no doubt continue to try and attract attention through entertaining and even shock-invoking commercials, it is unlikely that they expected the ad to be banned. Given their stated commitment to global expansion it would not be in Nike's best interests to create and invest financially in commercials that were not going to be aired. Clearly, this is a case where the global was being challenged and resisted at one particular locale. Notably, it is the specificity of the context that is central to understanding the complexity of the case. For example, New Zealand has long regarded itself as one of the most conservative nations with respect to its stance on media violence. Consequently, we should not be surprised to find that its media regulations are quite strict. However, the issue is not as simple as that. One only needs to examine the vast number of locally produced television commercials that, at face value, appear to be much more violent to find a number of contradictions. Thus, while this case study illustrates an example of how globalisation is being resisted within New Zealand, it also demonstrates potential contradictions in this resistance (Grainger & Jackson, 1999; 2000). Further research is required but there are some signs that there is a form of nationalism operating in New Zealand that seeks to challenge and resist global processes. Consequently, it raises some important questions. For example, who, for what reasons and under what conditions, is resisting which particular types of global commodities and processes? These types of questions are complex and require historical, political, economic and cultural analysis.

This vignette reveals cultural studies in action by examining the power, politics and resistance associated with global advertising, something that impacts on all our lives. It is theoretical to the extent that there are competing explanations as to its historical roots, its positive and negative effects and the sites at which we can see the interplay of theory and politics. It is, at its core, an interventionist intellectual practice. Although the case of a banned Nike advertisement in New Zealand may seem trivial, it does point out how everyday people (in this instance, the two complainants) can challenge a powerful, global company like Nike. One carefully crafted letter by a concerned citizen can subvert and terminate a multi-million dollar campaign. This not only demonstrates that people have a sense of agency, it also highlights both the diversity of the audience (that is, not everyone was offended by the advertisement) and the active versus passive manner in which media representations are interpreted (Ang, 1996). In many ways this particular example of resistance against Nike's advertising is what cultural studies is all about: gaining knowledge in order to challenge particular power structures in order that we will all be better off. As scholars and citizens, we have avenues of intervention at our disposal, though they are often overlooked. Teaching and listening to the ways in which students read advertisements critically while helping them identify strategies to challenge and resist are two basic ways. Likewise, our own research and writing can be used to both challenge policy makers and initiate fruitful dialogue that can improve existing social conditions.

Conclusion

Given this very political and historically specific nature of cultural studies, it is important to note that the cultural contexts into which sporting practices are articulated cannot be described or seen to pre-exist the elements that make it up. Too often within the sociology of sport, the context is simply seen as something already fully formed into which sporting practices are simply inserted. This is too simple, for while cultural practices are produced from specific social and historic contexts, they are also actively engaged in the ongoing constitution of those contexts. They are actively engaged in structuring the conditions out of which they emerge. So for cultural studies, "the context of a particular research is not empirically determined beforehand; it has to be defined by the project, by the political question that is at stake" (Grossberg, 1997c: 255).

Similarly, the theories appropriated by cultural studies practitioners are not "taken for granted, put in place, as it were, before the work of describing the context and transforming that description has begun" (Grossberg, 1997b: 10). Cultural studies is about the development and advancement of theory, about theorising through ongoing empirical critical research. And if we truly adhere to the fact that the meanings and effects of cultural practices cannot be interpreted ahead of the contexts in which they are located, we must then recognise that our own strategic commitments may have numerous, unintended and sometimes contradictory effects. In other words, just as the sporting practices we wish to study have no guaranteed effects, in that their place or position in the cultural field is not fixed once and forever, neither have our pedagogical and research practices. They, too, are caught up in the ongoing struggle to create connections, to articulate the meaning and effect of practices that are not guaranteed in advance. Here we come back to "theory and politics, the politics of theory" and the "deadly seriousness of intellectual work" (Hall, 1996: 274–275).

So, while we wholeheartedly endorse the 'turn' to cultural and sport studies, we wish to qualify our enthusiasm by asserting that cultural studies should not be seen as simply an alternative or "equivalent to critical or cultural theory" (Grossberg, 1997c: 245). In fact, this is our key point. We think there is a danger of those interested in the sociology of sport of conceiving of cultural studies as just another theoretical product to be pulled off the intellectual shelves of the orthodox academic grocery store. We say this because, for us, there is no real definable and coherent cultural studies product in the first place. But there is a cultural studies sensibility or project. In the process of analysing historically specific problems, cultural studies practitioners often draw upon elements shaped by encounters with sociology, philosophy, semiotics, history, psychoanalysis, Marxism and diverse feminisms. And while cultural studies practitioners might read and use a common, if not eclectic, set of terms and texts, that use and reading may be radically diverse, only to be truly understood in their relationship to the concrete ways in which they help intervene into a particular context and engage a specific strategic question.

Given its ingrained lack of consensus (political, substantive, and methodological), cultural studies cannot be imagined "as a whole" (Frow & Morris, 2000: 327). For this reason, we have made a conscious effort to avoid a discussion as to what scholarly sport studies work should, and should not be, categorised as cultural studies. Having said that, we recognise, like Grossberg (1997c), that

> cultural studies can be and needs to be defined or delineated; that
> it is not so broad as to encompass any critical approach to culture
> nor so narrow as to be identified with a specific paradigm or
> tradition. This is not a matter of a proprietary definition, or of
> "the proper" form of cultural studies, but of holding on to the
> specificity of particular intellectual trajectories (1997c: 245).

With this in mind, our intention has been very strategic in that we have focused on *certain features* of the history of cultural studies, *certain interventionist ways* into the culture power field, that we think are particularly relevant to the development of cultural and sport studies at *this particular juncture*. Ultimately, it is a call for those of us in sociology of sport to re-emphasise that cultural studies should not be conceived of as a coherent and structured discipline but rather as a contextual, specific and political intellectual practice.

References

Advertising Standards Complaints Board, Complaint: 94/152, July 18, 1994, Nike Rugby Coach advertisement. Complainants: A & R Garner, Wellington.

Andrews, D. (1999). Contextualising suburban soccer: Consumer culture, lifestyle differentiation and suburban America. *Culture, Sport, Society, 2*(3), 31–53.

Andrews, D., Pitter, R., Zwick, D., & Ambrose, D. (1997). Soccer's racial frontier: Sport and the segregated suburbanisation of contemporary America. In: G. Armstrong and R. Giulianotti (eds), *Entering the field: New perspectives on world football* (pp. 261–281). Oxford, England: Berg.

Andrews, D., Carrington, B., Mazur, Z., & Jackson, S. (1996). Jordanscapes: A preliminary analysis of the global popular. *Sociology of Sport Journal, 13*, 428–457.

Andrews, D. (1997). The (Trans)National Basketball Association: American commodity-sign culture and global-local conjuncturalism. In: A. Cvetovitch and D. Kellner (eds), *Politics and Cultural Studies Between the Global and the Local* (pp. 72–101). Boulder, CO: Westview Press.

Andrews, D., & Loy, J. (1993). British cultural studies and sport: Past encounters and future possibilities. *Quest, 45*(2), 225–276.

Ang, I. (1996). *Living Room Wars: Rethinking Media Audiences for a Postmodern World*. London: Routledge.

Anon. (1996, April 13). Major League Soccer: Growing stars. *The Economist* (p. 27).

Appadurai, A. (1996). *Modernity at Large: Cultural Dimensions of Globalisation*. Minneapolis: University of Minnesota Press.

Binford, H. (1985). *The First Suburbs: Residential Communities on the Boston Periphery 1815–1860*. Chicago: University of Chicago Press.

Bourdieu, P. (1978). Sport and social class. *Social Science Information, 17*(6), 819–840.

Bourdieu, P. (1984). *Distinction: A Social Critique of the Judgment of Taste*. Cambridge: Harvard University Press.

Bourdieu, P. (1986). The forms of capital. In: J. G. Richardson (ed.), *Handbook of Theory and Research for the Sociology of Education* (pp. 241–258). Westport: Greenwood Press.

Bourdieu, P. (1990). *In Other Words: Essays Toward a Reflexive Sociology*. Stanford: Stanford University Press.

Bourdieu, P. (1993). *The Field of Cultural Production*. New York: Columbia University Press.

Clarke, J., & Critcher, C. (1985). *The Devil Makes Work: Leisure in Capitalist Britain*. Houndsmills: Macmillan Press.

Cole, C. (2000). Our new wellness champions. *Journal of Sport and Social Issues, 24*(2), 91–95.

Cole, C., & Howell, J. (2000). Chelsea Piers: New York City's new point of pride. *Journal of Sport and Social Issues, 24*(3), 227–231.

Deem, R. (1986). *All Work and No Play?: The Sociology of Women and Leisure*. Milton Keynes: Open University Press.

Donnelly, P. (1996). The local and the global: Globalisation in the Sociology of Sport. *Journal of Sport and Social Issues, 23*, 239–257.

Duncan, N., & Duncan, J. (1997). Deep suburban irony: The perils of democracy in Westchester County, New York. In: R. Silverstone (ed.), *Visions of Suburbia* (pp. 161–179). London: Routledge.

Ehrenreich, B. (1989). *Fear of Falling: The Inner Life of the Middle Class.* New York: HarperCollins.

Ehrenreich, B. (1992, May/June). The morality of muscle tone. *Utne Reader* (pp. 65–68).

Featherstone, M. (1991). *Consumer Culture and Postmodernism.* London: Sage.

Featherstone, S., & Lash, S. (eds). *Global Modernities.* London: Sage.

Fishman, R. (1987). *Bourgeois Utopias: The Rise and Fall of Suburbia.* New York: Basic Books.

Frow, J., & Morris, M. (2000). Cultural studies. In: N. Denzin and Y. Lincoln (eds), *Handbook of Qualitative Research* (pp. 315–346). London: Sage.

Gardner, P. (1997, October 13). Soccer's place in the suburbs: Next up — soccer in the life of the Inuit in Greenland. *Soccer America* (p. 11).

Gilroy, P., Grossberg, L., & McRobbie, A. (eds) (2000). *Without Guarantees: In Honour of Stuart Hall.* New York: Verso.

Goldstein, R. (2000, 26 January–1 February). We got game: How sports took over American culture. *The Village Voice.*

Grainger, A., & Jackson, S. (1999). Resisting the swoosh in the Land of the Long White Cloud. *Peace Review, 11*(4), 511–516.

Grainger, A., & Jackson, S. (2000). Sports Marketing and the Challenges of Globalisation: A case study of cultural resistance in New Zealand. *International Journal of Sports Marketing & Sponsorship, 2*(2), 35–49.

Grish, K. (1998, April 15). Seven on soccer: On the road to strong sales, soccer manufacturers navigate Fashion Avenue. *Sporting Goods Business* (pp. 31, 34).

Grossberg, L. (1992). *We Gotta Get Out of This Place: Popular Conservatism and Postmodern Culture.* New York: Routledge.

Grossberg, L. (1997a). Cultural Studies, modern logics, and theories of globalisation. In: A. McRobbie (ed.), *Back to Reality?: Social Experience and Cultural Studies.* Manchester University Press: Manchester.

Grossberg, L. (1997b). *Dancing in Spite of Myself: Essays on Popular Culture.* New York: Routledge.

Grossberg, L. (1997c). *Bringing it all Back Home: Essays on Cultural Studies.* New York: Routledge.

Gruneau, R. (1983). *Class, Sports, and Social Development.* Amherst: The University of Massachusetts Press.

Gruneau, R. (ed.) (1988). *Popular Cultures and Political Practices.* Toronto: Garamond Press.

Hall, S. (1981). Notes on deconstructing "the popular". In: R. Samuel (ed.), *People's History and Socialist Theory* (pp. 227–240). Boston: Routledge & Kegan Paul.

Hall, S. (1986a). On postmodernism and articulation: An interview with Stuart Hall. *Journal of Communication Inquiry, 10*(2), 45–60.

Hall, S. (1986b). The problem of ideology-Marxism without guarantees. *Journal of Communication Inquiry, 10*(2), 28–44.

Hall, S. (1988). *The Hard Road to Renewal: Thatcherism and the Crisis of the Left.* London: Verso.

Hall, S. (1996). Cultural studies and its theoretical legacies. In: D. Morley and K.-H. Chen (eds), *Stuart Hall: Critical Dialogues in Cultural Studies* (pp. 262–275). New York: Routledge.

Hargreaves, J. (ed.) (1982). *Sport, Culture and Ideology.* London: Routledge & Kegan Paul.

Hargreaves, J., & McDonald, I. (2000). Cultural studies and the Sociology of Sport. In: J. Coakley and E. Dunning (eds), *Handbook of Sport Studies.* Thousand Oaks: Sage Publications.

Hargreaves, J. (1986). *Sport, Power and Culture.* Cambridge: Polity Press.

Harvey, J., & Cantelon, H. (eds) (1988). *Not Just a Game: Essays in Canadian Sport Sociology.* Ottawa: University of Ottawa Press.

Hayes-Bautista, D., & Rodriguez, G. (1994, July 4). L.A. story: Los Angeles, CA, soccer and society. *The New Republic* (p. 19).

Hebdige, D. (1986). Postmodernism and the 'other side.' *Journal of Communication Inquiry, 10*(2), 78–98.

Hersh, P. (1990, June 3). Soccer in U.S. at crossroads: World Cup seen as last resort to stir fan sport. *Chicago Tribune* (p. C1).

Holleb, D. (1975). The direction of urban change. In: H. Perloff (ed.), *Agenda for the New Urban Era* (pp. 11–43). Chicago: American Society of Planning Officials.

Houlihan, B. (1994). Homogenisation, Americanisation and Creolisation of sport: Varieties of globalisation. *Sociology of Sport Journal, 11*, 356–375.

Howell, J. (1991). A revolution in motion: Advertising and the politics of nostalgia. *Sociology of Sport Journal, 8*(3), 258–271.

Howell, J. (1996). The 1996 Surgeon General's report on physical activity and health. *Nurse Practitioner Forum, 7*(3), 104.

Howell, J., & Ingham, A. (2001). From social problem to personal issue: The language of lifestyle. *Cultural Studies, 15*(2), 326–351.

Ingham, A. (1985). From public issue to personal trouble: Well-being and the fiscal crisis of the State. *Sociology of Sport Journal, 2*(1), 43–55.

Ingham, A., & Donnelly, P. (1997). A sociology of North American Sociology of Sport: Disunity in unity, 1965 to 1996. *Sociology of Sport Journal, 14*(4), 62–418.

Ingham, A., & Loy, J. (eds) (1993). *Sport and Social Development: Traditions, Transitions and Transformations.* Champaign, IL: Human Kinetics.

Jackson, K. T. (1985). *Crabgrass Frontier: The Suburbanisation of the United States.* New York: Oxford University Press.

Jackson, S. J., & Andrews, D. L. (1999). Between and beyond the global and the local: American popular sporting culture in New Zealand. *International Review for the Sociology of Sport, 34*(1), 31–42.

King, A. (1990). *Culture, Globalisation and the World System.* Basingstoke, UK: Macmillan.

Klein, A. (1991). Sport and culture as contested terrain: Americanisation in the Caribbean. *Sociology of Sport Journal, 8,* 79–85.

Lasch, C. (1979). *The Culture of Narcissism: American Life in an Age of Diminishing Expectations.* New York: W.W. Norton.

Lash. S., & Urry, J. (1994). *Economies of Signs and Space.* London: Verso.

Leland, J., & Power, C. (1997, October 20). Deepak's instant karma. *Newsweek* (pp. 52–58).

Leonard, G., & Murphy, M. (1995). *The Life We are Given.* New York: Jeremy P. Tarcher/Putnam Book.

Lury, C. (1996). *Consumer Culture.* Cambridge: Polity Press.

Maguire, J. (1999). *Global Sport: Identities, Societies, Civilisations.* Cambridge: Polity Press.

Malone, M. (1994, May–June). Soccer's greatest goal: Cultural harmony through sports. *Americas,* (p. 64).

McKay, J. (1995). Just Do It: Corporate sports slogans and the political economy of enlightened racism. *Discourse: Studies in the Cultural Politics of Education, 16*(2), 191–201.

McKay, J., & Miller, T. (1991). From old boys to men and women of the corporation: The Americanisation and commodification of Australian sport. *Sociology of Sport Journal, 8,* 86–94.

McKay, J., Lawrence, G., Miller, T., & Rowe, D. (1993). Globalisation and Australian sport. *Sport Science Review, 2,* 10–28.

Miller, T., & McHoul, A. (1998). *Popular Culture and Everyday Life.* London: Sage.

Morley, D., & Chen, K. (1996). *Stuart Hall: Critical Dialogues in Cultural Studies.* New York: Routledge.

Murdock, G. (1997). Cultural studies at the crossroads. In: McRobbie, A. (ed.), *Back to Reality: Social Experience and Cultural Studies.* Manchester: Manchester University Press.

Perez, A. (1997, March 24). Soccer looks: Soccer fashion. *Sporting Goods Business, 30,* 44.

Robertson, R. (1992). *Globalisation: Social Theory and Global Culture.* New York: Russell Sage.

Rowe, D. (1996a). Editorial: Sport, globalisation and the media. *Media, Culture & Society, 18*(4), 523–526.

Rowe, D. (1996b). The global love-match: Sport and television. *Media, Culture & Society, 18*(4), 565–582.

Rowe, D., McKay, J., & Lawrence, G. (1997). Out of the shadows: The critical Sociology of Sport in Australia, 1986 to 1996. *Sociology of Sport Journal, 14*(4), 340–361.

Rowe, D., Lawrence, G., Miller, T., & McKay, J. (1994). Global sport? Core concern and peripheral vision. *Media, Culture & Society, 16,* 661–675.

Russakof, D. (1998, August 25). Okay, soccer moms and dads: Time out! Leagues try to rein in competitive parents. *Washington Post* (p. A1).

Schor, J. B. (1998). *The Overspent American: Upscaling, Downshifting and the New Consumer*. New York: Basic Books.

Steinbrecher, H. (1996, February 26–27). *Getting in on Soccer: The Hottest Sport to Reach International Markets*. Paper presented at the Marketing with Sports Entities, Swissotel, Atlanta, GA.

Struna, N. (1986). E. P. Thompson's notion of 'context' and the writing of physical education and sport history. *Quest, 38*, 22–32.

Theberge, N., & Donnelly, P. (eds) (1984). *Sport and the Sociological Imagination*. Fort Worth: Texas Christian University Press.

Thompson, E. P. (1972). Anthropology and the discipline of context. *Midland History, 3*, 41–55.

Thomas, G. S. (1998). *The United States of Suburbia: How the Suburbs Took Control of America and What They Plan To Do With It*. New York: Prometheus Books.

Turner, G. (1990). *British Cultural Studies: An Introduction*. Boston: Unwin Hyman

US Department of Health and Human Services (1992). *Healthy People 2000: National Health Promotion and Disease Prevention Objectives*. Sudbury: Jones and Bartlett Publishers.

Weaver, K. (1996). The television and violence debate in New Zealand: Some problems of context. *Continuum: The Australian Journal of Media and Culture, 10*, 64–75.

Zwick, D., & Andrews, D. L. (1999). The suburban soccer field: Sport and America's culture of privilege. In: G. Armstrong and R. Giulianotti (eds), *Football Cultures and Identities* (pp. 211–222). London: Macmillan Press.

Chapter 8

Postmodernism and Sport Studies

Geneviève Rail

In the last few decades, the nature of Western societies has changed radically. Sociologists have interpreted these changes through the development of concepts such as 'media society', 'society of spectacle', 'consumer society', 'postindustrial society', 'and post-Fordist society'. Cultural and sport critics have described our Western world as one dominated by capitalism, consumption and globalisation of mass communications and computer technologies. Also noted has been the blurring of the traditional distinctions between 'high' and 'mass' culture, and the resulting tendency for fragmentation and recombination through *pastiche* and *collage*. Evidence of the fragmentary has been detected in the theorisation of language, time, the human subject, and society itself. In relation to sport as well as other domains of cultural life, observers have commented on the fragmentation of monolithic political structures and the emergence of political initiatives made manifest through struggles over the body, gender, sexuality, ethnicity, race and the environment (Whitheford & Gruneau, 1993). Either at the local or the global level, the terrain of such discourses and struggles is now more complex than the traditional Marxist one of class conflict. In fact, it has become apparent that the plurality of social discourses and power relations cannot be simply unified by grand explanations of 'reality' such as those proposed by Marxist or liberal theory.

   In sociology as well as in sociology of sport, the critique of grand theories has expanded to include an interrogation of their modernist assumptions, particularly the belief that 'reason' and technological innovation can guarantee unlimited progress and universal emancipation. Classical theories such as those presented in the early chapters of this book are facing challenges that are diverse, but that commonly dismiss totalising theories and the idea of a universal 'truth'. These challenges also share a conviction that 'postmodern' times, sports and bodies are marked by a different cultural logic and thus require new social theories, epistemologies, methodologies and politics (Jameson, 1991; Kellner, 1989; Rail, 1995a). If sport writing has long been structured and constrained by modern, positivist, heterosexist, sexist and racist boundaries, then a blurring of these boundaries is needed, and greater attention must be paid to the ways in which differences — particularly those embedded in modern binaries such as man/woman, nature/culture, heterosexual/homosexual, white/other, normal/pathological — are constructed and maintained (Cole & Rail, 1994).

Conceptualising the contemporary as 'postmodern' suggests a break with the features of 'modernity.' However, this makes 'postmodernity' a problematic concept as we are only on the threshold of the shift, and not in a position to regard the postmodern as something that can be defined in a comprehensive manner. Bearing this in mind, the confusion that surrounds postmodernism is such that it is helpful to offer some preliminary understandings of this concept; this is the focus of the first two sections of this chapter. In the third section, I discuss the encounter between feminism and postmodernism. In the final section of the chapter, I provide examples of epistemological, methodological, discursive and political projects that may be envisaged when a postmodern perspective is used to study sport.

The Various Postmodernisms

Many attribute the origin of the term 'postmodernism' to Federico de Onis who, in the 1930s, used it to suggest a reaction to 'modernism'. The term became popular in the 1960s in New York when it was used by young artists and writers to refer to a movement against the institutionalised high modernism of the museum and the academy. It gained wider usage in architecture and the arts in the 1970s and 1980s (Jencks, 1987). Thereafter, European and North American debates multiplied as the search for theoretical explanations of artistic postmodernism widened to include discussions of postmodernity. Postmodernism, then, is not easily encapsulated in one phrase since it has been used in various disciplines (e.g., music, art, fiction, film, drama, architecture, photography, literary criticism, philosophy, sociology, anthropology, geography) to convey very different meanings. Furthermore, it is an amalgam of often purposely ambiguous and fluid ideas. It is nevertheless crucial to trace the contour of the postmodern since we are ill-served by the prevailing tendency to deploy 'postmodernism' as a totalising device that obscures the basic differences between the various postmodernisms. Although many existing variants are constantly altered, and despite the fact that other variants may emerge, I tentatively distinguish between the following five.

Postmodernism is at times used to describe a *style* qualifying the transformations in artistic representation inside architecture and generally including phenomena observed in the wider aesthetic field (Wood *et al.*, 1993).

The term makes evident the departure from the modern style and its elitism and authoritarianism. Postmodern style is rather inspired by aesthetic populism or the collapse of the hierarchical distinction between high and popular culture. As such, it involves pluralism, eclecticism, parody, playfulness, paradox, and irony.

Postmodernism, as *artistic practice*, refers to a structure of experience, a mode of sensibility. It often refers to the diverse contributions of literature, theatre, dance, and other 'performance' arts. While this mode of sensibility implies a radical break in artistic modes, there is no unity within or between postmodern artistic practices; as the term acquires common currency, it takes on new connotations.

Another variant is often associated with the idea that postmodernism represents an epochal transition, a radical break with the past. Fredric Jameson (1991) is the foremost supporter of postmodernism as *epoch* as he believes in the emergence of a new 'cultural logic' corresponding to a new type of social life, both being associated with a transition from a national system of s... capitalism to multinational corporate capitalism. The notion of an epochal break from modernity can also be detected in the writings of Jean Baudrillard (1981, 1983, 1988) and Jean–François Lyotard (1984). Baudrillard argues that new forms of technology and information are central to a shift from a productive to a reproductive social order in which the distinction between simulations and the real disappears. Lyotard is interested in the consequences of society's computerisation on knowledge; he stresses that in postmodernity the loss of meaning need not be mourned when it points to the replacement of classical theories or 'grand narratives' by a plurality of local narratives.

Postmodernism as *method* comes from literary theory and can be seen as a revolt against modernism and structuralism. Postmodernism, phenomenology and ethnomethodology emerged from similar sources, notably the philosophies of Friedrich Nietzsche and Martin Heidegger that rejected the Enlightenment's attempt to create a universal knowledge. Challenging the grand narratives of modernism, postmodernism as method favours a 'deconstruction' of linguistic structures and systems (Derrida, 1973, 1976).[1] The focus on language and text explains why the term 'poststructuralism' has often been preferred. Recent writing in the social and cultural domain has emphasised the transgression of boundaries between writing genres and the term postmodernism has also

[1]Although Derrida does not elaborate a single deconstructive method and refuses to associate himself with something as systematic as a method, literary critics prise out of Derrida a strategy of textual reading called deconstruction. This 'method' has spread through the Western academy, challenging the traditional literary and cultural criticism dominated by textual objectivism (see Agger, 1991; Leitch, 1992).

emerged to refer to a method which, not unlike that of radical feminism and feminist cultural studies, challenges the traditional ways of 'doing' social science. Denzin (1994), for example, has noted the importance of recognising the 'fictional' aspect of all social 'science' writing, including the ways in which researchers 'write' reality and people's understanding of it.

In the last sense of the term, postmodernism means a *theoretical reflection* on all the previous areas. I use the expression 'theoretical reflection' to bypass the ongoing debate raging over the existence, the possibility even, of a postmodern sociological 'theory'. Indeed, a good portion of the literature on postmodernism has, according to a number of conservative sociologists (e.g., structural functionalists), ventured quite far from sociology. Their concerns reflect what Agger calls the contemporary 'metatheoretical insecurities of the discipline' (1992). That is to say, although many writers of the postmodern have not brandished the banner of a new sociological theory, they have been accused of social theorising and contamination of the 'reasonable' discourse in sociology. At this point, it suffices to say that theoretical reflections on the postmodern are numerous and dissimilar, some being closer to social theorising than others.

The term postmodernism, then, is applied to a range of theoretical positions that escape disciplinary boundaries and vary to such an extent that they can at times be thought of as pragmatist (e.g., New Times theorists and other pragmatic 'truth-seekers') or anarchist (e.g., Arthur and Mary–Louise Kroker and other 'postmodern story-tellers'), from the Left (e.g., some neo–Marxists and critical theorists) or the Right (e.g., neo–conservative Baudrillard), and leaning toward economic reduction (e.g., Jameson) or semiotic dissolution (e.g., Lacan). Postmodernist positions are so diverse that any attempt to represent postmodernism in a unified way leads to exclusions and distortions. Attempting to establish one 'master' narrative on postmodernism would be highly paradoxical: a text that sets out to represent the postmodern in a structured and unambiguous fashion is by definition modern rather than postmodern in orientation. It follows that the exclusionary and modern bias of the present chapter cannot be avoided. At the outset, I should therefore mention that my discussion is partial to types of postmodern reflection that seem, to me, most useful and productive for scholars of sport. In selecting this way, I am ultimately producing a specific version of postmodernism that has theoretical inclinations and that can be used for sociopolitical analysis and cultural critique. My version has methodological and political implications that may differ from those of other types of postmodernism. I would argue, however, that most types of postmodernism share certain assumptions and features, which I now discuss.

Postmodernism as Theoretical Reflection

A brief discussion of postmodernism assumes that we can cleanly distinguish postmodernism from poststructuralism. Unfortunately, we cannot, since there is substantial overlap between the two perspectives. To characterise them simply, I would say that poststructuralism focuses on knowledge and language, as in the work of Derrida (1973, 1976, 1978) and other French theorists such as Lacan (1977), Kristeva (1981, 1982, 1984, 1986), Deleuze and Guattari (1972, 1987), Irigaray (1985a 1985b) and Cixous (1994). Postmodernism, meanwhile, is concerned with society, culture and history, as is evident in the writings of Lyotard (1984), Barthes (1975, 1977), Baudrillard (1983, 1988, 1989) and Jameson (1991). Of course, a large number of writings is claimed by either camp and this is notably the case for Foucault (1973b, 1979, 1981, 1986, 1988). For my purposes, I argue that postmodernism encompasses two important tendencies. The first emphasises the idea that the world is fragmented into many isolated worlds; it is a *collage*, a *pastiche* of elements randomly grouped in a plurality of local discourses that cannot be unified by any grand theory. The second emphasises a poststructuralist element; preoccupied with the problem of meaning, it results in a position that considers meaning as fundamentally elusive.

The two main tendencies present in postmodernism are interwoven by Lyotard in his book *The Postmodern Condition* (1984). According to him, there are two versions of narrative legitimating: the 'political narrative' which, since the 18th century Enlightenment, has promised progressive emancipation and freedom, and the 'scientific narrative', which has been considered a means to this end. Lyotard argues that there is a crisis in the legitimating of knowledge in the post-industrial age and thus a collapse of the grand theories or 'metanarratives' that have legitimated the 'truth' of history. Postmodernists, Lyotard suggests, question the assumptions of the modern age, notably the conviction that scientific progress is possible and desirable, and that rational thought and technology will bring advancement and enlightenment to humanity. They also refute the existence of a reality characterised by structure, patterns, and causal relationships; a reality that can be studied objectively and usefully represented by theories. Postmodernists dismiss large stories about history and the world as products of an era wherein Europeans and North Americans mistakenly believed in their own superiority and invincibility. Meta-narratives are no longer seen as truth, but rather as privileged discourses that deny and silence competing and dissident voices. Lyotard sees postmodernism as, above all, maintaining an incredulity toward meta-narratives.

Foucault has also emphasised the inadequacies of meta-narratives; he dismisses reason as a fiction and sees truth as simply a partial, localised version of reality (1972, 1973a, 1979). Foucault argues that discourse is the site where meanings are contested and power relations determined. He also points to the 'false' power of hegemonic knowledge and suggests that it can be challenged by counter-hegemonic discourses that offer alternative explanations of reality. Foucault's writings have drawn attention to the power of language and discourse, as well as to their impact on the way people understand and assign meaning to their lives. This has led to a call for the dismantling of language/ discourse in order to discover the way meanings are constructed and used.

Baudrillard (1983) suggests that reality is increasingly simulated for people, constructed by the mass media and other cultural institutions. This is what he calls 'hyperreality'. Derrida (1976) also focuses on the constructed nature of reality when he disqualifies the positivist model of researchers who simply reflect the world 'out there'. He and other postmodernists have called for the critical deconstruction of written and oral texts, and greater attention to the way modern binaries are produced and maintained. In particular, Derrida has called attention to the crucial role played by binary opposites (e.g., truth/falsity, unity/diversity, man/woman, culture/nature, normal/pathological), whereby the nature of the first term is seen as superior to, and depends on the definition of the second. Derrida's deconstruction challenges traditional assumptions about writing and reading science. He insists that every text is 'undecidable' since it conceals conflicts between the text and the 'sub-text'. What every text appears to say on the surface cannot be understood without reference to the assumptions it makes in presuming that it will be understood.

To use a simplified example in sport, I could read about the 'Athlete of the Year' and the 'Woman Athlete of the Year' in the newspaper. One deconstruction of these headlines could reveal the deep assumptions about the gendered nature of sport as well as about the male supremacy that underlies this choice of headlines in a newspaper. Among other things, the analysis could shed light on the powerfully ideologising sub-text that encourages readers to think that: (a) there is a unified notion of the social subject 'woman' and it is distinct from an equally unified notion of the social subject 'man'; (b) an athlete of the year is a man; (c) athletes are men; (d) women are not really athletes, they are just women athletes; (e) only men are/should be involved in sport; (f) male athletes are superior to female athletes; (g) there is a univocal and unchallengeable measure of that superiority; and (h) it is desirable to use this measure for comparative purposes.

For Derrida, deconstructive reading prises open unavoidable gaps of meaning that readers fill with their own meanings. Reading is thus a strong activity since readers give writing its sense. Language, in and of itself, is undecidable. Derrida uses the fictitious word *différance* to demonstrate this. *Différance* is pronounced the same way as the French word *différence*, but its fiction cannot be detected when speaking, only when writing. Derrida argues that language produces meaning only with reference to other meanings against which it takes on its own significance. In this sense, *différance* corresponds to the dual production of meaning through difference and deferral (see Johnson, 1997; Weedon, 1997). Derrida suggests that we cannot arrive at a fixed meaning as long as we use a necessarily differing as well as deferring language: every definition needs to be clarified and meaning always lies in the future.

For postmodernists, all of reality is based on language and can be thought of as text. Any text is 'inter-textual' in that it is inflected by other texts and therefore any text that attempts to represent anything is necessarily incomplete and biased. In sport studies, this means that there is no 'Truth' but rather many accounts of social experience emerging from multiple perspectives of discourse/ practice and different subject positions. Postmodernists consider science domineering and dangerous when it is treated as a privileged discourse because of its truth claims (i.e., science always claims an exemption from the rule of undecidability). Instead of building grand theories, then, postmodernists suggest the deconstruction of texts to reveal their assumptions and contradictions, and the construction of mini-narratives that make no truth claims and within which difference, pluralism, irrationality, and paradox can surface.

Epistemologically-oriented postmodernists characterise the postmodern mostly in terms of the breakdown of belief in scientific truth and objectivity. Other postmodernists see the global ravage of consumer capitalism as central. The ceaseless proliferation of products and images strongly figures in their story of the postmodern. For instance, thanks to Jameson (1991) and Harvey (1989), the term postmodernism has been equated with the late-capitalist or post-Fordist historical period and its industrial model of flexible specialisation and production.[2] Such ways of reading the postmodern are important precisely

---

[2]Originally theorised by Piore and Sabel (1984), 'flexible specialisation' is seen by optimists (e.g., Hall & Jacques, 1989; Lipietz, 1992) as the solution to the problems of mass production. For instance, reprogrammable computerised equipment revitalises small batch production, allowing producers to cope with the increased volatility and fragmentation of demand. Flexible machines and workers replace the dedicated equipment and deskilled workers of the Fordist production system. The Japanese 'just-in-time' management system fosters upgrading, stream-lining and cost control. Since workers work in teams and master a wide range of skills, rigid job descriptions and work rules become obsolescent. Large firms with a centralised decision-making structure and spatially dispersed production facilities disappear in favour of small firms that interact with each other in an array of supplier and purchaser relations. More pessimistic analysts (e.g., Harvey, 1989) rather see the outcome of post-Fordism in terms of a polarised labour force: a few highly skilled workers who enjoy 'yuppie' affluence and a huge number of unskilled casual workers who struggle at low wages to obtain the necessities of life. On the political level, these analysts also point to the massive retreat of the welfare state and the problematic reassertion of market relations in all spheres of social existence.

because they render contemporary cultural and political changes intelligible within a neo–Marxist framework. At the same time, they are somewhat problematic because they often ignore a growing body of cultural and ethnographic studies (e.g., Clifford, 1992; Clifford & Marcus, 1986; Mascia–Lees, Sharpe, & Ballerino Cohen, 1989; Marchand & Parpart, 1995; Smith, 1989, 1992; Smith, Tarallo, & Kagiwada, 1991) that describe how people's everyday practices and understandings of their conditions of existence often modify those very conditions and thereby shape rather than merely reflect new modes of culture. It seems also that efforts to subordinate cultural processes to the master discourse of classical Marxism downplay the ontological and epistemological challenges that postmodernism poses for modernist assumptions and all forms of essentialism.[3] In this regard, postmodernism and some types of feminist theorising share a common critique of the modernist *épistémè* (Foucault, 1972).

Postmodernism/s and Feminism/s

The encounter between feminism and postmodernism has led to many alliances and numerous debates. Feminists have both contributed and responded to postmodern thought in a number of ways. Some feminists (e.g., Butler, 1992; Flax, 1990a, 1992) believe that feminist theory has always dealt with postmodern issues and feel comfortable with the label 'postmodernist'. Others (e.g., Hartsock, 1990) recognise the problem associated with a division between many postmodernists and other theorists; a division continually reinforced by the obscure power language that has become increasingly present in academe and elsewhere. Yet other feminists (e.g., Finn, 1993) respond to postmodernism by concluding that feminist theory has more to offer women than male-centric postmodernist and poststructuralist writers.[4]

---

[3]As Smith (1992) explains, both liberal and Marxist theories of the subject are seen as essentialist because they offer a reductionist view of the relationship between consciousness, agency and social change. They offer abstract categories (i.e., the 'individual' and 'class') as carriers of coherent capacity for a universal and trans-historical agency. In contrast, postmodern social analysis considers the subject as decentred; there are no clear-cut 'roles' waiting for subjects to occupy in pursuit of their historical mission. Rather, there is a multiplicity of forms of agency that people come to experience in history.

[4]For a brief but insightful discussion of the theoretical difficulties involved in the encounter between feminism and postmodernism, see Geraldine Finn's chapter "Why are there no great women postmodernists?" (1993). Diane Elam's description of 'The Abyss' in her book *Feminism and Deconstruction* (1994) offers an insight into similar difficulties associated to the introduction of feminism to poststructuralism.

Not surprisingly, feminists working in the liberal or Marxist traditions — both of which are embedded in Enlightenment ways of thinking — are strongly opposed to postmodernism (e.g., Walby, 1990). The postmodern conceptualisation of subjectivity as permanently discontinuous, displaced and destabilised is problematic for them as well as for other feminists. For instance, standpoint feminists (e.g., Brodribb, 1992; Harding, 1986, 1987, 1990; Smith, 1990) who focus on women's lived experiences as the basis for feminist knowledge reject the postmodern 'assault' on the subject[5] since their critique of male hegemony is based on the authority of women's subjectivity as it is grounded in their daily lives.

Many feminist scholars (e.g., Bordo, 1989; DiStefano, 1990; Hartsock, 1987) depend on a relatively unified notion of the social subject 'woman'. These scholars remain profoundly wary of calls for a feminism whose foundation omits and/or excludes the possibility of a unified female subject. They have proposed two central problems with postmodernism's 'impossible subject' thesis. The first relates to what some feminists perceive to be a reaction against recent gains made by feminists and other marginalised groups. Hartsock resumes the first problem when she asks why the concept of the subject and the possibility of discovering a liberating 'truth' become suspect just at the moment in Western history when previously silenced populations have begun to speak for themselves. The second problem with the impossible subject thesis pertains to its possible andro-centric bias. In this regard, DiStefano wonders whether "the subject under fire from postmodernism may be a more specifically masculine self than postmodern theorists have been willing to admit" (1990: 75). Adding to these crucial questions, feminists of various persuasions have expressed concern about the political implications of a postmodernist feminist perspective (e.g., Hutcheon, 1989). Some (e.g., Bordo, 1992) have specifically suggested that the over-emphasis on difference leads to further political fragmentation within the feminist movement.

While agreeing with Nancy Hartsock (1990) that postmodernism taken to its extreme impermeable nature and as practised by a number of white, middle-class, male-centred proponents does nothing to further the feminists' search for a more egalitarian world, I support a growing number of feminists in their belief that postmodernist thought has much to offer feminist theorising and action. Many have come to appreciate the alternative ontology, epistemology, methodology

[5]Humanist discourses such as those adopted by standpoint feminists presuppose an 'essence' at the heart of the individual which is unique, fixed and coherent, and which makes her what she is. Postmodernism proposes that subjectivity is constructed. Postmodern subjectivity is thus precarious, contradictory and in process, constantly being reconstituted in discourse.

and politics inherent in postmodernism and have realised that attempts to challenge male hegemony within essentialist and male-centric Enlightenment thoughts are doomed to failure. For example, Butler (1990) points out that discursive power regimes, namely language, political processes and judicial systems, both produce and compel the subjects they come to represent. In this sense, such discursive systems are 'performative'. By virtue of being constantly subjected to the systems of power, the individual becomes defined, formed and reproduced in accordance with the requirements of those structures. An uncritical appeal to such judicial systems for the emancipation of women is therefore self-defeating, as the individual is discursively constituted by the very systems to which she is appealing. Postmodernism thus offers feminism a way to conceptualise its own ongoing dilemma: the desire to seek equality within the very institutions and discourses which feminists have attempted to challenge and dismantle. As for the notion of the universal and coherent female subject, Butler (1990) finds it problematic because: (a) the female subject is both regulated and constituted by the same performative discursive systems; and (b) the universal subject of some types of feminism is based on a fundamentally privileged occidental conception of power and oppression. Indeed, the early feminist claim of a universal woman's experience was based on a privileged range of Western women's experiences (e.g., white, bourgeois, heterosexual, able-bodied) and their corresponding experiences of oppression. Because the early feminist discourse relied on universal and coherent categories of femaleness, it invariably homogenised those within it and marginalised their differences.

Of course, to many feminists, one of the most appealing aspects of post-modernism is its focus on difference and its legitimisation of the search for the voice of displaced, marginalised and oppressed people. A number of feminists (e.g., hooks, 1984, 1991, 1994; Lorde, 1984) have argued for a re-conceptualisation of the subject as shifting and multiply organised across variable axes of difference (e.g., class, race, dis/ability, ethnicity, age, gender, sexuality). They have stressed how mobile subjectivities are embedded in the historical, spatial and institutional contexts of daily life and how they must be understood in this context. This approach has successfully integrated the position of standpoint feminists and the postmodernist perspective, as heterogeneity, discontinuity and displacement point to real elements of women's contemporary experience.

The attention to marginalisation and oppression allows a *rapprochement* between postmodernism and the relatively new 'postcolonial studies'. As Ashcroft *et al.* (1995: 117) note, "the major project of postmodernism — the deconstruction of the centralised logocentric master narratives of European culture — is very similar to the postcolonial project of dismantling the

Centre/Margin binarisms of imperial discourse".[6] Postcolonial studies is transforming the ways in which non-occidental scholars conceptualise cultural identities. Edward Said (1993, 1995), Gayatri Chakravorty Spivak (1987, 1995), Homi Bhabha (1990a, 1990b, 1995), Trinh Minh-ha (1989, 1995), hooks (1992), Audré Lorde (1990) and other notable postcolonial critics also seek to understand the complex processes of cultural construction and the power relations entangled in such processes. Feminist contributors to the post-colonial studies tradition draw attention to the postcolonial subject by questioning the essentialist assumption of a subject who speaks from a position of knowledge in terms of identity (race, gender, class, etc.) rather than difference (Harding, 1998). Postmodernist feminism and postcolonial studies thus converge to question the totalising or colonising tendencies of Western feminist scholarship. Proper critical attention is thereby paid to colonial subjects, doubly colonised by imperial as well as patriarchal ideologies.

The de-centring of the West makes it possible to integrate within one space apparently divergent epistemologies. In this sense, what postmodernism changes, at least at the epistemological level, is that what becomes important and significant is not so much what theories say, but what can be done with them. For instance, it is unimportant that Foucault was not concerned with women's issues; what is relevant is how one can make use of his research to say radically different things. Butler (1990), for instance, questions gender formations starting from Foucault and Lacan: mounted on them, she carries out a scathing attack on how patriarchal societies have dealt with the question of gender and the inscription of the body.

Weedon (1997) suggests that postmodernist feminists "have mobilised the postmodern critique of authority and status of science, truth, history, power, knowledge and subjectivity, bringing a transformative gender dimension to postmoden theory and developing new ways of understanding sexual difference" (1997: 171). In this sense, these feminists have much in common with queer theorists such as Sedgwick (1990), Fuss (1995), Butler (1990, 1992, 1993, 1997) and de Lauretis (1991, 1994), who are interested in deconstructing normalcy (particularly heteronormativity), interrogating the intersections between racial and sexual identities, and viewing any categorisation of identity along racial, gender, sexuality and other lines as inherently suspicious.[7] Queer

[6]Derrida calls 'logocentrism' the basic drive to ground truth in a single point, an ultimate origin, a center. Western thought has always been logocentric; secure foundations, logical principles and a notion of the center have been the groundings for all its inquiries and statements. *The Logos* (a Greek term that means 'word', 'reason') leads to the mistaken belief that meaning somehow exists 'out there' and guarantees the truth of our statements.
[7]For an excellent discussion of this point, see Weed and Schor's anthology entitled *Feminism Meets Queer Theory* (1997).

theory includes a critique of all forms of normalisation and calls into question all reigning schemes of sexual normativity. For queer theorists, Foucault's regulatory notions of sexuality not only refer to heterosexual culture but to gay conservative desires for normativity. In queer theory, the grand narrative referring to the emancipatory struggles of gay subjects is interrogated and so is the essentialist and biological construction of the homosexual subject (e.g., the 'gay gene'). Queer sexuality expresses a desire for polymorphous sexual configurations that do not stem from a need to regulate and control the sexual subject according to binary categories and compulsory identifications.

Finally, postmodernist feminists Donna Haraway (1985, 1989, 1991, 1997) and others (e.g., Balsamo, 1996) bring us what some have called 'cyberfeminism'. One of their many theoretical and political strategies has been to map the identity of woman onto the image of the cyborg. Cyborgs offer a particularly appropriate emblem of postmodern identity because they are predicated on transgressed boundaries: they do not belong entirely to either culture or nature, they are neither wholly technological nor completely organic. According to Haraway, the cyborg challenges feminism to study the body as it is both a social construction and a material fact of human life. The cyborg reminds us that the body cannot be reduced to a matter of discourse, but also that the search for a female 'nature' is a utopian quest since the body is not solely a matter of materiality either. The cyborg body is inscribed by science and technology, as systems of socially-constructed knowledge, myths and meanings that enact practices of domination and oppression based on gender, race and class distinctions. Haraway thus proposes a more important task for feminists: to form coalitions and alliances with other political groups based not on some natural gender identification, but on the necessity for shared political strategies.

Postmodernism and Sport Studies

In sport scholarship, few perspectives account for the growing cultural differentiation as well as the multiplication of marginally situated forms of social agency (see Cole, 1993). In this regard, postmodernism is promising because it considers subjectivity as mobile and culturally constructed at the intersection of various social categories. Below, I offer some reflections on postmodernism as a way to focus attention to such subjectivity and to political relations of power and struggle, particularly as these articulate with issues of race, ethnicity, class, age, dis/ability, gender and sexuality. I suggest that postmodernism follows the Gramscian quest for new forms of oppositional agency since it proposes the study of the culturally marginalised as well as of social movements and social forces in order to discern the formation of new subject positions and give voice to the 'polyphonic' (hooks, 1990) patterns of accommodation and resistance. Using examples from postmodernist writings found within the sociology of sport literature, I also argue that postmodernism is an intentionally provocative effort to transcend or blur the modernist binary oppositions of micro-analysis *versus* macro-analysis, structure *versus* agency, and science *versus* art in social analysis.

De-monopolising the Production of Knowledge on Sport and Sporting Bodies

In terms of theoretical implications, I suggest that to use a postmodern perspective to inform sport studies is to reject the view that 'science' (or the end product of our knowledge production efforts) can be spoken in a singular and universal voice. Sport studies become an accounting of social experience from multiple perspectives of discourse, rather than a larger cumulative enterprise committed to the inference of general principles of social structure and organisation. Although this risks losing the grand meta-narratives, it enables readers to deconstruct Enlightenment assumptions and uncover the class, race, sexuality and gender biases of Eurocentric rationality (see Agger, 1991). Such projects, then, help to demystify the whole institution of knowledge production.

Postmodernism allows sociologists of sport and other sport studies scholars to historicise the process of writing sport, by questioning Enlightenment notions of authorial objectivity and detachment from the 'discursive traffic'. In treating knowledge about sport as a social product emanating from and limited by culturally mediated discursive practices, postmodernism rejects both the rationalist quest for general laws of history or human behaviour, and empiricist efforts to ground knowledge in the 'hard facts' of an external material world (Cole & Rail, 1994). At the same time, the postmodernist perspective challenges sport scholars to recognise the class, race, gender, dis/ability, age and sexuality biases found not only in sport but in the forms of its analysis. Indeed, in 'regime[s] of reason' (Leitch, 1992), there are unacknowledged values attending to ethical, economic, political, philosophical, educational, legal, familial, religious and aesthetic representations. Such representations are operating everywhere, including in the sociology of sport. Postmodernism forces sport scholars to be reflexive about underlying values and their link to methodological choices.

For postmodernists, language is not a simple technical device for establishing stable meanings: it is a constitutional act. Using this starting point, postmodernists reject the false objectivism of positivism by calling attention to positivism's embeddedness in language. They see science as similarly embedded in method since method encodes certain assumptions and values about the social world. Postmodernism is useful in this sense, because it suggests ways of reading and reformulating the densely technical discourses of the social sciences, sociology of sport included. It proposes more accessible modes of writing[8] and it opens up to readers intrigued by its deep assumptions. Postmodernism helps sport scholars to identify and render explicit the literary involvements and investments in sport studies, ours and that of others. This deconstructive strategy politicises and democratises the process of knowledge production by opening its texts to outsiders, allowing them to engage with the surface rhetoric more capably and to contest the deep assumptions where necessary. This has the additional advantage of challenging singular methodologies, whether quantitative or qualitative. A postmodernist perspective on sport argues for multiple methodologies as well as multiple perspectives on issues. It empowers those who have been silenced to join discussions about sociology of sport issues, rendering legitimate their non-credentialed interventions into the scientific field, and de-privileging the positivist voice.

Struggling Against Corporate Epistemology as a Basis for Research in Sport

In most Western societies today, democracy is under the rule of big business (see Dobbin, 1998). One of the consequences of this is the paradoxical establishment of the 'business' of public education. Institutions of higher learning are currently being 'colonised' by corporations (Deetz, 1992) and multinational companies are progressively involved in the production of knowledge and associated discourses of truth, deviance and normalisation (Robertson, 1998; Tudiver, 1999). As far as research is concerned, the required patents, licensing, and intellectual property rights create new practices, patterns and systems of knowledge production. Furthermore, the private ownership of knowledge is now being made possible through the intellectual property regimes that are included in trade agreements such as the GATT (Global Agreement on Trade and Tariffs),

---

[8]Postmodernism proposes simpler modes of writing although writing on postmodernism has traditionally been anything but simple. On this subject, hooks (1990) rightfully deplores the fact that the contemporary discourse that talks the most about heterogeneity and the recognition of 'Otherness' still directs its critical voice primarily to a specialised audience that shares a common language rooted in the master narratives it claims to challenge. I would similarly argue that postmodernist scholars of sport should be concerned that their discourses not remain exclusively located in the predominantly white and elitist institution of the university.

NAFTA (North American Free Trade Agreement), APEC (Asian Pacific Economic Community), and the spectre of the MAI (Multilateral Agreement on Investment), the CBI (Caribbean Basin Initiative), and the AGOA (African Growth and Opportunity Act). The commodification of knowledge and technological innovations is also facilitated by multinational corporations; they are always on hand to develop the academics' skills to secure pre-venture funding and get their scientific discovery to market. Obviously, one does not have to go very far to find examples of what could be called 'corporate epistemology'. Transnational corporations such as Coke, Pepsi, McDonald's, and Nike, have already invested in a great number of universities and seriously impacted the processes of knowledge creation and dissemination, not to mention the semiotic environment.

Considering the corporate colonisation of universities, sport scholars who favour a postmodernist perspective are at least armed to interrogate the production of hegemonic and domineering knowledge. Postmodernism considers science dangerous when it is treated as privileged discourse. It renders explicit the ways in which particular truths are produced. This forces sport scholars to ask a number of necessary political questions: Who establishes these truths and in who's interest? Who controls science? And if science is such a powerful cultural site, how can its truths, meanings and knowledge become objects of resistance and struggle?

In the context of academic institutions becoming more and more a target for corporate take-over (Tudiver, 1999), it becomes crucial to ask ourselves whether sport scholars are immune to *corporatus epistemologitis.* A number of important and related questions also need to be addressed: to what extent are multinational corporations, their practices, their mediated presence and their financial assistance providing the impetus for the knowledge produced? To what extent are they controlling this produced knowledge, for instance, by threatening sport scholars who dare speak out against corporations or by pushing sport scholars and their academic organisations to censor themselves for fear of reprisal? What are the consequences of the relationships that are being established between sport scholars and the corporations that are clients or recipients of their knowledge? What are the implications for the public interest in knowledge creation and dissemination?

Acting on 'Outlaw Emotions' as an Epistemological Alternative in Sport Studies

Postmodernism is certainly not a panacea, but it may contribute to the comprehension and solution of the above questions/problems. This perspective not only facilitates epistemological inquiries, it also represents a new way of doing 'science', of producing a new kind of 'scientific' knowledge. Postmodernism legitimates otherwise disparaged discourses — for instance, those of people who are on the losing end of corporate ventures in universities and elsewhere — to give them the same epistemological status as the dominant discourse. It also necessitates that sport scholars blur these faculties that our culture has abstracted and separated from each other when it comes to knowledge production: emotion and reason, observation and action.

Jaggar (1992) argues that within a capitalist, racist, sexist and homophobic society, dominant values will tend to serve the interests of rich white men. She also suggests that within such a society, we are all likely to develop a particular emotional constitution:

> Whatever our color, we are likely to feel . . . . "visceral racism";
> whatever our sexual orientation, we are likely to be homophobic;
> whatever our class, we are likely to be at least somewhat ambitious
> and competitive; whatever our sex, we are likely to feel contempt
> for women (1992: 159).

However, the hegemony that society exercises over our emotional constitution is not total and we do not always experience the conventionally acceptable emotions. Some people feel "outlaw emotions" (1992: 160), to borrow Jaggar's expression. These people are often subordinated individuals who pay a disproportionate price for status quo. For instance, people of colour are more likely to experience anger than amusement when a racist joke is recounted. Their anger is an anti-racist anger. In this way, individuals may have anti-racist emotions, feminist emotions, queer emotions. What Jaggar suggests is that these outlaw emotions can and should motivate new investigations, can and should help to determine the selection of sociological problems. With regards to the epistemological point of departure in sociology of sport or in sport studies more generally, multinational corporations and hegemonic forms of reason can and should be *countered by outlaw* emotions.

Transgressing Boundaries between Writing Genres in Sport Scholarship

Postmodernism has emerged as a method that challenges the traditional ways of 'doing' social science and 'telling' research stories (see Richardson, 1990, 1992, 1994). Denzin (1991, 1992), for instance, has noted the importance of recognising the 'fictional' aspect of all social science writings, including the ways in which researchers write reality and people's understanding of it. Fiction is not seen as opposed to truth; rather, the use of fiction is seen as a recognition of reality as something always partial and constructed. Postmodernists always construct partial truths that inherently reflect their location and their subjects' locations within specific discourses organised across variable axes of difference (Denzin, 1994). Furthermore, since all forms of writing constrain the kinds of knowledge that are produced, postmodernists find possibilities for new insights in new ways of writing. This long overdue transgression of boundaries between writing genres involves, for example, writing drama, performed dialogue, poetry, polyvocal texts, cinematic reconstructions, and short stories.

In the sociology of sport, few scholars have experimented with such new writing genres. Postmodernist scholars who have contributed to the sociology of sport literature have rather addressed theoretical (e.g., Cole, 1993; Fernandez–Balboa, 1997; Morgan, 1995; Rail, 1991b, 1995b, 1998; Sparkes, 1991) and methodological issues (e.g., Bruce, 1998; Bruce & Greendorfer, 1994; Cole, 1991; Foley, 1992; McDonald & Birrell, 1999; Wright, 1995). Other postmodernists have realised Baudrillardian and/or Jamesonian types of cultural analysis to further the understanding of the Michael Jordan phenomenon (e.g., Andrews, 1996a, 1996b, 1998a; Andrews, Jackson & Mazur, 1996; Armstrong, 1996; Jackson & Andrews, 1999), of various elements related to the Olympics or other major Games (e.g., Andrews, 1998; Real, 1996; Redhead, 1998; Slowikowski, 1991; van Wynsberghe & Ritchie, 1998), and of other issues related to professional sports and their postmodern representation (e.g., King, 1996; Rail, 1991a; Slowikowski, 1993; Stranger, 1999).

Using postmodernist and deconstructive strategies, a number of scholars have written on the relation between 'scientific truths' and the production of difference and deviance through the sporting body (e.g., Cole, 1993; Davis, 1989; Duquin, 1994; Dworkin & Wachs, 1998; Theberge, 1991). Starting from Derrida's notion of *différance*, Cheryl Cole (1998), Brian Pronger (1995, 1999) and Heather Sykes (1998) have examined sport, physical activity, and physical education discourses and their articulation with various 'technologies of the body' that produce and classify bodies as normal or deviant. They and others have also discussed the sporting body and how it is branded by the inscriptions of cultural discourses organised around modern binaries (Andrews & Cole, 1999; Cole, 1996; Cole & Hribar, 1995; Cole & King, 1998; Lafrance, 1998; Markula, 1995; Pronger, 1998). Finally, several scholars have used a Foucauldian approach to investigate the issues of discipline, normalisation, rationalisation, surveillance, panopticism and other forms of power used to 'invest' sporting bodies (see reviews in Andrews, 1993; Rail & Harvey, 1995).

Sport scholars who have experimented with sport writing and transgressed the conventions associated with doing and telling social science, are still very few in number. Without being exhaustive, I provide three examples here to show some of the possibilities that may be envisaged. In her 1998 work, Toni Bruce provides an extensive discussion (to which I am very much indebted here) regarding postmodernist writing. She also offers 'experimental stories' about women sports writers. In one story, the voices of 22 women sports writers are melded in a monologue to illustrate key features of locker room life for women who interview male professional or college athletes. The story is constructed from personal interviews with women sports writers, newspaper and magazine articles, keynote speeches and a novel. In a second story, rather than constructing a coherent and linear narrative, Bruce uses story fragments to reflect the contradictions and inconsistencies in women sports writers' explanations for problematic locker room encounters. Again, the dialogue is re/constructed from the voices of women writers, but quotations stand isolated and without context. They jostle with and against each other, challenging the reader to make sense of them and offering multiple takes on the reality of problematic locker room encounters.

Boundaries of traditional social science writing genres are similarly transgressed by Kohn and Sydnor (1998) in the presentation of their postmodern dialogue. The latter constitutes a highly personal, ironic and reactionary account of their daily encounters with the 'hegemony of sport' and is a concrete example of a text which elicits emotion in the reader and which brings understanding to the postmodern sport culture. Furthermore, their dialogue offers seduction, melancholy, impatience, indifference and other original strategies for resistance to, and subversion of hegemonic forces found in everyday life.

A final example of violation of the prescribed conventions of traditional social science writing genres is the work of Robert Rinehart (1998), who has examined the world of private swimming lessons and used this experience as a starting point for his discussion of the place of the researcher in 'vital' stories. Throughout his lived experience of the swimming school and throughout his writing, Rinehart's location moves from outsider to observer as participant, to participant as observer, to complete participant. These epistemological shifts allow for a poignant postmodern story in which Foucault's ideas of disciplinary practices are brought forward, in order to shed light and understanding on the teaching of swimming and on the use of sport as an evangelical tool. Ultimately, by writing about the swim school's panopticism and the coaches' gaze, surveillance and discipline, Rinehart allows the reader to see the swimming lanes as small theatres of punishment, and sport as an ethically problematic ideology.

Resisting Exploitative Knowledges about Sport

A cursory look at writings in the sociology of sport and the other sport sciences leads one to believe that scientific knowledge is produced, but that this type of knowledge renders invisible and reproduces the oppressive systems of differentiation existing in our society. Indeed, if there is a terrain upon which the two concepts of knowledge and exploitation meet, it is most certainly that of the traditional researcher's relationship to his or her subjects. Abounding in the sport sciences, rationalist and positivist projects have naturalised the notion of the researcher's transcendence, objectivity and value neutrality. This often translates into an exploitative process where the researcher extracts information from the subject who is henceforth excluded from the research process.

In the sociology of sport, exploitation assumes various forms. For instance, a number of writings do not empower subjects but rather annihilate and erase them. hooks (1990) has eloquently discussed this issue. Mimicking the researcher speaking to subjects who have been 'othered', she says:

> No need to hear your voice when I can talk about you better than you can speak about yourself. No need to hear your voice. Only tell me about your pain. I want to know your story. And then I will tell it back to you in a new way. Tell it back to you in such a way that it has become mine, my own. Re-writing you, I write myself anew. I am still author, authority. I am still colonizer, the speaking subject and you are now at the center of my talk (1990: 343).

Another danger of exploitation occurs when the researcher assumes a position of authorial passivity to 'record' the supposedly pure, authentic voice of the 'marginal' or the 'different'. This temptation to 'capture' the 'essence' of a local voice, inscribed as a heroic challenge against oppressive forces precisely mirrors the problem of exoticising the other, or what hooks calls 'eating the other' (1991).

Rather than perspectives and methodologies yielding exploitative knowledge, postmodernism offers the possibility of an inclusive space wherein subjects and researchers move in solidarity to blur modern methodological boundaries between researcher/subject, recorder/recorded, objective/subjective and expert/ neophyte. Postmodernism also challenges the idea that identity is singular or monolithic, exploring instead the concept of a multiple, shifting, and often self-contradictory identity. Finally, postmodernism forces sport scholars to recognise the fact that subjects are as much embedded in historical time and space as they are. The idea of the subject's pure voice is thus demystified and subjects are considered as socially produced in the here and now, rather than archeologically salvaged from the past.

Blurring 'Science' and Politics in Endeavours to Further the Understanding of Sport

Beyond theory and method, there is the important issue of politics. The original sociologies of Comte, Durkheim and Weber established the positivist study of social facts and separated the vocations of science and politics (for further discussion see Chapters 2 and 3). Postmodernism blurs such categories. A postmodernist cultural politics (see Rail, 1995a) exposes the exclusions and silences of the past to give a voice to marginal sensibilities. Furthermore, its goal is to create a political space in which new connections across race, ethnicity, age, sexuality, dis/ability, gender and class can be constructed, alliances can be forged, and credible projects can be established in order to rally people and allow them to see that their efforts can and do make a difference.

Postmodernism has been interpreted as a conservative political position by some feminist and Marxist critics (e.g., Harvey, 1989; Lovibond, 1989). It has also been said to depoliticise the collective struggle against domination. This is because it gives priority to the plurality of the different over the duality of the other in constituting social relations of ethnicity, race, class, gender, sexuality and locality. In doing so, postmodernism rejects the political strategy by which the binary dualisms of capital-labour, center-periphery, assimilation-ethnic purity, and male-female are converted into an either-or logic (Smith, 1992). If, in much Marxist and feminist discourse, the marginal is turned into the 'Other', whose only self-respecting strategy is to displace the center by revolutionary struggle, postmodernism recognises instead that relations of domination-subordination exist but are always complexly constituted. As Smith suggests, "the identification of various modes of accommodation and resistance to similar structural constraints and forms of social control places the motif of power–domination–accommodation–resistance at the center of the postmodernist project" (1992: 509). Postmodernism makes explicit its value positions. Postmodernist scholars of sport carry a political project to effect radical changes in sport; changes to be guided by multiple voices. Postmodernist projects reflect the variety of subject positions from which ordinary people can speak about sport. They thus empower a variety of speakers and legitimize their non-credentialed interventions.

In sport studies, postmodernism means a number of possibilities: (a) to inscribe voices that until now have been silenced; (b) to conceive of science, culture, society and sport in a different manner; (c) to think of new forms of representation outside of the binary system that still characterises our culture; and (d) to listen to other forms of knowledge. 'Logocentrism' has meant a barrier or boundary between theory and practice for the sake of scientificity. Postmodernism, in contrast, pushes sport scholars to go beyond the barrier and to think beyond binarism. Bhabha (1994) speaks to this possibility in the following terms:

> The language metaphor opens up a space where a theoretical disclosure is used to move beyond theory. A form of cultural experience and identity is envisaged in a theoretical description that does not set up a theory-practice polarity, nor does theory become 'prior' to the contingency of social 'experience' that is particularly important for envisaging emergent cultural identities (1994: 179).

For postmodernist sport writers, the idea is to project alternative visions, analyses and actions that proceed from particularities and that arrive at political connectedness. This may sound utopian and fanciful. Recent cutbacks in Western societies in the areas of health, education and social programmes reinforce this perception. However, postmodernist politics must confront these enormous and urgent challenges. It is time for sport scholars to refuse to limit their visions, analyses and praxis to particular terrains. The aim is to dare to redefine and revise the very notions of mainstream, margin, difference, otherness. Modern sport has long been a project of differentiation and socio-cultural boundary maintenance. As Pronger (1998) argues, it is now time to think outside of modern binaries and to think of a postmodern type of sport as a wild, democratic, and transgressive event of boundary pollution, dedifferentiation, and celebration of the erotic ecstasy of the moving body.

(In) Conclusion

There can be no conclusion to a chapter that is so limited and that provides more questions than answers. However, I will offer a few final remarks. First, it is clear that postmodernism challenges the territoriality of sociology, including its differentiation from other scholarly disciplines. It redefines the human sciences and sport studies in ways that blur traditional disciplinary boundaries. Second, postmodernism enables us to recognise that the important questions today, in sport and in society, are hardly about sociological theory. They are about the complex intersections of discipline and deterrence, sexuality and desire, power, the body, simulation, and seduction. We seem to have reached a turning point as sport scholars. We can continue with traditional modes of analysis that perhaps are no longer adequate to their object. Alternatively, we can join in the effort to construct multiple and concrete languages, flexible enough to seduce and capture, however briefly, an object that is always elusive, always one step ahead of theory. Such an effort rests upon a recognition of "growing cultural differentiation and the multiplication of marginally situated forms of social agency as accompaniments of and potential modes of resistance to the homogenizing logic of global consumer society" (Smith, 1992: 503).

Finally, it should be noted that my reflections are made within the framework of my own account of postmodernism and that my attempt to represent this perspective is inexorably superficial, incomplete, and biased. Surely, then, the best way to speak of postmodernism is not to further develop my own reflections but rather to encourage others to speak/write their diverse narratives and stories of the everyday relations of power, domination, representation, resistance and struggle in sport, as they are articulated through a web of issues including age, race, class, ethnicity, dis/ability, gender and sexuality.

References

Agger, B. (1991). Critical theory, poststructuralism, postmodernism: Their sociological relevance. *Annual Review of Sociology, 17,* 105–131.

Agger, B. (1992). *Do Books Write Authors?* Durham, NC: Duke University Press.

Andrews, D. L. (1993). Desperately seeking Michel: Foucault's genealogy, the body, and critical sport sociology. *Sociology of Sport Journal, 10*(2), 148–167.

Andrews, D. L. (1996a). Deconstructing Michael Jordan: Reconstructing post-industrial America. *Sociology of Sport Journal, 12*(4), 315–318.

Andrews, D. L. (1996b). The fact(s) of Michael Jordan's blackness: Excavating a floating racial signifier. *Sociology of Sport Journal, 13*(2), 125–158.

Andrews, D. L. (1998a). Excavating Michael Jordan: Notes on a critical pedagogy of sporting representation. In: G. Rail (ed.), *Sport and Postmodern Times* (pp. 185–219). Albany, New York: State University of New York Press.

Andrews, D. L. (1998b). Feminizing Olympic reality: Preliminary dispatches from Baudrillard's Atlanta. *International Review for the Sociology of Sport, 33*(1), 5–18.

Andrews, D. L., & Cole, C. L. (1999). Performative cultures: Sport, masculinities, and consumption. *Men and Masculinities, 1*(3), 319–324.

Andrews, D. L., Jackson, S. J., & Mazur, Z. (1996). Jordanscapes: A preliminary analysis of the global popular. *Sociology of Sport Journal, 12*(4), 428–457.

Armstrong, E. G. (1996). The commodified 23, or, Michael Jordan as text. *Sociology of Sport Journal, 13*(4), 325–343.

Ashcroft, B., Griffiths, G., & Tiffin, H. (eds) (1995). *The Post-Colonial Studies Reader.* London: Routledge.

Balsamo, A. (1996). *Technologies of the Gendered Body: Reading Cyborg Women.* Durham and London: Duke University Press.

Barthes, R. (1975). *The Pleasure of the Text.* New York: Hill and Wang.

Barthes, R. (1977). *The Death of the Author* (Trans. Heath, S.) London: Fontana.

Baudrillard, J. (1981). *For a Critique of the Political Economy of the Sign.* St. Louis: Telos.

Baudrillard, J. (1983). *Simulations.* New York: Semiotext(e).

Baudrillard, J. (1988). *America.* New York: Verso.

Bhabha, H. K. (ed.) (1990b). *Nation and Narration.* London: Routledge.

Bhabha, H. K. (1994). *The Location of Culture.* London: Routledge.

Bhabha, H. K. (1995). Signs taken for wonders. In: B. Ashcroft, G. Griffiths and H. Tiffin (eds), *The Post-Colonial Studies Reader* (pp. 29–35). London and New York: Routledge.

Bordo, S. (1989). Reading the slender body. In: M. Jacobus, E. Fox Keller and S. Shuttleworth (eds), *Women, Science, and the Body Politic: Discourses and Representations* (pp. 83–112). New York: Methuen.

Bordo, S. (1992). Review essay: Postmodern subjects, postmodern bodies. *Feminist Studies, 18*(1), 159–175.

Brodribb, S. (1992). *Nothing Mat(t)ers: A Feminist Critique of Postmodernism.* Toronto, ON: James Lorimer and Co.

Bruce, T. (1998). Postmodernism and the possibilities for writing "vital" sports texts. In: G. Rail (ed.), *Sport and Postmodern Times* (pp. 3–19). Albany, New York: State University of New York Press.

Bruce, T., & Greendorfer, S. L. (1994). Postmodern challenges: Recognizing multiple standards for social science research. *Journal of Sport and Social Issues, 18*(2), 258–268.

Butler, J. (1990). *Gender Trouble.* New York: Routledge.

Butler, J. (1993). *Bodies that Matter: On the Discursive Limits of Sex.* New York: Routledge.

Butler, J. (1997). *Excitable Speech: A Politics of the Performative.* New York: Routledge.

Cixous, H. (1994). *The Hélène Cixous Reader* (ed. Sellers, S.) London and New York: Routledge.

Clifford, J. (1992). Traveling cultures. In: L. Grossberg, C. Nelson and P. Treichler (eds), *Cultural Studies* (pp. 96–116). New York and London: Routledge.

Cole, C. L. (1991). The politics of cultural representation: Visions of fields/fields of visions. *International Review for the Sociology of Sport, 26*(1), 37–51.

Cole, C. L. (1993). Resisting the canon: Feminist cultural studies, sport, and technologies of the body. *Journal of Sport and Social Issues, 17*(2), 77–97.

Cole, C. L. (1996). American Jordan: P.L.A.Y., consensus, and punishment. *Sociology of Sport Journal, 13*(4), 366–398.

Cole, C. L. (1998). Addiction, exercise, and cyborgs: Technologies of deviant bodies. In: G. Rail (ed.), *Sport and Postmodern Times* (pp. 261–275). Albany, New York: State University of New York Press.

Cole, C. L., & Hribar, A. (1995). Celebrity feminism: Nike style. Post-Fordism, transcendence, and consumer power. *Sociology of Sport Journal, 12*(4), 347–369.

Cole, C. L., & King, S. (1998). Representing black masculinity and urban possibilities: Racism, realism, and *Hoop Dreams*. In: G. Rail (ed.), *Sport and Postmodern Times* (pp. 49–86). Albany, New York: State University of New York Press.

Cole, C. L., & Rail, G. (1994). *La science comme pratique culturelle: vers une déstabilisation de l'objet des études du sport.* In: N. Midol, J. Lorant and C. Roggero (eds), *Sciences des activités physiques et sportives: Aspects épistémologiques, méthodologiques et impacts sociaux* (pp. 4–10). Paris and Nice: AFRAPS–LARESHAPS.

de Lauretis, T. (1994). *The Practice of Love: Lesbian Sexuality and Perverse Desire.* Bloomington, IN: Indiana University Press.

Deetz, S. (1992). *Democracy in an Age of Corporate Colonization.* Albany, New York: State University of New York Press.

Deleuze, G., & Guattari, F. (1972). *Anti-Oedipus: Capitalism and Schizophrenia.* New York: Viking.

Deleuze, G., & Guattari, F. (1987). *A Thousand Plateaus: Capitalism and Schizophrenia.* Minneapolis, MN: University of Minnesota Press.

Denzin, N. K. (1992). *Symbolic Interactionism and Cultural Studies: The Politics of Interpretation.* Oxford and Cambridge: Blackwell.

Denzin, N. K. (1994). The art and politics of interpretation. In: N. K. Denzin and Y. S. Lincoln (eds), *Handbook of Qualitative Research* (pp. 500–515). Thousand Oaks, CA: Sage.

Derrida, J. (1973). *Speech and Phenomena.* Evanston, IL: Northwestern University Press.

Derrida, J. (1976). *Of Grammatology* (Trans. Spivak, G.) Baltimore: Johns Hopkins University Press.

Derrida, J. (1978). *Writing and Difference.* Chicago: University of Chicago Press.

DiStefano, C. (1990). Dilemmas of difference: Feminism, modernity, and postmodernism. In: L. J. Nicholson (ed.), *Feminism/Postmodernism* (pp. 63–82). New York and London: Routledge.

Dobbin, M. (1998). *The Myth of the Good Corporate Citizen: Democracy Under the Rule of Big Business.* Toronto, ON: Stoddart.

Duquin, M. E. (1994). The body snatchers and Dr. Frankenstein revisited: Social construction and deconstruction of bodies and sport. *Journal of Sport and Social Issues, 18*(3), 268–281.

Dworkin, S. L., & Wachs, F. L. (1998). 'Disciplining the body': HIV-positive male athletes, media surveillance, and the policing of sexuality. *Sociology of Sport Journal, 15*(1), 1–20.

Elam, D. (1993). *Feminism and Deconstruction*. London: Routledge.

Finn, G. (1993). Why are there no great women postmodernists? In: V. Blundell, J. Sheperd and I. Taylor (eds), *Relocating Cultural Studies: Developments in Theory and Research* (pp. 123–152). London: Routledge.

Flax, J. (1990a). Postmodernism and gender relations in feminist theory. In: L. J. Nicholson (ed.), *Feminism/Postmodernism* (pp. 39–63). New York: Routledge.

Flax, J. (1992). Feminists theorize the political. In: J. Butler and J. W. Scott (eds), *Feminists Theorize the Political*. New York and London: Routledge.

Foley, D. E. (1992). Making the familiar strange: Writing critical sports narratives. *Sociology of Sport Journal, 9*(1), 36–47.

Foucault, M. (1972). *The Archeology of Knowledge and the Discourse on Language*. New York: Tavistock Publications and Harper Colophon.

Foucault, M. (1973a). *The Order of Things: An Archeology of the Human Sciences*. New York: Vintage Books.

Foucault, M. (1973b). *The Birth of the Clinic*. London: Tavistock.

Foucault, M. (1979). *Discipline and Punish: The Birth of the Prison*. New York: Vintage.

Foucault, M. (1981). *The History of Sexuality (Volume I: An Introduction)*. Harmondsworth: Pelican.

Foucault, M. (1986). *The History of Sexuality (Volume II: The Use of Pleasure)*. Harmondsworth: Viking.

Foucault, M. (1988). *The History of Sexuality (Volume II: The Care of the Self)*. Harmondsworth: Viking.

Fuss, D. (1995). Inside/Out. In: C. Caruth and D. Esch (eds), *Close Encounters: Reference and Responsibility in Deconstructive Writing*. New Brunswick, NJ: Rutgers University Press.

Haraway, D. J. (1985). A manifesto for cyborgs: Science, technology, and socialist-feminism in the 1980s. *Socialist Review, 80*, 65–107.

Haraway, D. J. (1991). *Simians, Cyborgs, and Women: The Reinvention of Nature*. New York: Routledge.

Haraway, D. J. (1997). *Modest_Witness@Second_Millennium. FemaleMan©_Meets_ OncoMouse™: Feminism and Technoscience*. New York and London: Routledge.

Harding, S. (ed.) (1987). *Feminism and Methodology*. Bloomington, IN: Indiana University Press.

Harding, S. (1990). Feminism, science, and the anti-enlightenment critiques. In: L. J. Nicholson (ed.), *Feminism/Postmodernism* (pp. 83–106). New York: Routledge.

Harding, S. (1998). *Is Science Multicultural? Postcolonialisms, Feminisms, and Epistemologies*. Bloomington, IN: Indiana University Press.

Hartsock, N. (1987). Rethinking modernism: Minority vs. majority theories. *Cultural Critique, 7*, 187–206.

Hartsock, N. (1990). Foucault on power: A theory for women? In: L. J. Nicholson (ed.), *Feminism/Postmodernism* (pp. 157–175). New York and London: Routledge.

Harvey, D. (1989). *The Condition of Postmodernity: An Enquiry into the Origins of Cultural Change*. Oxford: Basic Blackwell.

hooks, b. (1990). Marginality as site of resistance. In: R. Ferguson, M. Gever, T. T. Minh-ha and C. West (eds), *Out There: Marginalization and Contemporary Cultures* (pp. 341–344). New York and Cambridge: The New Museum of Contemporary Art and the Massachusetts Institute of Technology Press.

hooks, b. (1991). *Yearning: Race, Gender and Cultural Politics*. Boston: South End Press.

hooks, b. (1994). *Outlaw Culture: Resisting Representations*. New York and London: Routledge.

Hutcheon, L. (1989). *The politics of Postmodernism*. London: Routledge.

Irigarway, L. (1985a). *This Sex Which Is Not One* (Trans. C. Porter and C. Burke.) Ithaca, New York: Cornell University Press.

Irigarway, L. (1985b). *Speculum of the Other Woman* (Trans. Gill, G. C.) Ithaca, New York: Cornell University Press.

Jackson, S. J., & Andrews, D. L. (1999). The globalist of the all: The everywhere man, Michael Jordan and American popular culture in New Zealand. In: R. Sands (ed.), *Global Jocks: Anthropology, Sport and Culture*. Westport, CT: Greenwood Press.

Jaggar, A. M. (1992). Love and knowledge: Emotion in feminist epistemology. In: A. M. Jaggar and S. R. Bordo (eds), *Gender/Body/Knowledge: Feminist Reconstructions of Being and Knowing* (pp. 145–171). New Brunswick, NJ: Rutgers University Press.

Jameson, F. (1991). *Postmodernism, or, the Cultural Logic of Late Capitalism*. Durham, NC: Duke University Press.

Jencks, C. (1987). *Post-Modernism: The New Classicism in Art and Architecture*. London: Academy Editions.

Kellner, D. (1989). *Postmodernism, Jameson, Critique*. Washington: Maisonneuve Press.

King, A. (1996). The fining of Vinnie Jones. *International Review for the Sociology of Sport, 3*(2), 119–137.

Kohn, N., & Sydnor, S. (1998). 'How do you warm-up for a stretch class?': Sub/in/di/verting hegemonic tugs toward sport. In: G. Rail (ed.), *Sport and Postmodern Times* (pp. 21–32). Albany, New York: State University of New York Press.

Kristeva, J. (1982). *Desire in Language. A Semiotic Approach to Literature and Art* (Trans. T. Gora, A. Jardine and L. S. Roudiez). Oxford: Blackwell.

Kristeva, J. (1984). *Revolution in Poetic Language* (Trans. Waller, M.) New York: Columbia University Press.

Kristeva, J. (1986). *The Kristeva Reader* (ed. Moi, T.) Oxford: Blackwell.

Lacan, J. (1977). *Écrits*. London: Tavistock.

Lafrance, M. R. (1998). Colonizing the feminine: Nike's intersections of postfeminism and hyperconsumption. In: G. Rail (ed.), *Sport and Postmodern Times* (pp.117–139). Albany, New York: State University of New York Press.

Leitch, V. (1992). *Cultural Criticism, Literary Theory, Poststructuralism*. New York: Columbia University Press.

Lipietz, A. (1992). *Toward a New Economic Order: Postfordism, Ecology and Democracy*. New York: Oxford University Press.

Lorde, A. (1984). *Sister Outsider: Essays and Speeches*. Freedom, CA: Crossing Press.

Lorde, A. (1990). Age, race, class, and sex: Women redefining difference. In: R. Ferguson, M. Gever, T. T. Minh-ha and C. West (eds), *Out There: Marginalization and Contemporary Cultures* (pp. 281–289). New York and Cambridge: The New Museum of Contemporary Art and the Massachusetts Institute of Technology Press.

Lovibond, S. (1989). Feminism and postmodernism. *New Left Review, 178*, 5–28.

Lyotard, J. F. (1984). *The Postmodern Condition: A Report on Knowledge.* Minneapolis, MN: University of Minnesota Press.

Marchand, M. H. (1994). Latin American voices of resistance: Women's movements and development debates. In: S. J. Rosow, N. Inayatullay and M. Rupert (eds), *The Global Political Economy as Political Space.* Boulder, CO: Lynne Rienner.

Markula, P. (1995). Firm but shapely, fit but sexy, strong but thin: The postmodern aerobicizing female bodies. *Sociology of Sport Journal, 12*(4), 424–453.

Mascia-Lees, F. E., Sharpe, P., & Ballerino Cohen, C. (1989). The postmodern turn in anthropology. *Signs, 1*(Autumn), 7–33.

McDonald, M., & Birrell, S. (1999). Reading sport critically: A methodology for interrogating power. *Sociology of Sport Journal, 16*(4), 283–300.

Minh-ha, T. T. (1995). Writing postcoloniality and feminism. In: B. Ashcroft, G. Griffiths and H. Tifflin (eds), *The Postcolonial Studies Reader* (pp. 264–269). New York: Routledge.

Morgan, W. J. (1995). Incredulity toward metanarratives and normative suicide: A critique of postmodernist drifts in critical sport theory. *International Review for the Sociology of Sport, 30*(1), 25–45.

Piore, M., & Sabel, C. (1984). *The Second Industrial Divide: Possibilities for Prosperity.* New York: Basic Books.

Pronger, B. (1995). Rendering the body: The implicit lessons of gross anatomy. *Quest, 47*(4), 427–446.

Pronger, B. (1998). Post-sport: Trangressing boundaries in physical culture. In: G. Rail (ed.), *Sport and Postmodern Times* (pp. 277–298). Albany, New York: State University of New York Press.

Pronger, B. (1999). Outta my endzone: Sport and the territorial anus. *Journal of Sport and Social Issues, 23*(4), 373–389.

Rail, G. (1991a). *Technologie post-moderne et culture: Un regard sur le sport médiatisé.* In: F. Landry, M. Landry and M. Yerlès (eds), *Sport: The Third Millennium — Proceedings of the International Symposium* (pp. 731–739). Québec: Presses de l'Université Laval.

Rail, G. (1991b). The dissolution of polarities as a megatrend in postmodern sport. In: F. Landry, M. Landry and M. Yerlès (eds), *Sport: The Third Millennium — Proceedings of the International Symposium* (pp. 745–751). Québec: Presses de l'Université Laval.

Rail, G. (1995b). *Le Sport et la Condition Postmoderne. Sociologie et Sociétés, 27*(1), 139–150.

Rail, G. (ed.) (1998). *Sport and Postmodern Times.* Albany, New York: State University of New York Press.

Rail, G., & Harvey, J. (1995). Body at work: Michel Foucault and the sociology of sport. *Sociology of Sport Journal, 12*(2), 164–179.

Real, M. R. (1996). The postmodern Olympics: Technology and the commodification of the Olympic movement. *Quest, 48*(1), 9–24.

Redhead, S. (1998). Baudrillard, "Amérique", and the hyperreal World Cup. In: G. Rail (ed.), *Sport and Postmodern Times* (pp. 221–236). Albany, New York: State University of New York Press.

Richardson, L. (1992). The consequences of poetic representation: Writing the other, rewriting the self. In: C. Ellis and M. G. Flaherty (eds), *Investigating Subjectivity: Research on Lived Experience* (pp. 125–140). Newbury Park, CA: Sage.

Richardson, L. (1994). Writing: A method of inquiry. In: N. K. Denzin and Y. S. Lincoln (eds), *Handbook of Qualitative Research* (pp. 516–529). Thousand Oaks, CA: Sage.

Rinehart, R. (1998). Born-again sport: Ethics in biographical research. In: G. Rail (ed.), *Sport and Postmodern Times* (pp. 33–46). Albany, New York: State University of New York Press.

Said, E. (1993). *Culture and Imperialism.* New York: Random House.

Sedgwick, E. K. (1990). *The Epistemology of the Closet.* Berkeley: University of California Press.

Slowikowski, S. S. (1991). Burning desire: Nostalgia, ritual, and the sport-festival flame ceremony. *Sociology of Sport Journal, 8*(3), 239–257.

Slowikowski, S. S. (1993). Cultural performance and sport mascots. *Journal of Sport and Social Issues, 17*, 22–43.

Smith, D. E. (1990). *The Conceptual Practices of Power.* Toronto: University of Toronto Press.

Smith, M. P. (1992). Postmodernism, urban ethnography, and the new social space of ethnic identity. *Theory and Society, 21*, 493–531.

Smith, M. P., Tarallo, B., & Kagiwada, G. (1991). Colouring California: New Asian immigrant households, social networks, and the local state. *International Journal of Urban and Regional Research*, 250–268.

Spivak, G. C. (1987). *In Other Worlds: Essays in Cultural Politics.* New York: Methuen.

Spivak, G. C. (1995). Can the subaltern speak? In: B. Ashcroft, G. Griffiths and H. Tiffin (eds), *The Post-Colonial Studies Reader* (pp. 24–28). London and New York: Routledge.

Stranger, M. (1999). The aesthetics of risk: A study of surfing. *International Review for the Sociology of Sport, 34*(3), 265–276.

Sykes, H. (1998). Turning the closets inside/out: Towards a queer-feminist theory in women's physical education. *Sociology of Sport Journal, 15*(2), 154–173.

Theberge, N. (1991). Reflections on the body in the sociology of sport. *Quest, 43*(2), 123–134.

Tudiver, N. (1999). *Universities for Sale: Resisting Corporate Control over Canadian Higher Education.* Toronto, ON: James Lorimer & Company.

van Wynsberghe, & Ritchie, I. (1998). (Ir)relevant ring: The symbolic consumption of the Olympic logo in postmodern media culture. In: G. Rail (ed.), *Sport and Postmodern Times* (pp. 367–384). Albany, New York: State University of New York Press.

Weed, E., & Schor, N. (eds) (1997). *Feminism Meets Queer Theory*. Bloomington, IN: Indiana University Press.

Weedon, C. (1997). *Feminist Practice and Poststructuralist Theory*. London: Blackwell.

Whiteford, N., & Gruneau, R. (1993). Between the politics of production and the politics of the sign: Post-Marxism and "New Times". *Current Perspectives in Social Theory, 13*, 69–91.

Wood, P., Frascina, F., Harris, J., & Harrison, C. (1993). *Modernism in Dispute: Art Since the Forties*. London: The Open University.

Part III

Potential Syntheses

Chapter 9

Figurational Contributions to the Sociological Study of Sport

Eric Dunning

'Figurational' studies in the sociology of sport have now been carried out over more than four decades. In that time, the figurational tradition of sports studies has become reasonably well established in two countries — the United Kingdom[1] and the Netherlands[2] — and roots are beginning to be laid down in three more — France,[3] Canada[4] and Germany.[5] Norbert Elias was the founder. He was born in Breslau, Germany (which is now Wroclaw, Poland) in 1897. Elias was of Jewish descent. He left Germany in 1933 when the Nazis came to power, fleeing first to France, settling in England in 1935 and later becoming 'naturalized' as a British citizen. His mother was an Auschwitz victim but he survived the war, dying in Amsterdam in the Netherlands in 1990.

Elias spent his adult life striving to construct a reality-orientated, equally theory-centred and research-centred synthesis between a modified psycho-

---

[1] In the UK, there have so far been five generations of figurational sociologists of sport: (i) Norbert Elias; (ii) Eric Dunning; (iii) Patrick Murphy, Kenneth Sheard, and Ivan Waddington; (iv) Grant Jarvie and Joseph Maguire; (v) Sharon Colwell, Graham Curry, Dominic Malcolm, Louise Mansfield, Martin Roderick, and Stuart Smith. Christopher Brookes should perhaps be added to this list as should also Chris Rojek even though most of his work deals with leisure rather than sport. In the Far East, there is growing interest in this approach — see Kiku, 2001; Ichii, 2001; and Han, 2001.

[2] In the Netherlands, the main figurational sociologists of sport are Ruud Stokvis and Martin van Bottenberg.

[3] The main figurational sociologist of sport in France is Alain Garrigou of the University of Paris X, Nanterre.

[4] Kevin Young has endeavoured to introduce aspects of figurational thinking into his work but Michael Atkinson, an Assistant Professor of Sociology at Memorial University, is so far the most full-blown Canadian exponent of a figurational approach.

[5] See Michael Krüger, *Körperbildung und Nationalbildung*, Schorndorf: Karl Hofmann. Bero Rigauer has attempted to wed a figurational perspective with a Marxist one. See, for example, his 'Marxist Theories' in Jay Coakley and Eric Dunning (eds) (2000), *Handbook of Sports Studies*, London, Sage.

Theory, Sport & Society
Copyright © 2002 by Elsevier Science Ltd.
All rights of reproduction in any form reserved.
ISBN: 0-7623-0742-0

analysis and the best features of the classical and modern sociological traditions.[6] He attempted this because he strongly believed that such a synthesis would help practitioners of the subject:

i)   to withstand better the extreme shifts of ideological fashion, particularly political and philosophical shifts to which sociology has historically been subject. The most recent (which, of course, occurred mainly after Elias' death in 1990) is the shift towards 'postmodernism' and 'cultural studies', and involves the making of patently absurd claims such as that we are currently witnessing: 'the end of ideology' (Bell, 1961); 'the end of history' (Fukuyama, 1993); 'the end of racism' (D'Souza, 1995): that 'grand narratives are dead' (itself a grand narrative!); and that we now live in a world which is 'discontinuous' with the past (Giddens, 1984).

ii) to circumvent dualisms such as 'individual *versus* society' ('agency *versus* structure') and 'cooperation *versus* conflict' which have recurrently contributed to the fragmentation of sociology into rival schools such as those which promote 'action theory', 'symbolic interactionism', 'exchange theory', 'rational choice theory', 'structuralism', 'functionalism', 'conflict theory', etc. Dualistic thinking has also arguably contributed to the neglect of the study of sport in the parent discipline (Dunning, 1999). An example is provided by the 'work-leisure' dualism, the originally Puritan idea that human societies can be divided into two 'spheres'; a 'work sphere' which is valuable and productive, and a 'leisure sphere' which is basically 'a waste of time'. Seen in these terms, sport is part of the 'unproductive' leisure sphere, and a sport like soccer is conceived as 'nothing more' than twenty two players 'just kicking a ball about'. Such conceptualisations, unfortunately, remain paramount in sociology and arguably help to account for the fact that, despite its growing socio-cultural and socio-economic importance, the subject of sport hardly ever figures in general sociology textbooks.[7]

Elias also laid stress on the need to seek a balance between what he called 'involvement' and 'detachment' in sociological research, arguing that both — detachment *and* involvement — are necessary to obtain and accumulate reliable

---

[6] Also included in Elias' synthesis are elements of Gestalt theory, field theory and behaviourism.
[7] Anthony Giddens's *Society* (1997) is a good example of a text in which sport is not mentioned. This is surprising given that Giddens is a Tottenham Hotspur fan and that his 1961 MA thesis at the London School of Economics was on sport.

knowledge (Elias, 1987; Dunning, 1999).[8] In addition, Elias' synthesis was orientated towards the building-up of knowledge that is practically useful. He accordingly emphasised the construction of a sociology orientated towards the study of interdependencies and processes, especially long-term processes, and he condemned in this connection what he called 'the retreat of sociologists into the present' (Elias, 1983). It was another of Elias' contentions that the major forms of sociological explanation must be *relational* and, above all, *historical* in character; that is, they should involve references to relationships and ordered sequences over time (Abrams, 1982). Elias also developed a testable concept of power, holding it to be a universal property of human relations and best understood as relational and polymorphous (Elias, 1978; Dunning, 1999). In other words, he saw power as:

i)   a function of interdependency ties;
ii) a question of balances and ratios;
iii) not explainable satisfactorily solely by reference to single 'factors' such as ownership of the means of production or control of the means of violence. In addition, he took account of such bodily power resources of individuals as physical and intellectual strength. The reality-orientation of Elias' sociological synthesis is further underlined by the fact that, working together in the first instance with Eric Dunning, he was one of the pioneers of the sociology of sport (Dunning, 1971; Elias & Dunning, 1986).

Elias also paid rather more attention than is usual in sociology to what a human 'individual' is.[9] According to Elias, like the universe at large, each human person is a *process*. That is, biologically, we are born and, if we survive, we

---

[8]Briefly expressed, as Elias saw it, 'involvement' is necessary in sociological research for motivational purposes and as a source of detailed knowledge, whilst 'detachment' is necessary in order to avoid fantasy and ideology and to build-up a picture of things as they 'really are'. Elias spoke in this connection of the sciences — including the human and social sciences — as engaged in a quest to add to the 'object-adequacy' or 'reality-congruence' of human knowledge. It is a question, that is to say, of striving to make our representations — our concepts and theories — more 'adequate' as representations of, or more 'congruent with', what it is that we are trying to understand. Elias' position in this regard was based on a radical critique of the traditional dichotomy between 'subjectivity' and 'objectivity'. It is perhaps worth adding in this overall context that, in his training of post-graduate students, Elias invariably sought to persuade them to produce detached studies of an area of social life in which they were deeply involved. Thus, the actress, Ilse Seglow, produced a study of theatre, the photographer, Gisele Freund, a study of photography, and the university footballer, Eric Dunning, a study of football.
[9]Symbolic interactionism, based as it is largely on the works of writers such as G. H. Mead and C. H. Cooley, constitutes an obvious exception in this regard (see Chapter 4).

mature and eventually die. Whilst we are alive, not only do our bodies ingest food and drink, eliminate waste and automatically perform all sorts of vital functions, but we also constantly feel, think, move and act.[10] At the levels of personality, individual habitus and social habitus,[11] we also change and develop at a pace which is usually rapid in early life and slower later on. We are bound to others, furthermore, by fluid ties of interdependence which are a bio-social fact of life. That is, with the marginal exception of test-tube babies, we are born as a result of a/the sexual union between our parents. We also have a partly inborn tendency to seek the company of others, e.g., for sexual purposes but also as a pleasurable 'end-in-itself'. In addition we have an inborn capacity to speak languages but, just as we have to learn how to perform aspects of the sexual act, we also have to learn languages from other people. Another way of expressing this key fact would be to say that humans form dynamic '(con-)figurations' with each other.[12] Through this and similar formulations, Elias sought — I would argue on the whole successfully — to circumvent what philosophically-minded sociologists such as Giddens (1984) call 'the agency-structure' dilemma. That is a difficulty which philosophers have encountered for centuries and which sociologists have faced since the eighteenth/nineteenth centuries when their subject began to part from philosophy (Kilminster, 1999). It is the problem of coming up with formulations of the 'individual-society' relationship which avoid 'reductionism' on the one hand and 'reification' on the other, whilst simultaneously doing justice to both the individual and the social sides of the equation.[13]

The concept of figurations can be applied equally to such interdependency ties as those within and among 'dyads' (two-person groups), 'triads' (three-person groups),[14] small groups of varying sizes, cities, classes, tribes, ethnic groups, nations, nation-states and, indeed, humanity as a whole. Accordingly, it is a concept which points a way towards bridging the gap in sociology between explanations at the 'micro', 'meso' and 'macro' levels of social integration. It

---

[10]Even sleeping involves forms of movement, thinking and feeling — e.g., tossing and turning and dreaming.

[11]For Elias, each of us develops an individual habitus which is unique, as well as a series of social habituses — e.g., class, gender, and national habituses — which are shared with others who have been habituated through similar experiences and to common standards.

[12]After initially using the term 'configuration', Elias eventually settled on 'figuration' because the prefix 'con' (with) is literally redundant in phrases such as: 'the (con)figurations that interdependent human beings form with one another'.

[13]'Reification' is also called 'the fallacy of misplaced concreteness'. Philosophers deal with this issue under the heading of 'nominalism versus 'realism'.

[14]The reference here is to the concept developed by the nineteenth century German philosopher/sociologist, Georg Simmel, and not to Chinese criminal gangs!

does so by showing that these 'levels' are, at best, convenient fictions, and at worst, obstacles to understanding. Elias also succeeded in developing formulations which avoid the tendency to dichotomise 'body' and 'mind', that is to see humans as split into two: a 'physical' body and a separate 'spirit', 'mind' or 'soul'. More particularly, he conceptualised humans as a species of symbol-forming animals who are bodily equipped to 'feel' as well as 'think' and 'act', and which depend less than other animals on inherited drives and more on social learning (Elias, 1978).

Elias considered himself to be a human scientist (*Menschenwissenschaftler*). As such, to use the words of Johan Goudsblom (1977), he concerned himself with studying humans 'in the round'; that is, in their bio-, psycho-, socio-historical aspects and with the complex, not well understood ways in which these aspects are interconnected. Given such an orientation, it is not perhaps surprising that Elias made pioneering contributions to the sociological study of sport. He did not share the view of sport as a 'physical realm' of lesser value than the 'realm of mind' but, on the contrary, saw it as a kind of 'natural laboratory' for shedding light on key aspects of human existence — including, for instance, the universal but variable tension-balance between conflict and cooperation[15] — as well as constituting a problem area which merits investigation in its own right. However, since it is generally acknowledged that what he called the theory of 'civilising processes' is Elias' major contribution to the field, it is to that theory that my attention will now be turned.

The Theory of Civilising Processes[16]

Contrary to a popular misconception (Smith, 2001), Elias did not use the concept of a civilising process in a morally evaluative way. It was, for him, a technical term. That is, he did not suggest that people who can be shown to stand at a later, more advanced level in a civilising process than some others are in any meaningful sense 'better than' or 'morally superior to' the latter. That, of course, is almost invariably how the former view themselves. Many of the latter correlatively internalise a conception of themselves as 'inferior' (Elias & Scotson, 1965/1994).

The theory of civilising processes is a complex, in equal parts theoretical

---

[15]See, for example, the discussion of this issue by Elias and Dunning in relation to sport in their 'Dynamics of Sport Groups' (Dunning, 1971; Elias & Dunning, 1986).

[16]The plural, 'civilising processes', is used here in order to signal that there are differences between, for instance, the English, French, Dutch, and German civilising processes, as well as between those of, for instance, India and China. In short, Elias was not proposing some kind of linear progress theory.

and empirical construct. It was derived through a synthesis of deduction and induction in the course of an examination of a substantial body of data, principally books on manners from the Middle Ages to modern times. These indicate that, in the societies of Western Europe between the Middle Ages and the early decades of the twentieth century, a long-term process took place involving the elaboration and refinement of manners and social standards, together with an increase in the social pressure on people to exercise stricter, more continuous and more even self-control over their feelings and behaviour. As part of this unplanned process, there occurred a shift in the balance between external constraints and self-constraints in favour of self-constraints and, at the levels of personality and habitus,[17] an increase in the importance of 'conscience' or, in Freudian terms 'superego', as a regulator of behaviour. That is, social standards came to be internalised more deeply and to operate, not simply consciously and with an element of choice, but also beneath the levels of rationality and conscious control. An example would be the automatic arousal of feelings of anxiety, guilt and shame, often but not invariably accompanied by blushing, which takes place in the modern West when people see others violating a deeply internalised taboo or when they are seen violating one themselves, e.g., urinating or defecating in public.

An aspect of this process, which is of central relevance for understanding the development of modern sport, has been the increasing control of violence and aggression (Elias, 1939, 2000; Dunning, 1999). According to Elias, this took place together with a long-term decline in most people's capacity for obtaining pleasure from directly taking part in and/or directly witnessing violent acts. Elias refers in this connection to a 'dampening of *Angriffslust*' — literally to a dampening down or curbing of the lust for attacking; that is, a taming of people's conscious desire to obtain pleasure from attacking others and a reduction at the level of habitus in their capacity for doing so. This process has entailed at least two things:

i)   A lowering of what Elias called the 'threshold of repugnance' regarding bloodshed and other manifestations/consequences of physical violence, especially direct ones, but also involving, in some cases, manifestations of violence of a symbolic, pictorially, cinematically or televisually represented kind. As a result, according to Elias, most people nowadays tend to recoil more readily in the presence of such manifestations than may have been the case with people in the European Middle Ages.

[17]The concept of habitus has been popularised in recent years by Pierre Bourdieu, (see, for example, his *Distinction*, 1984). It was, however, a standard term in German Sociology before the Nazi era and was used by Elias in the first (1939) edition of *Über den Prozess der Zivilisation* (Basle, Haus zum Falken). In Elias' usage, it means 'second nature' or 'embodied social learning'.

ii) The internalisation of a stricter taboo on the use of violence. A consequence of this is that guilt-feelings are liable to be aroused in a person who violates this taboo. At the same time, said Elias, there has occurred a tendency to 'push violence behind the scenes' and, as part of this, to describe people who, like medieval knights, continue openly to derive pleasure from direct (as opposed to 'mimetic' [Elias & Dunning, 1986]) violence in terms of the language of psychopathology and to treat or punish them by means of stigmatisation, hospitalisation, imprisonment, or a combination of all three.

In popular understanding, the terms 'violence' and 'civilisation' are usually taken to be anti-theses, but the civilising processes of Western Europe were seen by Elias as the unplanned outcomes of violent struggles for supremacy among monarchs and other feudal lords. Elias called these struggles 'hegemonial', 'elimination' or 'survival struggles'. These struggles led — at different times, different rates and in more or less greatly differing ways — to the establishment within the emergent European nation–states of relatively stable and effective state monopolies of what Elias regarded as the twin major means of ruling: violence and taxation. In other words, states which remained externally embattled at each stage — and it is crucial to remember that external embattlement was emphasised by Elias — became increasingly pacified internally. That is to say, modern nation–states were formed largely for purposes of war.

Another way of putting it would be to say that, far from being simple anti-theses, violence and civilisation are interdependent in specific ways. More particularly, it was Elias' contention that a civilising process depends on the establishment of an effective monopoly of tax and violence at the centre and that this, in turn, facilitates among other things the following complex of developments: internal pacification, a lengthening (e.g., through trade) of what Elias called 'interdependency chains', an equalising change in the balance of power between classes and other groups — Elias (1978) referred to this as 'functional democratisation' — and economic growth. Forms of reciprocal 'cause and effect' between these part-processes were involved as well. For example, economic growth increased the revenue available to states through their tax monopolies, thus providing the wherewithal for state agents to buttress still further the monopolies of violence, and so on and so forth. At the risk of over-simplification, one could express Elias' theory by saying that he held civilising processes basically to be a function of state-formation, growing social differentiation, growing equality of power chances, and growing wealth. He also showed how, in the course of a civilising process, overtly violent hegemonial struggles tend to be transformed into relatively peaceful struggles for prestige and power in which, in the most frequent course of events, destructive urges are kept for the most part beneath the threshold of consciousness and not translated into overt action.

Established-Outsider Figurations

A theory closely related to the theory of civilising processes, especially to its stress on power, inequality and conflict, was called by Elias the theory of 'established-outsider figurations'. It grew most directly out of a study by Elias and John Scotson of a dominance-subordination figuration formed by two working class groups in a suburb of Leicester, a city in the English East Midlands (Elias & Scotson, 1965, 1994). According to Elias, these groups were near enough identical in terms of all conventional indices of social stratification (incomes, occupations, education), differing only in the fact that the 'established' group had lived in the community for several generations, whilst the 'outsiders' were relative newcomers. Yet a constellation of symptoms normally associated with class or racial/ethnic hostility and oppression was detectable in the relations between them. This led Elias to suggest that:

> As a rule, one encounters this kind of figuration in connection with ethnic, national and group differences (such as those between classes). . . . But here in Winston Parva the full armoury of group superiority and group contempt was mobilized in the relations between two groups who were different only in regard to the duration of their residence. . . . Here, one could see that 'oldness' of association . . . was, on its own, able to create the degree of group cohesion, the collective identification, the commonality of norms which are apt to induce the gratifying euphoria that goes with the consciousness of belonging to a group of higher value and with the complementary contempt for other groups (Elias & Scotson 1994: xvii).

According to Elias, the power of the 'established' group in 'Winston Parva' thus primarily depended on the fact that the length of time or 'oldness' of their association had enabled them to develop greater cohesion than the 'outsiders', many of whom started as strangers to each other, and this, in turn, enabled members of the 'established' group to monopolise, for example, official positions in local associations. Such greater cohesion of 'established' relative to 'outsider' groups is, Elias suggested, a common, 'purely figurational' component of power relations. Dunning (1999) has used this theory in an attempt to illuminate some of the problems of race and sport.

Although there is much more that could be said on the theory of civilising processes, the theory of established-outsider figurations and other aspects of Elias' work, I have now reached a point at which it is appropriate to consider, at some length, the contributions of figurational sociologists to the sociological study of sport.

Figurational Contributions to the Sociological Study of Sport

Figurational studies in the sociology of sport have so far been mainly concerned with making a contribution to understanding in nine problem areas: the development of modern sport in the context of European civilising processes;[18] the growing socio–cultural centraility of sport and its correlative 'monetarisation' (commodification, commercialisation, professionalisation);[19] football (soccer) hooliganism and sports spectator violence more generally;[20] the 'globalisation'/ international spread of sports;[21] sport and gender;[22] sport and 'race';[23] the dynamics of sport groups;[24] sport and drugs;[25] and the social aspects of sports injuries.[26] Given limited space, some of these problem areas will be dealt with at greater length and in greater detail than others.

The Development of Modern Sport

According to Elias (1971, 1986), the term 'sport' can be used in two main ways: in a general sense, to refer to non-work related forms of physical activity, with or without an element of competition. In terms of this rather abstract usage, sport is

[18]See, especially, Elias and Dunning (1986); Dunning and Rojek (1992); and Dunning (1999) for discussions of this issue. See also Dunning and Sheard (1979).

[19]See especially, Dunning and Sheard (1979); and Dunning (1999).

[20]Football hooliganism is discussed especially in Dunning, Murphy, and Williams; (1988), Williams, Dunning, and Murphy (1984, 1989); and Murphy, Williams, and Dunning (1990). See also Elias and Dunning (1986); Dunning and Rojek (eds) (1992); and Dunning (1999).

[21]See, especially, Maguire (1999).

[22]See, especially, Dunning in Elias and Dunning (1986); Dunning (1999); and Dunning and Maguire (1996).

[23]See, especially, Dunning (1999).

[24]See, especially, Elias and Dunning (1986); and Dunning (1999).

[25]See, especially, Waddington (2000).

[26]See, especially, Waddington (2000).

a socio–cultural universal. However, the term can also be used more concretely to refer to a group of competitive physical activities which are specifically modern in key respects and which first began to emerge in Britain and Ireland, above all in England, in the eighteenth and nineteenth centuries. Following Elias, figurational sociologists tend to favour the second definition.

It is Elias' contention that the word 'sport' first acquired its modern meaning in eighteenth century England. Aristocratic and gentry groups were centrally involved in this process of language development and it occurred, Elias suggested, correlatively with: (i) a change of habitus and, above all, conscience among these ruling groups; and (ii) a highly specific set of changes in English society at large. Elias coined the process term 'sportisation' as a shorthand way of conveying the central meaning of this complex set of changes which were, he claimed, closely connected with the English variant of the overall European civilising process. More particularly, Elias used the term 'sportisation' to refer to a process in the course of which the rules of sports came more and more to be written down, nationally (subsequently internationally) standardised, more explicit, more precise, more comprehensive, orientated around an ethos of 'fair play' and providing equal chances for all to win, and with eliminating, reducing and/or more strictly controlling opportunities for violent physical contact.[27] Non-playing officials such as referees, umpires, timekeepers and judges with an array of sport-specific sanctions such as 'penalties' and 'free kicks' at their disposal also began to be introduced and, at the same time, sportspersons began to be expected, in line with the direction of the overall national civilising process, to exercise stricter, more even and more continuous self-control both on and off the field of play. In the game-contests that came to be known as 'sports', a flexible balance also began to be established between the possibility of obtaining a high level of pleasurable combat- or contest-tension and what was regarded as reasonable protection against the chances of injury. This pleasurable contest-tension began to be described as 'good sport'.

Elias' explanation of why processes of sportisation occurred first of all in England goes beyond the 'economistic' explanation in terms of the 'industrial revolution' offered by Marxists such as Rigauer (1981), Brohm (1978) and Hargreaves (1986). It also goes beyond Guttmann's (1978) hypothesis of a correlation between the 'sports revolution' and the 'scientific revolution' by adding

---

[27]Sportisation processes and other forms of civilising process do not take place in a simple, linear and continuously 'progressive' manner. For example, short-term increases in violence frequently occur. If powerful groups respond to them by the imposition of civilising controls and these succeed, the overall process will continue in a civilising direction. If powerful groups do not respond in this way or if they attempt to respond and fail, changes in a de-civilising direction are liable to gather momentum.

references to comparative social structural and 'political' developments, especially processes of state-formation, into the equation. More particularly, Elias notes how Germany and Italy remained relatively disunited until well into the nineteenth century, while France and England became relatively united nationally as early as the seventeenth and eighteenth centuries. France, however, had become highly centralised and its people subject to a form of 'absolutist rule', one aspect of which was that the right of subjects 'to form associations of their own choosing was usually restricted . . . if not abolished' (Elias in Elias & Dunning, 1986: 38; Dunning, 1999). In England, by contrast, movement towards a highly centralised, 'absolutist' state was more or less destroyed in the seventeenth century by the Civil War (1632–1649) and the so-called 'Glorious Revolution' (1688). In that context, the country became caught up in a serious 'cycle of violence'. One consequence of these, what were among other things, early symptoms of democratisation, was the placing of restrictions on the powers of the monarch. Similarly, the reliance placed by the island-dwelling English on naval force meant that the sort of large centralised bureaucracy required to coordinate an army geared to defending land frontiers did not develop. In ways such as these, a variety of processes contributed in England to the landed classes retaining a high degree of autonomy *vis à vis* the monarchical state and also, *via* parliament, sharing with the monarch in the tasks of ruling (Dunning, 1999).

Further to this, according to Elias, as the feelings associated with the seventeenth century 'cycle of violence' began to calm down, the habitus of members of the English ruling classes underwent a 'civilising spurt', a process marked most notably in the emergence of ritualised political party forms of ruling. In the words of Elias:

> Military skills gave way to the verbal skills of debate . . . rhetoric and persuasion . . . which required greater restraint all round. . . .
> It was this change, the greater sensitivity with regard to the use of violence which, reflected in the social habitus of individuals, also found expression in the development of their pastimes. The 'parliamentarisation' of the landed classes of England had its counterpart in the 'sportisation' of their pastimes (Elias in Elias & Dunning, 1986: 34).

This initial sportisation of pastimes occurred in two main waves: an eighteenth century wave in which the principal pastimes which began to emerge as modern sports were boxing, cricket, fox-hunting and horse-racing; and a nineteenth century wave in which soccer, rugby, hockey, tennis, athletics and water sports, such as rowing and swimming, began to take on modern forms (Dunning, 1999; Elias & Dunning, 1986). Members of the aristocracy and gentry were primarily responsible for developments in the first wave; whilst in the second, members of the bourgeoisie — the industrial, commercial and professional middle classes — joined the landed classes in taking the lead. 'Clubs' were the organisational form of the first wave; 'associations' and 'unions' of the second (Dunning, 1999).

'Sport' in the Ancient and Early Modern Worlds

During the 1960s, Elias and Dunning began to test the hypothesis that central aspects of the early development of modern sports can be understood as a civilising process by undertaking comparative and developmental examinations of the Ancient Greek and Roman equivalents of modern sports (Elias [1971, 1986] called them 'agonistic game contests'), especially boxing, wrestling and 'the pankration' — an Ancient Greek equivalent of today's 'ultimate fighting'.[28] They also looked at the 'folk games' and other 'sports' of Medieval Europe, especially 'football', Cornish 'hurling', Welsh 'knappan' and their continental European equivalents (Dunning, 1999). What these studies revealed was that the sport-like activities of people at earlier stages in a civilising process differed considerably from the sports of today. Elias (1971, 1986) demonstrated, for example, how the agonistic games of Ancient Greece were used as a direct training for war and were based on a warrior ethos rather than an ethos of fairness. Hence, they involved higher levels of socially tolerated violence than are publicly permitted in sports today. In the pankration, for example, the contestants would bite and scratch and gouge out each others' eyes. In Greek boxing, there were no weight classes, and dodging and feinting were regarded as 'cowardly' with the consequence that boxers would stand toe-to-toe and slog it out. This is the sort of thing that Elias' theory of civilising processes would lead one to expect. The city–states of Ancient Greece were patriarchal societies with slave economies. They went frequently to war, were characterised internally by high levels of physical and material inequality and insecurity and were ruled by warrior elites. All this was reflected in the conscience and habitus of their people; above all, the fact that most of them had a lower threshold of repugnance regarding physical violence than tends to be the case among the peoples of Western Europe today.

In their work on the folk games of medieval and early modern Europe, Elias

---

[28]For a short figurational account of 'ultimate fighting', see Marc Howes, *Figurations*, No. 11, June, 1999.

and Dunning (Dunning, 1961; Elias & Dunning, in Dunning, 1971; Elias & Dunning, 1986) painted a broadly similar picture. More particularly, they showed how such games were not highly regulated and were played according to localised, orally transmitted customs rather than centrally determined written rules. They were also played over open countryside as well as through the streets of towns. Further to this, the numbers of participants were indeterminate and not equalised between the contending sides. Finally, these games involved a higher level of open violence than would be tolerated in comparable games today. In fact, although they were 'mock' or 'play-fights', they were considerably closer to 'real' or 'serious' fighting than their present-day counterparts are most of the time.

Elias and Dunning's work on the early development of football was extended by Dunning and Sheard in *Barbarians, Gentlemen and Players: A Sociological Study of the Development of Rugby Football* (1979).[29] In this book, using rugby as their principal example but dealing also with the bifurcation of rugby and soccer, the authors tackled four main themes: (i) the development of 'more civilised' team games; (ii) the trend towards the commercialisation and professionalisation of top-level sport; (iii) the correlative trend towards the cultural centrality of sport and the increasing seriousness of player and spectator involvement; and (iv) 'football (soccer) hooliganism'. This latter theme was treated only hypothetically in that context but the hypotheses that were formulated served as the basis of the 1980s work on football (soccer) hooliganism by what came to be known as 'the Leicester School'. Let me take the argument one step further by dealing with the first three of these issues.

Sport in the 'Civilising Process': The Incipient 'Modernisation' of Football and the Early 'Civilising' of the Game

In *Barbarians, Gentlemen and Players*, Dunning and Sheard sought to show how the incipient 'modernisation' and 'civilisation' of football took place in the English public schools in the first part of the nineteenth century as part of the second wave of 'sportisation'. This analysis was subsequently taken further by Dunning (1999) and further still by Curry (2001). At that time, there were seven public schools in England: Charterhouse, Eton, Harrow, Rugby, Shrewsbury, Westminster and Winchester. During the eighteenth and early nineteenth centuries,

---

[29]In his unpublished Ph.D thesis, 'Football: A Study in Diffusion' (University of Leicester, 2001), Graham Curry provides a more soccer-orientated counterpart of Sheard and Dunning's (1979), *Barbarians, Gentlemen and Players*.

these schools were transformed into fee-charging boarding establishments for boys from the upper and upper-middle classes. Two main consequences followed from this: (i) the class discrepancy between teachers and pupils inherent in the structure of a type of school where middle-class classical scholars endeavoured to cater for the parentally perceived educational needs of boys who mostly came from higher social backgrounds than themselves, meant that the teachers were unable to prevent the emergence of forms of boy self-rule; (ii) this class discrepancy also implied a power and status gap, and this contributed to chronic problems of indiscipline, regular bullying and not infrequent rebellions by the boys. The result was the gradual crystallisation of a system of dual control involving the dominance of senior over junior boys which came to be known as the 'prefect-fagging system' (Dunning & Sheard, 1979; Dunning, 1999).

This system was central to the early development of football. One of the customary duties which developed for the juniors or 'fags' was that of 'fagging out' at football. Fags were compelled to play and, unless they showed precocious courage and/or skill, were forced to play 'in goal', i.e., they were ranged *en masse* along the base lines. Public school football at that stage was based on oral rules and, by present standards, it was physically violent. The older boys would kick and trample on each other and the fags, and some of the former played in iron-tipped boots. At Rugby, they called them 'navvies'. According to a former Rugby pupil reminiscing in the 1920s, navvies had 'a thick sole, the profile of which at the toe much resembled the ram of an ironclad' (Dunning & Sheard, 1979: 55–57).

During the 1840s, newer forms of football, more appropriate to the emergent social conditions of an urbanising and industrialising society in which state-formation and civilisation were advancing, began to develop in the public schools. Centrally involved in this process were: (i) the committing of rules to writing; (ii) stricter demarcation and limiting of the size of pitches; (iii) the imposition of stricter limitations on the duration of matches; (iv) a reduction in the numbers taking part; (v) an equalisation in the size of contending teams;[30] and (vi) stricter regulation of the kinds and degrees of physical force that it was legitimate to use. It was in the course of this process that the soccer and rugby ways of playing began to emerge out of the matrix of locally differentiated public school games.

According to currently available data, the first public school to commit its football rules to writing was Rugby in 1845. The main precondition for the

---

[30]Adrian Harvey (1999) and John Goulstone (2000) have recently shown that football matches between teams of variable but equal size developed outside the public schools first. Such matches were mainly pub-related and stake money was usually involved.

occurrence of this process was reform of the prefect-fagging system there. This occurred under Thomas Arnold, Rugby Headmaster from 1828 to 1842. What Arnold achieved was the transformation of the Rugby variant of the prefect-fagging system from a system of dual control which was conducive to recurrent disorder, into a system of indirect rule which was conducive to greater harmony, both in staff-student relations and in those among the boys. Also achieved was the preservation of a substantial measure of self-rule for the boys. It was a 'Sixth Form Levee' (an assembly of the senior boys) which produced the written rules of 1845, and among the principal objectives which they hoped to achieve through this process of codification were: (i) legitimation of carrying the ball, or 'running in', a practice which had begun to grow more frequent in football at Rugby in the 1830s;[31] (ii) a reduction in the violence of the game, especially by placing restrictions on the practice of 'hacking over', i.e., kicking opposing players on the shins and knocking them to the ground; and (iii) elimination of the use of dangerous footwear. Both the reform of the prefect-fagging system at Rugby and the incipient modernisation of football which started there were small-scale 'civilising processes'.

The second public school to commit its football rules to writing — again according to the currently available data — was Eton in 1847, two years after Rugby. Interestingly, the Eton rules were in some ways diametrically opposite to their Rugby counterparts. More particularly, whilst carrying the ball and scoring by kicking above H-shaped posts were legislated for by the 1845 Rugby rules, the 1847 Eton rules decreed that carrying and striking the ball by hand were taboo, and that goals were to be scored by kicking the ball beneath an imaginary crossbar.

Why should the Eton boys have wanted to produce a game of this sort? Under Arnold, the fame of Rugby had begun to spread and, with it, the fame of their way of playing football. By developing a game which was equally distinctive but in key respects diametrically opposite to the Rugby game, it seems reasonable to suppose that the higher class Etonians were seeking to put the 'upstart Rugby provincials' in their place. If this hypothesis has any substance, it means that the compulsion leading to the initial bifurcation of soccer and Rugby stemmed from status rivalry between the leading English public school and what was, in the mid-nineteenth century, its leading contender (Dunning & Sheard, 1979; Dunning 1999).

[31]There is a widely believed myth that Rugby football originated from a single deviant act by a single individual. His name was William Webb Ellis and he is said to have inaugurated the game in 1823 by cheating through picking up and running with the ball. For a sociological critique of this myth, see Dunning and Sheard, 1979.

Growing 'Cultural Centrality' and the 'Monetarisation'
(Commercialisation and Professionalisation) of Modern Sport

In Britain and Ireland, starting in the 1850s, the embryonic soccer and rugby games spread into the wider society and became, like, for example, cricket, which had already become so in the eighteenth century, status-enhancing activities for adult 'gentlemen'. Two developments in particular underpinned this process: (i) an expansion of the middle classes and, with it, of the number of public schools. This was basically a consequence of continuing industrialisation, urbanisation, state-formation and 'civilisation'; and (ii) an educational transformation usually referred to as the 'public school games cult' (Marples, 1954; Mangan, 1981, 2000). What happened in this latter connection was that sports came to dominate the public school curriculum, the best sportsmen among the boys (the 'bloods') became an elite, and demonstrable sporting prowess (e.g., having been an Oxford or Cambridge 'blue') became as or more important than academic qualifications in securing a teaching position at a public school. Underlying this games cult was a belief that games, especially team games, are character-forming and more important than academic subjects for instilling into boys qualities such as leadership, subordination of self in the pursuit of collective goals, and fair play, qualities which were regarded as vital for the administration and defence of the expanding British Empire (Dunning, 1961).

The public school games cult represented an early stage in the growing cultural centrality and rising social significance of sport. As it continued, this process involved sport becoming an issue to which increasing time and space began to be devoted in the print and electronic media. It also became an issue of growing political concern, and can be said to have begun taking on increasingly the characteristics of a secular, non-theological 'religion' in Durkheim's (1915) sense (Dunning, 1979; Dunning & Sheard, 1979; Dunning in Elias & Dunning, 1986).

As the modern forms of sport grew culturally more central and socially more significant, so they became more popular and more exploitable for purposes of economic gain. As a result, they also underwent processes of commercialisation, professionalisation, and 'monetarisation' in the sense of generating cash in large amounts and becoming more and more subject to the constraints of what economists call 'the market'. Correlatively with all of this, sports grew more characterised by serious involvement. In short, modern sports ceased, especially at the top levels, to be forms of play and underwent processes of 'de-amateurisation' (Dunning & Sheard, 1979). This complex of processes is rightly seen by Marxists as a consequence of the capitalist mode of production (Rigauer, 1969, 1981; Hoch, 1972; Brohm, 1978; Hargreaves, 1986). However, figurational sociologists attribute it additionally to what Elias (1978) called 'functional democratisation' — that is, the reciprocal pressures and controls to which people become increasingly subject as chains of inter-dependence grow longer and denser. Thus, top-level sportspersons in modern societies are no longer independent and able to participate solely for 'fun'; that is, they are no longer able to play in order to please themselves. The sheer numbers of people involved in modern sports mean that achievement-orientation, a striving for success, is necessary if one is to stand a realistic chance of getting to the top. Moreover, top-level sportspersons can no longer participate just for themselves but are representatives of wider communities such as cities, counties and nations. This means that they are increasingly constrained to provide the sorts of satisfactions demanded by their patrons, 'owners', and supporters. For example, they are expected to provide them with pleasurable excitement and the satisfaction that comes from supporting a successful team. That is, top-level sportspeople have to validate in competition the community with which their supporters and patrons identify (Dunning & Sheard, 1976, 1979; Dunning in Elias & Dunning, 1986). More recently, Dunning has used this line of reasoning to urge the need for distinguishing between nine different types of sports professionalism (Dunning, 1999: 114).

Given such pressures, it is not surprising, according to Dunning and Sheard (1979: 272–89), that top-level sportsmen and women sometimes resort to the calculated use of illegitimate violence in order to achieve victory. This seems, at first sight, to be a contradiction of Elias' theory of civilizing processes. However, Dunning (in Elias & Dunning, 1986: 237) suggests that, in the course of a civilising process, there occurs in conjunction with an increase in socially produced competitive pressures, an increase in people's tendency and ability to renounce immediate gratification and to plan, use foresight and longer-term means for securing their goals. In this context, the deliberate, 'rational' use of violence to secure advantage or victory in a game is consistent with the personality and habitus of people today who consider themselves to be 'civilised' because it involves a high degree of control, relatively little pleasure from directly inflicting pain and is utilised in the achievement of specific ends. According to Dunning, in fact, in the course of a civilizing process, there tends to take place a shift in the balance between 'expressive' (affective) and 'instrumental' (rational) violence in favour of the latter (1986: 227). This is an appropriate point at which to turn to a discussion of the work on football hooliganism of 'the Leicester School'.

Football Hooliganism

The research findings of the Leicester group are set forth at greatest length in *The Roots of Football Hooliganism* (Dunning *et al.*, 1988).[32] These findings are essentially twofold:

(i) that what had been up until that time the dominant media, political and academic view was inadequate in crucial ways, above all in the belief that football hooliganism was an entirely recent phenomenon, a product of the 'permissiveness' of the 1960s with no precedents, forerunners or equivalents in the past at all. Counter to this, the Leicester group sought to demonstrate that, although they were not named as such until the 1950s/1960s, forms of hooligan-like crowd disorders had taken place in the context of British football since at least the 1870s and 1880s, the period when the modern professional game first started to emerge. They had encountered references to instances of these in their earlier researches and, so, using the records of the Football Association and data culled systematically from a variety of national and local newspapers, they gathered a body of data which enabled them to substantiate that every form of behaviour which, by the 1980s, had come to be labelled as 'football hooliganism' by the media and politicians — missile throwing, pitch invasions, attacks on match officials, attacks on visiting players, fights between rival fan groups — can be shown to have taken place in every decade since the 1870s/1880s, though at varying rates.

More particularly, it was shown that, plotted graphically, the incidence of reported 'football hooliganism' from the 1870s/1880s to the 1980s followed a U-shaped curve and that the balance between different reported types changed especially after World War II when improved transport and growing affluence formed pre-conditions for an increase of fan travel to away matches. That is to say, whilst sometimes serious attacks on match officials and opposing players predominated before the First World War, fights between opposing fan groups came to predominate from the mid-1960s. These fights were sometimes, but not invariably, as seriously violent as the media depicted them.

(ii) that English football hooligans come from all levels in the class hierarchy but that the overwhelming majority, some 80–85 percent, come from the 'rougher' sections of the working class. More particularly, according to 'the

---

[32]Joseph Maguire wrote his Ph.D thesis as part of this research under the supervision of Eric Dunning. See his *The Limits of Decent Partisanship: A Sociogenetic Investigation of the Emergence of Football Spectating as a Social Problem* (Ph.D, University of Leicester, 1985). Much valuable evidence was gleaned for the Leicester team by Maguire who also succeeded imaginatively in locating the problem of football hooliganism in the context of the 'civilising offensives' of English middle class groups such as the 'rational recreationists'.

Leicester School', if they are employed, football hooligans tend to work in manual occupations, especially manual occupations that require only low levels of formal education. They also tend to come from neighbourhoods that are characterised by the following constellation of interacting structural characteristics: relative poverty; mother-centred families; high levels of sex/gender and age-group segregation; male dominance; and, a tendency for children to be socialised as much if not more on the streets by older children and their age-peers than by parents and teachers in the home and school.[33] If we are right, the interplay of these characteristics leads to the regular production and reproduction of fighting/street gangs and aggressive masculinity. That is, the members of these street gangs develop a positive evaluation or 'love' of fighting and tend to use aggressive physicality in order to affirm their identities and resolve conflicts. They also tend to develop strong, positive feelings of attachment towards narrowly defined 'we-groups' and correspondingly strong negative feelings towards 'they-groups' or 'outsiders' (Elias, 1978). At the risk of being accused of anachronistic thinking, one could even hazard the suggestion that, because their social experiences habituate them to a love of violence and fighting, they are in this respect but, of course, not in others, similar to early medieval knights as Elias (1939, 2000) depicted them.

Such groups of 'segmentally bonded' males — males who bond primarily with others who are similar to themselves — tend to seek as their opponents and to fight with groups who also resemble themselves in many ways. However, just like the segmental lineages described by anthropologists such as Evans–Pritchard (1940) as characteristic of some tribal societies, these local 'segments' often combine to fight an external enemy, for example football fans from another town or country. Football is an attractive venue for acting out these masculinity rituals for three main reasons: (i) because football — the 'people's game' — is culturally important in working-class communities in England and the rest of Britain; (ii) because the game itself is a kind of play-fight with a stress on masculinity; and (iii) because football regularly produces opponents with whom to fight and regular opportunities for invading the football citadels and towns of others as well as of defending one's own. This analysis of football hooliganism is put forward by 'the Leicester School' as a contribution to understanding and not as the final, definitive answer.

More recently, Dunning (1999, 2000) has sought to apply a figurational framework to the study of football hooliganism as a global phenomenon. He

---

[33]Neighbourhoods of this kind tend to have wider ramifications, leading, for example, to children and adolescents from more respectable families, especially males, having to learn to defend themselves against physical attack at school, on the streets and, later on, in pubs and clubs.

suggests in this connection that the fact that violent spectator disorder occurs more frequently at or in conjunction with soccer than at or in conjunction with any other major sport appears to be centrally a function of the social composition of its crowds. Soccer is the world's most popular team sport and, worldwide, a majority of its spectators tend to be male and to come from the lower reaches of the social scale; that is, from social strata and social segments where social norms tend to legitimate a higher incidence of overt aggressiveness and violence in everyday social relations than tends to be the case among the middle and upper classes. Furthermore, in most societies, groups lower down the social scale are less likely to be so highly individualised and more likely readily to form intense 'we-group' bonds and identifications (Elias, 1978: 134–148) which involve an equally intense hostility towards 'outsiders' (Elias & Scotson, 1965, 1994) than is the case among the more powerful, more self-steering and usually more inhibited groups who stand above them. At a soccer match, of course, the outsiders are the opposing team and its supporters and, in some cases, the match officials.

According to Dunning, it would be wrong to view soccer hooliganism as always and everywhere a consequence solely or mainly of class stratification. As a basis for further research, he hypothesises that, other things being equal, the problem is fuelled and shaped by what might be called the major 'fault-lines' of particular countries. In England, that means class and regional differences and inequalities; in Scotland (at least in Glasgow) and Northern Ireland, religious sectarianism; in Spain, the partly language-based sub-nationalisms of the Catalans, Castilians and Basques; in Italy, city-based particularism and perhaps the division between North and South as expressed in the formation of the 'Northern League'; and in Germany, relations between the generations (Heitmeyer & Peter, 1992; Elias, 1996) and those between East and West. Religious, sub-national, city-based, regional and generation-based fault-lines may draw into football hooliganism more people from higher up the social scale than tends to be the case in England. Arguably, however, a shared characteristic of all these fault-lines — and, of course, each can overlap and interact with others in a variety of complex ways — is that they correspond to what Elias and Scotson (1965, 1994) called 'established-outsider figurations'; that is, social formations involving intense 'we-group' bonds and corres-pondingly intense antagonisms towards 'outsiders' or 'they-groups' ('them'). This is an appropriate point at which to turn to the problem of sport and 'globalisation' more generally.

Sport and Globalisation

Although Elias paid attention to the issue as early as the 1970s (Elias, 1971), figurational sociologists have recently begun working on the global spread of modern sports, seeking to shed light on correlations between this process, civilising processes and broader processes of globalisation. Joseph Maguire, sometimes working alone and sometimes with others, is generally acknowledged as the leading figure in this regard. The study of globalisation is, he contends, an area full of conceptual snares. These include: a tendency to think in terms of dichotomies rather than continua; the explanation of complex processes in monocausal (usually economic) terms; and a tendency to view global processes as produced *either* intentionally *or* as the unintended consequence of intended human actions instead of by a variable admixture of both. Maguire also distances himself from the equation of globalisation with homogenisation, i.e., the supposed disappearance of difference in a world where the members of non-Western societies are held to be modelling themselves increasingly on the West, especially the United States. Together with processes of 'Americanisation' — in sport as elsewhere — Maguire notes the prior occurrence of processes of 'Anglicisation' and, more recently, 'Japanisation'. These processes — or 'cultural flows' as Maguire calls them — depend fundamentally on the shifting balance of world power. Hence, the spread of English/British sport forms in the nineteenth and early twentieth centuries through the formal and 'informal' British Empires, of American sport forms in the twentieth century as American power gradually grew, and of Japanese 'sport' forms, such as 'sportised' martial arts, as the Japanese recovered from their defeat in World War II. Developing the earlier work of Elias and Dunning (1986) and Dunning (1999), these processes are conceptualised by Maguire as representing third, fourth and fifth stages of sportisation.

Maguire (1999) also makes use of Elias' (1939, 2001) contention that the civilising and state-formation processes of Western Europe have been neither purely 'homogenising' and 'massifying' as writers such as those associated with 'the Frankfurt School' of 'critical theory' have argued,[34] nor purely 'differentiating' as, for example, Durkheim (1896, 1964) can be interpreted as having claimed but, on the contrary, characterised by an admixture of 'diminishing contrasts' and 'increasing varieties'. Maguire expresses this empirically-based line of reasoning on the development of modern sport thus. Globalisation processes in the second half of the twentieth century, he suggests, have been 'powered' primarily by Western commercial and industrial interest groups

---

[34]See Horkheimer, M. and Adorno, T. W. (1947), *Dialectic of Enlightenment*, London, New Left Review Editions, 1979.

which, acting under the protective umbrella of US military hegemony, have spread Western products and a 'cult of consumerism' around the globe. This has led to a diminishing of contrasts between countries as the personnel involved in the 'media-sport production complex' have successfully marketed virtually identical sport-forms, products and images around the world. According to Maguire, however, the personnel at the hub of media-sport production and global marketing also attempt to celebrate difference. They do so, for example, by supporting the spread to the West of Eastern products and forms. The Japanese martial arts can serve as an illustration once again. An earlier example is the spread of polo from East to West. In a word, despite the dominance of the West over the past two or three centuries, such processes of cultural diffusion by no means simply involve one-way flows.

Also implicated in processes of globalisation are patterns of cultural interchange between more powerful and less powerful countries within the West itself. Examples are the spread of soccer to the USA and of revamped British sport-forms, e.g., American and Australian football, back to the 'mother country'. It is Maguire's contention in addition that the effects of the spread of sport from the British to their former colonial subjects have been double-edged. Although originally an index of the success of the British colonisers in spreading their civilisation and sport forms across the world, most former colonial peoples now regularly beat the English/British 'at their own games', in the process boosting their own self-confidence and sense of nationhood whilst simultaneously compounding the identity problems of the English/British that result from the loss of empire.

Some Other Figurational Contributions to the Sociological Understanding of Sport

Figurational sociologists have also sought to make contributions to the sociological understanding of such areas as sport and gender (Sheard & Dunning, 1973; Dunning in Elias & Dunning, 1986; Dunning & Maguire, 1996; Maguire & Mansfield, 1988; Colwell, 1999), sport and race (Maguire, 1988, 1991; Maguire & Stead, 1996; Malcolm, 1997a, 1997b, 2001; Dunning, 1999), sport and drugs (Waddington, 2000; Waddington & Murphy, 1992; Dunning & Waddington, forthcoming), sport and health (Waddington, 2000; Waddington, Malcolm, & Green, 1998), and sports injuries (Waddington, 2000; Waddington, Roderick, & Parker, 1999). There is only space here for a brief discussion of what 'figurationalists' have written about sport and gender, sport and race, and sport and drugs.

Contrary to the claims of Jennifer Hargreaves (1992, 1994) who argues that figurational sociologists have neglected the study of sport and gender, such issues have been central to their work since the 1970s. This was recognised by Susan Birrell when she wrote in 1988 that:

> Sheard and Dunning's 1973 article, 'The Rugby Club as a Type of Male Preserve', gained respect as a sub-cultural study, but because it focused so clearly on males, it was not fully recognised for its importance to feminist scholarship until gender relations were recognised as the proper focus for the field (Birrell, 1988: 481).

What Sheard and Dunning attempted in this article was to illuminate the behaviour of English male rugby players by locating them in the context of the changing balance of gender power. They hypothesised in this connection: (i) that the initial formation of rugby clubs as preserves where males could bolster their threatened egos by mocking and vilifying females and homosexual males in songs and drinking rituals took place in large measure in response to the growing power of females as expressed in the suffragettes movement; and (ii) that since the 1960s, the further (still so far in most, especially public, spheres, relatively slight) shift in the balance of gender power away from males as expressed, for example, in the rise and relative success of second-wave feminism, has contributed, along, for example, with the professionalisation of Rugby Union, to a weakening of the extreme forms of patriarchy once characteristic of rugby clubs. More recently, Dunning (1999) has endeavoured to show how this change in the power ratio of males and females is best explained largely as a consequence of the ways in which Western civilising processes have placed restrictions on the resort to violence against females by males, and how external constraints (*Fremdzwänge*) in this regard have been internalised as self-constraints (*Selbstzwänge*) by growing numbers of males. Dunning (1999) also uses this framework to explore the increasing direct involvement of females in sport, including in relatively violent contact/combat sports such as boxing, wrestling, soccer and rugby, and to examine the consequences for sport and the wider society, especially for gender identities and gender relations, of this female 'invasion' of what started out generally as a male preserve.

Figurational studies of race and sport started with Maguire's (1988) work on 'stacking' in English soccer, a theme more recently re-visited by Malcolm (1997a) in respect of cricket. More recently still, Dunning (1999) has sought to conceptualise race and sport in power terms and has applied Elias' conceptualisations of power and established-outsider figurations to the history and development of race and sport in the USA. He pays particular attention in this connection to the emergence of a black middle class ('black bourgeoisie') and to the recruitment into that class of professional sports personnel. He also seeks to synthesise the findings on sport and race in the USA of historians and sociologists.

The leading contributor to figurational studies of sport and health and sport and drugs is Ivan Waddington (2000), a scholar who specialised originally in medical sociology. As far as sport and drugs is concerned, he synthesises Dunning's (1986) work on the increasing seriousness of sports involvement with that of Illich (1975) on the 'medicalization of life' in modern societies in order to explain why the abuse of performance-enhancing drugs by top-level sportspersons/athletes is increasing. Waddington (Waddington & Murphy, 1992) also shows how a figuration of athletes, officials and medical personnel is involved in this connection and not just individual athletes. More recently, Dunning and Waddington (2002) have sought to illuminate the problem of sport and drugs by bringing alcohol into the overall equation, examining the shifting historical balance between 'Dionysian' and 'Puritanical' sports cultures, and looking at extreme forms of sports involvement as themselves forms of addiction.

Conclusion

Along with the protagonists of most of the other paradigms in the field, figurational sociologists of sport have sought to contribute to the body of knowledge and understanding of sport as a social phenomenon. In fact, most figurational sociologists would claim that the approach they inherited from Elias is a synthesis of most of the most valuable (i.e., reality-congruent) elements in all the major sociological and psychological positions and theories. Hence, they look forward to a day when contributors to our field no longer see themselves as adherents to warring schools but just accept each other as sociologists in much the same way as takes place in the natural sciences where the idea of, for example, a 'Marxist' physics or a 'conservative' chemistry is absurd. Hopefully, this chapter will help to persuade a growing number of students and their teachers of the value of such a synthesis and of the debilitating consequences that flow from paradigm wars. With this in mind, an attempt has been made to write this chapter in clear and jargon-free language in order to make the text an accessible and reader-friendly introduction to the complexity of the real social world of sport and not to the sometimes abstract and needlessly complex language of whichever 'postmodernist', 'poststructuralist' or 'social theorist' (read 'philosopher' as opposed to 'sociologist') whose work has most recently come into fashion.

References

Abrams, P. (1982). *Historical Sociology*. Wells, Somerset: Open Books.

Atkinson, M. (2001). *Miscreants, Malcontents and Mimesis: Sociogenesis, Psychogenesis and the Canadian Tattoo Figuration*. Unpublished Ph.D thesis, University of Calgary, Canada.

Bell, D. (1961). *The End of Ideology*. New York: Collier–Macmillan.

Bourdieu, P. (1984). *Distinction: A Social Critique of the Judgement of Taste*. London: Routledge.

Brohm, J. M. (1878). *Sport: A Prison of Measured Time*. London: Ink Links.

Brookes, C. (1978). *English Cricket*. London: Weidenfeld & Nicholson.

Curry, G. (2001). *Football: A Study in Diffusion*. Unpublished Ph.D thesis, University of Leicester.

D'Souza, D. (1995). *The End of Racism: Principles for a Multiracial Society*. New York: Free Press.

Dunning, E. (1961). *Early Stages in the Development of Football as an Organised Game*. Unpublished MA thesis, University of Leicester.

Dunning, E. (ed.) (1971). *The Sociology of Sport: A Selection of Readings*. London: Frank Cass.

Dunning, E. (1979). The figurational dynamics of modern sport: Notes on the sociogenesis of achievement-striving and the social significance of sport. *Sportwissenschaft, 9*, Jahrgang, 4, 341–359.

Dunning, E., & Sheard, K. (1976). The bifurcation of rugby union and rugby league: A case study of organisational conflict and change. *International Review of Sport Sociology, 4*, 31–72.

Dunning, E. (1986). Sport as a male preserve: Notes on the social sources of masculine identity and its transformation. In: N. Elias and E. Dunning (eds), *Quest for Excitement: Sport and Leisure in the Civilising Process* (pp. 267–283). Oxford: Blackwell.

Dunning, E. (1999). *Sport Matters: Sociological Studies of Sport, Violence and Civilisation*. London: Routledge.

Dunning, E., & Maguire, J. (1996). Aspects of sport, violence and gender relations: Some process sociological notes. *International Review for the Sociology of Sport, 31*, 295–321.

Dunning, E., Maguire, J., & Pearton, R. (eds) (1993). *The Sports Process*. Champaign, IL: Human Kinetics.

Dunning, E., Murphy, P., & Williams, J. (1988). *The Roots of Football Hooliganism*. London: Routledge.

Dunning, E., & Rojek, C. (eds) (1992). *Sport and Leisure in the Civilising Process: Critique and Counter-Critique*. London: Macmillan.

Dunning, E., & Sheard, K. (1979). *Barbarians, Gentlemen and Players: A Sociological Study of the Development of Rugby Football.* Oxford: Martin Robertson.

Dunning, E., & Waddington, I. (2002). Drugs in sport: Some neglected issues. In: H.-D. Horch, M. Schubert and M. R. Friederici (eds), *Sport, Wirtschaft and Gesellschaft.* Schorndorf: Hofmann (forthcoming).

Durkheim, E. (1896). *The Division of Labour in Society.* New York: Free Press (1964 edition).

Durkheim, E. (1915). *The Elementary Forms of the Religious Life.* London: Allen & Unwin (1976 edition).

Elias, N. (1939). *Über den Prozess der Zivilisation.* (2 Vols.) Basel: Haus zum Falken.

Elias, N. (2000). *The Civilizing Process.* Oxford: Blackwell (integrated edition, revised and edited by E. Dunning, J. Goudsblom and S. Mennell).

Elias, N. (1971). The development of sport as a sociological problem. In: E. Dunning (ed.), *The Sociology of Sport: A Selection of Readings.* London: Frank Cass. See also Elias and Dunning, 1986.

Elias, N. (1978). *What is Sociology?* London: Hutchinson.

Elias, N. (1983). The retreat of sociologists into the present. *Theory, Culture and Society, 4*(2–3), 223–417.

Elias, N. (1987). *Involvement and Detachment.* Oxford: Blackwell.

Elias, N., & Dunning, E. (1986). *Quest for Excitement: Sport and Leisure in the Civilising Process.* Oxford: Blackwell.

Elias, N., & Scotson, J. (1994). *The Established and the Outsiders.* London: Sage (1st edition, 1965).

Evans–Pritchard, E. E. (1940). *The Nuer.* Oxford: Oxford University Press.

Fukuyama, F. (1993). *The End of History and the Last Man.* London: Penguin.

Giddens, A. (1961). *Sport and Society in Contemporary England.* Unpublished MA thesis, London School of Economics.

Giddens, A. (1997). *The Constitution of Society.* Cambridge: Polity.

Giddens, A. (1997). *Society.* Cambridge: Polity.

Goudsblom, J. (1977). *Sociology in the Balance.* Oxford: Blackwell.

Goulstone, J. (2000), The working-class origins of modern football. *The International Journal of the History of Sport, 17*(1), 135–143.

Guttmann, A. (1978). *From Ritual to Record.* New York: Columbia University Press.

Han, K. L. (2001). A historical and sociological analysis of Taekwondo skill and rule as a process of civilization. Paper presented at the 1st World Congress of the Sociology of Sport ("Sociology of Sport and the New Global Order: Building Perspectives and Crossing Boundaries"). Seoul, South Korea, July 20–24.

Hargreaves, John (1986). *Sport, Power and Culture.* Cambridge: Polity.

Hargreaves, Jennifer (1994). *Sporting Females: Critical Issues in the History and Sociology of Women's Sports.* London: Routledge.

Harvey, A. (1999). Football's missing link: The real story of the evolution of modern football. *European Sports History Review, 1,* 92–116.

Hoch, P. (1972). *Rip Of the Big Game.* Garden City, New York: Anchor Books.

Horkheimer, M., & Adorno, T. W. (1947). *Dialectic of Enlightenment.* London: New Left Review Editions, 1979.

Howes, M. (1999). Ultimate Fighting. *Figurations,* No. 11, June 1999.

Ichii, Y. (2001). On the emotional habitus in Sociology of Sport and Leisure: A comparative study. Paper presented at the 1st World Congress of the Sociology of Sport ("Sociology of Sport and the New Global Order: Building Perspectives and Crossing Boundaries"). Seoul, South Korea, July 20–24.

Kiku, K. (2001). Sports fans, violence, and the modern body: From a viewpoint of historical sociology. Paper presented at the 1st World Congress of the Sociology of Sport ("Sociology of Sport and the New Global Order: Building Perspectives and Crossing Boundaries"). Seoul, South Korea, July 20–24.

Kilminster, R. (1998). *The Sociological Revolution: From the Enlightenment to the Global Age.* London: Routledge.

Maguire, J. (1985). *The Limits of Decent Partisanship: a Sociogenetic Investigation of the Emergence of Football Spectating as a Social Problem.* Unpublished Ph.D thesis, University of Leicester.

Maguire, J. (1988). Race and positional assignment in English soccer: A preliminary analysis of ethnicity and sport in Britain. *Sociology of Sport Journal, 5*(3), 257–269.

Maguire, J. (1991). Sport, racism and British society: A sociological study of England's elite male Afro–Caribbean soccer and rugby union players. In: G. Jarvie (ed.), *Sport, Racism and Ethnicity* (pp. 94–123). London: Falmer Press.

Maguire, J. (1999). *Global Sport: Identities, Societies, Civilisations* Cambridge: Polity.

Maguire, J., & Stead, D. (1996). Far pavilions?: Cricket migrants, foreign sojourns and contested identities. *International Review for the Sociology of Sport, 31*(1), 1–24.

Malcolm, D. (1997a). Stacking in cricket: A figurational sociological re-appraisal of centrality. *Sociology of Sport Journal, 14*(3), 265–284.

Malcolm, D. (1997b). Cricket, "racial" stereotyping and physical education. *Bulletin of Physical Education,* 1997, *33*(1), 8–14.

Malcolm, D. (2001). It's not cricket: Colonial legacies and contemporary inequalities. *Journal of Historical Sociology, 14*(3), 253–275.

Mangan, J. A. (2000). *Athleticism in the Victorian and Edwardian Public School.* London: Frank Cass (First published 1981).

Marples, M. (1954). *A History of Football.* London: Secker & Warburg.

Murphy, P., Williams, J., & Dunning, E. (1990). *Football on Trial,* London, Routledge.

Rigauer, B. (1981). *Sport and Work.* New York: Columbia University Press. (German edition, *Sport und Arbeit,* 1969).

Simmel, G. (1971). *On Individuality and Social Forms* (ed. Levine, D. L.) Chicago: University of Chicago Press.

Smith, D. (2001). *Norbert Elias and Modern Social Theory.* London: Sage.

Waddington, I. (2001). *Sport, Health and Drugs: A Critical Sociological Perspective,* London: Spon.

Williams, J., Dunning, E., & Murphy, P. (1984; 1989). *Hooligans Abroad*. London: Routledge.

Young, K. (2000). Sports violence and the criminal law: Cases, trends, issues. Paper presented at the Conference on 'Sport in the New Millennium', University College, Dublin, Ireland.

Chapter 10

Pierre Bourdieu's Sociocultural Theory and Sport Practice

Suzanne Laberge and Joanne Kay

Bourdieu is widely considered by many scholars to have been one of the most influential French intellectuals of the twentieth century. His interdisciplinary work, linking anthropology, sociology and philosophy, emerged as a genuinely innovative theoretical and methodological approach for understanding the pluri-dimensional aspect of social life. Bourdieu has addressed a broad range of theoretical themes and has confronted them through an impressive diversity of empirical research, developing at once a theory of social practice, a theory of culture, a theory of power, and a theory of sociological knowledge. Thus far, his major empirical works include studies as diverse as the ethnography of the Kabyle Berber of Algeria (Bourdieu, 1962 [1958]), the study of museum attendance (Bourdieu, Darbel, & Schnapper, 1990 [1966]), the uses of photography (Bourdieu, Boltanski, Castel, & Chamboredon, 1990 [1965]), the French educational system (Bourdieu & Passeron, 1977 [1970]), cultural tastes (Bourdieu, 1984 [1979]), uses of language (Bourdieu, 1991a [1982]), French academic life (Bourdieu, 1988a [1984]), writers (Bourdieu, 1995 [1992]), artistic production (Bourdieu, Haacke, & Johnson, 1995 [1994]), scientific production (Bourdieu, 1997), television (Bourdieu, 1998b [1998]), gender relations (Bourdieu, 1998c), and current economic discourse (Bourdieu, 1999 [1998]).

The complexity and scope of Bourdieu's conceptual work make synthesis difficult,[1] and therefore we will focus mainly on two of his pivotal concepts: 'habitus' and 'field', as well as on his socio-cultural theory of practice as applied

---

[1]There is now a growing body of literature introducing Bourdieu's work. For an accurate and well designed introduction to Bourdieu's social theory, see Swartz (1997) and Harker, Mahar and Wilkes (1990). As for its use in the sociology of sport, see Jarvie and Maguire (1994: 183–209), Defrance (1995), Clément (1995), and Ohl (2000). For its use in the sociology of the body, see Shilling (1993).

---

to sport and physical activities (SPA)[2]. In order to map out his sociological approach, we will begin with a brief exposé of the main theoretical traditions that have influenced his conceptualisation. We will then explore the concept of habitus, and present Bourdieu's analysis of the social distribution of SPA tastes using the notion of habitus which will lead to a discussion of the concept of field and its utilisation in understanding SPA supply. Bourdieu's particular mode of sociological inquiry will then be considered. Finally, we briefly survey the misreadings and major criticisms of his conceptualisation, concluding with what we believe to be its strength for capturing the social dynamic of SPA practice and contribution to the sociology of sport.

Theoretical Influences

Bourdieu's social theory draws from diverse intellectual sources such as Bachelard, Durkheim, Elias, Marx, Weber, Wittgenstein, and from schools of thought ranging from structuralism and phenomenology to analytic philosophy (Swartz, 1997; Brubaker, 1985). Rather than being characterised as merely eclectic, however, Bourdieu is seen to have insightfully and creatively woven core ideas of Western thought into a synthesis of his own, keeping what he sees to be their respective strengths, and discarding weaknesses. Here, we consider the influences of three critical classical social theorists: Marx, Weber, and Durkheim.

Although Bourdieu cannot be labelled a Marxist, his work is in keeping with at least three of Marx's key concerns. First, Bourdieu shares Marx's contention that social theory should not consist in discourse closed on itself, but should aim to reveal processes of domination. Second, like Marx, he recognises the primacy of class conflicts and material interests in the understanding of social inequalities. Third, he is a materialist in the sense that he roots human consciousness in practical social life. However, Bourdieu discards the concepts of exploitation and ideology central to Marxian theory. Indeed, he sharply criticizes Marx for his economism which recognises economic capital as the only form of power. One of Bourdieu's innovations is the recognition that many forms of power exist in social life. He terms all forms of power 'capital' (for instance, 'cultural capital', 'social capital', 'symbolic capital', and so forth) in order to suggest similar conceptual status. He rejects Marx's conception of

---

[2]From here on, we will use the acronym SPA to designate sports and physical activities, and will refer mainly to their leisure modality of practice. Institutionalised (amateur) sport will be considered in the section devoted to the concept of 'field'.

culture as 'superstructure', and therefore, secondary to economy. One hallmark of Bourdieu's theory is to consider culture and economics as equally important. Finally, Bourdieu departs from Marx's conception of social class. Bourdieu's social classes are not real groups mobilised for social struggles. Rather, classes are defined from a cultural and relational standpoint: for Bourdieu, a social class refers to a group of social agents who share the same social conditions of existence, interests, social experience, and value system, and who tend to define themselves *in relation* to other groups of agents. Social class excludes neither the diversity of members nor the existence of internal conflicts. Moreover, social classes can be characterised by any kind of socially constructed trait, such as gender, age or ethnicity.

Bourdieu also draws from the work of Weber. First, he shares with Weber his conceptualisation of social class, since Weber held that classes are aggregates of common life chances but not real social groups. Second, Bourdieu borrowed much from Weber's political economy of religion that applies a materialist analysis while still recognising the symbolic dimension. One of Bourdieu's aims is to extend this model to *all* cultural and social life (Bourdieu, 1990a: 36). Of particular inspiration for Bourdieu is Weber's study of 'interest' (Bourdieu, 1987). However, Bourdieu's social theory expands upon Weber's notion in that it includes non-material goods. For him, all practices are fundamentally 'interested' — that is, "oriented towards the maximisation of material or symbolic profit" (Bourdieu, 1990b: 209). Finally, Bourdieu draws from Weber's notions of charisma and legitimacy to construct his notion of 'symbolic capital' (Bourdieu, 1991b). Weber contends that the exercise of power requires legitimisation. Like Weber, Bourdieu's notion of symbolic capital refers to a form of power that is not perceived as power, but rather as a legitimate demand for recognition, deference and obedience.

As for Durkheimian influences, Bourdieu adopted as a fundamental principle Durkheim's stance that science must disconnect from common sense — or people's explanations for social life — and adopt an 'objective' approach. Durkheim's quantitative studies, such as that which demonstrated suicide as a social phenomenon rather than a purely individual one, are most illustrative in this regard. However, Bourdieu departs from the strict Durkheimian objectivism (and any type of objectivism that followed[3]) by integrating a 'subjectivist' perspective into his social theory. Indeed, he considers people's different

---

[3]Bourdieu calls 'objectivism' either the form of knowledge that focuses uncritically on the recording and statistical analysis of empirical regularities of human behaviour, or the form that tends to impute the properties of formal models to social realities such as Lévi–Strauss' structuralism.

representations and interpretations of reality as essential components for the scientific understanding of social life. Bourdieu also builds upon Durkheim's hypothesis of the social origins of schemes of thought, perception, and action, and of the existence of a correspondence between symbolic classification and social stratification. Indeed, Bourdieu sees symbolic systems as classification systems that fulfil a function of social integration, and aims to explore the mechanisms that link symbolic classification and social stratification. However, while for Durkheim, this integrative force operates to produce a desired consensual unity for the social order, for Bourdieu it produces differentiation and domination.

Bourdieu's intellectual project was also strongly shaped by the French sociology of the 1950s from which Lévi–Strauss (a structuralist epitomising an objectivist mode of knowledge) and Merleau–Ponty (a phenomenologist epitomising a subjectivist mode of knowledge[4]) emerged as towering figures (Defrance, 1995). Bourdieu retains from Lévi–Strauss' structuralism the 'relational' mode of knowledge; that is: "a mode of thinking that leads one to characterise every element by the relations that unite it to all the other elements in a system, and from which each element gets its meaning and its function" (Bourdieu, 1990b: 10). He steadfastly implemented this relational mode of knowledge throughout his empirical and theoretical work. However, he rejects Lévi–Strauss' reification of the mental structures, and its correlative exclusion of active social agents from social explanation. To overcome these shortcomings, Bourdieu draws selectively from phenomenology. He was attracted by Merleau–Ponty's idea that the body is the fount of one's social experience and understanding of the social world. Indeed, Bourdieu accords a central place to the body in his social theory. He nevertheless criticises phenomenology because it considers subjects to be undetermined, and to be empowered to construct the world according to their own vision. Thus, it forgets that 'the social world is in the body', that agents classify and construct their understanding of the world from particular positions in a *hierarchically structured social space*.

Hence, Bourdieu's ambitious programme was to elaborate a social theory of practice that builds upon the objectivist and subjectivist insights, transcending their alleged antagonism and the related 'false antinomies' that have characterised sociological traditions (such as structure/agency, determinism/ freedom, macro-analysis/micro-analysis). In order to do so, he forges a new conceptual apparatus, the two pillars of which are the notions of habitus and

---

[4]Subjectivism refers to forms of knowledge that focus on individual or inter-subjective consciousness and interactions.

field. These notions are constructed as the means for analysing and understanding the dialectical relationships between social agents and the social structure in which they evolve. More concretely, it involves, on the one hand, the investigation of how social agents incorporate, through socialisation, the system of relationships that structures society, and on the other hand, how agents participate in the social construction of these very structures. The focus is not placed on either the structures or the individuals themselves but, rather, on processes and mechanisms of construction. Indeed, when asked to play the *labelling* game, Bourdieu chooses the term 'constructivist structuralism' (Bourdieu 1990a: 14) to indicate his focus on the social construction of individuals and social groups, and on the genesis of (cognitive or social) structures.

SPA as Differentiating Cultural Practices

Although Bourdieu has not devoted a complete project to SPA, *Distinction* (1984), one of his most important works, gives major attention to SPA practice. Moreover, his two articles 'Program for a Sociology of Sport' (1988b) and 'Sport and Social Class' (1978) appear to be seminal works for sociologists of sport. Although his influence in the subdiscipline 'began' in France,[5] it is now spreading to North-America, Asia, as well as parts of continental Europe.[6] The fact that Bourdieu was a rugby player in his youth, combined with the pivotal role of the body in his understanding of social life, may partly explain his interest in SPA practices.

Consistent with the central place he devotes to culture in his understanding of social life, Bourdieu considers SPA as a cultural practice in the same way as, for example, listening to music, reading, home-decorating, or clothing. Given his anthropological interests, cultural practices manifest 'a vision and a division of the world',[7] and bear particular symbolic value. In his highly in-depth, wide-ranging analysis of French society's cultural consumption in the early 1970s, Bourdieu (1984) shows that different SPA practices are integral to more general cultural practices constituting what he calls 'lifestyles'. A substantive body of

[5]The anthology edited by Pociello (1981) and the collection of research on sport published in two issues of *Actes de la Recherche en Sciences Sociales* (1989, issues 79 and 80) are indicators of the impact of Bourdieu on sociologists of sport.
[6]See Gruneau (1993); Harvey and Sparks (1991); Laberge and Sankoff (1988); Matsumura (1993), Taks, Renson, and Vanreusel (1995); von der Lippe (2000); and White and Wilson (1999).
[7]Bourdieu endorses the conception of culture that refers to beliefs, symbols, language and traditions, all of these being an expression of a vision of the world which necessarily involves a division of the world.

interviews and a broad statistical data base on French society allowed him to sketch (via the application of statistical analyses of correspondence) a *spatial representation* of socially significant cultural practices (which he calls the 'space of lifestyles') and of the structure of French society of that period (which he calls the 'social space'). Bourdieu uses the term 'space' to depict the society because:

> the notion of *space* contains, in itself, the principle of a *relational* understanding of the social world . . . . individuals or groups exist and subsist through *difference*; that is, they occupy *relative positions* in a space of relations which, although invisible and always difficult to show empirically, is the most 'real' reality and the real principle of the behaviour of individuals and groups (Bourdieu, 1998a: 31; emphases in the original).

What emerges (Figure 1) is a depiction of the system of hierarchical relationships between the various lifestyles and between the various social positions (Bourdieu 1984: 129). It should be noted that Bourdieu's aim is not to identify patterns of consumption of social groups but rather to reveal structures of opposition through the mapping of the *relative distances* between social positions and between different cultural practices. This procedure is conceived by Bourdieu as a preliminary step towards what he terms the 'socio-logical' analysis that focuses on the different *meanings* that the different social groups give to the practices. Social classification of the given meanings further allows him to disclose the power relationships at work in the social formation.

   With regard to Figure 1, it is important to note that Bourdieu's conception of the social structure breaks with the linear conception that considers only the simple direct determination of economical asset. He accounts for two major 'principles of differentiation', or *sources of power* (forms of capital), effective in our advanced capitalist societies: economic capital and cultural capital (the latter includes academic background and all other education). His 'social space' is constructed according to three main dimensions: (1) the volume of the two kinds of capital represented by the vertical axis; (2) the relative composition of the capital (± economic capital and ± cultural capital) represented by the horizontal axis; and (3) the change in these two properties over time (manifested by past and potential trajectories in social space). This last dimension is not represented in our simplified version. Bourdieu employs occupational titles as the principal indicator of social groups, but they are conceptually 'decon-structed' in terms of the underlying volume and composition of capital they cover.

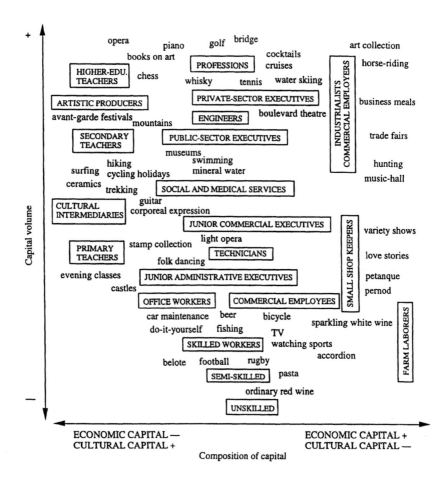

Figure 1. The Space of Social Positions and the Space of Lifestyles (simplified version of Bourdieu, 1984: 128–129 and 1998a: 5)

Taste

In order to uncover the power relationships at work in social formations, Bourdieu's analysis focuses on the study of 'taste' and judgement of taste; that is, the level of people's appreciation of certain lifestyles (e.g., snobbish/vulgar, dull/exciting, refined/crude). The expression of taste allows the social scientist to discern the generative principle that links the appreciation of various lifestyle practices, whether it be sports, food, clothing, etc. (Bourdieu, 1984: 173). For example, taste can reveal preferences for fitness activities rather than performance sports, for hardy rather than gourmet food, for low-maintenance rather than trendy clothing. Further, the judgement individuals apply to their own tastes and the tastes of others constitutes an act of classification; they differentiate and hierarchise them. Operating according to the principles of classification at work in their society, people choose the goods and practices that suit their taste. Hence, SPA, as part of classified lifestyles, acts as a symbol or a signifier for social groups.

In *Distinction* (1984), Bourdieu persuasively demonstrates that, in the struggle between them, social groups express distaste for the taste of other groups — the upper classes devalue the goods and practices associated with 'popular tastes', and reciprocally, the working classes reject the goods and practices presented to them as signs of 'good taste'. Similarly, older generations reject the goods and practices of youth culture, while adolescents might find those associated with their older counterparts to be 'uncool'. Taste is seen as an expression of the symbolic dimension of class relations. According to Bourdieu's relational approach, it matters little whether professionals prefer golf, hockey, boxing or rugby. What matters is that their preferences express systematic differentiation to those of other classes.

For Lash and Urry, one of Bourdieu's central claims is that "we consume not products but symbols with the intention of establishing social differentiation" (1987: 293). Bourdieu's relational approach then leads to the understanding of the space of lifestyles as an objective representation of a symbolic system, a system of socially classified and classifying practices (Bourdieu, 1984: 170–175). His notion of taste, therefore, permits a better understanding of the preferences in practices, including SPA, as being fundamentally social, rather than as the result of a 'natural' disposition or psychological trait, and as being involved, at the symbolic level, in the power relations between social groups.

What is at stake, then, for the social scientist is to construct a plausible mechanism or operator that could explain the relationship between practices and the positions in the social structure. In order to do so, Bourdieu developed the concept of 'habitus' to account for the dialectical relation between the social structure and individuals' practices and preferences (as objective manifestations of taste). Let us consider, first, the features of this concept, and second, the ways in which this concept can lead to a better understanding of the unequal distribution of SPA practices in society.

Habitus as the Mediating Construct Between Social Position and Social Practices

For Bourdieu, it is through the dynamic mediation of habitus, an embodied internalised system of schemes of dispositions, perceptions and appreciation, that positions in the social space are 'translated' into practices and preferences (Bourdieu, 1984: 170). Adopting a dynamic perspective, Bourdieu contends that habitus, on the one hand, is shaped by living conditions characteristic of a social position and, on the other hand, operates as a 'matrix', or generating principle, of classifiable practices and judgements of taste. The feature emphasised here is that habitus is a mediating construct, not a determined or a determining one.

Moreover, Bourdieu argues that different conditions of existence (linked to different positions in the social space) produce different habitus. In other words, life conditions and position in a social structure would fashion a certain sense of the world, and shape our perception and desires:

> Through the differentiated and differentiating conditionings associated with the different conditions of existence, through the exclusions and inclusions, unions (marriages, affairs, alliances, etc.) which govern the social structure and the structuring force it exerts, through all the hierarchies and classifications inscribed in objects (especially cultural products), in institutions (for example, the educational system) or simply in language, and through all the judgements, verdicts, gradings and warnings imposed by the institutions specially designed for this purpose, such as the family or the educational system, or constantly arising from the meetings and interactions of everyday life, the social order is progressively inscribed in people's minds. Social divisions become principles of division, organizing the image of the social world (Bourdieu, 1984: 470–471).

In addition, the internalisation of the classifications, codes and implicit rules that structure society are the means through which the individual constructs his/her social identity, the affirmation of his/her belonging to social groups (defined by sex, age, occupation, ethnicity, or other) and difference from others. Yet habitus is not only an internalisation of the social conditions into dispositions; Bourdieu conceives of it also as simultaneously a generating principle of practices expressed in 'taste'. Through socialisation and the learning (institutionalised or informal, discursive and bodily) it entails, social agents acquire a system of dispositions that leads them to act and react in a manner proper to his/her social group.

For Bourdieu, habitus provides the basic cognitive categories and action frames through which people think about and respond to the social world. It is a matrix, unconsciously at work and applicable to a variety of areas of life, that gives freedom within certain limits (Bourdieu, 1977: 95). Through habitus, social practices and lifestyles are understood as the outcomes of a dialectical relationship between social structure and social agency. For Bourdieu, what is at stake with this concept is to transcend the classical antinomies of structure/ agency, society/individual, determinism/freedom, and objectivism/subjectivism that he so adamantly rejects. The different habitus cannot easily be identified. Nevertheless, they are expressed through practices and, therefore, it is possible to 'reconstruct' theoretically the practice-generating principle through observation, relational analysis of the practices, tastes and judgement of tastes of members of the different social groups.

Given that Bourdieu attributes a corporeal dimension to his notion of habitus, presented as an *incorporation* of the hierarchised social structure and as *incorporated* schemes of dispositions, perceptions and appreciation, SPA constitutes, for Bourdieu, what Merton (1987) calls a 'strategic research site' for uncovering the different habitus specific to different social groups. But what is the heuristic value of habitus for sociologists of sport? We will see in the following section that the concept of habitus can be of great use in understanding how the differential appeal of SPA practices among social groups is linked to differentially acquired bodily dispositions, and to the differential benefits expected from the SPA practices. Habitus is also useful in highlighting the role of the SPA practices in the social relations of power.

The Relevance of Habitus for Understanding SPA Practices

It is in *Distinction* (1984, especially pp. 209–225), his wide-ranging analysis of lifestyles, and in his article, 'Sport and Social Class' (1978), that Bourdieu attempts to show that the classes' distinctive preferences in SPA practices are better explained by the differences in their *perception* and *appreciation* of the 'physical', social, educational, and economic investments required, and of the physical, social, economic and symbolic benefits expected from the different SPA practices. The following passage sketches what can be seen as a 'research programme' for a sociologist of sport:

To understand the class distribution of the various sports, one would have to take account of the representations which, in terms of their specific schemes of perception and appreciation, the different classes have of the costs (economic, cultural and 'physical') and benefits attached to the different sports — immediate or deferred 'physical' benefits (health, beauty, strength — whether visible, through 'body-building' — or invisible — through 'keep-fit' exercises), economic and social benefits (upward mobility, etc.) immediate or deferred symbolic benefits linked to the distributional or positional value of each of the sports considered (i.e., all that each of them receives from its greater or lesser rarity, and its more or less clear association with a class, with boxing, football, rugby or body-building evoking the working classes, tennis and skiing, the bourgeoisie and golf, the upper bourgeoisie), gains in distinction accruing from the different effects on the body itself (e.g., slimness, sun-tan, muscles obviously or discretely visible, etc.) or from the access to highly selective groups which some of these sports give (golf, polo, etc.) (Bourdieu, 1984: 20).

The Differentiating Bodily Dispositions

Of particular interest for the sociologist of sport is Bourdieu's 'phenomeno-logical' assessment of bodily practices. This leads him to argue that in order to thoroughly understand the logic of choice of a given SPA practice, one must delve into a person's deeper dimension; that is, the *'particular relation to the body'* or bodily disposition. For Bourdieu, it is assumed that the conditioning and education proper to a given position in the social structure generates a particular relation to one's own body which is, according to his conceptual-isation, the fundamental dimension of habitus:

> [. . .] the social conditionings linked to a social condition tend to inscribe the relation to the social world in a lasting, generalized relation to one's own body, a way of bearing one's body, presenting it to others, moving it, making space for it, which gives the body its social physiognomy (Bourdieu, 1984: 474).

A relational analysis of the variations in the type of corporal engagement in the degree of attention or interest that one has in one's body, in the degree of risk that one is ready to assume, in the conception itself of the body and its function, led Bourdieu to identify two opposing relationships to the body among the working class and professionals: the body as means versus the body as an end in itself:

> It is the relation to one's own body, a fundamental aspect of the habitus, which distinguishes the working classes from the privileged classes, just as, within the latter, it distinguishes fractions that are separated by the whole universe of a life-style. On one side, there is the *instrumental* relation to the body which the working classes express in all the practices centred on the body, whether in dieting or beauty care, relation to illness or medication, and which is also manifested in the choice of sports requiring a considerable investment of effort, sometimes of pain and suffering (e.g., boxing) and sometimes a *gambling with the body itself* (as in motor-cycling, parachute-jumping, all forms of acrobatics, and to some extent, all sports involving fighting, among which we may include rugby). On the other side, there is the tendency of the privileged classes to treat the body as *an end in itself*, with variants according to whether the emphasis is placed on the intrinsic functioning of the body as an organism, which leads to the macrobiotic cult of health, or on the appearance of the body as a perceptible configuration, the 'physique,' i.e., the body-for-others (Bourdieu, 1978: 838; emphases in the original).

Because SPA practices offer the possibility of shaping the body, they express the 'body for others', that is the bodily incorporation of social relations. In this regard, SPA practices are the visible manifestation of the impression one wants to give of oneself, of one's ethic or moral virtues (e.g., dignity, straightforwardness, toughness) or social value (e.g., virility, femininity). The differences hence "inscribed in the physical order of bodies" are raised "to the symbolic order of significant distinctions" (Bourdieu 1984: 175). Since they are perceived in their mutual relations and in terms of social classificatory schemes, classifiable worked-out body shapes become symbolic expressions of different positions in the social structure. Judgements of taste relating to body shaping are thus used as a means of legitimating and depreciating, and eventually naturalising, social differences.

Several French sociologists of sport have successfully used Bourdieu's conceptualisation of habitus. Clément (1981), for example, has shown how different types of relationships to the body can explain different social recruitment of three combat sports: wrestling, judo and aïkido.

Clément found that the distance separating the combatants, the emphasis put on dodging and avoidance techniques, the value put on aesthetics, and the linking of aesthetics to the efficiency of a movement are aspects of aïkido that match the relationship to one's body prevalent in the upper middle classes while, the full body contact, falls and aggressiveness in wrestling and judo are more appealing among the middle and popular classes (Clément, 1981). Focusing on one sport practice — rugby — Pociello (1983) provides an account of bodily dispositions and appreciation underlying three styles of rugby practice, each of them attracting different social groups. In North America, Wacquant's (1992b and 1995) ethnographic and participant observation study of a ghetto gym in Chicago shed light on how boxing was linked to the living conditions of young black males and their distinctive bodily habitus. Laberge and Sankoff (1988) studied the SPA practices of a sample of women of Montreal in light of their differentiating lifestyles and habitus. In different ways, these studies appear to attest to the fact that the compatibility of a given SPA practice with one's relationship to one's body is at the foundation of SPA selection and the manner of practice privileged by different social groups.

The Differentiating Profits Expected from SPA

Because people apprehend reality through the schemes of perception and appreciation of their habitus, it makes 'sociological' sense that different social groups do not agree about the profits (intrinsic or extrinsic, immediate or deferred) expected from SPA (Bourdieu, 1978: 834–7 and 1984: 211–5). Certain groups will seek external effects on the body such as a visible musculature. Others will seek internal profits; that is, physical and/or mental health or disease prevention. In assessing the distinctive habitus of the middle classes, Bourdieu provides us with an interesting explanation of why physical activity promotion strictly oriented toward health benefits mostly succeed among social groups with a high volume of cultural capital (such as professionals, teachers or junior executives). According to their position in the social structure, these social groups have internalised a distinctive ethic that leads them to find satisfaction in health-oriented activities like walking, jogging or aerobics,

> [. . .] which, unlike ball games, do not offer any competitive
> satisfaction, are highly rational and rationalized activities. This is

> firstly because they pre-suppose a resolute faith in reason and in
> the deferred and often intangible benefits which reason promises
> (such as protection against ageing, an abstract and negative
> advantage which only exists by reference to a thoroughly theo-
> retical referent); secondly, because they generally only have
> meaning by reference to a thoroughly theoretical, abstract
> knowledge of the effects of an exercise which is itself often reduced,
> as in gymnastics, to a series of abstract movements, decomposed
> and reorganized by reference to a specific and technically-defined
> end (e.g., 'the abdominals') (Bourdieu, 1978: 839).

These social groups would hardly see any value, nor wilfully enter into what they would consider as the 'self-destructive' practice of boxing. The different objectives from SPA are reflected in judgements of sport tastes. Pociello illustrated this when he quoted a discuss thrower's opinion of horseback riding: "The day when the jockey carries his horse on his back, then it will be a sport" (1999: 10). Judgements on SPA tastes, therefore, actively participate in the legitimation and devaluation of practices and thus in the struggles, transposed onto the cultural level, between social groups.

Finally, in addition to the intrinsic and extrinsic profits expected from SPA for the body itself, habitus allows us to take into account the 'social profits' (consciously or unconsciously) expected from SPA. For instance, golf, yachting and fencing offer the possibility of gaining social profits that are perceived and appreciated by the dominant social groups: practised in exclusive locations (private clubs), at a time one chooses, alone or with chosen partners and demanding a relatively low rate of physical exertion that is, in any case, freely determined but a relatively high investment of time and learning (Bourdieu, 1984: 215). Therefore, SPA practices participate in the process of inclusion and exclusion that contributes to the reproduction of a hierarchised social order. This can be done without any explicit segregation (in the context of leisure) because tastes and distastes translate the 'sense of one's place' into the social order. Indeed, Bourdieu (1984: 56) sees lifestyle differences as "perhaps the strongest barriers between the classes".

To sum up, Bourdieu's notion of habitus can help us to understand that the different tastes regarding SPA practices are generated by different relations to one's own body, and different perceptions and appreciation of the profits (intrinsic and extrinsic) expected from the practices. These dispositions, perceptions and appreciations are objective manifestations of generative and classificatory schemes acquired through social learning and socialisation relative to the position occupied in the hierarchical social structure. Because SPA practices are constitutive of lifestyles (classifiable practices) unequally distributed among the social classes, they act as social class signifiers or symbols of differentiating aesthetics and ethics, and thus are capable of fulfilling the social function of legitimating and naturalising social differences and maintaining a given social order. Bourdieu's analysis of SPA is in line with his broader effort to reveal the extent to which cultural practices embody power relations.

The Concept of Field and SPA Field Dynamics

Field, along with habitus, is the central organising concept in Bourdieu's theory of practice. For Bourdieu, practice emerges not simply from habitus, but from the encounter of habitus with competitive arenas called 'fields' (1990b: 56). In *Distinction* (1984: 101), he proposed the following equation as a way of summarising the intersection of habitus and field in his conceptualisation of the dynamics of practice: (habitus) (capital) + field = practice. However, this formula should be considered with caution[8] since it may incur two paradoxical effects: it objectifies Bourdieu's theory and it gives the image of a 'reductionist comprehension' of the social reality. Neither is intended by Bourdieu. With this equation in context, its formulation can be seen as Bourdieu's intention to stress the critical role of social fields, and their close connection to habitus in social practice. The assessment of a SPA field thus appears critical for our concern; but we must first ask if such a field exists. The existence of a SPA field will be explored after a brief overview of Bourdieu's notion of field.

A Working Definition of Field

The concept of field is less delineated than that of habitus, and Bourdieu develops it more as a 'general manner of thinking' — a device for the empirical study of various social arenas — than as a conceptual entity. As a 'working definition', a field in Bourdieu's work refers mainly to arenas of production, circulation, and appropriation of goods, services, knowledge, or status centred on a particular issue (e.g., literature, art, educational system, sport), *and* the network (or configuration) of historical relations of power between positions held by individuals, social groups or institutions (Bourdieu & Wacquant, 1992: 97). Like habitus, field is a *relational construct* in that, rather than referring to a delimited

---

[8]Swartz (1997: 141) and Harker, Mahar, and Wilkes (1990: 7) have underscored caution with regard to the interpretation and the use of this formula.

population of producers, it points to the relationships (such as alliances or oppositions) between various social agents occupying different positions in a structured network.[9] Moreover, the field concept gives insight into Bourdieu's understanding of macro structures. A critical characteristic of field is the existence of stakes for which people vie. For instance, in the field of art, these will be the 'legitimate' definition and function of art; in the field of sport, the 'legitimate' definition and function of sport, and so on. Each of the social agents participating in a field have specific interests, but share a common belief in it, or a 'passion' for it (Bourdieu, 1990a: 87–88).

A field is also simultaneously a space of competition for resources (economic capital) and rewards (symbolic capital) and of struggle for dominant positions. In an attempt to provide an understanding of the overall properties of field, Bourdieu often makes an analogy with games:

> We can indeed, with caution, compare a field to a game (*jeu*) although, unlike the latter, a field is not the product of a deliberate act of creation, and it follows rules, or better, regularities, that are not explicit and codified. Thus we have *stakes* (*enjeux*) which are, for the most part, the product of the competition between players. We have *investment in the game* . . .: players are taken in by the game, they oppose one another, sometimes with ferocity, only to the extent that they concur in their belief (*doxa*) in the game and its stakes; they grant these a recognition that escapes questioning. Players agree, by the mere fact of playing, and not by way of a 'contract,' that the game is worth playing . . . and this collusion is the very basis of their competition (Bourdieu & Wacquant, 1992: 98; emphases in the original).

Moreover, Bourdieu makes an analogy between the trump cards in a game and the particular species of capital (e.g., economic, social, cultural, symbolic) that are valued in a given state of a field. Individuals struggle to increase or conserve the defining forms of capital of the field (thus improving or keeping their position in the hierarchy of the field), but they can also work to change the relative value of the forms of capital recognised in the field. Thus, individuals' positions continually move in a field both as the outcome of the struggle for ascendancy

[9]Bourdieu often uses the term 'field' also to refer to 'social space' because both notions share similar properties: they involve relationships between different positions in a structured and hierarchised network, and they involve struggles for conserving or transforming a current state of the structure. To avoid ambiguity with 'specialised fields', we can see social space as the 'field of social classes', comprising also multiple specialised fields.

and/or eventually, as a consequence of the entry of new agents who modify the structure of the field. The notion of field, then, underlines the historical dynamism of a social arena, since it calls for both a *diachronic* and a *synchronic* analysis.

Although a field has a relative autonomy (it has its own history and specific culture), Bourdieu stresses that the hierarchies and dynamics of fields external to it (such as the field of power and fields overlapping it) can affect its internal dynamics. Finally, Bourdieu's empirical study of various fields have led to the recognition of the existence of 'subfields' within a field in-as-much as they have developed their own particular logic, stakes, and regulative principles.

The Constitution of the Sport Field

In the case of sports, can we speak of a field in the sense given by Bourdieu? For him, this means tracing the constitution of an arena of specific practices, "irreducible to a mere ritual game or festive amusement", endowed with its own logic, stakes and rules, and "where a whole specific competence or culture is generated and invested" (Bourdieu, 1978: 821).

Bourdieu argues (1978:822–833) that the importation, by aristrocratic and bourgeois families, of popular games into the English public schools of the nineteenth century, and their correlative change in meaning and function, produced a fundamental rupture which permitted the constitution of a relatively autonomous field of sports. In the school context, physical activities came to be endowed with educational functions, inserted into a specific calendar, and "converted into *bodily exercises*, activities which are an end in themselves, a sort of physical art for art's sake, governed by specific rules, increasingly irreducible to any functional necessity" (Bourdieu, 1978: 823). Bourdieu notes that this gradual autonomisation was accompanied by a process of *rationalisation* and the establishment of self-administered sports associations invested with the right to standardise rules, to exercise disciplinary power, and to award prizes and titles (symbolic capital). Moreover, he links the constitution of a sport field to the development of a *philosophy* of sport as a practice that promotes 'masculine' virtues and a sense of fair play (as opposed to the pursuit of victory at all costs). This initial phase is important to a sociological understanding of contemporary sport because "practice of sports such as tennis, riding, sailing or golf doubtless (*sic*) owes part of its 'interest', . . . to its distinguishing function and, more precisely, to the gains in distinction which it brings" (Bourdieu, 1978: 828).

However, the out-growth of sport as spectacle and its correlative popularisation process lead to the unfolding of new definitions, meanings and functions of sport. The field of sport thus becomes:

> the site of struggles in which what is at stake, *inter alia*, is the
> monopolistic capacity to impose the legitimate definition of
> sporting practice and of the legitimate function of sporting activity
> — amateurism versus professionalism, participant sport versus
> spectator sport, distinctive (élite) sport versus popular (mass)
> sport (Bourdieu, 1978: 826).

The entry of new social agents (sport events organisers, sporting goods manufacturers, the fitness industry and sport media) contributed to the transformation in the structure of the sports field, i.e., in the power relations between the various agents. Given the multiplication of new forms of physical activities and their link with more traditional sports, it seems more appropriate to speak of the SPA field.

Defrance and Pociello (1993) and Pociello (1999) deployed Bourdieu's concept of field in their analysis of the French sport field between 1960–1990. Although these authors discuss a case study, the general configuration they depicted can find obvious echoes in many Western countries. Figure 2 builds upon their diagram to illustrate the heuristic potential of the concept of field for sociological studies of the SPA 'supply'. This hypothetical structure of the SPA field proposes four main traits that can inform studies in other contexts:

- The field of SPA appears to be currently structured along lines of tension and conflict between various 'functions' of SPA, namely: an 'ethical' function (to promote the ideology of asceticism, self-improvement, and the cult of performance); an 'educational' function (to participate in the educational and social vocation of the school at a given time); a spectacular function (to promote performance and competition as a 'drama' and a show); a 'fitness/leisure' function (to promote health, body shape, hedonism); a commodity function (to promote SPA *via* consumption of goods and services relating to them); and a socio-political function (to promote the nationalistic value of high performance and a health value of SPA).
- The social groups and institutions associated with each of these functions "constantly interact, oppose each other, join together or adjust mutually, ensuring the dynamic of the system and regulating its evolution" (Defrance & Pociello, 1993: 4). They struggle for access to resources and for the maintenance and improvement of their competitive 'legitimacy' among the population. In the context of limited resources, what is at stake for each of them, then, is to get greater visibility in order to increase their economic profit or to improve the recognition of the specific social values (whether it

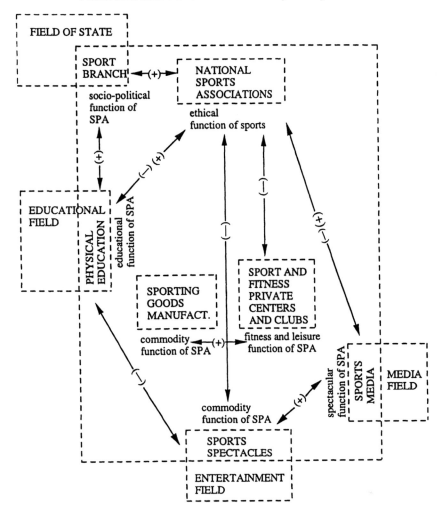

Figure 2. Diagram of a SPA Field and its Subfields (adapted version of Defrance & Pociello, 1993: 13)

be moral, economic, health-related, nationalistic, etc.) of the sport function they support. Hence, they develop strategies of alliance ('+' in the diagram) and opposition ('−' in the diagram).

The alliances proceed according to ideological relationships, but also according to common interests in a given state of the socio-economic context. For instance, one can notice 'logical' alliances between sport event organisers and sport media, as well as between the SPA branch of the State and both national sport associations and school physical educators. However, despite some ideological conflicts, national sport associations may develop alliances with the sport media due to budget cuts from the State. In contrast, the violence, drug use and unethical behaviours often displayed in certain sport settings generate opposition from school physical educators.

- It is possible to see overlaps of the SPA field and external fields (indicating that the strategies put forward by the social agents of the SPA field are affected by the stakes and dynamics of external fields), such as the international sport field, the educational field, the state field, the media field, and the entertainment field. We can even consider each of these overlaps as a subfield since each has its own history (e.g., the history of physical education, of state involvement in SPA), its own stakes (e.g., the legitimation of the 'educational' value of SPA versus other school disciplines, of the mediatic value of SPA versus that of other subjects likely to interest a large audience, of the nationalistic and socio-political value of sport versus that of other political issues).

- Finally, in all of these subfields as well as in the general SPA field there is also concurrence among the various forms of SPA, such as traditional sports versus new sports, men's versus women's sports, and so forth. Moreover, the struggle to maintain the current state of a sub-field may lead to an impediment to the entry of new SPA practices. Illustrations may be found in the recent fight against the recognition of 'sporting dance' as an Olympic sport and in the exclusion of boxing in Physical Education curricula.

As we can see, Bourdieu's concept of field encourages the researcher to investigate what is at stake in a given arena, to seek out the sources of conflict and collusion between social groups and institutions that interact, and to uncover the latent patterns of interest and struggle. It helps to understand how the structure of an arena produces inclusion and exclusion, selects forms of legitimate expression, and ultimately generates change in the 'products' supplied.

Bourdieu's Mode of Sociological Inquiry

Throughout his career, Bourdieu has continued to refine a distinctive approach to the production of sociological knowledge that unites theoretical reflection and empirical research. For Bourdieu, theory should always confront the world of observable phenomena (Bourdieu & Wacquant, 1992: 224–227). However, the thrust of his empirical investigation is less concerned with testing the 'validity' of his theory than it is with obtaining general empirical support for, and/or improving, his theoretical ideas. Indeed, his concepts are forged out from the process of empirical research and confrontation with opposing intellectual viewpoints. In accordance with his rejection of dogmatism, his concepts remain deliberately vague and malleable, encouraging their questioning and their adaptation to the specific domain to which they are applied. He calls them 'open concepts':[10]

> [. . .] the use of *open concepts* is a way of rejecting positivism. . . . It is, to be more precise, a permanent reminder that concepts have no definition other than systemic ones, and are designed to be *put to work empirically in systematic fashion*. Hence, such notions as habitus, field and capital can be defined, but only within the theoretical system they constitute, *not in isolation* (Bourdieu & Wacquant, 1992: 95; emphases in the original).

Consistent with his project to transcend the opposition between objectivism and subjectivism, his various field analyses blend ethnographic observations, open-ended interviews, and survey material together in a unique way. In *Distinction*, for example, he uses newspaper excerpts (articles, photographs, advertisements), and maps to support his analysis. In doing so, he contends that he "attempted to create a *discursive montage* that allows one to offer at once the scientific vision and the immediate intuition that this vision explains but also typically excludes" (Bourdieu & Wacquant, 1992: 66). Indeed, he considers to be valuable all types of data that could enlighten his sociological inquiry. However, this diversity of material is always subject to the epistemological principles that guide his approach, and to a critical vigilance with regard to 'pre-constructed' categories.

Concerning the qualitative part of his work, Bourdieu does not follow any methodological 'school' or tradition. For instance, one will never find in his account of interviews a description of his method of coding, organising, and analysing texts, as one can find in works using grounded theory or ethnomethodology. However, in *The Weight of the World* (Bourdieu *et al.*, 1999: 607–626), Bourdieu exposes in some detail the epistemological guidelines that ground his conception of the conduct and analysis of interviews.

[10]For an explanation of the distinction between 'open concepts' (or 'systemic concepts') and 'operational concepts', see Bourdieu, Chamboredon, and Passeron (1973: 53–54).

In the case of quantitative material, Bourdieu's use of statistical tools is quite different from (even opposed to) the common practice in sociology whereby attributes of individuals and groups are transformed into variables, hypotheses are tested, or the significance of factors is isolated. Bourdieu's claim for a relational approach leads him to reject linear modelling techniques (such as regression analysis) or predictive ones, in favour of a *descriptive* statistical procedure, namely correspondence analysis.[11] This procedure allows him to construct a *multidimensional* space (a space built with multiple axes of differentiation) that puts into light the configurations or structures of relations that characterise the data under study. One of the principles behind this statistical tool is that the data that are most often associated with one another in the target population will appear closer together (as a cluster of points) in the space, while those least often associated will be farthest away from one another. In Bourdieu's words:

> if I make extensive use of correspondence analysis, in preference to multivariate regression for instance, it is because corres-pondence analysis is a relational technique of data analysis whose philosophy corresponds exactly to what, in my view, the reality of the social world is. It is a technique which 'thinks' in terms of relation (Bourdieu & Wacquant, 1992: 96).

Bourdieu makes use of this technique in order to depict the struggles and oppositions present in social space (as can be seen in Figure 1). He also uses selected frequency tables derived from institutional surveys. Bourdieu uses these as a way to illustrate some of his arguments (see Bourdieu, 1984 and 1988a), but never discusses them as it would be done in the positivist tradition.

Finally, it is important to highlight a hallmark of Bourdieu's mode of sociological inquiry: his longstanding concern for a reflexive posture, what he calls 'reflexive sociology', or 'socio-analysis', or 'participant objectivation' (Bourdieu & Wacquant, 1992). These neologisms refer to the same concerns: on the one hand, for a critical reflection of the relationship of the researcher to the object of inquiry so that the position of the researcher is not unwittingly projected into the object of study; on the other hand, there is a concern for the validity of the categories used by the researcher to ensure that they are not socially but scientifically constructed. While Bourdieu provides no single methodological recipe for achieving a properly reflexive perspective, he offers few illustrations, notably that which appears in *Homo Academicus* (1988a),

[11]For more information on correspondence analysis as used by Bourdieu, see Rouanet, Ackermann, and Le Roux (2000); and Benzecri (1992).

his analysis of the French academic field (see Bourdieu & Wacquant, 1992: 62–74, 253–260).

Some Pitfalls in Bourdieu's Work

Bourdieu's work is not free from contradictions or shortcomings and has not gone without arousing controversy and critique.[12] However, Bourdieu himself considers that many objections and criticisms emerge from a degree of misapprehension or misreading.[13] Indeed, Wacquant notes that "the confounding variety of interpretations, the mutually exclusive criticisms, and the contradictory reactions it has elicited testify to this" (Wacquant, 1992a: 4). The causes of this situation can be partly located in what Bourdieu (Bourdieu, 1990a: 106) terms the 'production side', i.e., the author himself, and partly on the 'consumption side', the readers.

As for the author, we can identify at least three main difficulties that could lead to misreading. First, Bourdieu's writing style is tortuous. His sentences are often long and abstract, and charged with polemic, paradox, multiple negation and pun. All of this makes his work sometimes impenetrable to readers not familiar with a certain French writing style, and with the French intellectual context in which he is writing. Second, Bourdieu uses a variety of expressions or metaphors to designate the same concept without specifying that he wants to signal a nuance, an analytical refinement, or a change. For instance, 'habitus' is equally termed 'habit-forming force', 'generative principle of regulated improvisations', 'practical sense', and 'feel for the game'. A third and related difficulty lies in the deliberate vagueness of his concepts. Bourdieu is forcefully opposed to the dogmatism that eventually leads to a sclerosis of thought. Accordingly, his concepts are open, adaptable, even 'blurred', rather than operationally defined, and used rigidly. Yet, this is clearly at risk of generating confusion and ambiguity.

Still, numerous misunderstandings have also grown out of the way that Bourdieu has been 'read'. First, there is the fact that the fragmentary reading of

---

[12]There are too many critical reviews of Bourdieu's work to account for them in this limited space. His best known critics are, in English — Calhoun, LiPuma, and Postone (1993); and, in French — Mary, Caillé, Terrail, and Touboul (1991). The most recent collection of critical reviews is by Shusterman (1999).

[13]Bourdieu tries to resolve some misreadings, and responds to major criticisms of his theory in 1990a (106–122), in 1993 (263–275); and in Bourdieu and Wacquant (1992). Wacquant (1993) also offers an interesting analysis of the problems raised by the importation and adaptation of Bourdieu's theory by American scholars.

Bourdieu's work has led to serious misinterpretation of his concepts and mode of sociological inquiry. Indeed, it is difficult for someone to fully grasp his conceptual apparatus through the reading of a few works since Bourdieu constantly refines and develops his conceptualisation throughout his research. Second, major confusion stems from too literal a reading of his analyses. For instance, some scholars have interpreted *Distinction* as a book limited to showing that the driving force of social practice is the search for distinction, whereas Bourdieu used the term to designate the process of differentiation (deploying his relational mode of inquiry) at work in a social space (Bourdieu, 1998a: 9).

Similarly, literal readings have been applied to his notion of class, capital, and interest, while Bourdieu uses them in a sense that can be grasped only within his own epistemological framework. Another source of misapprehension undoubtedly comes from the fact that Bourdieu adopts a theoretical position that is unorthodox in the sociological tradition; that is, a position that attempts to integrate subjectivist and objectivist modes of knowledge, and to link structure and agency. Strict proponents of one mode or the other often see as weaknesses methodological and epistemological attempts to integrate these traditional oppositions.

An exhaustive account of the limits of Bourdieu's work is beyond the scope of this chapter. However, we would like to point to three main enduring shortcomings: first, the concept of habitus is so theoretically loaded and versatile that it becomes less effective for the empirical researcher who needs conceptual tools to identify specific dimensions of 'taste' and social practices as well as specific mechanisms at work in the internalisation and externalisation of the social structure; second, while Bourdieu's work offers a powerful demonstration of the mechanisms of social reproduction, it fails to provide a way to account for social movements of resistance and transformation. Although the concept of field allows one to assess the dynamic of transformation within an arena of social life, it can hardly be used for understanding collective action in the social space; finally, Bourdieu's treatment of gender as a 'secondary' constituent of social division (Bourdieu, 1984: 468) seems to contradict claims elsewhere in his work that gender is a major principle of social differentiation. Bourdieu's conception of social space is currently structured only by cultural and economic capital. In light of the importance that he gives to gender in the construction of social life, a more coherent approach would surely give gender an equivalent status in his conceptual system (McCall, 1992; Laberge, 1995).

Concluding Thoughts

The relevance of Bourdieu's social theory to the sociology of SPA is undeniable. Despite the theory's inherent complexity, his approach still constitutes a commanding and cogent resource for social scientists — or, simply, for human beings seeking to understand the 'social game' in which they take part. The main contributions of Bourdieu's social theory to the sociology of SPA can be summed up as follows.

First, it highlights SPA practices as bearers of particular symbolic value in a given society and thus, in their capacity as social group signifiers, to produce social differentiation. The theory, therefore, reveals the critical role played by SPA practices in the construction/affirmation of an individual's identity and difference. Second, Bourdieu's notion of habitus debunks the notion that one's taste for a particular SPA practice is the result of a 'natural' disposition or psychological trait. Rather, taste is generated by a class-specific relation to one's body, and by the different perceptions and appreciation of the profit expected from the practice. Habitus also transcends the traditional opposition between structure and agency by suggesting that dispositions, perceptions and appreciation with regard to SPA are generated by classificatory schemes acquired through socialisation specific to a given position in the hierarchical social structure. A third major contribution of Bourdieu's social theory to the sociology of SPA is the central role he accords to symbolic systems — or culture — in power relations. For Bourdieu, symbolic systems fulfil a political function by actively contributing to the legitimation and naturalisation of social differences, and thus, to the construction and maintenance of a given social order. Finally, the concept of field provides the SPA sociologist with a tool to recognise resources at stake in the SPA arena, to identify the sources of conflict and collusion between interacting social groups and institutions, and to uncover the latent patterns of interests and struggles in the definition of 'legitimate' SPA practices.

Ultimately, however, Bourdieu himself intends the primary contribution of his social theory to be to fight against social domination: "The true freedom that sociology offers is to give us a small chance of knowing what game we play and of minimising the ways in which we are manipulated by the forces of the field in which we evolve, as well as by the embodied social forces that operate from within us" (Bourdieu & Wacquant, 1992: 198).

References

Benzecri, J.-P. (1992). *Correspondence Analysis Handbook*. New York: Marcel Dekker.
Bourdieu, P. (1962 [1958]). *The Algerians*. Boston, MA: Beacon Press.
Bourdieu, P. (1977 [1972]). *Outline of a Theory of Practice*. Cambridge: Cambridge University Press.
Bourdieu, P. (1978). Sport and social class. *Social Science Information, 17*(6), 819–840. A slightly revised version was published on the title: How can one be a sportsman? In: P. Bourdieu (1993), *Sociology in Question* (pp. 117–132). London: Sage Publishers.
Bourdieu, P. (1984 [1979]). *Distinction: A Social Critique of the Judgement of Taste*. Cambridge, MA: Harvard University Press.
Bourdieu, P. (1987). Legitimation and structured interests in Weber's sociology of religion. In: S. Lash and S. Wimster (eds), *Max Weber, Rationality and Irrationality* (pp. 119–136). Boston, MA: Allen & Unwin.
Bourdieu, P. (1988a [1984]). *Homo Academicus*. Cambridge: Polity Press.
Bourdieu, P. (1988b [1983]). Program for a sociology of sport. *Sociology of Sport Journal, 5*(2), 153–161.
Bourdieu, P. (1990a [1987]). *In Other Words: Essays Toward a Reflexive Sociology*. Cambridge: Polity Press; Stanford: Stanford University Press.
Bourdieu, P. (1990b [1980]). *The Logic of Practice*. Stanford: Stanford University Press.
Bourdieu, P. (1991a [1982]). *Language and Symbolic Power*. Cambridge: Polity Press.
Bourdieu, P. (1991b). Genesis and structure of the religious field. *Comparative Social Research, 13*, 1–43.
Bourdieu, P. (1993). Concluding remarks: For a sociogenetic understanding of intellectual works. In: C. Calhoun, E. LiPuma and M. Postone (eds), *Bourdieu: Critical Perspectives* (pp. 263–275). Chicago: University of Chicago Press.
Bourdieu, P. (1995 [1992]). *The Rules of Art: The Genesis and Structure of the Literary Field*. Stanford: Stanford University Press.
Bourdieu, P. (1997). *Les Usages Sociaux de la Science: Pour une Sociologie Clinique du Champ Scientifique* [*Social Uses of Science: For a Clinical Sociology of the Scientific Field*]. Paris: INRA.
Bourdieu, P. (1998a [1994]). *Practical Reason. On the Theory of Action*. Cambridge, UK: Polity Press.
Bourdieu, P. (1998b [1998]). *On Television*. New York: New Press.
Bourdieu, P. (1998c). *La Domination Masculine* [*Masculine Domination*]. Paris: Seuil.
Bourdieu, P. (1999 [1998]). *Acts of Resistance. Against the Tyranny of the Market*. New York: New Press.
Bourdieu, P., Boltanski, L., Castel, R., & Chamboredon, J.-C. (1990 [1965]). *Photography: A Middle-Brow Art*. Cambridge: Polity Press.
Bourdieu, P., Darbel, A., & Schnapper, D. (1990 [1966]). *The Love of Art: European Art Museums and their Public*. Cambridge: Polity Press.

Bourdieu, P., Haacke, H., & Johnson, R. (1995 [1994]). *Free Exchange.* Stanford: Stanford University Press.

Bourdieu, P., & Passeron, J.-C. (1977 [1970]). *Reproduction in Education, Society and Culture.* London: Sage Publishers.

Bourdieu, P., & Wacquant, L. J. D. (1992). *An Invitation to Reflexive Sociology.* Chicago: The University of Chicago Press.

Bourdieu, P. *et al.* (1999 [1993]). *The Weight of the World: Social Suffering in Contemporary Society.* London: Polity Press; Stanford: Stanford University Press.

Brubaker, R. (1985). Rethinking classical sociology: The sociological vision of Pierre Bourdieu. *Theory and Society, 14*(6), 745–775.

Calhoun, C., LiPuma, E., & Postone, M. (eds) (1993). *Bourdieu: Critical Perspectives.* Chicago: University of Chicago Press.

Clément, J.-P. (1995). Contributions of the sociology of Pierre Bourdieu to the sociology of sport. *Sociology of Sport Journal, 12*(2), 147–158.

Clément, J.-P. (1981). La force, la souplesse et l'harmonie: Étude comparée de trois sports de combat (lutte, judo, aïkido) [Strength, flexibility, harmony: A comparative study of three combative sports (wrestling, judo, aïkido]. In: C. Pociello (ed.), *Sports et Société* [*Sports and Society*] (pp. 285–382). Paris: Vigot.

Defrance, J. (1995). The anthropological sociology of Pierre Bourdieu: Genesis, concepts, relevance. *Sociology of Sport Journal, 12*(2), 121–132.

Defrance, J., & Pociello, C. (1993). Structure and evolution of the field of sports in France (1960–1990). *International Review for the Sociology of Sport, 28*(1), 1–23.

Elias, N., & Dunning, E. (1986). *The Quest for Excitement. Sport and Leisure in the Civilizing Process.* Oxford: Basil Blackwell.

Gruneau, R. (1993). The critique of sport in modernity: Theorising power, culture, and the politics of the body. In: E. Dunning, J. A. Maguire and R. Pearton (eds), *The Sports Process* (pp. 85–110). Champaign, IL: Human Kinetics.

Harker, R., Mahar, C., & Wilkes, C. (1990). *An Introduction to the Work of Pierre Bourdieu. The Practice of Theory.* London: Macmillan Press.

Harvey, J., & Sparks, R. (1991). The politics of the body in the context of modernity. *Quest, 43*(2), 164–189.

Jarvie, G., & Maguire, J. A. (1994). *Sport and Leisure in Social Thought.* London and New York: Routledge.

Laberge, S. (1995). Toward an integration of gender into Bourdieu's concept of cultural capital. *Sociology of Sport Journal, 12*(2), 132–147.

Laberge, S., & Sankoff, D. (1988). Physical activities, body habitus, and lifestyles. In: J. Harvey and H. Cantelon (eds), *Not Just a Game: Essays in Canadian Sport Sociology* (pp. 267–286). Ottawa: University of Ottawa Press.

Lash, S., & Urry, J. (1987). *The End of Organized Capitalism.* Cambridge: Polity Press.

Mary, A., Caillé, A., Terrail, J.-P., & Touboul, H. (1991). *Lectures de Pierre Bourdieu* [*Lectures on Pierre Bourdieu*]. Caen: Ab Coedition Arcane–Beaunieux.

Matsumura, K. (1993). Sport and social change in the Japanese rural community. *International Review for the Sociology of Sport, 28*(2/3), 135–144.

McCall, L. (1992). Does gender fit?: Bourdieu, feminism, and conceptions of social order. *Theory and Society, 21*(6), 837–867.

Merton, R. K. (1987). Three fragments from a sociologist's notebook: Establishing the phenomenon, specified ignorance, and strategic research materials. *Annual Review of Sociology, 13*(1), 1–28.

Ohl, F. (2000). Are social classes still relevant to analyse sports groupings in "postmodern" society?: An analysis referring to P. Bourdieu's theory. *Scandinavian Journal of Medicine and Science in Sports, 10*, 146–155.

Pociello, C. (ed.) (1981). *Sports et Société: Approche Socioculturelle des Pratiques* [*Sport and Societies: A Sociocultural Approach of Practices*]. Paris: Vigot.

Pociello, C. (1983). *Le Rugby ou la Guerre des Styles* [*Rugby or the War of Styles*]. Paris: Métailié.

Pociello, C. (1999). *Sports et Sciences Sociales* [*Sports and Social Sciences*]. Paris: Vigot.

Rouanet, H., Ackermann, W., & Le Roux, B. (2000). The geometric analysis of questionnaires: The lesson of Bourdieu's *La Distinction. Bulletin of Methodological Sociology, 65* (http://www.ccr.jussieu.fr/bms/).

Shilling, C. (1993). *The Body and Social Theory*. London: Sage Pub.

Shusterman, R. (ed.) (1999). *Bourdieu. A Critcal Reader*. Malden, MA: Blackwell

Swartz, D. (1997). *Culture and Power. The Sociology of Pierre Bourdieu*. Chicago, London: University of Chicago Press.

Taks, M., Renson, R., & Vanreusel, B. (1995). Social stratification in sport: A matter of money or taste? *European Journal of Sport Management, 2*(1), 4–14.

von der Lippe, G. (2000). Heresy as a victorious political practice. *International Review for the Sociology of Sport, 35*(2), 181–199.

Wacquant, L. J. D. (1992a). Toward a social praxeology: The structure and logic of Bourdieu's sociology. In: P. Bourdieu and L. J. D. Wacquant (eds), *An invitation to Reflexive Sociology* (pp. 1–59). Chicago: The University of Chicago Press.

Wacquant, L. J. D. (1992b). The social logic of boxing in black Chicago: Toward a sociology of pugilism. *Sociology of Sport Journal, 9*(3), 221–254.

Wacquant, L. J. D. (1993). Bourdieu in America: Notes on the transatlantic importation of social theory. In: C. Calhoun, E. LiPuma and M. Postone (eds), *Bourdieu: Critical Perspectives* (pp. 235–262). Chicago: University of Chicago Press.

Wacquant, L. J. D. (1995). *Protection, discipline et honneur: Une salle de boxe dans le ghetto américain.* [Protection, discipline and honour: A boxing gym in an American ghetto]. *Sociologie et Sociétés, 27*(1), 75–90; special issue on sport and society edited by S. Laberge and J. Harvey.

White, P., & Wilson, B. (1999). Distinctions in the stands: An investigation of Bourdieu's 'habitus', socioeconomic status and sport spectatorship in Canada. *International Review for the Sociology of Sport, 34*(3), 245–264.

Chapter 11

Studying Sport from a Social Network Approach

Howard L. Nixon II

Undergraduate students often have difficulty grasping the subject matter of sociology. In the United States, a culture of individualism (Nixon, 1984: 17–19) encourages people to think more psychologically than sociologically about human behaviour, which contributes to difficulties or hesitation in thinking sociologically. Social network analysis provides a means of thinking about, studying, and analysing human behaviour sociologically. It provides a sociological framework for understanding human behaviour as *social* behaviour with *social* causes and implications.

Social network analysis is more than a framework, however, even though some (e.g., Scott, 1991: 38) have viewed it mainly as a set of methods for social research and analysis. Wellman (1988) argued that social network analysis is a comprehensive paradigm that focuses directly on patterns of social relations that become part of enduring social structures. Furthermore, he proposed that network analysis, which he called 'structural analysis', derived its strength from being "an integrated application of theoretical concepts, ways of collecting and analysing data, and a growing, cumulating body of substantive findings" (Wellman, 1988: 20).

Wellman has been a major proponent of this type of analysis for the social and behavioural sciences, and he has made important contributions to the development of the 'paradigm' and its body of knowledge. He identified five primary paradigmatic features of social network analysis. These features include emphases on: (a) structural constraints from positions in social networks rather than inner forces within social units, which might be persons, groups, organisations, or even nations; (b) relations between social units rather than the attributes of each independent unit; (c) how the patterned relationships among the variety of others with whom a social unit interacts jointly, rather than merely individually, affect the social unit; (d) structure as a network of networks that may or may not each have discrete group boundaries around them; and (e) analytic methods that focus explicitly on social structures as patterned social relations and supplement or replace conventional statistical methods that require independent units of analysis (Wellman, 1988: 20).

According to Wasserman and Faust (1994) in their text on methods and models for analysing social network data, the essence of social network analysis is its focus on social relationships between interacting units, or "actors", and how they become patterned and influence other relationships and actors. While conceptualising, measuring, mapping, and analysing social relations can pose difficult conceptual, methodological, and analytical challenges, these kinds of problems are central to the sociological enterprise. Sociologists may differ in the relative emphasis they place on the freedom or constraint of actors in society or in their specific theoretical or methodological approach to understand human social behaviour and society. Yet all sociologists share an interest in understanding patterns of human social relations. Social network analysis is defined by this interest, and its focus on *relational* data is consistent with the structural tradition in sociology that examines how enduring patterns of social relations — called 'social structures' — develop from interactions between people or other actors in different positions (Marsden & Lin, 1982; Scott, 1991).

Although a number of social network analysts are more interested in the structural causes and forms of network patterns than they are in their content or meanings (e.g., Lorrain & White, 1971; Fararo, 1973), the flow of content or meanings through network structures also interests network analysts (Wellman, 1988). In addition, a network-exchange perspective, inspired by Emerson's (1962) work on power-dependence relations, focuses on the flow of power through social exchange networks (e.g., Cook, 1982; Skvoretz & Willer, 1991). The question of whether social behaviour is influenced more by how social actors are linked together or what kinds of things flow through the links or relations between actors ultimately becomes a matter for researchers to resolve. All of these abstractions will become much easier to visualise or understand when we examine the key elements of social network analysis and the ways that network ideas and methods have been applied in actual sociological research. These topics will be considered after we look at a brief history of social network analysis. Following more general discussions of network analysis, we will consider how network ideas and methods could be applied to past and future work in the sociology of sport.

A Brief History of Social Network Analysis

We can trace the origins of formal analysis of social networks in sociology to Simmel and his studies of dyads, triads, conflict, and webs of group affiliation (Simmel, 1908, 1950). Simmel's work drew attention to the implications of structural factors such as group size on intimacy and other interpersonal relations in groups (Nixon, 1979: 9–12). Beyond the general foundation for social network analysis in Simmel's work, we can see the development of contemporary social network analysts follow three distinct historical paths in sociology and anthropology. According to Scott (1991: ch. 2), these historical paths are: (a) the study of groups from the sociometric perspective of Moreno (1934), which led to the application of graph theory, and the group dynamics research of Lewin (1951), who used the mathematics of topology and set theory to understand the interdependent relations between groups and their environment; (b) work by Harvard researchers in the 1930s that most prominently included Warner and Lunt's (1941, 1942) "Yankee City" community studies and Mayo and his colleagues' (e.g., Roethlisberger & Dickson, 1939) studies of the Western Electric Hawthorne plant focusing on informal relations and cliques in a large organisation; and (c) the work by British anthropologists Barnes (1954, 1972), Bott (1957), and Mitchell (1969, 1974), which examined structures of social relations in tribal and village communities. This work showed the imprint of the British social anthropologist, Radcliffe–Brown, in its emphasis on both social structure and power and conflict in social systems (Scott, 1991: 8). The work of these anthropologists was quite influential in Great Britain but, according to Scott, it tended to place attention on informal social relations of a 'communal' type and egocentric networks, which are conceptualised in terms of the social relations of particular individuals. A focus on more general qualities of whole networks of various types awaited the direction given by later Harvard investigators.

At Harvard, Homans (1950) sought to integrate the sociometric and anthropological approaches to structural analysis in his study of "the human group". This early work did not have the impact of his subsequent social exchange theory (Homans, 1961), with its roots in Skinnerian behaviourism and economic rational choice models, but his work on the human group still offers a good example of social network analysis in sociology at the middle of the twentieth century. Homans used matrices and carefully formulated hypotheses to achieve greater precision in the representation and understanding of social structures of groups. This emphasis on precision — reflected in a reliance on increasingly sophisticated mathematical techniques and models — is a distinctive feature of the development of social network analysis.

Homans' turn toward social exchange theory may have minimised his influence on the development of social network analysis, but subsequent Harvard scholars have had a major impact on the development of more rigorous, precise, and sophisticated methods and models for analysing large and small social networks of all kinds. For example, White trained a number of students at Harvard in the network approach to social structural analysis in the 1960s and 1970s (Wellman, 1988: 23) and made a strong argument that "network concepts may provide the only way to construct a theory of social structure" (White, Boorman, & Breiger, 1976: 732). White and his colleagues' work reflected the influence of prior structural analysis in the sociological and anthropological traditions, but according to Scott (1991: 32), this newer work provided a "breakthrough" in social network analysis. White's (1963) *An Anatomy of Kinship*, for example, illustrates how algebraic models of groups relying on set theory were used to represent patterns of social relations, in this case in kinship structures. In addition, sophisticated versions of block-models, earlier suggested by Homans' work on groups, were developed; various structural and network concepts were represented with mathematics and studied with mathematical techniques, and multidimensional scaling techniques were developed to represent and map previously elusive dimensions of social networks (Scott, 1991: 33–34).

Granovetter is one of the members of the 'Harvard network group' whose work may have had the widest influence in social science to date. Granovetter was interested in how people find jobs, and his influential analysis focused on the "strength of weak ties" (Granovetter, 1973, 1974, 1982). He proposed that weak ties perform an integrative function when they act as bridges between different networks. The importance of weak ties is that they are "disproportionately likely to be bridges, as compared to strong ties, which should be under-represented in that role" (Granovetter, 1982: 130).

Granovetter's work indicates how a social network approach can be applied to important matters of everyday life, such as securing a job. In the ensuing sections, we will examine key conceptual and methodological elements of the social network approach. The purpose of this discussion is not to convey the technical or quantitative details of the mathematics or methods of social network analysis, but instead to show in broad outline, the possibilities of network analysis for understanding the *sociology* of sport.

Key Elements of the Social Network Analysis Approach

Berkowitz was part of White's research group in the 1970s and wrote what may be the first general introduction to social network analysis. Berkowitz (1982) pointed out that the network approach to structural analysis did not constitute a single tightly integrated paradigm because its origins were diverse, as we noted. We can add that some network investigators were more heuristic or metaphorical in their use of a social network 'paradigm', while others were committed to representing and analysing the social world in terms of precisely formulated and formalistic models of social networks.

Wellman (1988: 40–47) identified some basic analytic principles shared by social network analysts:

1. Social relations or ties typically do not involve balanced exchanges, with the kinds of resources that are exchanged and intensity felt by the actors involved often being different; that is, "ties are usually asymmetrically reciprocal" (Wellman, 1988: 40).

2. Social ties linking members of a social network can be direct or indirect and voluntary or involuntary and should be seen in the context of larger social networks.

3. Social ties may be structured in ways that create clusters, boundaries, and cross-linkages, with individual actors often tied to a number of different social networks. According to Wellman, clustered networks create a paradox of integration for social systems; systems are highly connected at the level of the individuals who may be located in the midst of dense networks of direct and indirect social ties, but at the same time, at the level of the entire system, the social network may appear highly disconnected with many pairs of actors who are not directly or indirectly tied to one another (1988: 43).

4. Social ties connect clusters of actors, such as groups, corporations, and nations, as well as individual actors. Certain individual actors may be especially important because they link different clusters of actors, as in the case of interlocking corporate directorates in which an individual director is a member of the board of two or more different corporations. Being links between different clusters in such cases can give social actors special strategic and resource advantages in relations with other social actors, as when people who are uniquely positioned to have 'insider' information about relations between two different corporations use that information to affect stock transactions involving the corporations.

5. Resources do not flow evenly or equally to all actors in social networks because social ties are asymmetric, clusters of certain actors within networks may have boundaries around them, and certain actors may be located in parts of social networks that are less accessible than other parts are. Social networks with asymmetric ties between individual actors and clusters may become structured hierarchically and create cumulative inequalities in

access to resources. Asymmetric ties, hierarchies, and entrenched inequalities characterise networks of states, regions, nations, and multinational corporate actors. An example of the application of this conception of social networks is 'world-systems theory', which is based on assumptions of steeply hierarchical and highly unequal structures of relations among more and less industrially developed nations in the world network (Wallerstein, 1974). Certain actors gain power in social networks as a result of their structural location and the control over resources their position allows. For example, gatekeepers who control access to key network actors gain power, prestige, and use of valuable resources. Brokers gain their advantage from mediating between different clusters in social networks. They may derive a portion of their power from their marginality. They do not belong to the clusters whose relations they mediate and thus are not completely trusted because these clusters cannot control them. Thus, power derives from controlling the flow of resources through social networks. In some cases, people may flow through networks as they move from one position to another. In other cases, positions may be upwardly or downwardly mobile when people with different amounts of resources occupy them. White (1970) has studied how vacancies flow through social networks when actors vacate one position and move to another as part of a series of linked 'vacancy chains'. In this way, social network approaches can be used to study patterns of social mobility of persons and within occupations, organisations, and society.

6. Social networks create patterns of cooperation and competition among members seeking control over scarce resources. According to Burt (1992), competitive advantage in competitive settings goes to entrepreneurs who can serve as links filling 'structural holes', which are gaps between unconnected individuals with complementary resources or information. When social networks are hierarchical and social ties are asymmetric, coalitions or factions develop to enable less advantaged members to compete successfully for scarce resources. Thus, there is a structural basis for collective political behaviour. The formation and influence of political coalitions or clusters within social networks and their battles for resources can help us understand how networks become realigned and basic social structures change.

Throughout this discussion of network themes and analytic principles, a number of network concepts were explicitly or implicitly introduced. Wasserman and Faust's definition of the actor was previously cited, but the most fundamental concept is the social network idea itself. Social networks are collections of actors and the social ties and sets of ties in social relations that directly or indirectly link actors to one another (see Wasserman & Faust, 1994: 17–21). The social network analysis of social structure focuses on qualities of social ties and social relations, rather than on qualities of individual actors.

Social relations in social networks are channels for transmitting goods, services, information, influence, and sentiments. The social support that often flows through social relations can be a combination of some or all of these resources. The persisting patterns in the flow of resources through social networks become part of network structure. Most social network analysts have concentrated on the effects of network structure, but social network analysis can focus on various types of network properties and their implications for understanding social interaction patterns. Smith (1987: 382–405) summarised four major types of properties of social networks: (a) transactional content, which includes the meanings of messages or resources in social relations; (b) structural dimensions, which include size, density, centrality, reachability of other actors in a network, openness to links outside the formal or informal network boundaries, clustering or the number of highly connected or dense regions or subgroups in a network, and the stability of network patterns; (c) the nature of links, which includes the intensity, reciprocity, and multiplexity or diversity of ties between actors and the clarity of expectations about the relations; and (d) individual dimensions, which include roles of isolates, stars, gatekeepers, liaisons, and bridges and brokers linking different clusters.

The "tool box" of social network analysts contains methodological strategies and techniques as well as concepts (e.g., Berkowitz, 1982; Burt & Minor, 1983; Freeman, White, & Romney, 1992). The data from which sociograms and other maps of social ties and relations are derived for network analysis can be generated by a range of procedures, including social surveys, observational techniques, informant interviews, and archival studies (see Burt & Minor, 1983). A combination of ethnographic field methods and formal analysis may also be used to collect and interpret network data (Mitchell, 1994). The analysis of sociometric data is highly complex for larger networks. Therefore, the development of powerful computational aids, assisted by the computer, has made it possible to analyse network data for large networks.

Social network analysts have developed various forms of mathematics to manipulate the data in matrices, and they have used models of various kinds, such as block-models, which represent sets of nodes in a data network (Berkowitz, 1982: 133–137; Freeman, White, & Romney, 1992). While formalistic network analysts have developed and relied on formal models and mathematics, there have been other social network analysts, such as Wellman (e.g., 1979, 1982), who have relied less on mathematics than on the network-as-metaphor approach and have concentrated on egocentric — or personal —

networks. In both cases, though, there has been a basic focus on social positions and relations in social structures.

Current Directions in Social Network Analysis in the Social and Behavioural Sciences

Although the concepts, models, and methods of network analysis have been used in a wide range of disciplines, we will concentrate on examples of recent network studies with relevance to the sociology of sport. We will not pay attention here to the more technical work concerning mathematical and statistical models, methods, and procedures. Although this type of work can make social network analysis seem very inaccessible to sociologists as well as sociologists of sport, it should not dissuade sociologists or sport scholars from using less technical concepts, models, and methods of social network analysis to pursue their research.

New Theoretical Directions

In a keynote address to the International Sunbelt Social Network Conference in 1999, Lin (1999) proposed a social network theory of social capital. He observed that social capital had become a very important or, at least, frequently used concept in the social sciences and argued that social capital derived from embedded resources in social networks. He proposed that the roots of the social capital concept could be found in works ranging from the classical economic theory of Marx to more contemporary theoretical work by Bourdieu, Coleman, Burt, and Marsden (Lin, 1999: 30). This concept is related to notions of human and cultural capital, but it is distinguished by the assumption that investments in *social relations* have pay-offs for social actors. According to Lin, social capital consists of resources embedded in a social structure; access to these resources for social actors appropriately situated in the social structure; and use of these resources for purposive actions. Thus, social capital is integrally related to social structure and links structure to action. Social location becomes social capital at least in part when it provides social actors with the chance to exercise more control.

Lin used his own prior work on social resources theory (1982) to demonstrate the potential significance of structurally embedded social capital, noting his assumption that social capital derived from social networks and social relations can lead to enhanced socioeconomic status. This pattern was illustrated by Granovetter's (1973, 1974) work on the use of weak ties in social networks to secure jobs. Lin also cited Bourdieu's notion that the amount of social capital was affected by the size of social networks and the amount of economic, cultural, and symbolic capital possessed by other actors in an actor's network. He also mentioned Burt's idea that certain network positions, such as structural holes, may enable social actors to obtain better positions or other benefits in organisations. In general, a major contribution of Lin's network theory of social capital is to enable us to see how social actors can use the resources associated with their position and social contacts in social networks to gain various kinds of rewards, ranging from money, power, and prestige to better physical and mental health (Lin, 1999: 41). An important task in the development of this kind of theory is to clarify how inequalities in access to and mobilisation of social capital develop and become part of network structures and ultimately affect the overall life chances of social actors.

Social network ideas can be used in various ways to develop or extend sociological theory. For example, Carley (1999) proposed that the evolution of social and organisational networks can significantly affect how information is diffused through networks, how it is acquired and used, and how decisions are made. She pointed out that models of network evolution tended to ignore that networks tend to evolve in an environment of interdependent networks and that changes in any particular social network are likely to be shaped by how the various networks in its environment are interrelated. This is an important idea because it encourages us to look outside individual social organisations and other social networks for external structural relations as possible causes of the internal dynamics and structures of these networks. Examples of other recently published network-related theoretical work include studies of: (a) structural and strategic influences on collective action (Chwe, 1999); (b) the use of a firm's own social capital and the social capital of its organisational agents through collusion, contracts, strategic alliances, and interlocking directorates to gain competitive advantages in the marketplace (Galaskiewicz & Zaheer, 1999); and (c) how patterns of association with dissimilar others (heterophily) in organisations, which are much less common than the opposite patterns of homophily, are affected by the demographics of organisational memberships, how the relationship between heterophily and organisational heterogeneity is shaped by an organisation's position in its environment, and how the variety of organisations to which people belong affects the overall level of heterophily in their personal network (Popielarz, 1999).

Recent Research Directions

A search through the recent research literature suggests additional ways that social network analysis is currently being used to understand social structural patterns and influences. A sample of studies from this literature shows us that network researchers have been interested in: (a) how the strength of affective and supportive social ties in the social networks of runaway and homeless youths affected their engagement in risky behaviours (such as illicit drug use, multiple sex partners, and other types of sex) (Ennett, Bailey, & Federman, 1999); (b) the strategies used to coordinate home and work in dual-earning households affected by a "tangled web" of networks involving social and kin relations, resources, and information, knowledge, and learning (Jarvis, 1999); (c) how relationships between CEOs and outside directors involving independent control by the directors reduce the tendency towards strategic alliance formation by creating distrust among corporate leaders, while cooperation between CEOs and boards of directors in strategic decision making seems to encourage alliance formation by increasing trust (Gulati & Westphal, 1999); (d) how weak inter-unit ties in a multi-unit organisation speed up the search and transfer of knowledge and new product development when knowledge is not complex, but impedes communication and project development when knowledge is complex (Hansen, 1999); (e) how higher contact frequency and lower travel time to reach a network member increase the chances of continued relationships and how larger networks increase the likelihood that unbalanced exchanges will be terminated for older adults (Ikkink & van Tilburg, 1999); (f) how collaboration among firms in an industry creates a competitive advantage for individual firms and pushes the industry to develop and how collaborative learning through interorganisational networks eventually produces decreasing marginal returns for the organisation (Powell, Koput, Doerr *et al.*, 1999); (g) how gender may be more than a status attribute that people bring to the workplace in being structurally embedded in occupational environments, which makes it more difficult to remove gender influences or biases from the workplace (Talmud & Izraeli, 1999); (h) how the development of fraud networks in the securities industry depends on having highly centralised and intense communication relations as well as on being in a highly centralised decision making network (Zey, 1999); and (i) how structural holes in a network enhance the promotion opportunities for male, but not female, senior managers in the electronics and computing equipment industries and how earlier promotions were achieved by women who "borrowed" the social capital or networks of strategic partners, implying that insider–outsider differences play a bigger role than gender differences in the uses of social capital (Burt, 1998).

Applications of Social Network Analysis to the Study of Sport

Organisations are often the focus of social network analysis or the setting for social network research, with network analysts studying organisations as actors in social networks, social networks in organisations, social networks created by interorganisational ties and relations, and social ties linking different organisations. For example, in looking at economic organisations, Powell (1990) proposed that using a social network model of these organisations implies more established and diffuse ties than we associate with economic organisations when we see them mainly as competitors in the marketplace. In addition, he proposed that network models place more emphasis on reciprocal and egalitarian structures in organisations than hierarchical (or bureaucratic) models suggest and more emphasis on a relational perspective of communication and on organisational interdependence in making choices and acting than we find in either market or hierarchical perspectives (see Scott, 1998: 276, 277).

Although the landscape of sport is dotted with organisations and various types of interorganisational relations are an important part of this sports landscape, it is surprising that sociologists of sport have tended to relegate the study of organisations to sports management scholars. In view of the rich potential in social network analysis for understanding sports organisations, it is also surprising that sociologically-minded sports management scholars have not seemed to rely much on social network analysis. For example, a recent edition of a leading text on sports organisations that explicitly drew from the sociology of organisations' literature referred to networks only once and devoted only two pages to a discussion of how people in organisations can become more politically effective by building networks of contacts among sponsors, peers, and subordinates (Slack, 1997: 187–188). An important idea implied by this discussion is that networks that extend beyond the organisation's boundaries, as well as networks within the organisation, can enhance the political effectiveness of organisation members and the organisation as a whole. Slack gave the example of the Calgary Olympic Organising Committee for the 1988 Winter Games, which facilitated its organising efforts by using ties to International Olympic Committee, government, and corporate officials and others with international sports organising expertise and experience (King, 1991).

On reflection, the limited attention to social network analysis in the study of sports organisations is not really surprising. In fact, this relative inattention to social network analysis is found in the sociology of sport in general. With a few exceptions (e.g., Nixon, 1992, 1993a, 1993b, 1998; Walk, 1997; Roderick, 1998), we have not explicitly explored the value or use of social network analysis for conceptualisation, theory, or research in the sociology of sport. Yet, since sociology is fundamentally concerned with social structures and their effects, the sociology of sport could use social network concepts, models, and methods in many ways to enhance our understanding of sport. To recommend future work in this direction, I would like to review some extant network-related work in sport, including work only implicitly using a network approach, and then suggest where social network analysis could be used in the sociology of sport in the future.

We should keep in mind that insights about social relations in sport could come from network ideas, images, and models in narrative or descriptive form as well as from more rigorous, technical, mathematical, and formalistic network approaches. Slack's (1997: 187–188) brief discussion of building network contacts for political gains is an example of how the general and non-technical use of network concepts can provide insights about the political importance of social ties for sports organisations. Other applications of social network analysis to sport are suggested in a prior article (Nixon, 1993a). Part of the ensuing discussion in this section draws from that article.

In Baxter, Margavio, and Lambert's (1996) study of sanctions against National Collegiate Athletic Association (NCAA) member institutions from 1952 to 1990, we see how the density of the competitive environment affects a school's likelihood of being sanctioned for violating NCAA rules. Schools in less densely competitive environments were more likely to be penalised than were schools in more densely competitive environments. This research also indicated that variations in penalties could be explained in terms of the different structural properties, patterns of competition, legitimacy of regulatory bodies and rules, and resource exchange patterns of networks of NCAA institutions in different regions of the country, with penalties more likely in Division I schools in the South, Southwest, and Midwest than in the Mideast and East.

Frey (1978) studied the patterns of conflict and cooperation in inter-organisational relations in the amateur sports network in the US in the 1970s. In this network, individual sports federations exercised dominance in their relations with the various individual and organisational actors in their sports. They resisted efforts by the federal government to establish a more centralised national sports network because this change in power relations would threaten the dominance of these federations over their sport and could diminish their revenue potential.

Knoppers *et al.* (1990) studied gender and the distribution of power in intercollegiate athletic departments. Their research revealed why it is necessary to consider both the revenue-generating aspects of sport and the gender of coaches in explaining access to resources and resource mobilisation for the exercise of power within the social networks of athletic departments of individual institutions. A social network approach and power and network-exchange ideas would allow us to understand how resources are obtained and used in these social networks and how they affect the asymmetry of power relations between women and men and between others in differential status relations in these networks.

In another study, Knoppers *et al.* (1993) tested three alternative hypotheses about the effects of gender ratio on the frequency of interaction between men and women coaches: one predicted that increasing the gender ratio (proportion of women to men) in work groups will improve the work experiences of women and increase inter-gender interaction and reduce sex segregation (politics of optimism hypothesis); the second predicted that increasing the gender ratio will increase women's contacts with other women, decrease men's interaction with women, and have no effect on women's contacts with men or men's interaction with other men, resulting in an overall pattern of increasing sex segregation (politics of pessimism hypothesis); and the third predicted that situational factors affecting work groups could unite members and blur the effects of gender on patterns of interaction and work experiences for women and men, resulting in increases in all types of gender interactions except men with men (politics of transcendence hypothesis). The researchers studied nearly 950 Division I college coaches in the US, with the gender ratio based only on coaches of women's teams, since there is a very low gender ratio for coaches of men's teams. The focus on women's teams accounted for the prediction of no change in men's contacts with other men in the second and third hypotheses.

The research provided the most support for the politics of pessimism hypothesis, with an increased gender ratio associated with an increase in social interaction between women but no change in the frequency of interaction of women with men or of men with women or with other men. In comparing the interactions of women in the low and high ratio conditions, the researchers concluded that the increased entry of women into the male-dominated profession of coaching may have raised, rather than lowered, gender boundaries in social relations and thus, created more sex segregation. Social network analysis enables us to see the structure and evolution of patterns of interaction in social networks such as athletic departments, the clustering and isolation of actors in these networks, and the implications of different locations in these networks for access to and mobilisation of social capital.

In his case study of the day-to-day interaction in a small community-based track and field club in Canada, Pitter (1990) showed how power and control relations influenced interaction patterns. In particular, he found that interaction was influenced by a hierarchical and centralised power structure that favoured coaches and the most successful athletes. As a result, club members had different amounts of social capital, reflected in differential access to resources and control over the organisation.

In their article about change in sports organisations, Stevens and Slack (1998) proposed an explanatory model that integrated institutional theory with its focus on the structural constraints of the organisational environment and with more voluntaristic notions of strategic choice incorporated in a social-action perspective. In formulating their theoretical argument, Stevens and Slack noted the importance of seeing processes of organisational change embedded in contexts of social relations that shape both structural constraints and strategic choices (see Granovetter, 1985). Their research involved a case study of a women's ice hockey organisation that was supposed to promote and develop the sport in a western Canadian province. Their work suggests the importance of looking at how sports organisations in larger organisational networks, in this case involving other agencies and organisations in the larger hockey and amateur sports networks of their region, use their social capital to transform their organisation and create more legitimacy and new opportunities for themselves. At the same time, we can see how asymmetric power relations within these networks can shape the patterns of organisational change for individual social actors. In this case, the women's hockey organisation had to adapt to normative influences from the dominant men's hockey organisations. By making accommodations to become better integrated within the larger hockey network, the women's hockey organisation was able to secure more social capital, which enabled it to obtain more material resources, such as ice time and provincial government funding, and more administrative resources.

A special issue of the *International Review for the Sociology of Sport*, edited by Slack (1994), focused on sports organisations. The articles in this special issue drew attention to organisational structures and contexts in the national governing bodies of British sport, the effects of government financing on the autonomy of voluntary sports associations, organisational change, and rational planning systems as a source of organisational conflict. These articles reflect an interest in social structural analysis, even though there is little explicit attention to social network approaches. For example, Theodoraki and Henry (1994) draw from Mintzberg's (1979) work on the structuring of organisations to examine organisational types, the structural properties of organisations and their environments, strategic management styles, and organisational change. This work could be extended by taking a relational approach focusing on how the types and properties of intra-organisational and inter-organisational social ties and relations affect the patterns of change of the sports organisations that Theodoraki and Henry studied. An important focus of this research could be the identification and influence of the various social ties in the networks of these organisations. A major dimension of this kind of research is the interdependence of these various directly and indirectly connected networks to which individual organisational actors are tied and the impact of the flow of information and resources through these networks on the evolving structural relationships of individual actors and their networks.

In his study of German sports clubs, Horch (1994) proposed that cultural factors could minimise government interference when voluntary associations receive government financial support. By applying social network analysis, we could see how changes in the flow of resources between social actors alter the structure of their relations when the social networks of recipient actors differ in various ways, such as: size; density; clustering; social, economic, and political capital; and relations with agents, sponsors, and other mediating actors. These same kinds of perspectives could be applied to Saeki's (1994) study of organisational change in the Japanese Judo Federation caught in conflicts between the forces of tradition and modernisation. More specifically, the patterns of hegemony and control that produced conflict in relations among judo clubs could be understood in terms of how the asymmetry of power relations shaped network clustering and changed the organisational boundaries within the larger network of judo clubs in Japan.

Slack, Berrett, and Mistry's (1994) study of organisational conflict in a context of planning for change also shows how asymmetric organisational ties to external actors can be a source of conflict. Their research focused on a case study of a Canadian Olympic sports organisation and its relationship to the national sports body, Sport Canada. The researchers described how a number of volunteers from a particular city took over the governing board of a sport when its central offices were located in their city, rotated various board positions among themselves, exercised control over virtually all aspects of the sport, and disproportionately allocated organisational resources to themselves. This local dominance caused friction in the organisation, but board members from other regions were unwilling or unable to challenge the dominant coalition of directors until Sport Canada pressured the organisation to relocate to Ottawa as part of the government assessment and planning process. The organisation initially resisted the move, especially since its volunteer executive and a number of board members could not or did not want to relocate, but the threat of the loss of government funding ultimately overcame the resistance.

The effects of the move were to lessen the concentration of power within the organisation and create new specialised and interdependent subgroups in the organisation, which led to a period of conflict among subgroups. Conflicts developed in relations between the new highly paid foreign coaches and lesser paid professional staff members, between the volunteers who had dominated the organisation and staff members, and between the coaches and the athletes. The executive of the sports organisation attempted to mediate disputes, but after the 1988 Calgary Olympic Games, all of the coaches were released and the managing director resigned. As the organisation evolved, the regional resentments lessened, more trust developed in professional-volunteer relations, and the relationships between subgroups in the organisation evolved from conflict to more normalised relations.

Social network analysis would enable us to see how power was concentrated in a local cluster of positions or subgroups within the sports organisation and how relations of power with the external national body, Sport Canada, transformed the structure of power relations in the organisation. We could also see how Sport Canada, as a large and dominant actor in the national sports network, created conflicts in the individual sports organisation by involving the organisation in an assessment and planning process that pressured it to relocate, which led to changes in the composition of its governing board; to increase its task differentiation, which led to specialised and competing subgroups; to increase the number of coaching and professional administrative positions, which produced resentment and mistrust in the relations between these subgroups; and to increase the interdependence and amount of interaction between subgroups, including professionals and volunteers, which exacerbated tensions. Parenthetically, the evolution of network relations ultimately resulted in some stability.

There are a number of other applications of social network analysis to sport beyond organisational research and analysis, but the rich and extensive literature of network analysis of organisations makes it easy to see the relevance to network analysis to the sociology of sport. I do not intend to be exhaustive in my coverage of possible applications of network ideas to sport, but I would like to suggest a few more directions for such applications to make the range of applicability of this approach more apparent. For example, I have previously noted (Nixon, 1993a) that social network approaches could be used to study social relations within and between sports teams and sports subcultures; managerial recruitment and stacking; and social support networks to deal with pain and injury. In the latter regard, my own social network analyses of pain, injury, and the "culture of risk" in sport focused on how social relations in intercollegiate athletic networks (which I call "sportsnets") induce athletes either to accept or seek help for their pain and injuries.

This work prompted Walk (1997) to study how student athletic trainers mediate the pain and injury experiences of athletes within their sportsnets and how they navigate their sometimes conflicting ties to athletes and staff trainers.

In addition, my work prompted a summary and critique by Roderick (1998), who proposed using figurational analysis (Elias, 1978) to relate the analysis of the networks of athletes to broader social processes within a historical developmental perspective. In fact, figurational analysis has ideas that overlap with network analysis (see Chapters 9 and 13), including its basic conception of figurations as "historically produced and reproduced networks of interdependence" (Roderick, 1998: 70).

A related piece of research concerning social support networks in college sport focused on the types of social support provided by different types of social actors in male and female athletes' social networks. Survey research by Rosenfeld, Richman, and Hardy (1989) showed that coaches, teammates, friends, and parents provided various forms of support to these athletes. The sport-related support provided by coaches and teammates complemented the support from friends and parents that did not require sports expertise. The researchers found few differences between the support networks of athletes with low and high levels of stress.

Other sociology of sport research suggests a variety of additional future directions for social network analysis of sport. For example, Leifer (1990) created a computer programme and used National and American Football Conference schedules over 20 years to test the relative fairness of home-away schedules for networks that differed in size, density, and differentiation of actors. Sage (1999) used structural and interpretive perspectives to examine the organisational dynamics, actions, and consequences of a transnational advocacy network that was organised to protest the labour practices of Nike's athletic shoe factories in Asia. His structural analysis focused on how the coalition of organisational actors constituting this advocacy network grew through the extensive set of ties in the networks of individual network members. Sage's research revealed the difficulties of identifying the flow of communication in the network when a political advocacy network becomes very dense and diverse and is tied together by a large number of interlocking links.

Sage's analysis points to the importance of trying to understand social relations in sport in the context of global political, economic, and communication networks. Nauright and Black's (1994) study of rugby relations between New Zealand and South Africa during the period when other nations were attempting to isolate South Africa in the international sports network is an example of research of this type. In a related vein, Silk (1999) examined global and local communication flows in the telecasting of the 1995 Canada Cup (of soccer) and argued that forces of global capitalism influenced labour practices in the production of these Canada Cup telecasts. Diffusion of mass mediated influences to local or national contexts within global sports networks is also the theme of Jackson and Andrews' (1999) study of the spread of the National Basketball Association to local markets in New Zealand.

Another kind of research involving sports flows or movement within global networks involves the migration of athletes across national borders. Bale (1991) mapped the patterns of migration in the networks or "pipelines" that brought skilled foreign athletes to American intercollegiate athletic programmes, and critically examined the implications of these patterns for the athletes and their nations. He placed these migration patterns in the context of global networks of competition and sports organisation. He conveyed the extent of international athletic recruitment by citing statistics of foreign participation in intercollegiate football, ice hockey, basketball, soccer, tennis, swimming, golf, and track and field. Bale's case study of track and field showed the social ties in recruitment networks that linked athletes in various nations to colleges in less attractive areas of the United States that had difficulty recruiting American athletes.

Klein's (1991) study of the influence of American major league baseball on baseball in the Dominican Republic showed how American talent scouts developed ties with young Dominican baseball prospects and created pipelines to the United States' major league for such prospects. He noted that despite pride in accomplishments of their athletes in the major leagues, the Dominicans also displayed some cultural resistance to American domination of baseball in their nation. Like Bale's study of the "brawn drain", this kind of research could incorporate more explicit structural ideas about power and dependence in exchange relations among individual, organisational, and governmental actors in these international recruitment and migration networks.

Global migration patterns are also the focus of Maguire's research on Canadian ice-hockey players' migration to the United Kingdom (Maguire, 1996) and the migration of soccer players mainly between nations in the European Union (Maguire & Stead, 1998). In both cases, migration patterns could be understood in terms of chains of social ties between host and recipient nations, leagues, and teams over time. In regard to soccer, Maguire and Stead observed the parallels between patterns of player migration and television broadcast ties to various regions for individual teams. They also suggested that soccer players were motivated to move to another team because they were afforded the chance for a full-time career with more intense ties to their new team. The lure of money itself was not sufficient to explain these patterns of migration. In considering the more general patterns of movement within these international soccer networks, political and economic interdependencies of nations and their heritage of colonial ties, geographic proximity, and a nation's history of exploitative or supportive treatment of people from the migrant's nation all seemed to play a part in patterns of movement.

Conclusion

As it has evolved, the sociology of sport has shown the imprint of a variety of theoretical and methodological perspectives. The tensions between sociologists of sport with different disciplinary backgrounds and different theoretical and methodological orientations have sometimes obscured the significance of the sociology and even the sport in the sociology of sport. Indeed, in their sociological analysis of the sociology of sport on its 30th anniversary, Ingham and Donnelly (1996: 395) asserted that "the crucial question that North American 'sociologists' of 'sport' must address is whether the future of our 'community' will be anchored in *sociology* or in *sport* at all and, if not, what will be its alternatives?" I argue that a genuine *sociology of sport* requires both a focus on sport and an emphasis on sociological perspectives and methods. Whether or not major 'Sociologists of Sport' and their professional associations, most prominently the North American Society for the Sociology of Sport (NASSS) and the International Sociology of Sport Association (ISSA), emphasise sociological and sport perspectives, sport will always be a sufficiently important aspect of society to warrant serious scholarly attention. Furthermore, sociology will always be the primary means in social or behavioural science of understanding how sport is related to society. I do not want to exclude from the 'Sociology of Sport' studies of the body and physical activity or the use of cognate perspectives and humanistic approaches for understanding social aspects of "sport". Surely, the persistence of the sociology of sport requires both sociology and sport, however. Furthermore, I contend that the sociological study of sport necessarily directs attention to social structures and social processes, and social network analysis is an especially useful approach for understanding patterns and effects of social structures and processes of sport.

Social network analysis pushes the sociological analysis of sport beyond the mere aggregation, classification, or grouping of attributes of individuals such as age, gender, race, ethnicity, level of education, income, occupation, class background, academic performance, status on a team, and athletic performance. It directs attention instead to concepts, models, and methods that show how interacting individual persons and larger and more complex social actors, such as teams, leagues, corporations, sports federations, governing bodies, and international organisations, interact with other social actors in ways that become structured into consistent patterns. Social network analysis enables us to see how being embedded in particular structural locations in social networks creates opportunities and constraints for social actors through different amounts and types of social capital associated with those positions. Identifying the transactional content of social relations; the frequency, intensity, symmetry or asymmetry, and multiplexity of social ties; the size, density, complexity, composition, and openness of social networks; and the amounts and types of social capital embedded in social networks can reveal a great deal about relations among various types of social actors in sport.

We have considered many examples of social network research suggesting future directions for social network analysis of sport. By learning more about network analysis and creatively applying more rigorous models and methods or more metaphorical conceptions of social networks, sociologists of sport could look in new ways at familiar research topics. These topics could include socialisation and the diffusion of values, attitudes, and roles through sports networks; deviant actions by various types of social actors in sport; gender, race, and ethnic relations and patterns of segregation and discrimination; class relations and patterns of inequality in resource allocation; communication networks; media relations; relations among social actors in youth, interscholastic, intercollegiate, professional, and high-level amateur sports; the interrelationship of sport, government, and corporate actors in league expansion, stadium construction, selection of Olympic sites, and other major sports policy decisions; collective action in sport; and political and economic conflicts and relations of domination and exploitation between social actors in various sports networks. In addition, the emphasis on social ties, social relations, and social networks draws attention to less studied topics in contemporary sociology of sport, including sports groups and organisations; social ties among fans and between fans and other social actors in sport; networks of inter-organisational relations in sport; social support networks; patterns of athletic recruitment and migration; and links between household or family networks and the occupational networks of sport. Virtually any significant social structures and processes of sport could be studied with social network analysis, and the network approach will emphasise the social relational patterns of sport. The general past neglect among sport scholars of this increasingly popular approach in sociology and other social sciences implies that social network analysis offers potentially valuable untapped potential for seeing and understanding the *sociology* of sport.

References

Bale, J. (1991). *The Brawn Drain: Foreign Student Athletes in American Universities*. Urbana and Chicago: University of Illinois Press.

Barnes, J. A. (1954). Class and committees in a Norwegian Island Parish. *Human Relations, 7*, 39–58.

Barnes, J. A. (1972). *Social Networks*. Reading, MA: Addison–Wesley.

Baxter, V., Margavio, A. V., & Lambert, C. (1996). Competition, legitimation, and the regulation of intercollegiate athletics. *Sociology of Sport Journal, 13*, 51–64.

Berkowitz, S. D. (1982). *An Introduction to Structural Analysis: The Network Approach to Social Research*. Toronto: Butterworths.

Bott, E. (1957). *Family and Social Network*. London: Tavistock.

Burt, R. S. (1992). *Structural Holes: The Social Structure of Competition, Cambridge.* MA: Harvard University Press.

Burt. R. S. (1998). The gender of social capital. *Rationality and Society, 10*, 5–46.

Burt, R. S., & Minor, M. J. (eds) (1983). *Applied Network Analysis: A Methodological Introduction*. Beverly Hills, CA: Sage Publications.

Carley, K. M. (1999). On the evolution of social and organizational networks. *Research in the Sociology of Organizations, 16*, 3–30.

Chwe, M. S.-Y. (1999). Structure and strategy in collective action. *American Journal of Sociology, 105*, 128–156.

Cook, K. S. (1982). Network structures from an exchange perspective. In: P. V. Marsden and N. Lin (eds), *Social Structure and Network Analysis* (pp. 177–199). Beverly Hills, CA: Sage Publications.

Elias, N. (1978). *What is Sociology?* London: Hutchinson.

Emerson, R. M. (1962). Power-dependence relations. *American Sociological Review, 27*, 31–41.

Ennett, S. T., Bailey, S. L., & Federman, E. B. (1999). Social network characteristics associated with risky behaviors among runaway and homeless youth. *Journal of Health and Social Behavior, 40*, 63–78.

Fararo, T. J. (1973). *Mathematical Sociology: An Introduction to Fundamentals*. New York: John Wiley & Sons.

Freeman, L. C., White, D. R., & Romney, A. K. (eds) (1992). *Research Methods in Social Network Analysis*. New Brunswick, NJ: Transaction.

Frey, J. H. (1978). The organization of American amateur sport: Efficiency to entropy. *American Behavioral Scientist, 21*, 361–378.

Galaskiewicz, J., & Zaheer, A. (1999). Networks of competitive advantage. *Research in the Sociology of Organizations, 16*, 237–261.

Granovetter, M. S. (1973). The strength of weak ties. *American Journal of Sociology, 78*, 1360–1380.

Granovetter, M. S. (1974). *Getting a Job: A Study of Contacts and Careers*. Cambridge, MA: Harvard University Press.

Granovetter, M. S. (1982). The strength of weak ties: A network theory revisited. In: P. V. Marsden and N. Lin (eds), *Social Structure and Network Analysis* (pp. 105–130). Beverly Hills, CA: Sage Publication.

Granovetter, M. (1985). Economic action and social structures: The problem of embeddedness. *American Journal of Sociology, 91*, 481–510.

Gulati, R., & Westphal, J. D. (1999). Cooperative or controlling? The effects of CEO-board relations and the content of interlocks on the formation of joint ventures. *Administrative Science Quarterly, 44*, 473–506.

Hansen, M. T. (1999). The search-transfer problem: The role of weak ties in sharing knowledge across organization subunits. *Administrative Science Quarterly, 44,* 82–111.

Homans, G. C. (1950). *The Human Group.* New York: Harcourt, Brace, Jovanovich.

Homans, G. C. (1961). *Social Behavior: Its Elementary Forms.* New York: Harcourt, Brace, Jovanovich.

Horch, H.-D. (1994). Does government financing have a detrimental effect on the autonomy of voluntary associations?: Evidence from German sports clubs. *International Review for the Sociology of Sport, 29,* 269–285.

Ikkink, K. K., & van Tilburg, T. (1999). Broken ties: Reciprocity and other factors affecting the termination of older adults' relationships. *Social Networks, 21,* 131–146.

Ingham, A. G., & Donnelly, P. (1996). A sociology of North American Sociology of Sport: Disunity in unity, 1965 to 1996. *Sociology of Sport Journal, 14,* 362–418.

Jackson, S. J., & Andrews, D. L. (1999). Between and beyond the global and the local: American popular sporting culture in New Zealand. *International Review for the Sociology of Sport, 34,* 31–42.

Jarvis, H. (1999). The tangled webs we weave: Household strategies to coordinate home and work. *Work, Employment and Society, 13,* 225–247.

King, F. W. (1991). *It's How You Play the Game: The Inside Story of the Calgary Olympics.* Calgary: Writers' Group.

Klein, A. M. (1991). *Sugarball: The American Game, the Dominican Dream.* New Haven, CT: Yale University Press.

Knoppers, A., Meyer, B. B., Ewing, M., & Forrest, L. (1990). Dimensions of power: A question of sport or gender? *Sociology of Sport Journal, 7,* 369–377.

Knoppers, A., Meyer, B. B., Ewing, M. E., & Forrest, L. (1993). Gender ratio and social interaction among college coaches. *Sociology of Sport Journal, 10,* 256–269.

Lewin, K. (1951). *Field Theory in the Social Sciences.* New York: Harper.

Leifer, E. M. (1990). Enacting networks: The feasibility of fairness. *Social Networks, 12*(1), 1–25.

Lin, N. (1982). Social resources and instrumental action. In: P. V. Marsden and N. Lin (eds), *Social Structure and Network Analysis* (pp. 131–145). Beverly Hills, CA: Sage Publications.

Lin, N. (1999). Building a network theory of social capital. *Connections, 22*(1), 28–51.

Lorrain, F., & White, H. C. (1971). Structural equivalence of individuals in social networks. *Journal of Mathematical Sociology, 1,* 49–80.

Maguire, J. (1996). Blade runners: Canadian migrants, ice hockey, and the global sports process. *Journal of Sport & Social Issues, 20,* 335–360.

Maguire, J., & Stead, D. (1998). Border crossings: Soccer labour migration and the European Union. *International Review for the Sociology of Sport, 33,* 59–73.

Marsden, P. V., & Lin, N. (eds) (1982). *Social Structure and Network Analysis.* Beverly Hills, CA: Sage Publications.

Mintzberg, H. (1979). *The Structure of Organizations.* Englewood Cliffs, NJ: Prentice-Hall.

Mitchell, J. C. (ed.) (1969). *Social Networks in Urban Situations*. Manchester: Manchester University Press.

Mitchell, J. C. (1974). Social networks. *Annual Review of Anthropology, 3*, 279–299.

Mitchell, C. (1994). Situational analysis and network analysis. *Connections, 17*(1), 16–22.

Moreno, J. (1934). *Who Shall Survive?* New York: Beacon Press.

Nauright, J., & Black, D. (1994). It's rugby that really matters: New Zealand–South Africa rugby relations and the moves to isolate South Africa, 1956–1992. In: R. C. Wilcox (ed.), *Fitness Information Technology* (pp. 165–183). Sport in the Global Village, Morgantown, WV.

Nixon, H. L. II. (1979). *The Small Group*. Englewood Cliffs, NJ: Prentice-Hall.

Nixon, H. L. II. (1984). *Sport and the American Dream*. Champaign, IL: Human Kinetics.

Nixon, H. L. II. (1992). A social network analysis of influences on athletes to play with pain and injuries. *Journal of Sport & Social Issues, 16*, 127–135.

Nixon, H. L. II. (1993a). Social network analysis of sport: Emphasizing social structure in sport sociology. *Sociology of Sport Journal, 10*, 315–321.

Nixon, H. L. II. (1993b). Accepting the risks of pain and injury in sport: Mediated cultural influences on playing hurt. *Sociology of Sport Journal, 10*, 183–196.

Nixon, H. L. II. (1998). Response to Martin Roderick's comment on the work of Howard L. Nixon II. *Sociology of Sport Journal, 15*, 80–85.

Pitter, R. (1990). Power and control in an amateur sports organization. *International Review for the Sociology of Sport, 25*, 309–322.

Popielarz, P. A. (1999). Organizational constraints on personal network formation. *Research in the Sociology of Organizations, 16*, 263–281.

Powell, W. W. (1990). Neither market nor hierarchy: Network forms of organizations. In: B. M. Staw and L. L. Cummings (eds), *Research in Organizational Behavior* (pp. 295–336). Greenwich, CT: JAI Press.

Powell, W. W., Koput, K. W., Doerr, L. S. *et al.* (1999). Network position and firm performance: Organizational returns to collaboration in the biotechnology industry. *Research in the Sociology of Organizations, 16*, 129–159.

Roderick, M. (1998). The sociology of risk, pain, and injury: A comment on the work of Howard L. Nixon II. *Sociology of Sport Journal, 15*, 64–79.

Roethlisberger, F. J., & Dickson, W. J. (1939). *Management and the Worker*. Cambridge, MA: Harvard University Press.

Rosenfeld, L. B., Richman, J. M., & Hardy, C. J. (1989). Examining social support networks among athletes: Description and relationship to stress. *The Sport Psychologist, 3*(1), 23–33.

Saeki, T. (1994). The conflict between tradition and modernization in a sport organization: A sociological study of issues surrounding the organizational reformation of the All Japan Judo Federation. *International Review for the Sociology of Sport, 29*, 301–315.

Sage, G. H. (1999). Justice do it! The Nike transnational advocacy network: Organization, collective actions, and outcomes. *Sociology of Sport Journal, 16*, 206–235.

Scott, J. (1991). Social network analysis: A handbook. London, England: Sage Publications.

Silk, M. (1999). Local/global flows and altered production practices: Narrative constructions at the 1995 Canada Cup of Soccer. *International Review for the Sociology of Sport, 34*, 113–123.

Simmel, G. (1908). *Soziologie, Untersuchungen Uber die Formen der Vergeselschaftung.* Leipzig: Verlag van Duncker und Humboldt.

Simmel, G. (1950). *Sociology of Georg Simmel.* (Trans. Wolff, K. H.) Glencoe, IL: Free Press.

Skvoretz, J., & Willer, D. (1991). Power in exchange networks: Setting and structural variations. *Social Psychological Quarterly, 54*, 224–238.

Slack, T. (1994). Theoretical diversity and the study of sport organizations. *International Review for the Sociology of Sport, 29*, 239–242.

Slack, T. (1997). *Understanding Sport Organizations: The Application of Organization Theory.* Champaign, IL: Human Kinetics.

Slack, T., Berrett, T., & Mistry, K. (1994). Rational planning systems as a source of organizational conflict. *International Review for the Sociology of Sport, 29*, 317–328.

Smith, H. W. (1987). *Introduction to Social Psychology.* Englewood Cliffs, NJ: Prentice-Hall.

Stevens, J. A., & Slack, T. (1998). Integrating social action and structural constraints: Towards a more holistic explanation of organizational change. *International Review for the Sociology of Sport, 33*, 143–154.

Talmud, I., & Izraeli, D. N. (1999). The relationship between gender and performance issues of concern to directors: Correlates or institution? *Journal of Organizational Behavior, 20*, 459–474.

Theodoraki, E. I., & Henry, I. P. (1994). Organisational structures and contexts in British national governing bodies of sport. *International Review for the Sociology of Sport, 29*, 243–268.

Walk, S. R. (1997). Peers in pain: The experiences of student athletic trainers. *Sociology of Sport Journal, 14*, 22–56.

Wallerstein, I. 1974, (1976). *The Modern World-System, I.* Library and text editions. New York: Academic Press.

Warner, W. L., & Lunt, P. S. (1941). *The Social Life of a Modern Community.* New Haven, CT: Yale University Press.

Warner, W. L., & Lunt, P. S. (1942). *The Status System of a Modern Community,* New Haven, CT: Yale University Press.

Wasserman, S., & Faust, K. (1994). *Social Network Analysis: Methods and Applications.* Cambridge, England: Cambridge University Press.

Wellman, B. (1979). The community questions: The intimate networks of East Yorkers. *American Journal of Sociology, 84*, 1201–1231.

Wellman, B. (1982). Studying personal communities. In: P. V. Marsden and N. Lin (eds), *Social Structure and Network Analysis* (pp. 61–80). Beverly Hills. CA: Sage Publications.

Wellman, B. (1988). Structural analysis: From method and metaphor to theory and substance. In: B. Wellman and S. D. Berkowitz (eds), *Social Structures: A Network Approach* (pp. 19–61). Cambridge, England: Cambridge University Press.

White, H. C. (1963). *An Anatomy of Kinship*. Englewood Cliffs, NJ: Prentice-Hall.

White, H. C. (1970). *Chains of Opportunity*, Cambridge, MA: Harvard University Press.

White, H. C., Boorman, S. A., & Breiger, R. L. (1976). Social structure from multiple networks: I. Blockmodels of roles and positions. *American Journal of Sociology, 81*, 730–780.

Zey, M. (1999). The subsidization of the securities industry and the organization of securities fraud networks to return profits in the 1980s. *Work and Occupations, 26*, 50–76.

Chapter 12

Michel Foucault: Sport, Power, Technologies and Governmentality

Jennifer Smith Maguire

Students of sport might rightly ask, 'Why should I read Foucault?' After all, the French philosopher and social theorist is best known for his analyses of imprisonment, clinical medicine, madness, and sexuality. But what these studies have in common — and what makes Foucault such a significant theorist for the study of physical cultures — is his ongoing concern with the connections between the body, power, knowledge, subjectivity, and social management.[1] Broadly speaking, a Foucauldian analysis of sport is concerned with how relations of power target and shape the body through different types of practices, forms of knowledge, and sets of norms in order to produce specific bodily capacities and particular attitudes towards the body and self. For example, one might ask what kinds of knowledge are produced through different kinds of bodily training, and what other knowledges and training remain marginal? However, more than revealing the connections between bodies and power *within* sport, Foucault enables an analysis of the links *between* sport and other networks of power. Accordingly, a Foucauldian analysis treats sport as primary, rather than peripheral, in the social order.

The connections between bodies and power, which are central to understanding physical cultures, take two general forms. The first is largely institutional, and concerns how particular institutions, knowledge, and practices target the body to enable and discipline its productivity. This first connection, which Foucault calls 'technologies of domination', is the primary focus of his early work (1977, 1978).[2] In the later stage of his career, Foucault shifts his attention to the

---

[1] As Andrews (1993) has noted, Foucault's focus on the body, though exceptional, is not unique. Other social theorists who have taken the body as central to the social order and social reality include Elias (1939/1978); Bourdieu (1984); and Douglas (1966).
[2] A careful reading of *The History of Sexuality, Volume 1* (1978) most appropriately places it as the point of transition between these phases of his career.

second connection between bodies and power, 'technologies of self', which refers to the ways in which we construct ourselves through knowledge of, and work on, the body (1985, 1986, 1988a, 1988e). His later work also concerns the inter-connections between these two body/power modes in the governing of society (1988e, 1991). While the sociology of sport has drawn fruitfully from the 'early' Foucault (see Rail & Harvey, 1995: 171–173), it is only just beginning to take notice of his later work (e.g., Chapman, 1997; Shogan, 1999). As a result, Foucault remains an incomplete figure for the field, to its detriment.[3] First, without an equal emphasis on the technologies of self, Foucauldian analyses of physical cultures seem overly deterministic. Indeed, there is a persistent misreading of Foucault, in which bodies are passive cogs and power is simply a repressive force. Second, without equal attention to the interaction of the forms of body/power — the connections between technologies of domination and technologies of the self — analyses of physical cultures cannot fully appreciate the ways in which sport is implicated in the larger networks of power and social management.

Foucault's *oeuvre* is too vast and complex to submit easily to a brief summary. This chapter is not intended as a comprehensive review; other sources admirably fulfil this role (Danaher *et al.*, 2000; Diamond & Quinby, 1988; McNay, 1994; Rail & Harvey, 1995). Rather, this chapter provides a thematic discussion of Foucault, tracing the broad threads that traverse his career. These general themes provide the context from which many of Foucault's concepts — such as discipline, surveillance, and biopower — have been plucked.[4] First, *power* is conceptualised as positive and relational within the historically specific context of non-coercive social orders. Second, *technologies of domination* centre on the disciplining and regulating of bodies. Third, *technologies of the self* are those ways in which we produce ourselves. Fourth, *governmentality* weaves these other threads together, implicating sport and its participants in the social order of neo–liberal democracies.

Power

There is perhaps no concept more commonly associated with Foucault than power. His contribution to our understanding of power in modern society lies, in part, in

[3]The incompleteness of Foucault is certainly not limited to the sociology of sport. The sociology of the body, for example, has also tended to regard Foucault as a theorist of disciplined or regulated bodies, neglecting his potential contribution to theorising bodily practices as contingent upon autonomy and resistance (e.g., Frank, 1991; Turner, 1984).
[4]A critique of the misuse of Foucault's concepts, removed from their historical context, and apart from an understanding of Foucault's methods, can be found in Kendall and Wickham (2000).

a refusal to take power as a *thing*, possessed by some groups which control other, powerless groups. In rejecting this repressive model of power, Foucault also rejects the traditional assumption that power and freedom are mutually exclusive. As such, understanding Foucault's analysis of power requires us to set aside our commonplace associations between power and political structures or dominant classes. While the state and the bourgeoisie are certainly more able to mobilise power, Foucault is suggesting that focusing solely upon these groups or entities obscures the ways in which power actually works. His analyses encourage us to shift our attention to the impact of everyday interactions and intermediate institutions — such as the school, army, or factory — in order to grasp the basis of social order and the active part played by individuals. This is not simply a micro-level approach to understanding social reality (as we might associate with interactionism, for example). Rather, this is an understanding of social reality as being contingent upon both institutions *and* individuals, each the product of power relations.

In contrast to the repressive model of power, Foucault lays out an explicit definition of power as relational and positive.[5] In its basic form, power exists only in the context of a relationship in which one individual attempts to direct the behaviour or actions of another. Hidden within such a simple definition, however, are a number of important assumptions.

First, in a power relationship, one person acts upon the *actions* of another, rather than directly on the other person. Thus, power is a matter of how we try to influence or "act upon the possibilities of action of other people" (Foucault, 1983: 221). If we try to direct the actions of another by inflicting or threatening bodily harm, we are no longer in a power relation, but a relation of violence. We can influence the behaviour of others, however, without recourse to violence. By drawing on systematic knowledge and discourses, we frame some actions as more acceptable than others, thus indirectly constraining the available avenues of action. For example, consider a coach who wants her athletes to respect a curfew. The coach can't force the athletes to go to bed at a certain time, but she can persuade them. With reference to the ill effects of sleep-deprivation or to their responsibility to be at their best for the team, the coach can convince the athletes that it is in their own interests to do as she suggests. The relation is not repressive in that the athletes ideally have the option of refusing or resisting the coach's influence. Moreover, the relation is *productive,*

---

[5] Like his focus on the body, Foucault's understanding of power as relational and positive is unusual, but not unique. Readers of Elias will certainly recognise an affinity between the two thinkers in this respect, as noted by van Krieken (1998) and others. Other connections may be made, in large part due to the influence of Elias, to the work of Bourdieu (1984).

generating the ideal of (and a self-identity as) a 'committed athlete'. Positive power constrains, but is predicated on the other being able to choose; it is both restrictive and productive. Thus, when Foucault writes that "where there is power, there is resistance" (1978: 95), he establishes the baseline requirement for a relation of power. Where there is no potential for choice, alternatives, or resistance, there is no power — only domination.

The second assumption, then, is that the prerequisite of power is the potential for resistance. That is, power exists only between free subjects (Foucault, 1983: 220–221). Foucault is not suggesting that all power relations are equal. All relations involve some degree of domination, and in some cases the potential for resistance may be severely limited (Foucault, 1988b: 12). Nor does he suggest that resistance is always a matter of refusal or revolution; resistance is largely a matter of choosing one's response to the influence and overtures of the other:

> Consequently, there is no face-to-face confrontation of power and freedom which is mutually exclusive (freedom disappears everywhere power is exercised), but a much more complicated interplay. In this game, freedom may well appear as the condition for the exercise of power (at the same time its precondition, since freedom must exist for power to be exerted, and also its permanent support, since without the possibility of recalcitrance, power would be equivalent to physical determination) (Foucault, 1983: 221).

If the possibility of refusal ceases to exist (as in the case of the slave), power disappears and, necessarily, so does freedom. Violence, not power, is freedom's irreducible opposite. Incomplete readings of Foucault have characterised his statement that "power is everywhere" (1978: 93) as nihilistic, or deeply pessimistic (e.g., Andrews, 1993: 153). Such readings stem from a fundamental misunderstanding of what Foucault means by power and freedom. Power is not an evil to be escaped, but a matter of strategic games, which can be played with more or less domination. If power is everywhere, so too is freedom — not some essential freedom (which Foucault rejects as idealist fantasy), but a freedom that exists only in a reciprocal and often agonistic relationship with power (1983: 222). The case of the athlete provides an excellent metaphor for this point. For example, in the late 1880s, while playing for the Boston Beaneaters, Mike 'King' Kelly made the most of his knowledge of the rules of baseball when he substituted himself from the bench as catcher, in order to catch a 'foul ball'. As we know of baseball today, the rules of the game change in response to such creative challenges. Nevertheless, the player that is most free is the one that best knows the rules, and thus can stretch them to greatest advantage.

Underlying Foucault's positive and relational analysis of power is a third premise. In differentiating power from violence, and in placing power and freedom in a dynamic, inseparable relationship, Foucault is making a statement regarding the historically specific context of modern, non-coercive societies. In his examinations of the prison (1977), sexuality (1978), and neo–liberal democracy (1988c, 1988d, 1991), Foucault traces the historical emergence of the positive exercise of power and the free subjects who are its prerequisite. Prior to the 16th century, power was largely repressive; the sovereign's right to take the life of a lawbreaker assured the continuity of his or her rule and the basis of social order. However, the demographic expansion and economic diversification of the 18th century not only rendered this mode of governing inadequate, it also raised the need for a productive population. For Foucault, the growth of capitalism was contingent upon a positive model of power and this problematisation of productivity, and not, as Weber suggests, the Protestant ascetic morality (Foucault, 1978: 141). Such a model of positive power centres on the productive capacities of individuals. Of interest are not the variations between individuals, but the norms or standards to which their productivity might reasonably be held or trained. Thus, the emergence of a non-coercive society requires that the purpose or rationale of government shifts from the continuity of a ruler's tenure to the optimisation of the population's capacities through better management and normalisation (1991: 95). However, the state's agenda for economic efficiency must be balanced with the need for social order. That is, the state "had to have methods of power capable of optimizing forces, aptitudes, and life in general without, at the same time, making them more difficult to govern" (Foucault, 1978: 141).

Thus, the preconditions for (and consequences of) the shift to liberal government are two-fold. First, power now works through an affirmation of life and its capacities. Individuals are of interest to the state insofar as they are productive. The creation and collection of knowledge thus focuses on the productive capacity of humans, on establishing a norm of productivity and training individuals to meet (or exceed) this standard. While this results in the exclusion of other targets for knowledge production, one must bear in mind that a vast range of seemingly unrelated topics affect an individual's proficiency. For example, as the state can no longer rely on coercive means of ensuring productivity, there is an increasing interest in how best to manage, motivate, or otherwise entice humans through non-coercive means, such as advertising and promotion.

The affirmation and optimisation of bodily capacities thus produces a store of information, rules of inquiry, and discourses which make the body knowable in new ways. Certain capacities and characteristics are rendered measurable, and therefore, subject to comparison and standardisation. Not only is the state interested in such knowledge, but so too — crucially — are we. Individuals come to know and construct themselves in new ways. This brings us to the second consequence of the shift to non-coercive societies: the governability of the free subject. Like Elias' emphasis on the personality structure as a necessary corollary to new social bonds (see Chapter 9), Foucault focuses on the emergence of a new subjectivity that is formed through the process of self-management. In taking responsibility for following the social rules and regulations on their own, individuals are thus freed from the coercive application of those rules by an external agent (the state, the police). The freedom of the modern individual, then, is contingent upon knowing, monitoring, and improving oneself. This self-directed attention gives rise to a self-managing subject. In short, we become our own rulers.

Again, freedom is not the opposite of power in modern societies. Freedom, *as self-management*, is the prerequisite of power. The state relies on individuals to keep themselves in line, and thus doesn't routinely require force for the reproduction of its rule and authority. Moreover, our subjectivities are such that we define ourselves through this self-managing freedom. The capacity to choose, to resist, ensures our autonomy, while our choices are constructed in ways that rarely challenge the status quo.[6] Knowledge, then, is only part of the exercise of positive power; individuals must recognise themselves as governed and self-governing subjects.[7] As such, an analysis of the state is hardly adequate to capture the workings of power, which infiltrate every aspect of our public and (supposedly) private lives.

The productive body and self-managing subjectivity, married in the modern individual, are the results of particular technologies or "ways . . . that humans develop knowledge about themselves" (Foucault, 1988e: 18). Foucault's earlier work concentrates on technologies of domination, while his later work revolves around technologies of the self, and the interaction of the two in the social order. These themes, and their place within the sociology of sport, constitute the remainder of the chapter.

[6]Rose's work (1990, 1996) on the autonomous self and its implication in the reproduction of the social order provides an excellent extension of Foucault's thoughts on the self-managing subjectivity. As Rose makes clear, in liberal society, it is not only that we are free to choose, but that we are *'obliged to be free'* (1996: 17).

[7]As Cole (1994) has noted, this aspect of Foucault's work recalls Althusser's discussion of ideological state apparatuses and the process of interpolation. Not coincidentally, Althusser had been Foucault's teacher and friend (Eribon, 1991).

Technologies of Domination

Recall that the exercise of power in non-coercive societies involves both the optimisation of bodily capacities *and* the production of a self-managing subjectivity. In each instance, the individual is taken as an object — something knowable, measurable, comparable — by the state, institutions, and by individuals themselves. Technologies of domination refer to the modes of knowledge production and organisation that "determine the conduct of individuals and submit them to certain ends or domination, an objectivizing of the subject" (Foucault, 1988e: 18). As their name suggests, technologies of domination are used to constrain choices, such that individuals are productive and active in ways that, more often than not, reproduce the social order. As the range of choices narrows, the degree of domination rises. However, technologies of domination are exercises and implementations of *positive* power. That is, they are means of affirming and optimising life and bodily capacities. The question of *which* capacities are affirmed, and which are ignored or cast as deviant, points to how positive power constrains just as it enables.

Systematic knowledge, particularly what we think of as expertise, is central to the identification and categorisation of particular aspects of human existence, and is thus central to social management. This role of knowledge is admirably demonstrated with respect to sexuality (Foucault, 1978). According to Foucault, sexuality has no objective reality, but exists only insofar as it is constructed. However, an interplay of power relations and knowledge production centres on sex, rendering it knowable, measurable, and *normal* by specific criteria. Through the mobilisation of knowledge, particular bodies (man, woman, child) and bodily functions and practices (such as heterosexual intercourse or masturbation) are categorised as normal or pathological, resulting in the illusion of a (hetero)sexuality that is natural and universal. Both 'good' and 'bad' bodies are invested with power relations, making them the legitimate target of the interventions of medicine, education, and economics. Sexuality, then, is a mode of objectivising the individual, rendering him/her knowable and manageable.

If the state is interested in individuals only insofar as they are productive, the concern then becomes establishing a baseline expectation — a common denominator — for productivity. But at the same time as treating all individuals as interchangeable (and maximisable) productive bodies, the state requires that each individual take it upon him/herself to control counter-productive impulses and to find contentment in the productive life. Technologies of domination thus fall into two broad modes, reflecting the ongoing tension between, on the one hand, the state indirectly relying upon individuals to maintain social order, and on the other, the state directly governing the productivity of the population as a whole. That is, technologies of domination work in both *individualising* and *totalising* modes, producing different, interrelated bodies of knowledge that work through the same rationality of optimisation through normalisation. The first of these modes, an 'anatomo-politics of the human body',

> centred on the body as a machine: its disciplining, the optimiza-
> tion of its capabilities, the extortion of its forces, the parallel
> increase of its usefulness and its docility, its integration into
> systems of efficient and economic controls, all this was ensured
> by the procedures of power that characterized the *disciplines*
> (Foucault, 1978: 139, emphasis in original).

This is an individualising mode of power; disciplines separate individual beings and capacities from each other in order to better train, discipline, and optimise them.

Physical Education (PE) is an excellent example of a disciplinary technology of domination. In a Foucauldian analysis, PE is analysed as a strategic intervention of knowledge into our bodily existence, in the interests of economic productivity and the maintenance of social order. In his study of the British case, Hargreaves (1986) demonstrates how PE "constitutes a programme of control through sustained work on the body" (1986: 163). Targeting working class bodies in particular, British progressive PE was a disciplinary mechanism "for the production of normal individuals" (1986: 161), largely shaped in response to high unemployment and potential political unrest. Hargreaves demonstrates how practices of PE inculcate in children qualities such as flexibility, independence, and co-operation, qualities deemed necessary to meet market needs. That is, the discipline of PE is not simply about the optimisation of physical abilities (such as endurance or strength), but the optimisation of the productive individual, one who is well suited to participation in productive life.

PE is an example, then, of the positive exercise of disciplinary power, producing individual responsibility and competence such that the effects far outlast the individual's mundane participation in gym class. In connecting PE to broader power networks and political agendas, Hargreaves provides a key insight into the sustainability of the effects of disciplines: the active involvement of the individual means that disciplines give rise to self-discipline. Such an analysis could well be extended to contemporary PE, in which different perceived market needs lead to an emphasis on health-related fitness.

The goal of a Foucauldian analysis, therefore, is not simply to critique PE as a mode of control, but to reveal how and to whose benefit very specific bodily capacities are produced through forms of knowledge and training. This attention to the effects of disciplines can be applied more broadly to the study of physical culture. That is, we must look beyond the typical separation of control and freedom, work and play, to address how disciplinary techniques work in everyday life. Consider, for example, the development of the rational recreation movement in Victorian England. Bailey (1978) observes that the mid-Victorian bourgeoisie were concerned about the development of not only a work discipline, but also a 'play discipline', which would reinforce each other. Leisure, then, becomes a technology for the reproduction of the status quo.

As individuals take on the responsibility of their own management through disciplinary technologies, the state largely ceases to interfere in individuals' daily lives. Instead, the state's enduring interest in the productivity of its population means that its interference in everyday life occurs at a more general level. This brings us to the second mode of the technologies of domination, which works through totalisation. Originally spurred in part by new modes of collecting data about the population as a whole (notably, statistics), there emerged a 'bio-politics of the population', which focused on:

> the body imbued with the mechanics of life and serving as the basis of the biological processes: propagation, births and mortality, the level of health, life expectancy and longevity, with all the conditions that can cause these to vary. Their supervision was effected through an entire series of interventions and *regulatory controls* (Foucault, 1978: 139, emphasis in original).

The population, like the individual body, is rendered knowable (and thus subject to regulation via normalisation) through the production of knowledge. But if the state is interested in the productivity of its population, its interest is not merely in measures of economic output. A large range of information about the state of health, bodies, and abilities becomes relevant to the problem of productivity. Consider, for example, the production of data and expert knowledge around the question of weight. When we accept as common sense that inactivity and excess weight are 'bad', we fail to question how weight and fitness came to be designated as a problem, worthy of monitoring and intervention. Stearns (1997), for example, suggests that the North American social disdain for fat, starting at the end of the 19th century, was a symptom of cultural anxiety over the new excesses afforded by capitalism and consumption (see also Schwartz, 1986). However, what Stearns and others fail to acknowledge is that the very problematisation of fat — as a sign of moral corruption, hindrance to productive labour, or symptom of national weakness — presupposes an objectification of the body through a cataloguing of fat.

The collection of statistical data on population weight and fitness is a regulatory technology of domination that makes possible the strategic use of fat in the management of social life. For example, North American governmental programmes, such as the US Healthy People and Canadian ParticipACTION initiatives, set national health and fitness goals, including reducing the number of inactive and overweight people. While the benefits of such initiatives are many — and should not be discounted — the more difficult task is to question how our bodies are consequently made more knowable and thus further subject to regulation. We can see here the connection between the two forms of technologies of domination. The problematisation of fat involves both the totalising regulation of the population (we are all knowable and comparable by our fat content) and the individualising of discipline and responsibility (we each must control our weight or suffer social, psychological, and economic penalties). Although technologies of domination work to constrain our choices, they are neither deterministic nor repressive, provided their exercise continues to depend on the participation of free subjects. In this way, disciplines invoke an individual's autonomy just as they are attempts to circumscribe his/her choices.

Technologies of the Self

In order for individuals to be entrusted with their own management — in order for them to be free — they must recognise themselves within the social order so that they enact their freedom appropriately. Recognition of oneself as both governed and self-governing is contingent upon knowing and defining oneself in certain ways that are historically specific to modern, non-coercive societies. The production of subjectivity occurs through technologies of the self, ways of developing knowledge of oneself. These technologies:

> permit individuals to effect, by their own means or with the help of others, a certain number of operations on their own bodies and souls, thoughts, conduct, and way of being, so as to transform themselves in order to attain a certain state of happiness, purity, wisdom, perfection, or immortality (Foucault, 1988e: 18).

The 'certain number of operations' that we may draw upon in forming ourselves are also historically specific. The existence and acceptance of particular modes of thought and conduct is always limited through relations of power, such that we exercise our autonomy within the bounds of the existing social order. Thus, individuals form their own subjectivity, but within the context of existing patterns of interaction, codes of behaviour, and bodies of knowledge. Athletes, for example, make their own performances, but within rules and traditions not of their choosing. Subjectivity is not an ascribed structure, but we do not make ourselves simply as we please.

Physical cultures are an excellent example of the ways in which knowledge of one's body shapes one's sense of self and mode of conduct. Through work on and with the body, we experience, establish, and extend our limits and abilities, while placing them in the context of a number of rules and styles that make up our social circumstances. This is not simply a matter of doing exercises, but of monitoring and refining, keeping training records and making confessions, giving and taking up different behaviours. Our bodily knowledge is not total, but reflects the particular aspects and values on which we focus, and for which we are rewarded. For example, the value placed on brute strength is different from the value placed on flexibility. Each bodily characteristic stems from a different set of experiences: for example, boxing and weight-lifting provide different sensations and awareness than gymnastics or running. And, each characteristic is deemed more or less of a virtue in light of the historically specific situation, such as changing market needs for labour, or national needs for military defenders. This is especially relevant in an era in which the decline of manual labour in developed societies has meant that the rules and styles shaping the experience of one's bodily existence come increasingly from within the realm of leisure and recreation.

The historically specific context of self-formation means that we, as 'free subjects', are not formed in a vacuum, unfettered by social context, history, and constraints. At the same time, however, we must not fall prey to a deterministic reading of Foucault. Just as there is no sovereign subject who stands outside of power in his/her resistance, there is no predetermined 'automaton' passively funnelled into the appropriate production circuits and patterns of consumption. Foucault employs neither a simplistic functionalism (we always choose appropriately) nor a pessimistic determinism (we are always produced appropriately). The knowledge, institutions, and power relations that predate our individual lives make possible, but do not determine, the form of our subjectivity. It is by no means clear which modes of knowledge will be produced, for how long they will be accepted as legitimate, or to what effect they will be adopted by individuals. Foucault's investigations were of specific, contested, unpredictable histories of modes of knowledge production, and Foucauldian analyses must do likewise if they are not to make gross generalisations that obscure the uncertainties of history (Kendall & Wickham, 2000: 119–120).

Subjectivity, then, is a dynamic mechanism of social management because it is a self-managing subjectivity. For Foucault, this capacity for self-regulation is always a matter of practical ethics, in which we problematise, monitor, and work on our own conduct (as, for example, when we 'watch what we eat'). Such self-regulation may be directed by particular authorities towards specific ends, such as when a coach guides an athlete's weight-monitoring towards a goal of efficiency. However, technologies of the self, although self-regulatory, are not reducible to social control; they always involve a compromise between regulation and autonomy. Thus, while authorities may hope to use an individual's subjectivity as an instrument of social management, technologies of the self are also, always, a potential means of resisting that social management. For example, Chapman's study of elite women rowers (1997) reveals how athletes participate in self-regulatory techniques such as weight control to ambivalent effect. Lowering their weight to increase speed, the women follow the established, disciplinary training pattern. However, they do so critically, employing the very knowledge produced through their training, such as of their own strengths and the harms of dieting, to question, manipulate, and even abandon the conditions of being an elite athlete. Thus, we may think of sport as a set of activities and practices through which we develop and exercise our capacity for self-management. And, as such, we may think of sport as an ethical technology of self.

The contradictory or ambivalent effects of disciplinary technologies of power highlighted by Chapman are what lie at the heart of opportunities for resistance. That is, discipline and training generate 'solutions', which then generate new and different problems. Generally:

> mastery and awareness of one's own body can be acquired only through the effect of an investment of power in the body: gymnastics, exercises, muscle-building, nudism, glorification of the body beautiful. . . . But once power produces this effect, there inevitably emerge the responding claims and affirmations, those of one's own body against power, of health against the economic system, of pleasure against the moral norms of sexuality, marriage, decency. Suddenly, what had made power strong becomes used to attack it. Power, after investing itself in the body, finds itself exposed to a counterattack in that same body (Foucault, 1980: 56).

For athletes, for example, the bodily capacities of strength and speed produce results such as better and faster performances, but they also expose the body to new problems, injuries, and risks. Technologies of the self (such as the self-discipline involved in training) are not reducible to technologies of power (the established training techniques), and the effects of power are never fully predictable. The contradictory effects of training — virtuosity and vulnerability — create the possibility of athletes challenging the ends to which their competence is put, and directing their capacity for self-management towards ends and goals quite different from those originally intended.

Foucault's notion of self-management as a matter of practical ethics opens up the possibility of a radical ethical practice of the self, or ethics of existence, in which we more deliberately practice our freedom to question and choose (Foucault, 1985, 1988a, 1988b). In this distinctive formulation, Foucault defines ethics as a critical, self-reflexive practice. Foucault is not suggesting that ethics are the solution to the widespread imbalance in power relations (1988b: 14). The strategic co-ordination of resistance, like co-ordination of power relations, is necessary to effect institutional changes (Foucault, 1978: 96). While such changes are necessary, they will reconfigure — not dissolve — the power relations that shape the strategic games of social life. The problem thus remains of equipping oneself with the knowledge of both the rules of play and an ethics of practice, "which would allow these game to be played with a minimum of domination" (Foucault, 1988b: 18).

If we are formed through technologies of the self in ways that are harnessed (to contradictory effect) by technologies of domination, then a radical ethical practice of self involves questioning how our self-discipline comes to be and to what ends it is put. Such a practice requires a critical attitude towards the very codes and norms through which we form ourselves, and a sceptical treatment of those objects and tenets we typically regard as natural and commonsensical. Such an ethics would be an ongoing "investigation, not only of one's relationship to moral codes, but a . . . tracing of the events that have constituted us" (Shogan, 1999: 90). Foucault's work thus highlights the "obligation to face the endless task of reinventing" ourselves (Shogan, 1999: 90). Perhaps the greatest ethical challenge facing sociologists of sport and athletes alike is to question the very rationale that supports and legitimises sport. Participation in the disciplinary and regulatory practices of sport is most often justified and naturalised through the 'will to win' (Heikkala, 1993). A Foucauldian analysis of competitiveness would take its cues from Foucault's treatment of sexuality, asking how power and knowledge centre on the body and its capacities to direct it to the particular ends of categorisation and normalisation. How does the discourse of competitiveness valorise some attributes while ignoring or denigrating others? How is the desire to win promoted ahead of the pleasure of participation? How does the rationale of competition produce knowledge in the form of records and comparative scales; institutions such as sporting leagues; discourses such as 'sportsmanship' and teamwork; and disciplines such as training and judging? In short, the ethical athlete must question the very conditions that frame him/her as an 'athlete'.

Governmentality

Technologies of domination and technologies of the self do not work in mutual isolation. Rather, they are deeply interconnected, each forming the condition for the other. Without the support and participation of free subjects, disciplinary and regulatory mechanisms devolve into oppression. Without the resources and rules of institutions and bodies of knowledge, self-managing subjectivities would not be formed. Over time, the forms of these technologies have changed, as have their points of intersection in changing institutions and modes of authority. For example, PE programmes have reinforced different overriding objectives through different pedagogical methods over time, leading individuals to know and value different aspects of themselves, and to act accordingly.

The point of contact between technologies of domination and of the self — between discipline and self-discipline, regulation and freedom — is ultimately what gives shape to the social order and ensures its reproduction. That is, the social order rests on the self-managing individual choosing to act in a way that reproduces the status quo. As such, the government — the influencing and directing — of individual conduct becomes a matter that reaches deep into everyday life. It is this insight, into the way the modern, non-coercive social order works, that leads Foucault to distinguish between the state and government:

> It is certain that in contemporary societies . . . in a certain way all other forms of power relation must refer to [the state]. But this is not because they are derived from it; it is rather because power relations have come more and more under state control. . . . In referring here to the restricted sense of the word *government*, one could say that power relations have been progressively governmentalized, that is to say, elaborated, rationalized, and centralized in the form of, or under the auspices of, state institutions (Foucault, 1983: 224, emphasis in original).

Here, Foucault is making explicit the need to look beyond the state for an explanation of power and the social order. In the administration of society, the state relies on a vast array of behaviours and power relations that fall outside of its immediate parameters, such as the ways in which individuals care for their bodies, teachers promote self-esteem, consumers choose products, parents pass on values, and so forth. Thus, the traditional view of the state as synonymous with the government is too narrow to grasp how the social order works. Foucault proposes a much broader understanding of what the government of society involves, an understanding in which our everyday beliefs, hopes, and actions become relevant to the state. Thus, the governmentality perspective connects "questions of government, politics and administration to the space of bodies, lives, selves and persons" (Dean, 1999: 12). This is a particularly relevant perspective for our current era of neo–liberalism, in which the social order increasingly rests on self-government; how we choose to regulate and improve ourselves lies at the heart of the social order, and its potential transformation.

Since the 1970s, North America and the United Kingdom have been characterised by a neo–liberal style of government, which comes out of critiques of the welfare state and massive changes in the global economic order. This era is characterised by a withdrawal of the state from interfering in the market, and a growing reliance on free competition and market rationality to ensure the optimal outcomes from both markets and individuals. The logic of the market comes to permeate all sectors of life, as individuals are exhorted to become more competitive, efficient, and responsible. This extension of an economic rationality is perhaps most notable for our manner of choice, in that it encourages us to adopt an entrepreneurial attitude towards ourselves (Burchell, 1996: 28–29). As the burden of responsibility for social order falls ever more on the shoulders of individuals, so too does the responsibility for one's own improvement, competitiveness, and optimisation.

Governmentality, then, refers to a 'mentality' or way of thinking about the administration of society, in which the population is managed through the beliefs, needs, desires, and choices of individuals. If the state is indirectly involved in the management of our everyday lives, it is not disinterested. Rather, the state is all the more interested in the various means (authorities, agencies, techniques, and knowledges) by which individual beliefs and actions are directed towards specific ends through the fostering and promotion of such qualities and capacities as self-improvement and entrepreneurialism. The state, ideally, wants to fix power relations in order to make their outcomes more regular and predictable; if we are free to choose, we are to choose appropriately. This is not to suggest that our choices themselves are predetermined. Rather, our mode of choice is what is at issue.

Foucault's thoughts on governmentality illuminate the diffuse ways in which social management is carried out. The concept of governmentality has already been immensely effective in the study of health and illness. For example, programmes such as health education are questioned for their effects of empowerment, but also categorisation and control (Gastaldo, 1997; Lupton, 1995; Petersen & Bunton, 1997). As a conceptual tool, governmentality directs our attention to the ways in which a variety of authorities attempt to act upon our actions in the name of certain objectives, such as economic prosperity, social harmony, and individual fulfilment and happiness (Rose, 1996: 29). Accordingly, analyses of physical cultures, as governmental technologies, must take a more 'nuanced' view of the causes and consequences of participation. Participation in aerobics, for example, is neither a matter of being duped into working out nor an expression of some natural desire for physical exertion. Rather, it is a matter of both regulation and autonomy. Aerobics participation may reinforce a discourse of personal improvement and responsibility, but this has (at least) two potential effects. First, such a discourse may constrain choices regarding how one spends one's time and money, promoting time spent on improving one's body rather than, for example, on collective political action. But aerobics participation may also lead to a greater sense of self-awareness and self-knowledge, which may enable individuals to challenge the ends to which their 'improved' bodies are put.

Of the many insights from Foucault's work on governmentality, there are three that are most relevant to the study of physical culture. The first concerns the role of physical culture as a governmental technology, mobilised to educate citizens in how to manage their own behaviour. The governmentalised state draws on non-political (and thus non-publicly accountable) technologies to educate free, active, democratic citizens to enact their freedom in accordance with broader social objectives. In this way, personal values and goals reinforce social values and goals. The point is not to abandon all activities that may be used against us as means of management (as that would leave us with very little). Rather, the question is how we recognise our values and goals, and identify the vested interests in, and various consequences of, our participation in cultural forms.

Investigations of physical culture and technologies of domination (such as Hargreaves' analysis of PE (1986)) represent existing work in this first vein. What is still lacking, however, is a full interrogation of the ways in which the many forms of physical culture are brought within the realm of government and used in the exercise of political power. We must question the strategic alliances between the state and culture, as Ingham (1985) does in his critique of lifestyle and bodily fitness as the individualised solutions to the crisis of the welfare state. Political rationalities are brought to bear upon physical cultures — elite, popular, mass, folk — such that the pleasure of participation is displaced by criteria of economic efficiency, such as fewer medical claims and increased productivity. The consequences of our participation in sport and fitness are often obscured, if not disguised, by the subtle array of interests at work in the development, promotion, support, and application of specific physical programmes. Consider, for example, the vested interests of medical insurance companies and sporting goods manufacturers such as Nike and Adidas. We must flesh out the connections between sport and other networks of power if we are not to be idle participants in our own management.

If the first application of governmentality concerns, in top-down fashion, the vested interests behind our 'education' through physical culture, the second looks at the bottom-up implications of the exercise of our autonomy for social management. Rose (1990, 1996), following Foucault, explores the ways in which our autonomy — like our culture — is instrumentalised in the governmental state:

> Such a [self-regulating] citizen subject is not to be dominated in the interests of power, but to be educated and solicited into a kind of alliance between personal objectives and ambitions and institutionally or socially prized goals or activities. Citizens shape their lives through the choices they make about family life, work, leisure, lifestyle, and personality and its expression. Government works by 'acting at a distance' upon these choices, forging a symmetry between the attempts of individuals to make life worthwhile for themselves, and the political values of consumption, profitability, efficiency, and social order. Contemporary government, that is to say, operates through the delicate and minute infiltration of the ambitions of regulation in the very interior of our existence and experience as subjects (Rose, 1990: 10).

The objective, here, is to demystify the consequences of our actions for our selves and for the social order. In his comprehensive introduction to the governmentality literature, Dean (1999) links this form of analysis to Foucault's notion of critical, self-reflexive ethics. The goal, suggests Dean, is not an escape from power or domination; as we have discussed, Foucault regarded such a state of pure freedom as an impossible fantasy. Rather, an analysis of governmentality allows us to understand how it is that we govern ourselves and others: "It thus enhances human capacity for the reflective practice of liberty, and the acts of self-determination this makes possible, without prescribing how that liberty should be exercised" (Dean, 1999: 37–38). In short, such research reveals not only how our choices are influenced and constrained, but also enables us to demand new and different choices.

The sociologist, then, must question the effects of sport, health, and fitness at the point of intersection between self-formation and domination: how do physical culture activities call upon our autonomy in ways that accomplish social management and social goals? Such questioning is particularly necessary in the case of initiatives and activities regarded as unquestionably 'good' because they empower the individual, such as health education and physical fitness promotion. The positive effects, such as decreased morbidity, are not to be discounted; however, governmental technologies are double-edged swords, and we must look to the compromises we make in our pursuit of a healthy lifestyle. For example, we might ask to what extent the choice to 'get fit' is an implicit agreement to shoulder the responsibility — and hence the blame — for one's health, and what social, psychological, and economic forms such responsibility takes.

The third insight from Foucault concerns the fundamental instability of governmentality. This is especially important, as an incomplete analysis of neo–liberal social orders can easily lead to a pessimistic picture in which every action appears to reinforce the status quo. For Foucault, the foundations of the neo–liberal state provide the grounds for its own disruption. The state makes its own functioning and legitimacy the intimate affair of every individual. Doing so means that the state's rationality must be "credible to the governed as well as the governing" (Gordon, 1991: 48). Thus, social order is not solely a matter of top-down law and control, but is increasingly contingent upon all individuals and their self-managing activities. But this makes the social order a multifaceted and diffuse process, far too vast and tenuous in its networks for seamless management or guaranteed stability. The co-ordination of individual and institutional objectives is never perfect or total; there are always breakdowns in the intended flow of influence. The more government works through practices of self-management, the greater the consequences of these practices going awry, be it for resistance and disruption, or discipline and punishment.

In the governmental state, the intersections between technologies of domination and technologies of the self are increasingly crucial. We must look to this interface of the individual and the institution, as that is where our freedom is enacted, and where "malfunctionings, malaise, and, perhaps, crises are born" (Foucault, 1988d: 162). As Foucault writes:

> We must refuse the division of labor that very frequently is proposed to us: it is the job of individuals to become indignant and to speak out; it is the job of governments to reflect and to act. ... The will of individuals must be inscribed in a reality that the governments want to monopolize. This monopoly must be wrested from them bit by bit, each and every day (1981, quoted in Eribon, 1991: 279).

Contemporary society depends on our freedom. Foucauldian analyses offer an account of the radical potential of that freedom, and an illumination of the possibilities that lie within the complex interrelation of our autonomy and our governance. If we are each the site of social order, if we adopt an ethics of existence, if we refuse the standardisation of our self-formation, then our autonomy can be used to different, and perhaps radical, effect.

Conclusion

This chapter has sought to introduce the broad, interconnected themes of Foucault's writings that help us to think about sport, power, and the body; ideally, it will spur students to read the works themselves. Five points may be made in conclusion. First, Foucault's understanding of power in modern, non-coercive societies allows us to grasp the diffuse and subtle ways in which institutions, individuals, and the state interrelate, if not always co-operate, in the maintenance of social order. Second, Foucault's concept of technologies of domination highlights the linkages between the means of disciplining the individual body and those of regulating the population body, pointing to the varied uses to which knowledge is put. Third, his thoughts on technologies of the self and the positive model of power help us to appreciate the agency and autonomy of individuals, without falling into idealist fantasies of sovereign subjects and pure, utopian freedom. Fourth, the analysis of governmentality provides us with a comprehension of the multifaceted relations of power in the liberal state and the individualisation of social management, which opens up possibilities for ethical challenge and instability.

Finally, and in light of the preceding points, Foucault's work represents a challenge to sociologists of sport and physical cultures to interrogate their fields and subject matters for their disciplinary *and* ethical practices and potentials. Moreover, we are challenged as participants in physical culture to question our own motivations, and treat with scepticism the taken-for-granted 'truths' that valorise some pursuits, goals, skills, and bodies over others. Foucault encourages us to take up the obligation to question those who govern us, and to enact the autonomy that our system of governance affords us, in order for the games of life to be played with a minimum of domination.[8]

[8]An earlier version of this chapter was presented at the 1999 North American Sociology of Sport Conference in Cleveland, Ohio (Smith,1999). I would like to thank the Graduate Center of The City University of New York and the Social Sciences and Humanities Research Council of Canada for their funding during the time of writing.

References

Andrews, D. L. (1993). Desperately seeking Michel: Foucault's genealogy, the body, and critical sport sociology. *Sociology of Sport Journal, 10*(2), 148–67.

Bailey, P. (1978). *Leisure and Class in Victorian England: Rational Recreation and the Contest for Control, 1830–1885.* London: Routledge & Kegan Paul.

Bourdieu, P. (1984). *Distinction: A Social Critique of the Judgement of Taste.* (Trans. Nice, R.) Cambridge, MA: Harvard University Press.

Burchell, G. (1996). Liberal government and techniques of the self. In: A. Barry, T. Osborne and N. Rose (eds), *Foucault and Political Reason: Liberalism, Neo–Liberalism and Rationalities of Government* (pp. 19–36). Chicago: University of Chicago Press.

Chapman, G. E. (1997). Making weight: Lightweight rowing, technologies of power, and technologies of the self. *Sociology of Sport Journal, 14*(3), 205–223.

Cole, C. L. (1994 [1993]). Resisting the canon: Feminist cultural studies, sport, and technologies of the body. In: S. Birrell and C. L. Cole (eds), *Women, Sport, and Culture* (pp. 5–29). Champaign, IL: Human Kinetics.

Danaher, G., Schirato, T., & Webb, J. (2000). *Understanding Foucault.* London: Sage.

Dean, M. (1999). *Governmentality: Power and Rule in Modern Society.* London: Sage.

Diamond, I., & Quinby, L. (eds) (1988). *Feminism and Foucault: Reflections on Resistance.* Boston: Northeastern University Press.

Douglas, M. (1966). *Purity and Danger: An Analysis of Concepts of Pollution and Taboo.* New York: Praeger.

Elias, N. (1939/1978). *The Civilizing Process.* (Trans. Jephcott, E.) New York: Urizen Books.

Eribon, D. (1991). *Michel Foucault.* (Trans. Wing, B.) Cambridge, MA: Harvard University Press.

Foucault, M. (1977 [1975]). *Discipline and Punish: The Birth of the Prison.* (Trans. Sheridan, A.) New York: Vintage Books.

Foucault, M. (1978 [1976]). *The History of Sexuality: An Introduction. Volume 1.* (Trans. Hurley, R.) New York: Vintage Books.

Foucault, M. (1980 [interview 1975]). Body/Power. In: C. Gordon (ed.), *Power/Knowledge: Selected Interviews and Other Writings, 1972–1977* (pp. 55–62). New York: Pantheon Books.

Foucault, M. (1983 [1982]). The subject and power. In: H. L. Dreyfus and P. Rabinow (eds), *Michel Foucault: Beyond Structuralism and Hermeneutics* (pp. 208–226) (2nd Edition). Chicago: University of Chicago Press.

Foucault, M. (1985 [1984]). *The Use of Pleasure: The History of Sexuality, Volume 2.* (Trans. Hurley, R.) New York: Pantheon Books.

Foucault, M. (1986 [1984]). *The Care of the Self: The History of Sexuality, Volume 3.* (Trans. Hurley, R.) New York: Vintage Books.

Foucault, M. (1988a [interview 1984]). An aesthetics of existence. In: L. D. Kritzman (ed.), *Politics Philosophy Culture: Interviews and Other Writings, 1977–1984* (pp. 47–53). New York: Routledge.

Foucault, M. (1988b [interview 1984]). The ethic of care for the self as a practice of freedom. In: J. Bernauer and D. Rasmussen (eds), *The Final Foucault* (pp. 1–20). Cambridge, MA: The MIT Press.

Foucault, M. (1988c [lecture 1979]). The political technology of individuals. In: L. M. Martin, H. Gutman and P. H. Hutton (eds), *Technologies of the Self: A Seminar with Michel Foucault* (pp. 145–162). Amherst: University of Massachusetts Press.

Foucault, M. (1988d [interview 1983]). Social Security. In: L. D. Kritzman (ed.), *Politics Philosophy Culture: Interviews and Other Writings, 1977–1984* (pp. 159–177). New York: Routledge.

Foucault, M. (1988e [seminar 1982]). Technologies of the self. In: L. M. Martin, H. Gutman and P. H. Hutton (eds), *Technologies of the Self: A Seminar with Michel Foucault* (pp. 16–49). Amherst: University of Massachusetts Press.

Foucault, M. (1991 [lecture 1978]). Governmentality. In: G. Burchell, C. Gordon and P. Miller (eds), *The Foucault Effect: Studies in Governmentality: With Two Lectures by and an Interview with Michel Foucault* (pp. 87–104). Chicago: University of Chicago Press.

Frank, A. W. (1991). For a sociology of the body: An analytical review. In: M. Featherstone, M. Hepworth and B. S. Turner (eds), *The Body: Social Process and Cultural Theory* (pp. 36–102). London: Sage.

Gastaldo, D. (1997). Is health education good for you? Re-thinking health education through the concept of bio-power. In: A. Petersen and R. Bunton (eds), *Foucault, Health and Medicine* (pp. 113–133). London: Routledge.

Gordon, C. (1991). Governmental rationality: An introduction. In: G. Burchell, C. Gordon and P. Miller (eds), *The Foucault Effect: Studies in Governmentality: With Two Lectures by and an Interview with Michel Foucault* (pp. 1–51). Chicago: University of Chicago Press.

Hargreaves, J. (1986). *Sport, Power and Culture: A Social and Historical Analysis of Popular Sports in Britain*. New York: St. Martin's Press.

Heikkala, J. (1993). Discipline and excel: Techniques of the self and body and the logic of competing. *Sociology of Sport Journal, 10*(4), 397–412.

Ingham, A. G. (1985). From public issue to personal trouble: Well-being and the fiscal crisis of the state. *Sociology of Sport Journal, 2*(1), 43–55.

Kendall, G., & Wickham, G. (1998). *Using Foucault's Methods*. London: Sage.

Lupton, D. (1995). *The Imperative of Health: Public Health and the Regulated Body*. London: Sage.

McNay, L. (1994). *Foucault: A Critical Introduction*. New York: Continuum.

Petersen, A., & Bunton, R. (eds) (1997). *Foucault, Health and Medicine*. London: Routledge.

Rail, G., & Harvey, J. (1995). Body at work: Michel Foucault and the sociology of sport. *Sociology of Sport Journal, 12*(2), 164–179.

Rose, N. (1990). *Governing the Soul: The Shaping of the Private Self*. London: Routledge.

Rose, N. (1996). *Inventing our Selves: Psychology, Power, and Personhood*. Cambridge: Cambridge University Press.

Schwartz, H. (1986). *Never Satisfied: A Cultural History of Diets, Fantasies, and Fat.* New York: Anchor Books.

Shogan, D. (1999). *The Making of High-Performance Athletes: Discipline, Diversity, and Ethics.* Toronto: University of Toronto Press.

Smith, J. (1999). *Foucault, Fitness and the Disciplined Body: Technologies of Power and the Self.* Paper presented at the Annual Meetings of the North American Society for the Sociology of Sport, Cleveland, OH, 3–7 November.

Stearns, P. N. (1997). *Fat History: Bodies and Beauty in the Modern West.* New York: New York University Press.

Turner, B. S. (1984). *The Body and Society.* Oxford: Blackwell.

van Krieken, R. (1998). *Norbert Elias.* London: Routledge.

Part IV

Future Directions

Chapter 13

Feminist and Figurational Sociology: Dialogue and Potential Synthesis

Louise Mansfield

This chapter draws on feminist and figurational ('Process') sociology in order to promote a more informed dialogue between the two. Offering a preliminary synthesis, the chapter is designed as a way of making sense of the sports and exercise experiences of women[1] and of furthering an understanding of sport, exercise and gender relations. What is on offer is not a 'feminist-informed' figurational sociology, although it might represent a step in that direction. Rather, the aim is to examine the *overlapping* themes, issues and concepts of both feminism and figurational sociology that would underpin a feminist figurational approach. This approach can enhance the present state of knowledge in theoretical and empirical investigations of gender relations in 'sporting' spheres.

The ideas contained in this chapter will no doubt challenge those guardians of feminist and figurational sociology who adhere to a fairly rigid view of social theory and doctrinal purity. Yet, I do not claim to have all the answers to complex questions about sport, gender and society. Further empirical research and refinement of the theoretical proposals are needed. To this end, both the strengths and weaknesses of a feminist figurational approach are highlighted using investigations of physically active women as a case study.[2]

[1]The term 'women' is not meant to portray females as a homogeneous whole. My comments reflect particular women with whom I have spoken during fieldwork encounters. Their experiences, actions and emotions are both similar to and different from other women in my studies. These women reflect a range of socio-cultural backgrounds. For further information about some of them, see Mansfield and Maguire (1999). To protect the identities of respondents, pseudonyms are used.
[2]The examples are drawn from interview and observed evidence during the course of my own fieldwork with females involved in sport and exercise.

Developments in Feminist and Figurational Sociology

Feminism

Contemporary Western feminism grew out of the women's movement of the 1960s which was politically oriented towards women's liberation and equality (Beasley, 1999; Hargreaves, 1994; Scraton, 1992; Sharpe, 1994; Kemp & Squires, 1997). Feminist research continues to form the core of a great deal of scholarly activity in mainstream sociology and the sociology of sport, and attracts much attention in everyday discourse. Yet, taken-for-granted assumptions about what is meant by 'Feminism' and 'Feminist' have created confusion about these terms; it is not always clear what is meant when they are used. As indicated in Chapter 5, defining the term 'Feminism' is problematic and controversial. Arguably, feminist analyses of sport should be thought of as encompassing a complexity of approaches, positions and strategies that are both temporally and culturally grounded.

In terms of extant feminist literature in the sociology of sport, three key characteristics can be identified. Firstly, feminist research represents a departure from a traditional sociological focus on men's experiences. On this basis, feminism is characterised by critical explorations of and challenges to traditional notions of women as inferior and subordinate to men. Secondly, feminism places the experiences of women as central to an understanding of gender relations. The focus of attention is on female subjectivity and reflexivity, such as on the development of women's notions of self identity in sport and exercise practices. Thirdly, feminist theorising is grounded in evidence and practice, and politically committed to transforming dominant patterns of gender inequality in sport and the broader social sphere.

Figurational ('Process') Sociology

The genesis of figurational sociology lies in the extensive writings of Norbert Elias (Elias, 1978, 1983, 1987, 1994, 1996) (see Chapter 9). Elias' theories and concepts of the history of the emotions, identity construction, the body, violence and state formation have been utilised by several researchers in relation to a diversity of topics and disciplines within sociology and the sociology of sport.[3]

---

[3]For examples of in-depth 'Process' sociological investigations into sport, see Dunning (1999); Dunning and Maguire (1996); Dunning and Rojek (1992); Dunning and Sheard (1973); Dunning, Maguire, and Pearton (1993); Elias and Dunning (1986); Maguire (1999); and Waddington (2000).

One of the main characteristics of figurational sociology is its emphasis on the dynamic and relational character of social life. The focus is on studying intended and unintended social processes over time so as to further an understanding of the networks of human interdependence in social contexts. This focus dovetails well with a theme that underlines a great deal of feminist thinking. As Hargreaves (1992) explains, to understand the oppression of women we must "confront actual, existing social situations and historical processes which have produced current gender inequalities and constraints in leisure and sport" (1992: 166). One of the hallmarks of a feminist figurational approach, then, is the extent to which gender power relations are understood as structured processes located in time and space.

In what follows, I elaborate on the overlapping principles and concerns within feminism and figurational sociology. The ways in which each perspective can fruitfully draw on the other in understanding gender relations in sport, exercise and wider social life are highlighted. Some of my own research findings on women's experiences of sport and exercise are used to illustrate the arguments presented (Maguire & Mansfield, 1998; Mansfield & Maguire, 1999).

A Preliminary Synthesis

The work of Elias is increasingly being applied to a wide range of debates in the sociology of sport (Dunning, 1986, 1999; Dunning & Maguire, 1996; Mansfield & Maguire, 1999; Maguire, 1999; Waddington, 2000). Apart from Jennifer Hargreaves' (1992) critique of figurational sociology, feminist references to Elias have been sparse and few analyses of his work have been made from a 'gender conscious' perspective (van Krieken, 1998). Yet, it is not the case that the present state of knowledge about gender relations, in either feminism or figurational sociology, has reached the end point of theoretical or empirical development. Each has something to offer the other in this regard, as a modest literature has begun to demonstrate.

For example, a concern for gender relations has, arguably, been an important aspect of some figurational work since the 1970s (Dunning & Sheard, 1973; Maguire, 1986). While these studies have focused on men's experiences of sport at the expense of women's, more recent literature has highlighted the fact that changing relations between the sexes represent a key area for sociological investigation (Dunning, 1986; Dunning & Maguire, 1996; Dunning, 1999). In addition, one of North America's leading feminist scholars (Birrell, 1988) notes the relevance of the early contributions of Dunning and Sheard (1973) to feminist research.

Researchers working with figurational sociology have begun to broaden their focus of investigation and explore issues of women in sport, albeit in a preliminary way (Dunning, 1986, 1999; Maguire, 1999). Female scholars from mainstream sociology have also made positive reference to the work of Elias (Lupton, 1996; Tseëlon, 1995). It is my contention that those who study sport and gender relations could fruitfully develop these explorations.

Thinking about women's sporting experiences, rituals and practices in relation to aspects of feminism and figurational sociology may shed further light on the gendered nature of social life. Drawing on Bourdieu, Jarvie and Maguire (1994) observed that competing theoretical perspectives see differently due to the conceptual ground they occupy. In Bourdieu's words, "every sociologist would do well to listen to his/her adversaries as it is in their interest to see what he/she cannot see, to observe the limits of his [sic] vision, which by definition are invisible to him [sic]"(1990: 36).

Feminist and Figurational Sociology: Sport and Gender Relations

There are at least four main ways that we can begin to understand questions of gender relations using a feminist figurational analysis of sports practices. Firstly, we can use this framework to develop an understanding of the relative empowerment of females in the 'male preserve'[4] of sport, and the extent to which they might challenge and change existing male-dominated organisations and values. The critical investigation of and challenge to the dominance of males and masculine ideology lie at the heart of feminist scholarship. Using a 'Process' sociological approach to the analysis of gender power relations may help to unravel these complexities.

In this regard, the following figurational understandings of power are pertinent: (1) power is relational in that no individual woman or man, or group of women or men, has total control over another in particular social settings. Rather, people hold more or less power in relation to others; (2) power networks are dynamic in that they shift and change in a fluid set of human relations; and (3) power is thought of as multi-dimensional. That is, it is possible to define several interconnected dimensions of power, including economic, political, cultural and, for the purposes of this analysis, gender.

---

[4]The term 'male preserve' is used by authors studying sport and gender relations from several perspectives. It denotes those social institutions honoured, demarcated, and dominated both organisationally and ideologically by males.

Reflecting gender power relations in a wider social context, sport and exercise settings are marked by inequality in which the balance of power has predominantly rested with 'established' men. Through long-term processes, specific male/masculine traditions and values have become dominant, at least in Western societies, and these are reproduced in the 'male preserve' of sport (Dunning, 1986; Hargreaves, 1994). Since the rise of modern sport, women have, in the main, been afforded an inferior status in sports practices. As Hargreaves (1994) explains, a dominant bourgeois ideology, centring upon the biological functions of women, has been effective in sustaining long-term, unequal gender relations.

Of course, established beliefs and values are never static. Gender relations represent a network of processes that constantly undergo challenge and transformation. At any time, for example, established notions of femininity co-exist with emergent and residual notions of what 'feminine' means to various groups. There are many social spheres that provide particular women with the opportunity to act back upon, or resist, dominant power structures. Indeed, research has shown several ways in which some active women have the potential to resist traditional ideals of femininity (Bùnel, 1991; Miller & Penz, 1991; St. Martin & Gavey, 1996; Obel, 1996). In addition, it is also the case that some women are involved in the process of subordinating other women in specific sporting spheres (Maguire & Mansfield, 1998). In this regard, the figurational concept of 'established-outsider relations' is a useful aid in explaining the balance of gender power between dominant and non-dominant groups, including both women and men. These ideas are explored below.

Secondly, we can investigate the motivations, meanings and significance of sport and exercise for women, and the impact of their involvement on the construction of their sense of self identity. This central theme of feminist research is something that figurational sociologists could, more extensively, examine, since it is *both* women's and men's experiences of sport and exercise that impact on the social and sociological significance of sport. On this basis, there are connections to be made between the central figurational theory of civilising processes, and the development of unequal gender relations. Issues of sport and gender in the civilising process are discussed later in this chapter.

Thirdly, 'doing' feminist-figurational work should focus on the active role that women have to play in interpreting their experiences in the 'sporting' arena. Encouraging women to speak for themselves about sport and exercise is a focal point of 'doing' feminist research. While figurational sociologists may have begun to highlight gender issues in their work, it is not the case that the subjective experiences of females have been adequately explored. I would advocate an approach that emphasises the importance of women's sentiments, thoughts and emotions; one which hears their private voices, and allows them a more public place to speak.

Central to this feminist methodological point is the figurational idea of 'involvement and detachment' (Elias, 1987). Social researchers cannot escape being involved with their subjects and the research context if they want to understand the pattern of human relations that they wish to study. As a sports woman, participating with and studying other active women, I am necessarily involved with them. Yet, a balance between involvement and detachment can, from a figurational viewpoint, allow further insights into the pattern and dynamics of people's interactions. In the case of my own research, adopting, as Elias (1987) explains, a 'detour via detachment', means being simultaneously, but in varying degrees, close to and distant from the women and the social context under investigation. Developing research methods that interweave female dialogue with observations of women's particular sport practices in an historical, developmental and critical analysis, would be a key feature of feminist figurational work.

Fourthly, a feminist figurational approach is shaped by feminism's political commitment to identifying the diverse social encounters and conditions of women and transforming unequal gender relations. Seeking to increase our fund of knowledge about networks of gender power in sport settings should be combined with a commitment to facilitate social change. If this approach can indeed illuminate resistant sporting practices, structures, and ideologies in terms of what actions and emotions count as 'feminine/female', it should, in my view, also be concerned with sharing and disseminating the knowledge generated in ways that assist the transformation of gender inequalities.

Key Concepts in the Application of a Feminist Figurational Approach

The Figuration

Arguably, analysing women's physically active experiences using the proposed perspective requires a focus on the concept of 'figuration'. That is, women's participation in any game such as netball, hockey, soccer, rugby, and basketball or their involvement in activities like aerobics, circuit training and weight training, takes place within sport and exercise *figurations*. As a key analytical tool of process sociology, this concept allows us to understand social life in terms of a network of interdependent, mutually-oriented people. To clarify this idea, I refer to my research on women's experiences of aerobics.

Elias' (1978, 1994) work explains that human beings are bonded, in both enabling and constraining ways, to the social relations they form between each other in any social setting. In this sense, the aerobics class represents an exercise figuration in micro context, but one that is located within a wider network of social relationships. Participants[5] interact with each other in face-to-face contact, but they are also interdependently influenced by such institutions as education, the family, the media, diet and health technologies, sport sciences and the fitness industry. For example, the women I observed formed 'cliques' within the aerobics studio. They physically gravitated towards other participants, or the instructor, by communicating verbally and acknowledging people with spoken words, body language and gestures in a 'reciprocal exchange' of signs and symbols (Maguire, 1995). One could almost see them forming a dynamic figuration of bodies (Elias & Dunning, 1986).

Active in defining their sense of self identity, many of my respondents experienced liberating feelings of increased self confidence and emotional release in and through aerobics. Yet this exercise figuration is by no means isolated from the broader social, economic, and political context. For instance, intensely aware of their own bodies, and those of others in the aerobics setting and in their broader lived experience, these women predominantly shaped their bodies and their sense of self in relation to established codes of (hetero)sexual feminine beauty. They expressed aspirations to achieve a slim, toned 'look', identified by them as feminine. Wider commercialisation processes were at work in perpetuating established and socially acceptable ideals of femininity. 'Established' bodies, for example, revealed their lean, tanned and toned skin, in tight lycra clothing 'branded' with Nike, Adidas, Reebok, and other such seals of approval.

Whatever the characteristics of these direct and indirect bonds, they are not fixed or static. Rather, they are fluid and change in connection with the many and varied relationships that these women have with other women in the aerobics class, and women and men in a broader cultural context. These 'interdependencies'[6] change in relation to shifting balances of power between individuals and groups within any figuration. Simply put, people live out their lives in an interwoven network of relationships, which are historically developed and marked by both the enabling and constraining characteristics of the gender power balances. In the aerobics figuration, women form interdependencies with

---

[5]While men also participate in aerobic exercise classes, it is the case that women dominate this type of activity; it remains widely viewed as a 'woman's preserve'.
[6]The term 'interdependencies' is used in figurational sociology to denote the human bonds that develop within figurational networks (Elias, 1978).

others in a multitude of complex and dynamic ways that reflect both personal and public social processes.

In the next section, I draw on figurational sociology's theory of established-outsider relations, and identify a specific power dynamic at work in the micro context of aerobics, which impacts upon the relationships between 'established' and 'outsider' participants. In addition, I suggest that there are broader established-outsider relations at work between and within groups of women and men in society which are reflected in the thoughts, actions and emotions of the female aerobicisers. The examples seek to illustrate that the notion of figurational power dynamics can be a useful aid in feminist interpretations of women's sport and exercise experiences.

Established-Outsider Relations

'Established-outsider theory' is a central component of figurational sociology and was derived from a study of two neighbourhoods in the English East Midlands (Elias & Scotson, 1994; Mennell, 1992). Focusing on power balances between dominant and non-dominant groups, this approach has considerable potential where the study of gender power dynamics is concerned. Examining women's actions and emotions in sport and exercise, it is evident that while some women hold an inferior status in relation to other women and men, greater power chances are afforded to particular groups of active women. 'Established' women are relatively empowered in the aerobics context, for example, through access to exercise knowledge, increased fitness, and the ownership of 'appropriate' bodies. These characteristics often serve to differentiate higher status women from lower status women in the exercise setting.

Though it may not be generalisable to other exercise contexts, my fieldwork suggests that an established clique tends to dominate the space around the aerobics instructor, excluding 'outsiders' from seeing the routines effectively and, thus, hindering their mastery of movement patterns. Indeed, the degree of 'fitness' and competence in performing the exercise routines also helped to maintain the central status of particular women. A distinct type of status rivalry existed between these women in their quest for the 'body beautiful'. They competed against their 'opponents' without using force, but clearly gauged their levels of fitness, expertise, and appearance, in relation to other performers. This was highlighted by Ruth who explained, "I do try to emulate people who have good technique. I think if they are going well and jumping a bit higher, then I'll keep going." Commenting on processes of self and other surveillance, Claire "always notice[d] what other people look like. They look better than me."

Sarah echoed this sentiment when she exclaimed, "There are one or two women who come down here who look absolutely fabulous. I don't know how they do it!"

It was evident that 'established' women embodied societal values of thinness, and tone, which 'outsider' women desired. Setting the standards of appearance, 'established' women wore clothing that revealed their skin surface, and drew attention to themselves, by adorning their bodies with jewellery and make-up. At the front of the class, a 'chorus line' of tanned, toned bodies performed knowingly for the viewing of 'outsiders'. In contrast, 'insider' women in no way considered their bodies to be complete. They engaged in continual bodywork in order to maintain their appearance. For example, Beth reinforced this idea when she explained her intention to remain slim. Indeed, she echoed the sentiments of all of the 'insider' women I talked to by emphasising her goals thus: "I saw (sic) exercise as making me look good. I am nine stone now. My goal is eight and a half stone. Then I won't have any flesh/fat on me. I just want to stay lean".

Displaying desirable standards of bodily appearance, 'established' participants were also knowledgeable about the routines, exercises and the music associated with the aerobics class. At every session they showed familiarity with the music, and shouted, cheered and clapped enthusiastically as they performed. They incorporated an energetic and vocal dominant group charisma (Mennell, 1992). In this sense, a 'We' image tended to be developed and internalised by 'established' group members, and a 'They' image was constructed and more commonly embodied in relation to 'outsider' participants. It is important to re-emphasise here that the power networks which characterise insider-outsider relations are not absolute or static. Rather, they are relational and subject to change. 'Outsiders' were active in achieving the bodily standards of the established group by watching, listening to and talking with those 'who know'. Dominant group members had all, in varying ways and to differing degrees, experienced the intimidation and discomfort of being 'outsiders'. On this basis, they demonstrated some understanding toward the needs of less powerful participants.

Nevertheless, women who performed in the 'outsider' group, more often than those who participated in the 'insider' group, expressed internalised feelings of inferiority and embarrassment; they realised how great the gap was between their current appearance and performance levels, and the demanding ideals they faced within the exercise context. The sense of discomfort in non-dominant participants was summed up by Wendy who, when questioned on this matter, shook her head and whispered, "I can't see myself in any of those leotards. I just haven't got the body for it". Wendy, like other 'outsiders', had not, as yet, acquired competency in the movement patterns of the class and, hence, was too timid to move to the front. She remained, perhaps temporarily, part of the 'outsider' group.

These brief fieldwork episodes illustrate some aspects of the power dynamics that characterise the exercise figuration in question. Yet, the women who participated in this type of exercise were not isolated human beings. Their exercise experiences were interconnected with the way in which they lived out other parts of their lives. 'Higher status' women tend to hold a relatively privileged position in the aerobics dance studio. In more recent research, this is also the case in other fitness settings such as the gym, or the swimming pool. In addition, the achievement of the 'body beautiful' is commonly revered by women, and men, and socially approved by the images and messages of dominant institutions such as the media, the sport sciences, and the fitness industry.

Exploring established-outsider relations more broadly, it seems to be the case, in Western culture at least, that gendered ideology and action manipulates many women into the 'They' image of those women and men committed to traditional notions of socially acceptable femininity. The latter tend to hold a more favourable 'We' image and perpetuate established notions of what constitutes 'femininity'. It should be re-emphasised that such gender processes are not static. Balances of power are marked by negotiation, resistance and change. However, there is little evidence of resistant practices in activities such as commercial aerobics. I would argue that traditional pressures to discipline, control and ultimately 'correct' the female body are evident in the organisation and ideologies of such regimes. This can detract from the emancipatory potential of participating in this type of exercise. The power inequalities at work in the micro context of sport and exercise, and in the wider social sphere, impact on the ways that women come to live in female/feminine ways. My respondents seem to have developed, and internalised, particular gendered identities in the context of aerobic exercise. The following section draws on the concept of habitus to shed light on the development and characteristics of 'female/feminine' identities.

Gender Identity and Habitus Codes

Several authors have used the concept of 'habitus' in explaining issues of identity construction (Bourdieu, 1978; Dunning, 1999, Elias, 1978, 1939/1994,1996; Maguire, 1993b,1999; Mauss, 1973; van Krieken, 1998). Drawing on Elias' use of the concept, a figurational perspective argues that a person's habitus is characterised by the enduring dispositions that are laid down deep within us through ongoing socialisation processes (Elias, 1996). For example, throughout the life course, established ideals of gender are internalised within human beings as part of their 'second nature'.

Specific, enduring and socially acceptable characteristics of femininity and masculinity can be identified in people's actions and emotions in social contexts. With respect to 'female/feminine' habituses and sport settings, traditional ideas continue to reinforce the notion that grace, poise, a passive demeanour, and a caring attitude are preferable female traits. A feminine 'look' is associated with being slim and petite, with curves in the 'right' places. Girls tend to be directed away from sports and exercise that require strength, power, aggression, and muscularity. Of course, it is also the case that women are involved in some countries, indeed in rapidly growing numbers, in physical activities such as football, rugby, and weight training, which have historically been considered as male preserves (Hargreaves, 1994; Henry & Comeaux, 1999; Scraton *et al.*, 1999; Wright & Clarke, 1999). This is certainly a challenge to established gender codes. Yet, at the level of habitus, established notions of feminine beauty prevail.

Aerobics, for example, is one social dimension through which the women I have observed and interviewed develop and internalise deeply layered and symbolic notions of traditional femininity. These ideals of feminine beauty are evident in common characteristics of appearance, bodily deportment, gestures, actions and emotions. Performance routines in aerobics are organised in a strict, precise fashion according to dominant ideas about what type and intensity of exercise will ensure fat loss and improved muscle tone. These women are encouraged that continual rhythmic exercise will help them achieve a slimmer form. The toning exercises focus upon isolated body parts that, in a sense, define women's 'hetero-sex' appeal. In aerobics, much time is invested in 'working on' the thighs, bottom, stomach and breasts in order to tighten, tone and reduce. In my own fieldwork, it has been clear that the women who have spoken to me consciously shape their bodies according to (Western) societal values of feminine beauty.

Apparently, many women view physical activity as a means of reducing the size and changing the shape of their bodies in pursuit of the 'body beautiful'. In this regard, they have a particular dislike of fat. This was highlighted by Penny, who expressed her intense distaste for many aspects of her body in the following way:

> Ultimately, I do exercise for weight reasons. I hate my legs and
> my bum and my arms because they are fat! I go to the gym every

> day, I wouldn't want to stop. I want to come out of a class and
> feel that I've worked [out] and burned fat. If I was really thin, I
> don't think I'd go at all.

I would argue here that strongly built, muscular and aggressive women are still
not *'de rigueur'* in sport, exercise, or the wider society. Images of young, sleek,
lithe women, such as tennis player, Anna Kournikova, or beach volleyball
professional, Gabrielle Reese, are the preferred images of media and advertising
material, and are part of the taken-for-granted picture of feminine heterosexuality
that many women and men accept.

The women I have spoken with are not always *consciously* aware of the
female/feminine habituses I have described. Yet, these enduring features of
gender are central to their embodied experiences, and are a focal point of
common beliefs about women and gender power relations. Everyday behaviours
and experiences like exercise, dieting and beauty treatments, for example,
become so familiar that the women in my studies consider them to be 'natural',
normal' and rational aspects of being 'female/feminine'.

I do not wish to imply that habitus codes are fixed and unchallenged. There is
no genetically coded 'female/feminine' habitus. Women and men play an active
role in the pattern and meaning of social relations, and the construction of their
gendered identities. My respondents reinforced and challenged feminine habitus
codes, in varying degrees and in terms of the meaning they attached to the
techniques, practices and ideologies of aerobics. Yet, traditional notions of what
constitutes socially acceptable femininity (Hargreaves, 1994; Scraton, 1992;
Willis, 1994) still dominate these women's lives and are revealed in their bodily
size, shape, volume, postures, gestures, and expressions. This leads me to
conclude that 'female/feminine' habitus are characterised by the desire to be
slender, slim, lean and toned, and to exhibit graceful, controlled bodily movement.

Feminine identities are developed and inscribed upon women's 'sporting' bodies
in complex, shifting and dynamic ways. In this sense, gendered identity-construction
is also a feature of wider, long-term social development. A pivotal concept of
figurational sociology, that of the 'civilising process', is especially helpful in
understanding such long-term social development of gender power relations.

Gender, Civilised Bodies and Civilising Processes

Though it has been rarely acknowledged in the literature, the body is central to
the figurational perspective (Maguire, 1993a; Shilling, 1993). Elias argues that
the historical development towards more controlled behavioural and emotional

acts involves wide and diverse changes in standards of conduct for human bodies at individual and societal levels. Taking a long-term developmental view, he emphasises that human beings learn to control their bodily appearance, actions, and emotions according to changing social environments. 'Civilised' bodies, at least in contemporary Western societies, are characterised by internal pacification, rationalisation, self-restraint, and regulation, learned through processes of human interaction.

I suggest that these historical transformations are indicative of *gendered* civilising processes. Social codes and sanctions with respect to what constitutes acceptable female/feminine looks and demeanour, for example, are learned, internalised, and become self-imposed. Sport and exercise contexts show evidence of such gendered civilising processes at work. Shilling's (1993) account of civilised Western bodies makes it readily apparent that female bodies are socially managed. They are 'civilised' in accordance with established ideals of feminine beauty. In the micro context of aerobics, for example, feminine bodies are shaped by processes of self and other forms of monitoring. These self- and other-surveillance tactics extend to wider socio-cultural experiences, images, and ideologies, both past and present. 'Civilised' female bodies, in the case of aerobics, are symbolised by a rationalised command of the techniques, practices and rituals of exercise, and by an established bodily appearance (Shilling, 1993, 1997). The dominant aspiration of the women in my studies is to be slim and toned. This 'look' is revered within the aerobics context and wider society, and is status-enhancing. Achieving the 'body beautiful' is associated with the desire for bodily control, discipline and heterosexual feminine beauty.

This 'look' may well represent the enhanced social liberation of some women in contemporary societies, which is evident in personal feelings of self confidence, and in the admiration from others. Yet, it also masks a more private discrimination. Some of the women I spoke to were publicly empowered through the achievement of the 'body beautiful', perceived by them to be liberating on a number of fronts. Yet, these same women privately feared that their bodies might not measure up to acceptable standards. One aerobiciser, Sarah, had much to say on this issue: ". . . women are under so much pressure to conform to a fashionable shape. It's difficult to maintain, it's a constant battle. There isn't a day that goes by when I don't think about it. I feel guilty when I don't do my stomach exercises and it becomes deeply ingrained".

Both 'established' and 'outsider' women had come to *know* what shape, size and weight counted as feminine and 'attractive'. It seems that these women internalised and adhered to a set of rules, individually contoured, yet pertaining to socially acceptable notions of contemporary feminine beauty. Feelings of shame, embarrassment and repugnance were expressed when these women did not successfully control the shape and tone of their bodies.

Regarding the relative subordination of women in sport and the wider society, the theory of civilising processes and, in particular, the ideas which pertain to violence control, may enhance an understanding of long-term, changing relations of power between the sexes. Proponents of figurational sociology would argue that there is evidence of long-term controls and taboos regarding the practise and observation of violent acts. On this basis, social and psychological sanctions have developed in contemporary Western societies that mean it is decreasingly acceptable for males to use violence against women. Yet, the domination and subordination of some women clearly exists in many social settings including sport. Sometimes, this process is explicit and sometimes it is 'pushed behind the scenes' (Dunning, 1992, 1999), such as in specific coaching 'practices' and training regimes (Brackenridge, 1997; Nelson, 1994).

If sport does indeed remain as one legitimate sphere for the expression of masculine aggression and violence (Dunning, 1999), then the theory of civilising processes may explain why sexual assault and verbal vilification of women by male athletes is evident in some sport subcultures (Brackenridge, 1997; Nelson, 1994). The theory may clarify the ways in which traditionally male institutions, such as sport, serve as 'masculinity-validating' experiences (Dunning, 1999). That some arenas of sport represent havens for the expression of masculine dominance and the (re)production of traditionally male/masculine habituses, may help to explain why the numbers of women in positions of power in some sports has not increased proportionally with participation rates, and why women's performances continue to be marginalised and trivialised by powerful institutions such as the media (Creedon, 1994; Hargreaves, 1994; Dunning, 1999). It is this evidence which leads me to re-emphasise that in and through sport and exercise, and in their lived encounters, the women in my studies have undergone a gendered civilising process.

Concluding Remarks

The principal aim of this chapter has been to outline a preliminary synthesis between feminism and figurational or 'process' sociology. This approach represents a vehicle for shedding light on issues of gender power relations in the context of sport and exercise. There are several overlapping themes in feminist and figurational sociology that underline the need for such a synthesis. The central point of common ground is that both approaches emphasise the importance of understanding the relational nature of social interaction through time and space. A feminist focus on female subjectivity and experience can add to the existing knowledge about the balance of power between the sexes, and between established and outsider women and men in specific figurations. In the context of women's experiences of sport and exercise, this endeavour could fruitfully be fulfilled by drawing on figurational ideas about gender power relations, established outsider theory, notions of habitus and 'I/We' images, and the theory of the 'civilising process'.

A feminist commitment to challenging and transforming gender inequality must be central to this approach if we are to develop an understanding of the social and sociological significance of sport practices in the lives of *both* women and men. I emphasise that adding to our fund of knowledge about gender relations should be based on theoretically-informed empirical research. Given this, strong links should be developed between theory, evidence and political action if the proposed synthesis is to offer ways in which gender inequality within sporting spheres can be challenged in any meaningful way.

I do not suggest that a feminist figurational perspective can provide all the answers to complex questions about gender relations. It can, however, make a contribution. On this basis, I take Elias at his word and present this theoretical approach as symptomatic of a beginning in wider and growing investigations of women's experiences of sport and exercise. I am aware that there are defenders of both feminism and figurational sociology whose minds are closed to this inter-theoretical approach. Yet, it is arguably 'un-Eliasian' and even asociological to read either perspective as if it were the final word, and that collaborative ventures are not possible. This closed position represents an insufficiently 'detached' consideration of the relative benefits of a dialogue, and potential synthesis between feminism and figurational sociology. It seems to me that thinking in conjunction with, and in opposition to, both of these approaches has much to offer in understanding the ways in which female participation, opportunity, and experience in sport and exercise can be improved.

References

Beasley, C. (1999). *What is Feminism?* London: Sage.
Benson, S. (1997). The body, health and eating disorders. In: K. Woodward (ed.), *Identity and Difference* (pp. 121–183). London: Sage.
Birrell, S. (1988). Discourse on the gender/sport relationship: From women in sport to gender relations. *Exercise and Sports Science Review, 16*, 359–503.
Bourdieu, P. (1978). Sport and social class. *Social Science Information, 17*, 819–840.

Bourdieu, P. (1990). *In Other Words: Essays Towards a Reflexive Sociology.* Cambridge: Polity Press.

Brackenridge, C. (1997). He owned me basically: Women's experience of sexual abuse in sport. *International Review for the Sociology of Sport, 32,* 115–130.

Bùnel, A. (1991). The recreational physical activities of Spanish women: A sociological study of exercising for fitness. *International Review for the Sociology of Sport, 26,* 205–213.

Creedon, P. (1994). *Women, Media and Sport: Challenging Gender Values.* California: Sage.

Dunning, E. (1986). Sport as a male preserve: Notes on the social sources of masculine identity and transformation. *Theory, Culture and Society, 3,* 79–90.

Dunning, E. (1999). *Sport Matters: Sociological Studies of Sport, Violence and Civilization.* London: Routledge.

Dunning, E., & Maguire, J. (1996). 'Process' sociological notes on sport, gender relations and violence control. *International Review for the Sociology of Sport, 31,* 295–323.

Dunning, E., & Rojek, C. (eds) (1992). *Sport and Leisure in the Civilizing 'Process': Critique and Counter Critique.* London: Macmillan.

Dunning, E., & Sheard, K. (1973). The rugby club as a type of male preserve: Some sociological notes. *International Review for the Sociology of Sport, 8,* 5–24.

Dunning, E. Maguire, J., & Pearton, R. (eds) (1993). *The Sports Process: A Comparative and Developmental Approach.* Champaign, IL: Human Kinetics Publishers.

Elias, N. (1978). *What is Sociology?* London: Hutchinson.

Elias, N. (1983). *The Court Society.* Oxford: Blackwell.

Elias, N. (1987). *Involvement and Detachment.* Oxford: Blackwell.

Elias, N. (1994). *The Civilising Process: The History of Manners and State Formation and Civilization* (single integrated edition). Oxford: Blackwell.

Elias, N. (1996). *The Germans: Power Struggles and the Development of Habitus in the Nineteenth and Twentieth Centuries.* Oxford: Blackwell.

Elias, N., & Dunning, E. (1986). *Quest for Excitement: Sport and Leisure in the Civilising Process.* Oxford: Blackwell.

Elias, N., & Scotson, J. (1994). *The Established and the Outsiders.* London: Sage.

Hargreaves, J. (1992). Sex, gender and the body in sport and leisure: Has there been a civilising 'Process'? In: E. Dunning and C. Rojek (eds), *Sport, Leisure and the Civilising 'Process'* (pp. 161–183). London: Macmillan.

Hargreaves, J. (1994). *Sporting Females.* London: Routledge.

Henry, J., & Comeaux, H. (1999). Gender egalitarianism in coed sport: A case of American soccer. *International Review for the Sociology of Sport, 34*(3), 277–291.

Jarvie, G., & Maguire, J. (1994). *Sport and Leisure in Social Thought.* London: Routledge.

Kemp, S., & Squires, J. (eds) (1997). *Feminisms.* Oxford: Oxford University Press.

Lupton, D. (1996). *Food, the Body and the Self.* London: Sage.

Maguire, J. (1986). Images of manliness and competing ways of living in late Victorian and Edwardian Britain. *British Journal of Sport History, 3*(3), 265–287.

Maguire, J. (1993a). Bodies, sport cultures and societies. *International Review of the Sociology of Sport, 28*(1), 33–51.

Maguire, J. (1996). Globalization, sport and national identities: 'The empire strikes back'. *Society and Leisure, 16*(2), 293–322.

Maguire, J. (1995). Sport, the stadium and metropolitan life. In: J. Bale and O. Moen (eds), *The Stadium and City Life* (pp. 45–57). Keele, UK: Keele University Press.

Maguire, J. (1999). *Global Sport: Identities, Societies, Civilizations.* Cambridge: Polity.

Maguire, J., & Mansfield, L. (1998). "No-body's perfect": Women, aerobics and the body beautiful. *Sociology of Sport Journal, 15*, 109–138.

Mansfield, L., & Maguire, J. (1999). Active women, power relations and gendered identities: Embodied experiences of aerobics. In: S. Roseneil and J. Seymour (eds), *Practicing Identities: Power and Resistance* (pp. 81–106). London: Macmillan.

Markula, P. (1995). Firm but shapely, fit but sexy, strong but thin: The postmodern aerobicizing female bodies. *Sociology of Sport Journal, 12*, 424–533.

Mauss, M. (1973). Techniques of the body. *Economy and Society, 2*, 70–88.

Mennell, S. (1992). *Norbert Elias. An Introduction*, Oxford: Blackwell.

Miller, L., & Penz, O. (1991). Talking bodies: Female body builders colonize a male preserve. *Quest, 43*(2), 148–164.

Nelson, M. (1994). *The Stronger Women Get, the More Men Love Football: Sexism and the American Culture of Sport.* New York: Harcourt–Brace.

Obel, C. (1996). Collapsing gender in competitive bodybuilding: Researching contradictions and ambiguities in sport. *International Review for the Sociology of Sport, 31*, 185–201.

Scraton, S. (1992). *Shaping up to Womanhood: Gender and Girls Physical Education.* Buckingham: Open University Press.

Scraton, S., Fasting, K., Pfister, G., & Bùnel, A. (1999). It's still a man's game?: The experiences of top-level european women footballers. *International Review for the Sociology of Sport, 34*(2), 99–111.

Sharpe, S. (1994). *Just Like a Girl: How Girls Learn to Be Women.* London: Penguin.

Shilling, C. (1993). *The Body and Social Theory.* London: Sage.

Shilling, C . (1997). The body and difference. In: K. Woodward (ed.), *Identity and Difference* (pp. 63–121). London: Sage.

St. Martin, L., & Gavey, N. (1996). Women's bodybuilding: Feminist resistance and/or femininity's recuperation. *Body and Society, 2*, 45–57.

Tseëlon, E. (1995). *The Masque of Femininity.* London: Sage.

Waddington, I. (2000). *Sport, Health and Drugs.* London: E & F N Spon.

Willis, P. (1994). Women in sport in ideology. In: S. Birrell and C. Cole (eds), *Women, Sport and Culture* (pp. 31–47). Champaign. IL: Human Kinetics.

Wright, J., & Clarke, G. (1999). Sport, the media and the construction of compulsory heterosexuality: A case study of women's rugby union. *International Review for the Sociology of Sport, 34*(3), 227–245.

Chapter 14

The Political Economy of Place: Urban and Sport Studies Perspectives

Kimberly S. Schimmel

For the past twenty years, academic research on urban (re)development has been characterised by a curious and troubling disjuncture between urban studies and sport studies. While sport studies scholars routinely situate their work within urban studies frameworks and have made important contributions to our overall understanding of urban political economy, those contributions remain largely unrecognised within urban studies.[1] While urban studies scholars are beginning to acknowledge the significance of sport as a cultural and economic formation, they seem unaware of the ways in which sport studies itself has conceptualised that significance. In short, sport studies scholars are rarely consulted by colleagues in other disciplines as they (co-)investigate sport and urban development.

In this paper, I illustrate this disjuncture by drawing on one conceptual framework that addresses urban (re)development: the so-called 'growth machine' perspective.[2] Developed within urban studies and considered by some an 'academic tour de force' (Jonas & Wilson, 1999), the growth machine perspective has been utilised by scholars in sociology, political science, cultural geography, economics, and history, among others. What have been the contributions of sport studies scholars? Since Gregory Stone's influential work on sport and community in 1981, a number of conferences and symposia within sport studies have addressed the relationship between sport and the political economy of urban space (cf. Ingham & Donnelly, 1997). In this chapter, I draw primarily on work within the sociology of sport to illustrate the contributions

---

[1] For an important exception see Charles Euchner's (1993) *Playing the Field: Why Sports Teams Move and Cities Fight to Keep Them.*

[2] The growth machine perspective is not, obviously, the only theoretical framework which sheds light on patterns and rationales of urban (re)development, nor am I suggesting that it is necessarily the 'best'. However, it was both highly influential and remains remarkably durable as a way to conceptualise urban change. Furthermore, as I suggest in this paper, the sociology of sport has made significant contributions to the development of this perspective.

---

that have been made — and should be more widely recognised — to the growth machine perspective. In doing so, I hope to draw connections between urban studies and sport studies that will inform future ways of thinking about urban (re)development.

In the following two sections, I briefly examine the emergence of the concept of 'place' in theories of political economy, followed by a discussion of the growth machine thesis. In subsequent sections I address the varied contributions of sociologists of sport to this thesis despite little reciprocal recognition from most urban studies scholars of the existence or relevance of those contributions. Before beginning, however, I must offer several caveats to the reader. First, given space limitations, my discussion will necessarily be simplified, and at times I am forced to overlook important nuances within various growth machine perspectives. Second, rather than a comprehensive meta-analysis of the literature, I am selecting key works in the sociology of sport to illustrate disciplinary connections. Finally, I am not suggesting that the explicit purpose of the works selected was to contribute to the growth machine thesis; in fact, some authors might disagree with its basic tenets. Rather than a definitive statement, then, this chapter should be read as an attempt to open a more reciprocal dialogue between sport and urban studies scholars.

Putting 'Place' in Political Economy

In the 1970s, a leftist-oriented urban framework emerged in the United States as a challenge to mainstream urban social science, which assumed that business participation in local development policy was inherently "apolitical" (see especially Peterson, 1981, pp. 142). Henri Lefebvre's book *La Revolution Urbaine* (1970), David Harvey's critical articles published in *Social Justice and the City* (1973), and Manuel Castells' book *City, Class and Power* (1978) were landmarks in the development of an alternative to both traditional urban sociology and to neo–classical explanations of urban development in the United States.[3] Their work embodies the principles of Marxist structuralism in which economic processes or the "laws of motion" of capitalism are perceived to be the basic engines of urban change (see Smith, 1988; Swanstrom, 1993).

In a direct challenge to mainstream urban social science, leftist-oriented

---

[3]In short, a neo–classical perspective holds that government intervention into the forces of the free market is unnecessary, wasteful, and possibly even harmful to the general welfare of society. See Smith (1988); and Swanstrom (1993) for a comparison of leftist-oriented urban sociology and neo-classicism.

scholars stressed the conflictual nature of class struggle in the control and enhancement of urban space. Harvey (1986), for example, argued that power is structured hierarchically within urban areas, resulting in the local state having to assume the role of manager of class conflicts and economic contradictions. Due to the necessity of maintaining capital accumulation (i.e., generating profit), the local state favours the capitalist class. The logic of capital accumulation, therefore, limits the options for local governments and largely determines local policy (Leitner, 1990: 150–152). The result is uneven urban and regional development that is an inevitable reflection of national and global economies. In this view, urban politics is largely irrelevant to the laws of motion of economic development: "politics and society are reduced to the 'bearers' of inexorable economic and technological forces" (Smith, 1988: 4). The structural features of capitalism leave little (or no) room for local-level actors to influence urban development.

In the late 1970s and early 1980s, critical urban scholarship flourished in the United States, as scholars, influenced by the work of Lefebvre, Harvey, and Castells, began articulating a paradigm that emphasised the importance of analysing particular features of capitalism in any assessment of urban life. The richness and depth of Marxist thought inspired a variety of neo–Marxist approaches to urban analysis. Scholars debated the relative significance of the economy, the social production of space, competition for capital investment, significance of political processes, and the role of the state in urban development (see Feagin, 1988).

Just as neo–Marxist urban theory developed as a critique of mainstream sociology, so too emerged an alternative to the view that cities are 'held captive' (Peterson, 1981) to the capitalist mode of production. The 'capital logic' perspective was criticised for introducing politics only after the fact, as an urban reaction to economic forces. So-called 'urban praxis' scholars, for example, recognise the influence of broader economic processes, but assert that politics matters in the economic development of local-urban economy (Smith, 1988). This perspective allows for much greater local autonomy, and puts significantly more emphasis on the need to include 'place-specific' contingencies in the study of local development policy (Leitner, 1990). Thus, urban praxis scholars argue that the logic of capital accumulation can never fully determine specific social, political, and cultural formations (Smith, 1988). Instead, theorists began to emphasise the duality of social structure and human agency (see Giddens, 1984). Rather than focusing only on the ways in which structures *constrain* opportunity, these theorists also recognise their *enabling* features. In this view, urban economies are loosely coupled with broader national and global forces, leaving room for both cultural variety and political leadership. While the difference may seem subtle, in this new perspective, the focus is not on the economics of political relations — what is examined instead is the politics of economic relations (Swanstrom, 1993).

Local political power was conceptualised at this time primarily through community power studies, an approach exemplified by Dahl's (1961) work on New Haven where local power is viewed as a mechanism for social control: the exertion of issue-by-issue (e.g., political, electoral) domination over subordinate groups. Molotch (1976) criticised this approach, however, for granting too much autonomy to local actors and ignoring systemic constraint. His thesis forged a middle ground between community power studies and structural Marxism, and shifted the focus of local power to a more facilitative concept. He followed a social production model of power based on the question, "How, in a world of limited and dispersed authority, do actors work together across institutional lines to produce a capacity to govern and bring about publicly significant results?" (Stone, 1989: 89). In this model, power is enacted through what Molotch (1976) called 'growth machines' (see also Logan & Molotch, 1987). Other terms for this collectivity of social actors include 'growth coalitions' (Mollenkopf, 1983; Swanstrom, 1985), 'governing coalitions' (Stone, 1987), and 'urban regimes' (Elkin, 1987; Fainstein & Fainstein, 1983).

While there are variations in meanings underlying these terms, they all have in common a basic premise: local-level policy development is not an inevitable result of broad structural forces; rather, it is produced through the proximate actions of interested actors. As an empirical matter, adherents to this general paradigm assert that local development policy has real consequences for various groups in cities that may be problematic (Molotch, 1993). In the following section, I outline key themes of the growth machine thesis.

Understanding Local Power: The Growth Machine Thesis

Among the various perspectives for understanding the nature of place-based political economy, perhaps none has been more influential than Harvey Molotch's growth machine thesis. Appearing in 1976, his paper, "The City as Growth Machine", was a watershed event in the history of urban political economy. Unique in both scope and vision, it established and propelled a research agenda that now extends across multiple disciplinary boundaries; it also provided a basis for critical re-evaluation of work on the politics of local economic development (Cox, 1999; Jonas & Wilson, 1999). Molotch argued that the day-to-day actions of urban elites had not been taken into account in any substantive and relevant way. On the one hand, community power studies had failed to recognise structurally embedded aspects of power and resources that support the development of urban places. On the other hand, with their preoccupation with the Marxian concept of social class, leftist scholars "gave short shrift to the agents, processes, and consequences of city building" (Molotch, 1999: 247).

Jonas and Wilson (1999) point out that at various stages in its development, the growth machine thesis has drawn conceptual support from a complex mix of scholarly traditions. It has been informed and inspired by critical understandings from urban ecology, community power analysis, and neo–Marxism and structuration theories. In *Urban Fortunes* (1987), Logan and Molotch attempt to find a middle ground "between the voluntarism and structuralism, the micro and the macro, and the contextual and the compositional" (1987: 5). Though two decades of new concepts and empirical study of urban politics have called into question many of his original claims, at the very center of Molotch's 1976 thesis is a fundamental insight that has stood the test of time: "Coalitions of land-based elites, tied to the economic possibilities of places, drive urban politics in their quest to expand the local economy and accumulate wealth" (1987: 3). More recently, Molotch (1993, 1999) has reasserted the importance of the "agency-centered localism" (Jessop, Peck, & Tickell, 1999) of the growth machine thesis, ushering in renewed discourse about its limits and possibilities but attesting to the remarkable influence and durability of his ideas.

Clearly, I am not attempting to present all of the themes of the growth machine thesis. Rather, my choices are based upon my reading of the past two decades of sport studies scholarship that connect, either directly or indirectly, to some of the central concerns of a growth machine perspective of urban political economy. In doing so, I suggest that sport studies scholarship can count among its strengths a body of literature containing conceptualisations and empirical themes that address some of the very 'problems' with which urban studies scholars struggle or, in fact, overlook altogether. Among the issues I address below are: a) the extent to which sport-related actors exert influence in urban growth policy decisions; b) how sport has been used by various growth coalitions to construct an agenda for urban growth; and most notably, c) a conceptualisation of why both of these things are possible.

City Space as Commodity

In 1976, the growth machine model was believable, but untested. In the subsequent two decades, its principles have been intensively discussed and considerable new evidence has been

marshalled both for and against its conclusions. What, we now
ask, is the evidence for its core hypothesis? More specifically, is
the growth machine the predominant actor in local politics?
(Logan *et al.*, 1999: 75).

In *Urban Fortunes* (1987), Logan and Molotch hypothesise that the development
of cities is largely determined by two groups of people who act on inherently
conflicting 'forces' and whose interests, therefore, are often at odds with one
another: 'rentiers' and residents. The potential conflict centres on the highly
commodified arena of urban place production, or more simply stated, between
the use of land (use value) and its exchange for profit (exchange value). The
rentier class, consisting mainly of developers, realtors, and financial institutions,
is driven to intensify land use and improve the exchange value of local property.
Rentiers are supported by secondary groups located in the media, universities,
utilities, professional sport franchises, chambers of commerce, and elsewhere.
This blend of actors pushes for growth in order to increase the value of land and
enhance the financial position of growth machine members. The potential for
conflict exists because the actions of rentiers, who see 'place' as little more than
a commodity to sell, may threaten local residents' enjoyment and use of urban
space, as well as their ability to live comfortably. Both groups seek the powers
of the local government to protect and pursue their interests. For example, while
rentiers attempt to harness state and local resources for land clearance and site
assembly, local residents push for growth control through restrictive zoning or
suburban incorporation (Boyle, 1999; Jonas & Wilson, 1999).

However, use value opposition to growth projects is both rare and difficult.
Before local residents band together to resist urban development, they must have
a *desire* to do so. Growth machines act to unite local residents in pro-growth
causes, thereby proactively addressing conflict. This is accomplished by
utilising discourses of community, and fostering a belief that growth benefits
everyone in the long run. I address this 'ideology work' below. In addition to
the desire to oppose local development, residents must have the *capacity* to
influence decision-making. Sometimes, growth coalitions are able to undermine
residents' oppositional abilities by keeping growth plans away from public
scrutiny until 'deals are done'; when the plans are revealed, it is too late for
local residents to mount formidable resistance (see Elkin, 1987). Also, Logan
and Molotch (1987) suggest that the capacity to resist development is both race-
and class-bound; "poorer and 'black' neighborhoods apparently being rendered
impotent in the decision-making process" (see Boyle, 1999: 57).

In summary, the growth machine thesis offered a significant departure from
both structuralist–Marxian and community power studies perspectives. The

growth machine perspective stresses that it is the actions of human agents (for Logan & Molotch, rentiers and local residents, with the local state) along with structurally conditioned power and resources that determine local development. In this view, the city is a place where land and buildings operate as commodities and where groups of actors bond together in an attempt to protect and pursue their own interests. Furthermore, because of the differing interests of growth coalition members and local residents, and because growth outcomes usually benefit rentiers and burden residents, urban development may create conflict. Therefore, the growth coalition works to avoid and manage opposition to its plans. In other words, in the now familiar phrase of Stone (1989), 'politics matters' in local development.

Sociologists of sport have elaborated on the growth machine thesis in a variety of ways and provided empirical support, through case studies, for the idea that growth coalitions form and act in ways that advance their own interests. In some cases, rather than being mere 'auxiliary players', sport-related actors (e.g., professional sport franchise owners) have become key members of growth coalitions. In these cases, urban development plans centre on a specific project that utilises more space, leverages more public financing, and alters the landscape perhaps more than any other development project: sport stadium and sport facility construction.

In one of the first sport studies articles to address stadium construction, Riess (1981) presented an historical account of the interests that combined in the 1920s and 1930s to build and operate the Los Angeles Coliseum. Written prior to the mid-1980s wave of growth machine-oriented scholarship, Reiss's analysis bears some theoretical markings of community power studies, but it also contributed to emerging perspectives about the construction of coalitions for urban growth, the ways in with opposition to growth is circumvented, and the ways in which sport is utilised in the commodification of the city. According to Reiss, rather than publicly elected officials, the group that championed the LA Coliseum was made up of newspaper publishers, bankers, and real estate developers. It was a group of "confident and accomplished men, people who believed they knew what was in the best interests of the community, especially when the 'public interest' coincided with their own" (Reiss, 1981: 63). This 'local power elite' successfully circumvented opposition from the white, middle-class Municipal League, and in 1923, Los Angeles was the first major metropolitan area in the US to complete its municipal stadium.

Following Reiss, in 1984 George Lipsitz analysed the ways in which stadium construction in the 1960s was used in three US cities as a tool for promoting public and private spending for urban development. In all three cities — St. Louis, Houston and Los Angeles — promoters of stadium construction presented themselves as proponents of the welfare of all residents, while understating the extent to which specific local interests either benefited from, or would be burdened by, their plans. One of the major contributions of Lipsitz's work is his analysis of the role that sport can play in the ideological legitimacy of economic and political power. Another contribution concerns the commodification of urban space and the role stadium construction may play in altering urban environments. Though he does not use the term explicitly, Lipsitz shows how growth coalitions, comprised of public and private actors, used stadium construction to reclaim the built environment in ways that biased financial capital, service sector capital, and affluent populations. In all three cases, the major beneficiaries of stadium construction were professional sport franchise owners who, rather than being merely supportive of the agenda for local growth, were major players in constructing it.

Ingham *et al.* (1987) extended this line of argument in vignettes concerning professional sport team franchise relocation. The authors focused more attention than either Reiss or Lipsitz on the mobility of private capital and the competition within and between cities for capital investment. They also go farther than Lipsitz in exploring the ideology that underlies growth policy, a central theme in the growth machine perspective. More importantly for the purposes of this chapter is the fact that while they did not use the term 'growth machine' explicitly, the authors draw upon urban studies literature that is subsequently recognised as part of the growth machine tradition.

Taken together, these three articles provide insight into patterns of urban development and the role that economic and political actors play in them — a growing theme in the 1980s in urban studies research. In each city, the method of financing stadium construction and the particular sites chosen for stadium location grew out of the specific local legacy of urban history (a point made explicitly by Lipsitz). Public discourse about stadium development was couched in issues addressing the nature of each metropolis, and the new stadium was presented as part of an urban development solution to various problems that each city faced. In other words, though the 'problems' may have varied in these cities, the 'solution' to them was very similar: growth. As discussed below, similar, too, was the ideology that buttressed them.

Growth-talk: All Growth is Good!

> In most cities where case studies have been conducted, whether in the context of de-industrialization or of population boom, the most pressing issue of local politics is growth. . . . Growth is not

the only local issue, nor is it inherently and necessarily the key one. . . . Rather, its privileged status should be understood as an accomplishment for those groups whose mobilization into politics is grounded in their place-based interests (Logan, Whaley, & Crowder, 1999: 89; emphasis in the original).

This quotation illustrates the claim that an emphasis on growth in public discourse about urban development routinely overshadows other potentially relevant urban concerns (see Elkin, 1987). Though the hegemonic[4] status of growth is created and maintained in a variety of ways, I will focus only on two broad aspects: first, the material benefits of growth that supposedly extend to all urban residents; and second, the affective benefits that supposedly result from the solidarity created by a vibrant and growing 'community'.

In his 1976 article, Molotch argued not that growth machines actually *effect* growth, but only that they *attempt* to do so, because it is the existence of a growth ideology, rather than growth itself, that is important. In part, the hegemony of the growth model relies on the assertion that the material benefits of urban development do not merely accumulate within the rentier class, but extend to all city residents. One of the key ideological props is the claim that growth "makes jobs" (Molotch, 1976: 320). According to this claim, private investment in urban land and socio-spatial development produce an increase in tax revenues and jobs, which in turn produce an increased per capita spending that results in less citizen dependency on government funds. The premise that growth is the social tide that lifts all boats is used in the attempt to enlist the support of subordinate groups (Smith & Keller, 1983). Though two decades of social science research criticises the efficacy of this model, supposed 'trickle-down' and 'spin-off' effects have become taken-for-granted features in the dominant discourse about urban development.

It is to this fact that growth machine theorists refer when they speak of the growth ideology as being an 'accomplishment' for growth coalitions. When consensus is constructed around the idea that growth is good for everyone in the city, even if only in the long run, the potential for conflict between rentiers and residents is lessened. Not only do rentiers have an interest in promoting the idea that 'any growth is good growth', local politicians both help create and respond to the pro-growth ideology. One of the more troubling aspects of the

[4]Throughout this chapter I use the term 'hegemony' to refer to the process by which subordinated groups are led to consent to the system(s) that subordinate them. Rather than domination manifested through force or coercion, it is achieved through building consensus around belief-systems that seem 'natural' or 'inevitable' (see Gramsci, 1971).

US urban context is the perception that social problems should be handled at the local levels and that 'more development' is the solution (Molotch, 1993). Local level politicians are expected to 'do something' about the impact of broad-scale social problems that manifest themselves in local areas. Coupled with this expectation is the fact that locally elected officials are held accountable for problems that are authentically place-related, such as a declining infrastructure. The solution, for many politicians, is to 'do something' by manipulating the use and regulation of land, one of the few autonomous realms of local-level governance.

The result is the dominance of growth politics and the use of public subsidies for enterprises such as convention centres, urban shopping malls, retail anchors, and cultural centre development. In many cases, these projects are trumpeted as successful, not because of any objective assessment about their benefits to local residents, but because of the symbolic power of the edifices themselves. What they point to is a 'something' that can be done, and their mere presence colours local perceptions and builds political careers (Molotch, 1993; Zukin, 1991). More recently, Molotch (1999) points out that in the US, and to some extent in Europe, the growth ideology extends into all realms of urban life. Increasingly, all policies must justify themselves in terms of the growth agenda.

Sport studies researchers have extended this argument in important and convincing ways, all of which evidence some connection to the growth machine thesis. Through a number of case studies, the sociology of sport has shown that the growth discourse is dominant in urban politics and that sport gets linked to it in 'common sense' ways that are as problematic as they are powerful. With respect to the supposed tangible benefits of urban development, sport studies researchers have provided empirical evidence for how sport stadium and facility construction is promoted as job 'engines' and economic development 'magnets'. Within sport studies, stadium construction has been contextualised in a number of different ways. For example, in addition to those studies already discussed, Sage (1993), Schimmel *et al.* (1993), Schimmel (1995, 2000), and Brown and Paul (1999) explore how stadium construction is connected to inter-city competition for professional sport franchises. Whitson and Macintosh (1993, 1996), Rowe and McGuirk (1999), Heitzman (1999) and Lenskyj (1996) focus on the construction of sport facilities and the hosting of sport 'mega-events'. In the cities explored in these case studies, from Baltimore to Bangalore, Calgary to Cleveland, and Cincinnati to Sydney, sport facility construction is touted as being part of a larger urban growth scheme that would provide real benefits to the 'city-as-a-whole'. However, scholars in sport economics have refuted the claim that sport facilities and/or events generate economic benefits that trickle-down, percolate-up, spin-off, or multiply across various city segments.

Relatedly, the sociology of sport provides evidence that the socio-spatial consequences of this type of growth have regressive effects on local populations. Nevertheless, the pro-sport/pro-growth linkage remains strong, and the sociology of sport has contributed much to an understanding of why this is so.

The Discourse of Community

In addition to the claim that growth has tangible benefits for all, the growth machine toils to foster a sense of solidarity based on territory. It attempts, in other words, to bring together otherwise antagonistic interests and create a local sense of community, "a territorial bond" that, rather than being inevitable, is "socially organized and sustained" (Molotch, 1976: 315). Molotch viewed the propagation of the ideology of 'community' to be a prominent feature of growth machine politics; this idea has garnered considerable attention from both urban and sport studies scholars. For example, in his book *The Urban Experience* (1989), urban studies theorist, Harvey, notes that under conditions of late capitalism, the "ideology of locality, place and community has become central to the political rhetoric of urban governance" (1973: 14). Indeed, as his colleague Boyle suggests (1999: 55), it is difficult to read any recent analysis related to contemporary Western cities without encountering such phrases as "civic jingoism", "local boosterism", "flagship projects", "urban spectacle", "hallmark events", "and "place promotion". A growing cohort of urban theorists, Boyle informs us, are identifying these projects as attempts by urban elites to assert new forms of civic identity and pride.

While not disputing the accuracy or relevance of these claims, I would like to suggest that urban studies scholars are relative 'johnnies (or joanies)-come-lately' to the understanding of sport's significance in the development of growth machine politics. While urban studies scholars routinely mention sport in their discussions of urban (re)development (including Molotch in his 1976 article), their analyses are surprisingly superficial. Most disturbing, perhaps, is that urban studies scholars seem uninformed by the writings of sport studies scholars who have spent the past twenty years conceptualising the sport-community relationship. For example, in discussing the connection between sport and growth, Rosentraub (1996) writes about "sport as coalition glue" and "sport as cultural icon" without citing a single work of academic scholarship in the sociology of sport (though, somewhat inexplicably, American novelist, James Michener, is quoted at length). On the other hand, this is not to suggest that sport studies scholars always utilise urban studies theory in ways that reflect its richness and depth. There seems to be an unfortunate tendency for sociologists of sport (and I illustrate this in my own work below) to select contradictory ideas and concepts from urban studies without fully addressing the theoretical traditions from which they derive.

However, I believe that one of the most significant contributions the sociology of sport *has* made to understanding urban (re)development has been in conceptualising the ways in which sport as a *dominant cultural form* is mobilised by pro-growth coalitions in their attempts to construct and maintain the hegemony of a pro-growth ideology, achieved in part through a discourse of 'community', 'civic pride', 'major league city', 'world class city', and so on. The issue really does boil down, I argue, to hegemony (as an ideological construct) — and the sociology of sport has contributed important work to the understanding of hegemony in the way that Gramsci originally intended it, as a quest for consensus rather than coercion (see Note 4).

As one example of sport studies scholars' contributions in this regard, consider Ingham *et al*'s influential 1987 essay on professional sport and community which recasts the concepts of ritual and symbol from Cohen (1985), and community from Turner (1974), from the perspective of hegemony. They suggest that sport, as 'serialised civic ritual', can be viewed as one of the ways in which cultural relations and ideological assertions are a part of the social reproduction of political economy. Their ambitious essay draws upon Marxian notions about community formation in social class structuration, classical sociological theories of community, and the emerging growth machine perspective in urban studies. Professional sport can, they suggest, contribute to our imagination of the community as a whole, but the discourse of community is constructed in ways to naturalise the private interest of capital to appear in the public good.

These arguments provide the foundation for a subsequent article by Schimmel *et al.* (1993), which focuses more explicitly on growth politics and the inter-city competition for capital investment. Specifically, we link the internal reorganisation of the economy of sport leagues and the termination or relocation of professional sport franchises to broader forces that contour capital investment/disinvestments decisions. Revisiting this article, my own assessment is that our analysis suffers somewhat from theoretical eclecticism by being framed by both Marxist–structuralism (specifically Castells' 1979 work on 'the urban question') and urban praxis perspectives (specifically the work of urban growth theorists). However, we do attempt to make connections between the sociology of sport and urban studies literature, and open up space for the theoretical possibility that sport may play an influential role in the political economy of place.

We are not alone in this attempt. Several case studies have recently appeared in the sociology of sport literature that examine the ways in which sport is utilised by local growth, interests through appeals to 'civic pride' and the social construction of 'major league status'. For example, in their work concerning the (Australian) Newcastle Knights, Rowe, and McGuirk (1999) analyse the significance that sport plays as a marker of civic progress and as a locus of community affect. Sage (1993) shows how pro-growth groups in Denver leveraged public funds in pursuit of private profit by legitimising stadium construction as a community-as-a-whole benefit. Similarly, Brown and Paul (1999) illustrate how, in Cincinnati, a group ('Citizens for a Major League Future') that campaigned to pass a tax increase for a new stadium was funded by the very people who had the most to gain from the stadium's construction — including the owner of the local professional sport franchise. According to post-election surveys, 'civic pride' was an important element in garnering support for the referendum. Voters passed the referendum because they had been convinced the stadium was important to the area's economic future. As the authors note, "loyalty to community was a bigger factor than team loyalty" (Brown & Paul, 1999: 233). The connection between community, urban growth politics and sport-related projects is also examined by Lenskyj (1996) in her analysis of the ways in which sports leaders, corporations, and the media attempted to manufacture public consent to bid for the Olympic Games in Sydney and Toronto. In sum, in both intended and perhaps unintended ways, the sociology of sport is contributing significantly to an understanding of the discourse of community in an urban context.

Future Directions for Sport and Urban Studies

Among the most recent debates in urban studies is the extent to which the growth machine thesis applies to urban contexts outside the United States. The critique that urban growth perspectives are ethnocentric is often accompanied by calls for cross-cultural analyses which can identify more clearly the conditions under which growth coalitions are formed, sustained, and either evolve or degenerate. Such work is beginning to emerge in 'regime theory', the most recent iteration of the growth machine perspective and (arguably) the most dominant in urban studies today for analysing local power. For example, Henry and Paramio–Salcines's (1999) case study of Sheffield explores whether certain aspects of regime theory apply in an European context. Their work reveals striking similarities between Sheffield, UK, and Indianapolis, USA (see Schimmel, 1995) in terms of both the cities' shared economic context (e.g., de-industrialisation, job loss, city 'image' problems), and growth leaders' response to it — using sport as a key element in pro-growth strategies. However, scholars have yet to conduct an explicitly comparative analysis of the two cities; in fact, as of this writing, few studies compare two cities in different countries with an in-depth focus on sport and urban change.

However, there is emerging in the sociology of sport a body of literature that addresses sport and urban growth strategies against a larger international backdrop. Much of this work focuses on the ways in which various local actors draw upon the omnipresent theme of 'globalism' to market 'their' cites in the international competition for capital investment. For example, Whitson and Macintosh (1993, 1996) examine sport events and international urban marketing strategies in the context of global tourism and flexible capital accumulation. Heitzman (1999) explores the connections between urban planning, the projection of a nationalist ideology, and the National Games in Bangalore where, he suggests, the US model for urban growth is in experimental stages. These studies contribute to an understanding of the local-global connection and the extent to which US models for urban growth can be adopted elsewhere. But there is much work yet to do. As Molotch recently stated, the idea that "US-style urban entreprenuerialism sweeping the world is a consequence of new and inescapable conditions needs critical evaluation, not deferential acquiescence" (1999: 259).

This focus on globalisation is obviously only one direction in which sport and urban studies is headed, albeit one of the most popular ones currently. I suggest that in order for this research trajectory (and others) to be fully informed, we must engage in reciprocal bridge-building with colleagues in other disciplines. With the goal of 'making connections/making futures', I have sketched some ways in which sport and urban studies scholars have talked both 'to' and 'past' one another in the last twenty years. As a (sub)discipline, we are challenged to find ways to ensure that our colleagues in urban studies become more aware of our contributions to the political economy of place, and the particular role that sport plays within it.

References

Boyle, M. (1999). Growth machines and propaganda projects: A review of readings of the role of civic boosterism in the politics of local economic development. In: A.E.G. Jonas and D. Wilson (eds), *The Urban Growth Machine: Critical Perspectives Two Decades Later* (pp. 55–70). Albany, New York: State University of New York Press.

Brown, C., & Paul, D. M. (1999). Local organized interests and the 1996 Cincinnati sports stadia tax referendum. *Journal of Sport & Social Issues, 23*, 218–237.

Castells, M. (1978). *City, Class, and Power*. London: Macmillan.

Castells, M. (1979). *The Urban Question*. Cambridge, MA: MIT Press.

Cohen, A. P. (1985). *The Symbolic Construction of Community*. Chichester and London: Ellis Horwood & Tavistock.

Cox, K. R. (1999). Ideology and the growth coalition. In: A.E.G. Jonas and D. Wilson (eds), *The Urban Growth Machine: Critical Perspectives Two Decades Later* (pp. 21–36). Albany, New York: State University of New York Press.

Dahl, R. A. (1961). *Who Governs?* New Haven, CT: Yale University Press.

Elkin, S. L. (1987). *City and Regime in the American Republic*. Chicago and London: University of Chicago Press.

Euchner, C. (1993). *Playing the Field: Why Sports Teams Move and Cities Fight to Keep Them*. Baltimore, MD: Johns Hopkins University Press.

Fainstein, S. S., & Fainstein, N. I. (1983). Economic change, national policy, and the system of cities. In: S.S. Fainstein, N.I. Fainstein, R.C. Hill, D.R. Judd and M.P. Smith (eds), *Restructuring the City: The Political Economy of Urban Development* (pp. 1–26). New York: Longman.

Feagin, J. R. (1988). *Free Enterprise City: Houston in Political–Economic Perspective*. New Brunswick, NJ: Rutgers University Press.

Giddens, A. (1984). *The Constitution of Society: Outline of the Theory of Structuration*. Oxford: Basil Blackwell.

Gramsci, A. (1971). *Selections from the Prison Notebooks* (Trans. Hoare, Q. and Nowell–Smith, G.) New York: International Publishers.

Harvey, D. (1973). *Social Justice and the City*. Baltimore, MD: Johns Hopkins University Press.

Harvey, D. (1989). *The Condition of Postmodernity: An Inquiry into the Origins of Cultural Change*. Oxford: Blackwell.

Heitzman, J. (1999). Sports and conflict in urban planning: The Indian national games in Bangalore. *Journal of Sport & Social Issues, 23*, 5–23.

Henry, I. P., & Paramio–Salcines, J. L. (1999). Sport and the analysis of symbolic regimes: A case study of the city of Sheffield. *Urban Affairs Review, 34*, 641–665.

Ingham, A. G., & Donnelly, P. (1997). A sociology of North American Sociology of Sport: Disunity in unity, 1965 to 1996. *Sociology of Sport Journal, 14*, 362–418.

Ingham, A. G., Howell, J. W., & Schilperoort, T. S. (1987). Professional sports and community: A review and exegesis. *Exercise and Sport Science Reviews, 15*, 427–465.

Jessop, B., Peck, J., & Tickell, A. (1999). Retooling the machine: Economic crisis, state restructuring, and urban politics. In: A.E.G. Jonas and D. Wilson (eds), *The Urban Growth Machine: Critical Perspectives Two Decades Later* (pp. 141–159). Albany, New York: State University of New York Press.

Jonas, A. E. G., & Wilson, D. (1999). The City as growth machine: Critical reflections two decades later. In: A.E.G. Jonas and D. Wilson (eds), *The Urban Growth Machine: Critical Perspectives Two Decades Later* (pp. 3–18). Albany, New York: State University of New York Press.

Lefebvre, H. (1970). *La Revolution Urbaine*. Paris: Gallimard.

Leitner, H. (1990). Cities in pursuit of economic growth. *Political Geography Quarterly, 9*, 146–170.

Lenskyj, H. J. (1996). When winners are losers: Toronto and Sydney bids for the summer Olympics. *Journal of Sport & Social Issues, 20*, 392–410.

Lipsitz, G. (1984). Sports stadia and urban development: A tale of three cities. *Journal of Sport & Social Issues, 8*, 1–18.

Logan, J. R., & Molotch, H. (1987). *Urban Fortunes: The Political Economy of Place.* Berkeley, CA: University of California Press.

Logan, J. R., Whaley, R. B., & Crowder, K. (1999). The character and consequences of growth regimes: An assessment of twenty years of research. In: A.E.G. Jonas and D. Wilson (eds), *The Urban Growth Machine: Critical Perspectives Two Decades Later* (pp. 73–93). Albany, New York: State University of New York Press.

Mollenkopf, J. (1983). *The Contested City.* Princeton, NJ: Princeton University Press.

Molotch, H. (1976). The city as growth machine: Toward a political economy of space. *American Journal of Sociology, 82*, 309–330.

Molotch, H. (1993). The political economy of growth machines. *The Journal of Urban Affairs, 15*, 29–53.

Molotch, H. (1999). Growth machine links: Up, down and across. In: A.E G. Jonas and D. Wilson (eds), *The Urban Growth Machine: Critical Perspectives Two Decades Later* (pp. 247–265). Albany, New York: State University of New York Press.

Peterson, P. E. (1981). *City Limits.* Chicago, IL: University of Chicago Press.

Riess, S. A. (1981). Power without authority: Los Angeles' elites and the construction of the Coliseum. *Journal of Sport History, 8*, 50–65.

Rosentraub, M. S. (1996). Does the Emperor have new clothes?: A reply to Robert J. Baade. *Journal of Urban Affairs, 18*, 23–31.

Rowe, D., & McGuirk, P. (1999). Drunk for three weeks: Sporting success and city image. *International Review of the Sociology of Sport, 32*, 125–141.

Sage, G. H. (1993). Stealing home: Political, economic and media power and a publicly-funded baseball stadium in Denver. *Journal of Sport & Social Issues, 17*, 110–124.

Schimmel, K. S. (1995). Growth politics, urban development, and sports stadium construction in the United States: A case analysis. In: J. Bale and O. Moen (eds), *Stadium and the City* (pp. 111–155). Staffordshire, UK: Keele University Press.

Schimmel, K. S. (2000). Take me out to the ball game: The transformation of production–consumption relations in professional team sport. In: C.L. Harrington and D.D. Bielby (eds), *Cultural Production and Consumption: Readings in Popular Culture* (pp. 36–52). Oxford, England: Blackwell.

Schimmel, K. S., Ingham, A. G., & Howell, J. W. (1993). Professional team sport and the American city: Urban politics and franchise relocations. In: A.G. Ingham and J.W. Loy (eds), *Sport and Social Development* (pp. 211–244). Champaign, IL: Human Kinetics Publishers.

Smith, M. P. (1988). *City, State, and Market: The Political Economy of Urban Society.* New York, New York: Basil Blackwell.

Smith, M. P., & Keller, M. (1983). Managed growth and the politics of uneven development in New Orleans. In: S.S. Fainstein, N.I. Fainstein, R.C. Hill, D.R. Judd and M.P. Smith (eds), *Restructuring the City: The Political Economy of Urban Development* (pp. 126–166). New York: Longman.

Stone, G. (1981). Sport as a community representation. In: G. Luschen and G. Sage (eds), *Handbook of Social Science and Sport* (pp. 214–245). Champaign, IL: Stipes.

Stone, C. N. (1987). The study of the politics of urban development. In: C.N. Stone and H.T. Sanders (eds), *The Politics of Urban Development* (pp. 3–24). Lawrence, KA: University of Kansas Press.

Stone, C. N. (1989). *Regime Politics: Governing Atlanta, 1946–1988.* Lawrence, KA: University Press of Kansas.

Swanstrom, T. (1985). *The Crisis of Growth Politics: Cleveland, Kucinich, and the Challenge of Urban Populism.* Philadelphia: Temple University Press.

Swanstrom, T. (1993). Beyond economism: Urban political economy and the postmodern challenge. *Journal of Urban Affairs, 15,* 55–78.

Turner, V. (1974). *Dramas, Fields, and Metaphors: Symbolic Action in Human Society.* Ithaca, New York: Cornell University Press.

Whitson, D., & Macintosh, D. (1993). Becoming a world-class city: Hallmark events and sport franchises in the growth strategies of Western Canadian cities. *Sociology of Sport Journal, 10,* 221–240.

Whitson, D., & Macintosh, D. (1996). The global circus: International sport, tourism, and the marketing of cities. *Journal of Sport & Social Issues, 20,* 278–295.

Zukin, S. (1991). *Landscapes of Power.* Berkeley and Los Angeles, CA: University of California Press.

Chapter 15

Symbolic Interactionism and Cultural Studies: Doing Critical Ethnography

Becky Beal

At the heart of my interest in sociology is the desire to create better conditions for human life. Therefore, my research interests have centred on understanding the (de)construction of social barriers with the intent that this knowledge will give people hope and practical strategies to create more egalitarian social practices. The concepts and methods used by symbolic interactionism and cultural studies have been crucial to this endeavour, an endeavour that is shared by those who call themselves 'critical ethnographers'.

The purpose of this chapter is to illustrate the main ways in which critical ethnography has drawn from both symbolic interactionism and cultural studies.[1] In order to foreground this synthesis, a brief overview of symbolic interactionism and cultural studies will be presented.[2] This is followed by a review of shared concepts that are foundational to critical ethnography. The chapter concludes by discussing the intentions, methods, and scope of critical ethnography, paying particular attention to its uses in the sociology of sport.

Symbolic Interactionism[3]

Symbolic interactionism claims that humans create meanings through social interaction, and that these meanings are validated when people agree on a

[1]This chapter originated from a conversation and ultimately a manuscript with Todd Crosset about research using the concepts of 'subcultures' and 'subworlds' (see Crosset & Beal, 1997).

[2]Because both of these theories have been covered in other chapters in this volume (see Chapters 4 and 7), the overview is brief.

[3]Most of my discussion of symbolic interactionism is developed from Blumer's (1969) *Symbolic Interactionism: Perspective and Method* which itself draws primarily from George Herbert Mead. As has been noted by other scholars (Douglas, 1980; Prus, 1996; Denzin, 1992), there are a variety of styles or types of symbolic interactionism, yet much of the basis of that approach is exemplified in Blumer's discussion.

definition of a social phenomenon (see Chapter 4). The process of mutual definition is referred to as 'intersubjectivity'; this is what constitutes human social reality. In other words, the more the definition of the social phenomenon is shared, the more significant the meaning of that phenomenon will be. However, social reality is neither static nor unambiguous. Through interaction, various meanings are continuously being refined or altered. Symbolic interactionism tends to locate the foundation of human culture, the symbolic world, in small group interaction. Culture is viewed as a *process*, constantly being built 'from the ground up' as opposed to being imposed 'from above' as a coercive social structure.

Blumer's Three Premises of Symbolic Interactionism

Herbert Blumer (1969) identified three premises of symbolic interactionism which highlight the interpretive and negotiated processes in the construction of social reality. To illustrate these processes, the debate around the meanings and uses of Native American symbols to represent sport teams will be used. Blumer's first premise refutes the idea that humans automatically respond to stimuli. Instead, he claimed that humans interpret the meaning of objects or actions before acting accordingly: "The first premise is that human beings act toward things on the basis of the meanings that the things have for them" (1969:2). For example, not all people interpret in the same manner the use of a Native American religious symbol to represent a sport team. It is common in the United States to use eagle feathers or tomahawks as part of the team mascot. Some people view this use as a misrepresentation and ultimately as disrespect for Native Americans. Others view it as a way of honouring Native Americans (see Staurowsky, 1998, 1999). This example illustrates that humans respond differently to the same symbol on the basis of the meaning it has for them.

The next two premises highlight that there are no inherent meanings of symbols; rather, meanings are generated through human interaction and are negotiated over time. In Blumer's words, "The second premise is that the meaning of such things is derived from, or arises out of, the social interaction that one has with one's fellows" (1969:2). Using this premise, one can explain how differences in opinion about the meanings and appropriate use of Native American symbols have occurred. In the history of the US, Native Americans have been a segregated and often marginalised group, reducing the degree of direct interaction with other groups. Because of this segregation, there has been little social and symbolic interaction, resulting in a lack of 'intersubjectivity' or consensus on the meaning of such things as eagle feathers and tomahawks. In this manner, a lack of interaction between groups is one way to explain divergent meanings. For those who have not 'interacted' with traditional meanings of Native American symbols, the tendency is for them to interpret their use as mascots as harmless. This, in turn, results in indifference and the continuation of that practice.

Blumer's third premise addresses how change can occur through social interaction. He suggests that meanings change due to the context in which the individual interprets the symbol: "meanings are handled in, and modified through, an interpretative process used by the person in dealing with the things he (sic) encounters" (1969: 2). If those who view the use of Native American symbols as harmless are educated about the ways in which such mascot use can be interpreted as disrespectful, then they may change their minds about the meanings and, therefore, the use of those symbols. Such a process is currently underway as reflected by a growing number of schools changing their mascots from using Native American imagery (for instance, from 'Redman' or 'Redskin' to 'Red Hawks').

Key Interactionist Concepts

Symbolic interactionists study the processes by which people create identities, meanings, and relations. To this end, several key concepts are *social worlds*, *social objects*, and the *self*. The first two concepts are integrally related. Social worlds are groups of people who share the purpose and the actual processes of creating social objects. Blumer (1969) suggested three categories of socially defined objects: physical, social, and abstract. Abstract objects are represented by philosophical concepts such as 'fair play'; social objects are represented by various social roles and social relations people have such as athlete, manager, or referee; physical objects are represented by the more concrete aspects of daily life such as a football or the yellow card used by football referees. As noted previously, through Blumer's three principles, these social worlds are constantly being modified and challenged through various forms of social interaction. In the sociology of sport, the symbolic and interactive dynamics of many social worlds have been studied including those of women's professional golf (Crosset, 1995), male pre-adolescent 'little league' (Fine, 1987), swimming (Chambliss, 1989), and bodybuilding (Klein, 1993).

When the self is the concept under study, it is often investigated in terms of how various identities are formed. A number of sport-related studies examine the processes by which various athletic identities are (re)created. These include studies which explore the transition from novice to experienced athlete (Donnelly & Young, 1988), the conflict between student and athletic identities in American universities (Adler & Adler, 1985), the identities of Christian athletes (Stevenson, 1998), and the identities of women athletes with disabilities (Henderson & Bedini, 1996). A common focus here is the ongoing process of forming one's identity through the interpretation and response to problematic situations. These and other projects consider humans to be creators of their own identity. As Blumer noted (1969):

> The key feature in Mead's analysis is that the human being has a self. This idea should not be cast aside as esoteric or glossed over as something that is obvious and hence not worthy of attention. In declaring that the human being has a self, Mead had in mind chiefly that the human being could be the object of his (sic) own actions. . . . Mead regards this ability of the human being to act toward himself (sic) as the central mechanism with which the human being faces and deals with the world. This mechanism enables the human being to make indications to himself (sic) of things in his (sic) surrounding and thus to guide his (sic) actions by what he (sic) notes (pp. 79–80).

Symbolic interactionism assumes that symbols are the very foundation of our social reality. As indicated in the above passage, this perspective also assumes that humans have the capability as reflective agents to create and manipulate symbols which, in turn, enables us to change our identities and social worlds. Symbolic interactionism is, in brief, a perspective that grants humans, irrespective to their social location, a significant amount of power in the creation of social 'realities'.

Cultural Studies

As Howell *et al.* indicate (see Chapter 7), cultural studies is an interdisciplinary approach to analysing culture, especially the struggle over meanings which occurs in all cultural practices. Central to cultural studies is investigating relations of power, and how those relations are contested in the everyday lives of people. A variety and mix of disciplines and techniques characterises cultural studies, which have created some ambiguity as to what exactly cultural studies is. Nonetheless, there are some generally agreed upon concerns and concepts that do identify a cultural studies approach which will be described below. In brief, cultural studies draws from Marxist and interpretive traditions in both the assumptions it makes about what constitutes culture, and in the analysis of it. Culture is both ideological and material. It is the site of contested power.

Key Cultural Studies Concepts

Storey (1996) provides a thoughtful review of key cultural studies concepts. Not surprisingly, the notion of 'culture' itself is central. Culture is viewed as political, ideological, and inseparable from history and economics. It is also seen as encompassing all levels of the social strata as opposed to involving solely elite or upper class society. The political nature of culture is not limited to formal systems of governance, but instead encompasses other social institutions including popular culture. Ideology is seen as a set of meanings, socially constructed yet grounded in an economic and historical context. Ideologies are not only central aspects of culture, but crucial for the analysis of power because the values that are prioritised in social settings encourage specific behaviour and limit what is perceived as possible behaviour. Therefore, the significance of ideologies is that they constrain people's actions. Cultural studies has used Antonio Gramsci's (1971) notion that power is strongest when subordinate groups consent to the dominant groups' ideology. Yet, this consent is never complete because people will challenge dominant ideologies. Therefore, power is analysed as a process of legitimising the dominant groups' position as opposed to viewing power as a direct manipulation of the subordinate groups (Lears, 1985). To analyse power is to investigate the ways in which ideologies are contested, in process, and struggled over (see Chapter 16).

In an attempt to examine the creation and contestation of ideologies, cultural studies examines the relationship between social structure and human action. This is often referred to as the 'structure/agency' dynamic, where agency refers to human freedom and choice. The key issue is that humans have some degree of freedom, yet we are always constrained by our social context. Accordingly, human action is not completely determined by the social structure; in fact, we are able to have some effect on it. In cultural studies, this dynamic is referred to as 'articulation'. It is the point at which humans 'read' a social phenomenon and, therefore, create a specific meaning on the basis of it. That meaning is not predetermined by the phenomenon, but is created through human interpretation. As Storey (1998) summarises: "using the concept of 'articulation', therefore, is to insist that a cultural text is not the issuing source of meaning but a site where the articulation of meaning . . . can be produced in a specific context for particular competing social interests" (pp. 167). In this vein, cultural studies investigates the sites in, and the processes by which, ideologies are created, accepted, and challenged, and how they affect the structure of people's everyday lives.

Cultural studies adopts three main methods of investigating the struggle over meanings and related issues of power relations: textual analysis, interviews and observation, and political economic analysis (Johnson, 1996). With regard to current research on sport, textual analysis is perhaps the most prevalent and political economic perhaps least prevalent. Textual analysis is a method derived from interpretive traditions in sociology, especially hermeneutics. Cultural products are viewed as 'texts' that embody dominant sets of meanings where the ideologies can be inferred through 'decoding'. The goal is to infer the values that shape different cultural products such as sport. Media representations are most often the subject of textual analysis. Two examples are Armstrong (1996) and McDonald's (1996) work on the meanings of the mediated image of basketball player, Michael Jordan.[4] Another popular cultural studies approach is to use interviews and observation to investigate how groups of people create and refine various meanings of cultural products. For example, Chapman (1997) investigated the gendered notions of weight management techniques on a women's rowing team, Markula (1995) investigated the struggles over body image for women in an aerobics class, and Wilson and Sparks (1996) investigated how the racialised images of sneaker commercials were interpreted by young male consumers. A political economic analysis looks at the actual construction of cultural products. For example, Laurel Davis (1997) investigated the social and political production processes of the *Sports Illustrated* Swimsuit Issue. Similarly, Mark Lowes (1997) described the daily operations of a major newspaper in his analysis of its sports page production. For an excellent example of a synthesis of all three types of analyses, see Davis' (1997) work.[5]

Common Links between Symbolic Interactionism and Cultural Studies: The Foundation for Critical Ethnography[6]

Critical ethnography is based on the core concepts and approaches of symbolic interactionism and cultural studies which include hermeneutics, pragmatism, and human agency.

[4]For a current collection of textual analysis research, see Birrell and McDonald (2000).
[5]See Andrews and Loy (1993) for an historical overview of cultural studies research that has focused on sport.
[6]For different perspectives on the linkages between symbolic interactionism and cultural studies, see Denzin (1992); Becker and McCall (1990); and the *Journal of Contemporary Ethnography* (1999) ("Ethnography: Reflections at the Millennium's Turn").

Hermeneutics and Pragmatism

Symbolic interactionism and cultural studies both view humans as symbolic beings who create meaning through social interaction. Therefore, both have been identified as part of the interpretive tradition in sociology.[7] The roots of the interpretive tradition draw on hermeneutics as represented by the works of William Dilthey. Hermeneutics initially was a form of identifying the meanings of written texts. According to Prus (1996), it was Dilthey who applied techniques of interpreting texts of various sorts to other forms of human behaviour, much as cultural studies does today. In addition, Dilthey viewed individuals as beings who create and are motivated by meaning. Because Dilthey acknowledged that the context of social interaction would affect the meanings derived, he concentrated on the actual lived experiences of humans as the way to understand their world perspectives (Fontana, 1980).

Pragmatism emphasises that meaning is generated through human action. Scholars such as Charles Peirce, William James, and John Dewey developed pragmatism in the late nineteenth and early twentieth centuries.[8] Generally, "pragmatism is the doctrine that the function of thought is to guide action and that truth is known by testing the practical consequences of a belief" (Thomas, 1983: 31). We create knowledge by our practical engagement in the world. Knowledge is validated through its usefulness in solving problems, as opposed to being judged by a fixed standard. Therefore, pragmatism considers human lives as an emergent process, one in which ideas and their subsequent actions could potentially improve human life (Maines, 1992: 1531–1532). Symbolic interactionism draws more explicitly on pragmatism than cultural studies (Charon, 1998; Denzin, 1992; Prus, 1996), but I contend that it is implied in some of the cultural studies work, and is essential in critical ethnography because of its emphasis on political action (see also Chapter 7).

Human Agency

The notion of human agency underscores that human beings are active in the construction of their worlds through their ability to create meaning and act according to that meaning. Symbolic interactionism was in part a response to

---

[7]For an excellent review of the interpretive tradition in the sociology of sport, see Donnelly (2000).

[8]The connection between pragmatism and symbolic interactionism is evident in some professional relations. While at the University of Michigan, Dewey and George Herbert Mead were colleagues.

earlier theories that viewed humans similarly to other physical matter where behaviour was a result of either internal or external forces such as biological drives or one's economic status. Symbolic interactionism and cultural studies view humans as symbolic creatures who act with intention and some degree of freedom, not as objects passively responding to various stimuli in determined ways. Paul Willis (1980), a central figure associated with the Centre for Contemporary Cultural Studies at the University of Birmingham, England, specifically points to the Chicago School of symbolic interactionism and later American practitioners such as Howard Becker as precursors to the work done at the UK Centre. Researchers at the Centre have investigated the role of human agency in terms of resistant and oppositional behaviour (e.g., Hall & Jefferson, 1976; Hedbidge, 1976; Willis, 1977). Because the tools used to study the natural physical world cannot fully explain socially constructed meanings at work in human agency, a methodology that was attentive to the actual process of creating meaning and the resultant social relations was called for.

The Ethnographic Imperative

Practitioners of both symbolic interactionism and cultural studies engage in ethnography in order to investigate how those meaning systems are created in the everyday lives of people. Blumer (1969) argued for a methodology of social science that corresponded with the nature of humans and their social life. He argued against the traditional experimental design approaches of the natural sciences because they could not adequately explain social behaviour. Because symbolic reality is created, refined, and lived out through social interaction, the data that should be used to explain human group life must be constituted by the everyday actions of people. Blumer also called for a method where the investigators are immersed in the situation they study. The investigator would have to be able to understand the perspective of the participants and be able to identify the social objects and social action that constitute that group's social world. Techniques of participant observation and in-depth interviewing are seen as essential to provide an insider's view. For example, one could only penetrate the ethos of a group by identifying its priorities and by exploring what is problematic for that group and the common ways used to resolve those issues.

Because the symbolic world is an emerging process of human interaction, Blumer thought that is was extremely important not to enter social settings with a predetermined hypothesis or view. Instead, he argued for an inductive means of generating theory. This stands in stark contrast to traditional experimental studies that require an hypothesis before gathering data, and where the validity of the data gathered is often determined by a prearranged mathematical equation. Instead, Blumer argued that the everyday lives of people, their social interactions, should tell the researcher about human group life. This is similar to Glaser and Strauss'(1967) notion of 'grounded theory' where explanations and concepts are derived principally from the data by identifying social objects and related patterns of social interaction.

What Makes Ethnography Critical?

Although critical ethnography shares with symbolic interactionism and cultural studies the definition of social reality and the methodology needed to access that reality, it has developed in response to criticisms aimed at both of those traditions. A long-standing critique of symbolic interactionism is that it does not explicitly focus on structural issues or social inequities, even though it does not inherently preclude an analysis of power (Adler & Adler, 1980). Incorporating a cultural studies perspective helps to focus the researcher on the processes around the negotiation of power which provides ethnography with a critical perspective. On the other hand, cultural studies has come under fire for often being too subjective in that one individual's (i.e., the researcher's) interpretation of a cultural product (being examined) is deemed sufficient sociological 'data'. A related concern is that cultural studies loses its politically reforming potential by not involving the subjects of the study more directly. These criticisms underline a need for practical change, and there has been debate about whether research from cultural studies is in fact aiding in policy change (McRobbie, 1996; Sugden & Tomlinson, 1999). Unlike cultural studies, critical ethnography argues the necessity to include, at all turns, participants' voices. In sum, critical ethnography's focus is in part defined by the criticisms stated above. It addresses those criticisms by promoting an explicit political agenda and by grounding their analysis of power negotiation in an empirical investigation of the groups involved.

Critical Ethnography

Those who practice critical ethnography are primarily concerned with power issues and processes and tend to focus on the ways in which people accept or contest specific sets of power relations in their everyday lives. As noted earlier, ethnographic research may have an emancipatory potential, in that the research it produces may have a practical effect on the researcher and those studied (Kincheloe & McLaren, 1994; Quantz, 1992). In order for the research to effectively challenge unequal relations and the ideologies that justify them, it must be grounded in the examination of the historical and material relations as well as the actual processes by which people come to accept or challenge those relations. As Quantz stated, the research focus is not on proving a group's subordinate status, but "[The] question is, rather, how are marginalized people positioned in material and symbolic relations, how do they participate in these relations, and how can our understanding work towards the restructuring of those relations?" (1992: 468). For critical ethnographers, the key to change is to engage in a critical dialogue. It is assumed that this type of conversation will raise awareness of how dominant ideologies are implicated in preserving unequal relations. Engaging with subjects is essential in developing common ground for communication. In a sense, this research is akin to a consciousness-raising exercise; one that opens the discussion about possible lines of action, but does not prescribe a specific set. This premise, that people have the ability to reflect and change behaviour for better life experiences, corresponds with the pragmatic approach inherent in symbolic interaction.

Social Reality: A Mediated Empiricism[9]

The key for critical ethnographers is to probe the everyday interpretations of various social conditions, and how these affect the perceived range of options and subsequent actions people take. There are two main components in critical ethnography. The first is a description and critique of the social political context, which often incorporates previous political economic research. The second is an examination of the ways in which humans interpret, and act, within that context. This is assessed through ethnography. Critical ethnographers rely on a mediated version of empiricism, one in which the negotiation of the social structure is central. This approach draws from the hermeneutic tradition, noting that social reality is always mediated by humans' interpretation (including the researcher's). Comstock (1982) comments on this mediated version of empiricism:

> While positivist social science studies human behaviour, critical social science studies human action and seeks to make manifest the processes by which social structures are constructed by human action and ordered by inter-subjective meanings. Critical accounts relate social conditions to the subjects' actions, not

[9]For a thorough review of the ontological and epistemological position described here, see Carspecken (1996).

directly or mechanically, but as they are interpreted and ordered by their understandings and motives. Since all human actions are consequences of socially interpreted sets of conditions, we cannot predict behaviour directly from social conditions. Instead, critical explanations must recognize the mediation of meaning by which members make sense of their own and others' acts (1982: 375).

The above discussion is similar to the cultural studies concept of 'articulation'; that is, the construction of social meaning comes through the interaction of humans and their social structure. To understand the construction of social reality, we must address human agency by investigating the process of interpretation. Human agency, the ability to redefine and reconstruct our social worlds, is a crucial assumption for critical social scientists because they ground their work in the desire to promote democratic social change.

Affecting Change: Exposing Contradictions through Critical Dialogue

Exposing contradictions between the dominant ideologies and actual cultural practices is one way of raising consciousness. This is usually done by examining the surface level explanations of social relations, and comparing this to the day-to-day actions that distribute resources and opportunities in order to participate fully in public life. For example, in 'democratic' societies, there is usually a publicly stated commitment to equal opportunity in employment. Yet, in most of these countries, it can be shown that minority groups do not have the same levels of opportunity. Willis (1980) noted that the strength of a critical ethnography is in identifying moments of contradiction. It is these moments where new insights about the ways in which power is challenged or maintained can be developed. One clear example of this type of illumination has occurred in the work examining the labour practices of the sports clothing and equipment company, Nike. Starting in the early 1990s, Nike ran a series of advertisements that highlighted how sport empowers women. At the same time, however, Nike's sub-contractors were exploiting Indonesian female labourers in the actual production of their athletic shoes. In this case, buying Nike products for personal empowerment reinforced the exploitation of other women. This is an obvious contradiction in Nike's message of female empowerment and the actual labour practices. There is also a contradiction for those consumers who want to promote female empowerment. These debates have led to groups, such as Students Against Sweatshops at Duke University, applying pressure against exploitative companies (Sage, 1999).

The Researcher's Role

The critical ethnographic researcher's primary goal is to conduct a thorough analysis of the political context in which people live, and the participants' negotiation of it. In addition, the researcher seeks to engage subjects in ways that may challenge unequal relations. As mentioned previously, one avenue is to expose contradictions within the dominant groups. Yet, contradictions happen not only in the dominant groups, but in subordinate groups as well. Dealing with the contradictions that arise within the group one studies can be challenging. The difficulty is in maintaining a mutually respectful atmosphere, while engaging in a critical dialogue. If the goal is to engage in research for political change, then one will face many decisions in how to handle exposing and challenging the *group's ideology*. In my research with skateboarders (Beal, 1995, 1998), I was faced with confronting a rather insidious sexism. The contradiction for the skateboarders was that they believed that skateboarding was a sport open to all those who are willing to try. Yet, the vast majority of participants were male. When I asked them why so few females skated, their responses relied heavily on dominant gender ideology; that females were naturally less likely to take physical risks and to disfigure their bodies through the bruising and scarring. Even though the participants felt strongly that they were being discriminated against by the dominant culture because they did not conform to 'military-like' bureaucratic standards, they did not readily see their activity (and their gendered ideology) as discriminating against females. Although I challenged their reasoning by providing examples of figure skating and gymnastics as similar types of sports (also emphasising balance, agility, strength, and high risk) in which women have a long history, I do not think the majority of my respondents accepted the premise that they were similar types of sports. Therefore, they could not conceive that something other than natural aptitude kept females from participating. The conversation was difficult because I wanted to engage the skaters in reflection without having them become defensive and withdrawn by my criticism.[10]

Another problematic issue of the relationship of the researcher and the participants is the inequity in power relations. For an academic to enter the lives of another group of people, and then present her findings as a 'better' representation of those people is a form of power relations because the published view is often seen as the legitimate source. Those who use cultural studies are concerned with this tendency to 'colonise', and try to guard against coming

---

[10]I do want to note, however, that several male skateboarders were concerned about the lack of female participation, and talked about the sexist representation of skateboarding in the trade magazines.

across as the 'authority' on other people's lives. Their concern with traditional ethnographies is that the researcher presents herself as a neutral viewer of another's reality and simply records, describes, and explains that situation. Frequently, one reads this as a concern about portraying a 'realist' presentation of someone else's life when, in fact, it too is an interpretation of the events.

Those who practise critical ethnography seek to address these concerns. First, this type of research is meant to be an analysis (an interpretation) of data using social scientific concepts. The goal is not to colonise, but to develop and refine sociological interpretations. Second, critical ethnographers seek to enact a form of 'reflexivity'. The goal is to explicitly state the social position of the researcher, and to note the contradictions that arise from her interaction with the subjects of the study. Part of examining how power relations are reproduced is to examine one's own assumptions about reality, and how, and why, those are shared or not shared with the group under study. In other words, to apply the critical method seeks to examine the contradictions between the researchers' world and the subjects' world (Denzin, 1992; Foley, 1990; Quantz, 1992; Willis, 1980).

Critical Ethnography in Action

The research identified below uses critical ethnography to illustrate the ways in which sport is a contested cultural practice, a social site where dominant ideologies are reproduced and challenged. Therefore, the dynamics that underpin issues of race/ethnicity, socio-economic status, and gender/sexuality have been the focus of attention of such critical ethnographic research. For example, the work of Curry (1991) and Anderson (1999), examines gender relations while addressing other constraints. The work of Klein (1991) and Paraschak (1997) highlights issues of ethnicity and race. Sugden and Tomlinson's (1998) work focuses on economic power dynamics of elite governing organisations, while Walk's (1997) study considers various levels of power in an academic sport setting. Critical ethnographers are also concerned about the political implications of new sport forms; that is, the ways they support an emancipatory practice and the ways in which inequitable relations are reinforced (Beal, 1995; Donnelly, 1993; Wheaton & Tomlinson, 1998). The following discussion highlights three examples in the sociology of sport that have explicitly drawn from both cultural studies and used the methodology of ethnography.

Susan Birrell and Diana Richter (1987: 396–397) specifically identified using feminism and 'interactionist principles and cultural studies approach' as the conceptual base for their investigation of feminist softball: "Feminist softball is not a *product* turned out by inventive minds but rather an ongoing *process of invention*, and that process can be observed." Over a four year period, they interviewed self-identified feminist softball players and observed them during games. They chose a group of people who intentionally challenged dominant (e.g., masculinist and rationalist) practices of sport to investigate how those with an alternate ideology lived it out. For these women, the mainstream traditional sport was considered the male model of sport, primarily because men tended to derive the most benefits through participation and administration of these programmes. The benefits also extended to the ideological realm; the 'real' athlete was associated with a male athlete. In other words, this model legitimised male privilege ideologically and materially. In addition, players were also critical of the structure of the traditional male model, that Birrell and Richter labelled 'rationalist'.

This is a model where the outcome was more important than the process, a sport where winning at the expense of relationships with other players and one's own body is acceptable. Not only did these women criticise this male model, they wanted to create an alternative. So the participants worked on creating a sport that focused on women's relations and experiences. To ensure the quality of the game, they intentionally tried to create the most competitive game by ensuring that the outcomes of games were uncertain by exchanging positions on the field or playing positions with which they were not familiar if a game appeared to be lop-sided. To distribute authority, teams would often rotate the coaching position. These, and other practices, were conscious decisions designed to resist the autocratic and hierarchical practices of sport associated with the male model. This does not mean to say that everything went smoothly. There were disagreements about such things as the oppressiveness of elite skill, and divisions around other forms of oppression such as race and sexuality. This acknowledges the various contradictions that arise in a group which is pursuing more democratic social practices. This research demonstrates that raising consciousness of various unequal relations can lead people to create alternatives, and this is certainly an ongoing process, one which is pushed on by trying to resolve its contradictions between democratic ideals and practices which inhibit them.

Ben Carrington (1998) conducted his ethnographic work in Yorkshire, England, on one specific cricket club in which the participants were predominately Black. Carrington placed this ethnographic data in a larger historical and political context of race relations in England. He drew from cultural studies by focusing on how cricket was a racially contested social practice, and was interested in the ways in which the local Black community identified the social significance of cricket. He found that the cricket players labelled the cricket club a Black space (similar to feminists using softball to create their own space). It was a project that was created by, and for, the local Black community, and was identified as a safe space where Blacks could be themselves. This Black space was seen as a form of resistance to White racism because it was an autonomous area that acted as a cultural site that positively sanctioned expressive behaviour.

From Carrington's interviews, it was evident that contests between White and Black teams were 'racially loaded'. For the Black players, competition in cricket embodied the historically exploitative relations between England and the colonies. The Blacks wanted to beat the Whites at their own game, as noted by one informant: "You think, 'let's show these lads who's the boss here' " (1998: 290). The Black participants were aware that White teams were very concerned about being beaten by Black men:

> Given the racial signification of the contests, the immense emotional and personal investment made in the games for the Black men was significant. At both a symbolic and very real level, winning became a way of challenging the logic and efficacy of the racism they faced in their day-to-day lives, even if the victories were always, ultimately, transitory (Carrington, 1998: 290).

Carrington highlights the problems with this type of resistance, again deriving from some of the contradictions within the cricket club. First, the role of women is often marginalised at the club, thus excluding the needs of Black women as part of the challenge to White racism. In addition, there was concern that the type of resistance expressed resembles war, proving one's worth through competition and physical domination. This type of empowerment could have a high price to pay because of its association with aggressive versions of competition.

Whereas the studies above focused on the partial success of creating alternative relations within sport (albeit, with their own serious contradictions), critical ethnography also looks at the ways in which challenges to the dominant relations are not successful. The following study demonstrated the enormous power of historical rituals to override various types of resistance. Anthropologist Doug Foley (1990) wrote about life in a small town in Texas, USA, focusing on the social significance of the high school, but grounded in a political and historical setting of the town. Influenced by Paul Willis' work, Foley wanted to explore the ways in which a mainstream sport could act as a contested political site. His work focused on sport (1990b) in that town and described the social interactions around football to discern in what ways those were challenging or reinforcing dominant social relations associated with race, class, and gender. He spent one year in the field interviewing and observing those involved in the high school sport scene. In addition to observing football players and coaches during practices, bus rides, and games, Foley examined the rituals around football such as the pep rally, and its supporting cast of the band and cheerleaders, the homecoming ceremonies, and the 'powder puff' football game. Foley's investigation identified many isolated moments that challenged dominant practices, such as the players refusing to comply to rationalist training practices. However, his conclusion remains thus: "In North Town, football is still a popular cultural practice deeply implicated in the reproduction of the local ruling class of white males, hence class, patriarchal, and racial forms of dominance" (1990: 133).

Recent Developments: Cultural Consumption, Agency, and Identity Formation

The scholarly focus on cultural consumption has become more popular in the past decade. This research has specifically connected the formation of identity, traditionally a symbolic interactionist concept, within the political context of consumer culture. It investigates the creation of culture through the reciprocal processes of production and consumption. Cultural products are produced, we consume them, and when we give meaning to that consumption, we create identities and social relations. Belinda Wheaton's (2000) ethnographic study examines how windsurfers consume cultural products as part of the process of creating their subcultural identity. She found that the use and display of windsurfing equipment affected one's subcultural status. Primarily, there was necessity to have equipment, but conspicuous display was frowned upon. Instead, commitment to the practice of windsurfing was more significant to membership status than the brand used. Wheaton concludes that identities are not simply a matter of purchasing and displaying of products, but are the meanings developed by the use of those products.

Consumption, then, is the active process of creating meaning within the constraints of a specific political and social context. Researchers in this vein tend to stay away from labelling acts of agency as either resistance or co-option. Instead, they tend to look at the creative and constraining processes of identity formation. For critical ethnography, this type of research can be very important in illustrating contradictions. Critical ethnographers who focus on consumption need to continue to engage with their participants and use the results of the study to critique inequitable and dis-empowering relations. In this respect,

Beal and Wheaton (2000) investigated how skateboarders and windsurfers consumed mediated images of their sport. They were particularly interested in examining the processes of inclusion and exclusion, and found that gender and race impacted inclusion.

Conclusion

Critical ethnography relies on the conceptual bases of symbolic interactionism and cultural studies, but strives for an application of this knowledge in the form of emancipatory practices. It synthesises symbolic interactionism and cultural studies with its assumption that humans are active agents in the construction of their social worlds. In addition, the methodology of ethnography enables one to access the everyday processes of this social construction. Symbolic interactionism provides the essential elements of ethnography, and cultural studies provides the critical perspective; a concern for how power is negotiated. Critical ethnography goes beyond these by explicitly claiming a commitment to do research that can change unequal social relations. This process involves consciousness-raising, where we recognise contradictions and create alternative relations.

One of the main criticisms of critical ethnography is that there is a tendency to romanticise the revolutionary aspects of marginalised groups, or 'to side with the underdog'. It is significant to note that researchers in this tradition are very aware of the limitations, both material as well as ideological (e.g., internal contradictions), of the groups they study. Nonetheless, these limitations do not detract from recognising the ways in which people negotiate power in their attempts to create social change.

My assumption is that purposeful change has to be driven by intention. In this sense, critical ethnography's emphasis on consciousness-raising can be a significant tool in encouraging emancipatory actions. My goal has been to exemplify the ways in which people create social relations that meet their needs as a way to provide hope and strategies for other people to do the same. Nonetheless, I had concerns about the effectiveness of my research project. For example, I had hoped the skateboarders would critically reflect on some of their own forms of discrimination. Some did, but I do not know whether there was a long-term effect and whether the skateboarders transferred that knowledge to other settings. In addition, I did not actively pursue opportunities for long-term political support, such as encouraging skateboarders to connect with community services or other potentially supportive agencies (they certainly did some of this on their own). Ideally, critical ethnography could not only raise people's consciousness, but aid in linking various constituencies in supportive networks.

Maintaining long-term relations with the groups people study would help to create community links, and to identify and analyse the long-term effects of the research/political action.

A related challenge to this type of research concerns the issue of time commitment. With the university standards for hiring and promoting professors, young professionals may be discouraged from engaging in critical ethnography because of the pressure to publish frequently. In addition, research which challenges the status quo is not always well received or well funded. Nonetheless, the quality of life will always be an issue for the vast majority of people and to various degrees is an issue for governments. Therefore, there will be a desire to conduct this type of research as well as a demand for it, and there are educational, governmental, and private research institutions that support this type of research. Seeking those institutions and fostering relationships among those working in these entities will be extremely helpful. With these issues in mind, to conclude, I will cite the observations of David Rowe which summarise my main sentiments for future research:

> sport sociologists should be involved not only in building up the sub-discipline but also in the promotion of social justice in their field of inquiry ... Of course, we should not exaggerate the capacity for sociology to be able to change the world, but it should, I believe, at least be out in the public sphere presenting a sociologically informed and, it is to be hoped, ethically derived perspective (Rowe, 1998: 250).

References

Adler, P., & Adler, P. (1980). Symbolic interactionism. In: J. Douglas *et al.* (eds), *Introduction to the Sociologies of Everyday Life* (pp. 20–61). Boston: Allyn and Bacon.

Adler, P., & Adler, P. (1985). From idealism to pragmatic detachment: The academic performance of college athletes. *Sociology of Education, 58*, 241–250.

Anderson, K. (1999). Snowboarding: The construction of gender in an emerging sport. *Journal of Sport and Social Issues, 23*, 55–79.

Andrews, D., & Loy, J. (1993). British cultural studies and sport: Past encounters and future possibilities. *Quest, 45*, 255–275.

Armstrong, E. (1996). The commodified 23, or, Michael Jordan as text. *Sociology of Sport Journal, 13*, 325–343.

Becker, H., & McCall, M. (1990). *Symbolic Interaction and Cultural Studies*. Chicago: University of Chicago Press.

Beal, B. (1995). Disqualifying the official: Exploring social resistance through the subculture of skateboarding. *Sociology of Sport Journal, 12*, 252–267.

Beal, B. (1998). Symbolic inversion in the subculture of skateboarding. In: M.C. Duncan, G. Chick and A. Aycock (eds), *Play and Culture Studies, Volume 1: Diversions and Divergences in Fields of Play* (pp. 209–222). Greenwich, CT: Ablex Publishing.

Beal, B., & Wheaton, B. (2000). Images of lifestyle sports: The audience view. Paper presented at the annual conference of the North American Society for the Sociology of Sport, Colorado Springs, CO.

Birrell, S., & McDonald, M. (2000). *Reading Sport: Critical Essay on Power and Representation.* Boston: Northeastern University Press.

Birrell, S., & Richter, D. (1987). Is a diamond forever?: Feminist transformations of sport. *Women Studies International Forum, 10,* 395–409.

Blumer, H. (1969). *Symbolic Interactionism: Perspective and Method.* Englewood Cliffs, NJ: Prentice–Hall.

Carrington, B. (1998). Sport, masculinity, and Black cultural resistance. *Journal of Sport and Social Issues, 22,* 275–298.

Carspecken, P. F. (1996). *Critical Ethnography in Educational Research: A theoretical and practical guide.* New York: Routledge.

Chambliss, D. (1989). The mundanity of excellence. *Sociological Theory, 7,* 70–86.

Chapman, G. (1997). Making weight: Lightweight rowing, technologies of power, and technologies of self. *Sociology of Sport Journal, 14,* 205–223.

Charon, J. (1998). *Symbolic Interactionism: An Introduction, an Interpretation, and Integration.* Upper Saddle River, NJ: Prentice Hall.

Comstock, D. (1982). A method for critical research. In: E. Bredo and W. Feinberg (eds), *Knowledge and Values in Social and Educational Research* (pp. 370–390). Philadelphia: Temple University Press.

Crosset, T. (1995). *Outsiders in the Clubhouse: The World of Women's Professional Golf.* Albany, New York: State University of New York Press.

Crosset, T., & Beal, B. (1997). The use of 'subculture' and 'subworld' in ethnographic works on sport: A discussion of definitional distinctions. *Sociology of Sport Journal, 14,* 73–85.

Curry, T. (1991). Fraternal bonding in the locker room: A profeminist analysis of talk about competition and women. *Sociology of Sport Journal, 2,* 119–135.

Davis, L. (1997). *The Swimsuit Issue and Sport: Hegemonic Masculinity in Sports Illustrated.* Albany, New York: State University of New York Press.

Denzin, N. (1992). *Symbolic Interactionism and Cultural Studies: The Politics of Interpretation.* Oxford, UK: Blackwell.

Donnelly, P. (1993). Subcultures in sport: Resilience and transformation. In: A. Ingham and J. Loy (eds), *Sport in Social Development: Tradition, Transitions, and Transformation* (pp. 119–145). Champaign, IL: Human Kinetics.

Donnelly, P. (2000). Interpretive approaches to the sociology of sport. In: J. Coakley and E. Dunning (eds), *Handbook of Sports Studies* (pp. 77–92). London: Sage.

Donnelly, P., & Young, K. (1988). Construction and confirmation of identity of sport subcultures. *Sociology of Sport Journal, 5,* 223–240.

Douglas, J. (1980). Introduction to the sociologies of everyday life. In: J. Douglas et al. (eds), *Introduction to the Sociologies of Everyday Life* (pp. 1–19). Boston: Allyn & Bacon.

Ethnography: Reflections at the millennium's turn [Special issues] (1999). *Journal of Contemporary Ethnography, 28,* 5 & 6.

Fine, G. A. (1987). *With the Boys: Little League Baseball and Preadolescent Culture.* Chicago: University of Chicago Press.

Foley, D. (1990a). *Learning Capitalist Culture: Deep in the Heart of Texas.* Philadelphia: University of Pennsylvania Press.

Foley, D. (1990b). The great American football ritual: Reproducing race, class, and gender inequality. *Sociology of Sport Journal, 7,* 111–135.

Fontana, A. (1980). Toward a complex universe: Existentialist sociology. In: J. Douglas et al. (eds), *Introduction to the Sociologies of Everyday Life* (pp. 155–181). Boston: Allyn & Bacon.

Glaser, B., & Strauss, A. (1967). *The Discovery of Grounded Theory.* Chicago: Aldine Publishing.

Gramsci, A. (1971). *Selections From Prison Notebooks of Antonio Gramsci.* New York: International Publishers.

Hall, S., & Jefferson, T. (1976). *Resistance Through Rituals: Youth Subcultures in Post-war Britain.* London: Hutchinson.

Hebdige, D. (1979). *Subculture: The Meaning of Style.* London: Methuen.

Henderson, K. A., & Bedini, L. A. (1995). "I have a soul that dances like Tina Turner, but my body can't": Physical activity and women with mobility impairments. *Research Quarterly for Exercise and Sport, 66,* 151–161.

Johnson, R. (1996). 'What is cultural studies anyway?'. In: J. Storey (ed.), *What is Cultural Studies?* (pp. 75–114). London: Arnold.

Kincheloe, J., & McLaren, P. (1994). Rethinking critical theory and qualitative research, In: N. Denzin and Y. Lincoln (eds), *Handbook of Qualitative Research* (pp. 138–157). Thousand Oaks, CA: Sage Publications.

Klein, A. (1991). *Sugarball: The American Game, the Dominican Dream.* New Haven: Yale University Press.

Klein, A. (1993). *Little Big Men: Bodybuilding Subculture and Gender Construction.* Albany, New York: SUNY Press.

Lears, T. J. J. (1985). Concept of cultural hegemony: Problems and possibilities. *American Historical Review, 90,* 567–593.

Lowes, M. D. (1997). Sports page: A case study in the manufacture of sports news for the daily press. *Sociology of Sport Journal, 14,* 143–159.

Maines, D. (1992). Pragmatism. In: E. Borgatta and M. Borgatta (eds), *Encyclopedia of Sociology, 3* (pp. 1531–1536). New York: MacMillian Publishing.

Markula, P. (1995). Firm but shapely, fit but sexy, strong but thin: The postmodern aerobicizing female bodies. *Sociology of Sport Journal, 12,* 424–453.

McDonald, M. (1996). Michael Jordan's Family Values: Marketing, meaning, and post-Reagan America. *Sociology of Sport Journal, 13,* 344–365.

McRobbie, A. (1996). All the world's a stage, screen, or magazine: When culture is the logic of late capitalism. *Media, Culture, & Society, 18,* 335–342.

Paraschak, V. (1997). Variations in race relations: sporting events for native peoples in Canada. *Sociology of Sport Journal, 14,* 1–21.

Prus, R. (1996). *Symbolic Interaction and Ethnographic Research: Intersubjectivity and the Study of Human Lived Experience.* Albany, New York: State University of New York Press.

Quantz, R. (1992). On critical ethnography (with some postmodern considerations). In: M.D. LeCompte, W.L. Millroy and J. Preissle (eds), *The Handbook of Qualitative Research in Education* (pp. 448–505). San Diego: Academic Press.

Rowe, D. (1998). Play up: Rethinking power and resistance in sport. *Journal of Sport and Social Issues, 22,* 241–251.

Sage, G. (1999). Justice do it! The Nike transnational advocacy network: Organization, collective actions, and outcomes. *Sociology of Sport Journal, 16,* 206–235.

Staurowsky, E. J. (1998). An act of honor or exploitation: The Cleveland Indians' use of the Louis Francis Sockalexis story. *Sociology of Sport Journal, 15,* 299–316.

Staurowsky, E. J. (1999). American Indian imagery and the miseducation of America. *Quest, 51,* 382–392.

Stevenson, C. (1997). Christian athletes and the culture of elite sports: Dilemmas and solutions. *Sociology of Sport Journal, 14,* 241–262.

Storey, J. (1996). *Cultural Studies and the Study of Popular Culture: Theory and Methods.* Athens, GA: University of Georgia Press.

Storey, J. (1998). *Cultural Consumption and Everyday Life.* London: Arnold.

Sugden, J., & Tomlinson, A. (1999). Digging the dirt and staying clean: Retrieving the investigative tradition for a critical sociology of sport. *International Review for the Sociology of Sport, 34,* 385–398.

Sugden, J., & Tomlinson, A. (1998). Power and resistance in the governance of world football: Theorizing FIFA's transnational impact. *Journal of Sport and Social Issues, 22,* 299–316.

Thomas, C. (1983). *Sport in a Philosophic Context.* Philadelphia: Lea & Febiger.

Walk, S. (1997). Peers in pain: The experiences of student athletic trainers. *Sociology of Sport Journal, 14,* 22–56.

Wheaton, B. (2000). "Just do it": Consumption, commitment, and identity in the windsurfing subculture. *Sociology of Sport Journal, 17,* 254–274.

Wheaton, B., & Tomlinson, A. (1998). The changing gender order in sport? The case of windsurfing subcultures. *Journal of Sport and Social Issues, 22,* 252–274.

Willis, P. (1977). *Learning to Labour: How Working Class Kids Get Working Class Jobs.* New York: Columbia University Press.

Willis, P. (1980). Notes on method. In: S. Hall (ed.), *Culture, Media, Language: Working Papers in Cultural Studies* (pp. 88–95). London: Hutchinson.

Wilson, B., & Sparks, R. (1996). "It's gotta be the shoes": Youth, race, and sneaker commercials. *Sociology of Sport Journal, 13,* 398–427.

Chapter 16

Bodies, Subcultures and Sport

Michael Atkinson and Brian Wilson

In mainstream sociology, conceptions of 'subculture' and the 'body' have changed in recent years. The adoption of the term subculture, which has a continued association with British studies of spectacular 'resistive' youth groups of the 1970s such as Punks and Skinheads, has since been expanded to account for the ways that social groups express themselves through a variety of practices and styles. Conventional views of the body, which have focused on how bodily shape, size, appearance, movement, and experience influence and are influenced by one's interaction with others in society, have also been revised and updated. Approaches now attempt to explain the ways that the body and body image have become commodities to be sold through advertising and other discourses of influence, the ways that biological and societal 'risks' have created a perceived need to intensify the monitoring and maintenance of the body, and the ways that increasingly global cultures (where people are exposed to diverse cultural norms) have created a blurred sense of the appropriate uses/presentations of the body.

In the sociology of sport, these ideas have also received increasing attention. Research on sport subcultures has included examinations of alternative leisure groups (e.g., surfers, climbers) and mainstream sport cultures (e.g., rugby, ice hockey, and football players), work on the various social rituals and processes associated with sport involvements (e.g., initiations into sport, retirement from sport, informal norms of sport subcultural conduct), and research on the ways that sport subcultures simultaneously resist and reproduce dominant sport norms. Sport-related research on the body includes studies of self-esteem and athlete body image, body rituals and displays in sport, gender construction in sport, and more recently on the cybernetic (e.g., bio-medically and chemically enhanced) body and related issues surrounding personal risk (Cole, 1993, 1998; Rail & Harvey, 1995; Theberge, 1991; Young & White, 1995; Young, White & McTeer, 1994). However, and despite the apparent centrality of both subcultures and the body to understandings of sport/leisure involvements, we argue that these concepts, as they exist in contemporary research in the sociology of sport, could benefit from more attention to developments that have taken place in mainstream sociology and elsewhere. We also suggest that there are multiple possibilities for progressively integrating these two literatures that have not been adequately explored in the sociology of sport context to date.

These contentions are presented and developed in four sections. First, the concept of subculture as it has been used in mainstream sociology and in the sociology of sport is critically examined. Second, this is followed by a parallel overview of work on the body. Third, suggestions are offered for ways in which these concepts may be progressively integrated. The final section discusses future directions/considerations for research on subcultures and the body.

Subculture: Definitions and History

Classic definitions of the concept of subculture build on fundamental understandings of the root term 'culture'. Culture, which has traditionally meant the "peculiar and distinctive 'way of life' of the group or class" (Hall & Jefferson, 1976: 10; see also Williams, 1977), was amended by British theorists at the Centre for Contemporary Cultural Studies (CCCS) in Birmingham, England in the 1970s, who explained how culture is the 'battleground' where struggles between dominant and marginal groups take place.

Building on this explanation, Hall and Jefferson (1976: 13) defined subcultures as "subsets — smaller, more localised and differentiated structures" within the larger cultural class configuration. In this context, Hall and Jefferson (1976) suggested that (youth) subcultures are "focussed around certain activities, values, certain uses of material artefacts, territorial spaces, etc., which significantly differentiate them from the wider culture" (1976: 14). Moreover, youth subcultures were specifically characterised by their 'double articulation' — that is, their relationship to their 'parent' culture (e.g., a working class youth's relationship to working class culture) and to the dominant culture (e.g., the sometimes contentious relationship between working class culture and the dominant class culture). In this way, subcultures have been understood for both their internal configuration and their relationship to the broader society.

The British development of the concept of subculture can be traced back to earlier American explorations of the term at the University of Chicago in the 1920s and 1930s (Shaw & McKay, 1927; Sutherland, 1947), Merton's (1938) 'strain' theory, and Albert Cohen's (1955) update of Merton's theory. While American deviance/subcultural theorists focused largely on the ways that youth react to their class positioning, and the later symbolic interactionist theories of subcultural involvement (see Prus, 1996) were concerned with describing small group characteristics and micro-processes, British subcultural theorists at the CCCS in the 1970s developed a more sophisticated stance on subcultural activity, by focusing on the ways that youth *reactively* and *proactively* resist their social positioning, and express tension/displeasure in purposeful, often spectacular ways. Although there were two diverse methodological and related theoretical strands that characterised the CCCS's approach to studying youth subcultures,[1] its exponents were largely interested in how youth, particularly working class youth, creatively find 'magical solutions' that allow them to symbolically resist and (temporarily) escape from their marginalised class and occupational positions (Cohen, 1972).

According to Hall and Jefferson in their seminal volume, *Resistance Through Rituals: Youth Subcultures in Post-War Britain* (1976), it was through leisure activities (e.g., dance, drug use) and subcultural style (e.g., of music, language, hairstyle, clothing) that youth articulated their dissatisfaction with the dominant social order. In essence, these styles and activities took on oppositional meanings. Of particular significance was the CCCS's use of 'homology' and 'bricolage' as concepts to explain the logic of youth consumption and display. 'Homology' refers to the way that the various styles and actions of subculture members work together to reflect, express, and symbolise "the typical concerns, attitudes, and feelings of the social group" (Willis, 1978: 191). For example, the Skinheads' shocking shaved heads, aggressive music, and profane language aggregately represented an expression of the group's anger with their social conditions (according to CCCS theorists). 'Bricolage' is the process of taking existing social objects and giving them new (and often counter-cultural) meanings. An example of bricolage is when sport team jackets (normally worn as a symbol of team support) are used to represent gang affiliation for some youth. That is, a conventional market item is adopted and given a new and modified meaning. While not all of the research at the CCCS was focused on spectacular subcultures such as Punks and Skinheads *per se* (e.g., Willis, 1977; McRobbie, 1977), the Centre is most well-known in youth studies for its theoretical treatment of overtly stylistic displays of resistance.

The CCCS interest in the division between dominant and subordinate cultures is largely informed by the notion of 'hegemony' that was originally developed by the Italian Marxist, Antonio Gramsci (1971) (see Chapter 1), and later by the 'neo–Marxists' at the CCCS. Hegemony refers to the domination that is

[1]One strand was focused on the use of traditional ethnographic methods (e.g., Willis, 1977), while the other (Hebdige, 1979) drew from various information sources (e.g., interviews that appeared in popular music magazines, mass media reports, record albums, music lyrics), piecing together cultural artefacts from diverse genres and times and producing 'readings' of style and culture.

consented to by subordinate groups or, to put it another way, it is when the dominant class has successfully persuaded subordinate classes to accept mainstream cultural/political values. Subcultures, as subordinate groups, are important to the study of hegemonic processes because they are the groups predominantly responsible for direct opposition or resistance toward the ideology of ruling groups. Subcultures become a viable counter-hegemonic and resistant force by challenging social leadership of the hegemonic power-bloc, and by presenting alternative social ideologies and (sub)cultural practices. However, theorists often point out that such popular cultural solutions (e.g., symbolic resistance solutions) are mainly 'magical' because they do little to concretely alleviate problems experienced by the group in larger society; indeed, at times, they actually serve to reproduce existing social relations and dominant cultural ideologies (cf., Willis, 1977).

The CCCS model arguably suffered several difficulties. For example, it over-emphasised the impact of social class and to a certain extent race (largely ignoring gender and the leisure/cultural activities of females). It romanticised and glorified youth style and behaviour (e.g., finding resistance in most subcultural activities), despite the likelihood that many youth subculture members do not interpret their behaviour in the way that the theorists assumed they did. In fact, many youth potentially conform to the 'cool' alternative/subcultural norms with little consideration for the symbolic implications of their behaviour (Gruneau, 1988; McRobbie, 1987; Tanner, 1996). Furthermore, CCCS research on subcultures was overly concerned with subculture formation and representation in the United Kingdom (England, specifically), tending to overlook subcultural expressions in other, more global, contexts.

In the 1980s and 1990s, researchers such as McRobbie (1993, 1994) attempted to retain the powerful theoretical foundations of CCCS theory, while overcoming the limitations of the original class-based model. To do this, McRobbie de-emphasised the spectacular aspects of culture, concentrating instead on the ways that subcultural resistance is played out on an everyday basis. As she explained:

> If, for the moment, we deconstruct the notion of resistance by removing its metapolitical status (even when this exists in some disguised, magical, or imaginary form, as it did in CCCS theory), and if we reinsert resistance at the more mundane, micrological level of everyday practices and choices about how to live, then it becomes possible to see the sustaining, publicizing and extending of the subcultural enterprise (1993: 162).

McRobbie's position is akin to Willis' (1990) argument that 'common' youth use more subtle cultural strategies for negotiating their identities and resisting (or temporarily escaping) oppressive circumstances that frame their lives.

Recently, the term 'subculture' has been updated and revised to more adequately account for the socio-cultural and socio-historical conditions characteristic of the 1990s. For example, Muggleton (1997) has argued that with the development of more eclectic and fragmented mainstream styles, it has become difficult to resist symbolically when the distinction between alternative and mainstream symbols has become blurred. For example, shaved heads, dyed hair, ripped clothes, and/or tattoos, once considered symbols of resistance, have become commonplace and are integral to a variety of subcultural styles. Muggleton (1997), Redhead (1990, 1997a, 1997b) and others argued that the 1990s was a postmodern, post-punk period characterised by a loss of meaning (e.g., a loss of resistance), nostalgia (e.g., a return by subcultural members to music/clothing styles of the past), and unoriginality/inauthenticity. Redhead (1990) has suggested that the CCCS model was no longer appropriate for analysing 1990s culture because it overstated the extent to which subcultures are able to (or even attempt to) effectively create authentic expressions of resistance. Quite simply, subcultures of the 1990s (according to these theorists) were guided by the marketplace. Any opposition expressed by subcultural groups is usually focused on other subcultures since the dominant culture and alternative culture have become almost indistinguishable.

In summary, it is clear how the term subculture has developed from an American sociological perspective that viewed subcultures as groups that are reacting to their marginalised status (e.g., Cohen, 1955), to a symbolic interactionist perspective focused on the way groups are characterised by their insider vantage points, activities, identities, relationships, and commitments (e.g., Prus, 1996), to the early British (CCCS) subcultural theorists who focused on the proactive, spectacular forms of subcultural resistance (e.g., Hebdige, 1979). More recently, subculture has been characterised by its association with subtle forms of common, everyday resistance (e.g., Willis, 1990). Subculture has also been conceptualised in-line with a post-punk view of subcultures as non-resistant and largely consumer-oriented (e.g., Redhead, 1997a). Furthermore, postmodern 'readings' of subculture suggest that groups are unable to culturally resist because the distinctions between the oppositional and the mainstream have become increasingly blurred (e.g., Muggleton, 1997).

Subcultures and the Sociology of Sport

The history of work on subcultures in the sociology of sport reflects many of these developments. Symbolic interactionist studies on the social processes of sport involvement and socialisation in and through sport, in particular, have been widespread. In his work on interpretive approaches to sport, Donnelly (2000) outlines these developments, examines the origins and evolution of work on sport careers (Ingham, 1975), and identifies seminal work on sport-careers. This includes Weinberg and Arond's (1952) work on boxing, Stone's (1972) research on wrestling, Scott's (1968) study of horseracing, Polsky's (1969) work on pool hustling, Faulkner's (1975) examination of hockey player careers, and Haerle's (1975) study of baseball players. Perhaps most importantly, Donnelly identifies three notable trends that emerged from these early works. First, the notion of 'career', a term previously associated with more conventional occupational models of sport involvement, had become loosely defined as, "any time spent progressing in sport . . . [such as] a competitive swimmer who began at age 6, retired at age 14, and never earned any money" (Donnelly, 2000: 83). Donnelly went on to explain how subcultures were also being studied for their 'non-career'-related characteristics, such as in his own (1980) work on climbers, Albert's (1991) examination of cyclists, and Pearson's (1979) study of surfers.

Second, Donnelly points out how research on subcultures in the 1980s used more in-depth qualitative methodologies to provide detailed, 'thick' descriptions (Geertz, 1973) of subcultural groups and contexts. Third, sport subculture research began to draw on British subcultural theory as part of a move toward providing critical analyses of sport subcultures. In other words, studies were now focusing not only on the cultural characteristics of subcultures and the meanings people give to their activities, but also on the ways that sport may be both constraining and enabling for participants, and how sport subcultures simultaneously resist and reproduce existing patterns of social domination. As part of this trend, a corpus of research on subcultural struggle that adopted this critical position emerged, including work on rugby players (Young, 1983), football players (Foley, 1990), women's hockey (Theberge, 1995), male locker room culture (Curry, 1991), boxing (Sugden, 1987), soccer hooligans (Giulianotti, 1995), bodybuilders (Klein, 1993), and skateboarders (Beal, 1995). So, while studies focused on processes of involvement are still a central part of the sociology of sport (see Coakley & Donnelly's (1999) edited volume *Inside Sport*), this critical focus underlies many of the recent ethnographies of sport subcultures.[2]

[2]Donnelly has also pointed out that while most of these studies were conducted in Canada, Britain and the United States, France has also produced a series of studies influenced primarily by the work of Pierre Bourdieu (e.g., Wacquant's (1995) work on boxing).

Although this breadth of critical ethnographic work on sport is impressive, more contemporary 'mainstream' approaches to studying subcultures, such as those adopted by McRobbie, Muggleton, and Redhead, are rarely acknowledged or implemented. For example, in Crosset and Beal's (1997) recent examination of, and proposal for clarifying the concept of subculture, these recent formulations were not considered. While the adoption of postmodern theoretical perspectives has become commonplace in the sociology of sport generally, seldom is this literature linked with sport subculture research.

Extant studies in the sociology of sport advancing current understandings of sport subcultures beyond the conventional subculture model include Foley's (1992) work on writing ethnographies, where the author argued for pushing the boundaries of the ways we write about subcultural groups — encouraging ethnographers to make themselves 'more visible' in portrayals of subcultural groups, and to acknowledge their influence on the setting and groups under study (cf., Bruce, 1998; Richardson, 2000). Some recent work has also usefully acknowledged the contradictory character of subcultures in a highly commercial era. Humphries (1997, 1998), for example, explored the tentative and conditional resistances (e.g., 'commercialised rebellion') that exist in the now 'pseudo–mainstream' snowboard culture.

Wheaton and Tomlinson's (1998) work on female windsurfers is one of the few studies of sport subcultures that examines the complexities of identity (e.g., the various female, sport-related identities) from various theoretical positions (borrowing from feminist, postmodern, and symbolic interactionist theory). Redhead (1997a, 1997b), Reynolds (1998) and others drew parallels between British football (soccer) culture and the rave subculture, arguing that in 1980s Thatcherism, the "soccer match and the warehouse party offered rare opportunities for the working class to experience a sense of collective identity" (Reynolds, 1998: 64).

Following these and other projects in the sociology of sport, we suggest that the field would benefit from more attention: to mainstream sociology and cultural studies-based conceptions of subtle resistance; to the contradictory nature of resistance in postmodern times; and, to the relationship between cultural authenticity (and inauthenticity) and the oppositional potential of subcultural groups. Of course, many of these themes are played out in other areas of the sociology of sport, particularly in work on the body and body culture. Before examining the ways that the sport subculture literature can be integrated with and borrow from work on the body, an overview of mainstream and sport-related conceptions of the body is provided.

Bodies and Sociology

It has been 18 years since Bryan Turner's seminal work, *The Body and Society* (1984), helped to rejuvenate an interest in corporeality within sociology. Following Turner's lead, social theorists have become increasingly mindful of the myriad of ways in which bodies are constructed, understood, and ultimately integrated in representing identities in the 'high modern era' (Shilling, 1993). As a result, the sociology of the body has become one of the most substantively and theoretically *avant garde* sub-fields within the parent discipline. As an offshoot of the growing interest in the body, sociologists of sport have also been particularly attentive to bodily construction and representation. In introducing several of the ways that sociologists of sport study the body, it is useful to briefly mention three principal reasons why sociologists (in general) have become more cognizant of embodied experience.

First, the contemporary explosion of sociological research on the body has been inspired by several prevalent sociological theories. While authors may debate the specific aetiology underlying the growth in research on the body, it is evident that feminist theories (Bordo & Jaggar, 1989; Butler, 1993), Foucault's post-structuralism (1977, 1988, 1990), Baudrillard's postmodernism (1983), phenomenology (Merleau–Ponty, 1962), Goffman's dramaturgy (1959), and figurational/process sociology (Elias, 1978; Elias & Dunning, 1986) are enduring influences. Emphasising different foci of inquiry and promulgating various interpretations of the body, all of these theoretical perspectives unequivocally advocate studying the body as a 'text of culture' (Bordo, 1989: 14) — how bodily shape, size, appearance, movement, and experience influence (and are influenced by) one's interaction with others in society (Bourdieu, 1984).

Second, the proliferation of research on the body has been driven by a recognition that recent socio-cultural transformations in Western societies have fostered new sensibilities about appropriate bodily construction and display. For example, Giddens (1991) suggests that there is escalating disbelief in dominant cultural 'meta-narratives' (e.g., religious, medical–scientific) that impose universal guidelines for understanding the 'nature' of the body. Correspondingly, individuals are now more reflexive and simultaneously uncertain about what their bodies can be used to achieve, evidenced by the veritable gamut of non-traditional manipulations and (re)presentations of the body which Westerners currently explore (Atkinson, 2001). Expanding upon this idea, Maguire (1999) suggests that the cross-cultural exchange intrinsic to globalisation processes effectively erodes barriers between cultures. As a result, traditional uses/understandings of the body in the West have become questioned and uncertainties about the body exacerbated. Similarly, Beck (1991) mentions that the post/high-modern epoch is characteristically an era of risk in which individuals are more conscious of the multiplying social (e.g., discrimination, poverty, crime) and biological (e.g., AIDS, pollution) perils that underscore a demand for meticulous bodily monitoring, maintenance, and defence. Finally, Featherstone (1991) argues that the heightened attention granted to the body both inside and outside of the academy is a direct consequence of Western cultural attitudes about the body as a site of commodity consumption. As the physical body can be altered, modified, or re-structured with the aid of a wide range of commercial products, individuals are able to explore a multitude of ways for manipulating their bodies and social selves (Shilling, 1993).

Third, in seeking to develop analytical templates for studying bodily practices and experiences, sociologists have proposed several typologies of the body. In effect, these efforts encourage sociologists to become aware of the existing research on the body and the sociological essence of corporeality. Turner's (1984) description of the body as a site of order and nexus of culture was one of the first attempts to develop such an analytical framework. As perhaps the second major, and most often cited, typology of the body, Frank's (1991) model of bodily control elucidates the ways in which bodies are central in shaping individual and cultural understandings of the world. More recently, Maguire's (1993) synthesis of research on the body identifies limitations in both Turner's (specifically) and Frank's typologies, while suggesting an agenda for future research on the body. Even though each typology is ultimately oriented toward explicating a particular sociological theory (functionalism, phenomenology, and figurational/process sociology respectively), each is central in bringing together seemingly disparate substantive research on the body, while highlighting the principality of the body in all sociological analysis.

In sum, the sociological discipline appears to have been affected by the contemporary boom in research on the body. Although there is an apparent concern for issues of corporeality across sub-disciplines within sociology, several have stood out as pioneers in this area of research — including the sociology of sport. Of central importance, then, is what impact the sociology of sport has had on research on the body in the parent discipline, and the sociological impact of the types of theory and research on the body sociologists of sport have tendered in the past two decades.

Bodies and the Sociology of Sport

Since athletic events consist of moving, performing, and competing bodies, one of the clear mandates of the sociology of sport is the analysis of how bodies are 'used' in and through sport and play. It is not surprising, then, that sociologists of sport would extensively study both athletes' relationships with their bodies and what an athletic body can symbolise within a given culture.

Much of the early sports-related research on the body tended to focus on how one's 'body image' is inextricably linked to one's notion of self. Describing the body as a social fact, Heinemann (1980) called for a need to examine how 'body ethos' develops in sport — how participation in sport affects one's level of satisfaction with one's body. Pursuing this idea, a series of sports studies in the 1980s utilised survey questionnaires and quantitative strategies to explore how athletes' identities and self-esteem may be bolstered because of their socially-admired athletic appearance and enhanced physical capabilities (Balogun, 1987; Bednarek, 1985). Also inspired by Goffman's (1959) discussion of how individuals present images of the self through bodily performance and display, sports researchers began to appreciate the ways in which athletes' identities are partly shaped by their relationships with, and understandings of, their own bodies.[1]

In the 1990s, a distinctive turn to the writings of Michel Foucault (1977, 1988, 1990) heralded in a new era of sports research on the body (see Chapter 12). Deciphering the origins of Foucault's influence, Rail and Harvey (1995) argue that his work was imported by sociologists of sport directly, and indirectly filtered into sports research on the body via a burgeoning interest in cultural studies or Foucault-informed feminist theory. Focusing on the concepts of discourse, power, and discipline in particular, sociologists of sport adopting a Foucauldian perspective have attended to the ways in which individual bodies are both socially 'enabled' and 'constrained' through participation in sport. Along these lines, it has been argued that athletes may reproduce or resist hegemonic codes about the body via their involvement in sport — in particular, by challenging dominant ideologies about gender (Cole, 1993; Hall, 1996), sexuality (Pronger, 1998), and race/ethnicity (Andrews, 1993). In studying how the body is disciplined into a passive or 'docile' entity in sport (and is thus 'constrained'), or how athletes may confront hegemonic ideologies and discourses through body use and display in sport (and is thus 'enabled'),

---

[1]In many ways, a pastiche of interests and theories about the body began to develop in the 1980s. Important during this period was the work of Elias (1978); Elias and Dunning (1986); Bourdieu (1984), and several streams of feminist thought (see Theberge, 1991).

research informed by Foucault's writings has been central in explaining how dominant cultural norms, values, and beliefs are literally inscribed and contested on the physical body.

Even more recently, sociologists of sport have debated the nature of the postmodern/high-modern sports body. One issue in the debate involves the varying ways in which athletes' bodies are progressively becoming 'cybernetic'. For example, in addressing how pain/injury is routinely rationalised as an aspect of athletic involvement (Hoberman, 1992; Young & White, 1995), sport scholars have uncovered the litany of bio-medical and chemical methods employed for re-structuring, modifying, enhancing, or rehabilitating 'broken-down' athletic bodies. Referring to this as a defining feature of the 'post-human' era in sport (Cole, 1998; Haraway, 1991; Pronger, 1998; Rintala, 1995), sociologists of sport have been keenly critical of the social, physical, emotional, and psychological risks associated with cybernetic reconstitution of the body.

Body image, disciplined/resistant bodies, and the cybernetic body are only three of the dominant areas of inquiry in sport-related research. Summarising extant studies on the body in a very general way, Maguire (1993) notes that sociologists of sport tend to focus on the 'symbolic', 'commodified', 'biomedical', or 'disciplined' nature of athletes' bodies. Using this framework to review existing research, he argues that sociologists of sport have mainly analysed these dimensions of the body in isolation, failing to consider how each dimension may relate to the others. Unfortunately, this practice does not promote cross-comparison between existing studies on the body, nor does it typically encourage sociologists of sport to integrate studies of the body in previously untapped ways.

One might argue that given the relative lack of cross-comparison between case studies (and loyal adherence to specific, mainly postmodern, theories about the body), research within the sociology of sport is currently in a state of stagnancy. While sociologists of sport have unquestionably furnished the parent discipline with a rich collection of research on the body, we must question the usefulness of treating the current/dominant research on the body as unproblematic. A more fruitful and innovative approach to the study of the body might involve linking research on sporting practices to research *within* and *outside* of the literature on sport (including as yet untapped or under-developed areas, issues, theories, and concepts). This might help to promote continued research on the body while pushing sociologists of sport to develop and consider new theories about bodily experience.

Therefore, we now move on to consider how research on the body could be linked to the study of sports subcultures. As we have noted, in viewing the concept of 'subculture' as a similarly rich but under-used sociological tool, studies of the body employing the concept of subculture could explore how 'subculture' may be re-invigorated/revived in the sociology of sport. However, we also propose that research efforts integrating subculture and the body might simultaneously press for much needed cross-comparison and theoretical innovation within research on the body.

Subcultures and Bodies: Toward Integration

In this section, we explore the possibilities for integrating conceptions of 'subculture' and the 'body', and discuss the benefits of these connections for the study of sport-related practices and involvements. In doing so, we wish to broaden current understandings of the way that sport is both enabling and constraining for its participants, and provide frameworks and study ideas for future examinations of substantive topics related to subcultures and the body. Within this context, a series of theoretical and methodological suggestions are made.

The first suggestion for integration derives from two related strands of research. The first of these includes work on the ways that members of sport subcultures express themselves with (and resist constraints imposed by the dominant culture through) relatively 'free' or liberating body movements. The second strand examines how bonds established within many subcultural groups relate to shared bodily experiences (experiences that are not completely regulated/monitored by mainstream discipline agents). From these developments emerge a multitude of possibilities for demonstrating how an integration of subculture and body theory/literature can enhance our understanding of sport-related cultural phenomena. For example, while body theorists might be concerned with the ways that alternative sport groups (e.g., skateboarders, snowboarders, and surfers) are disciplined and controlled because they have been positioned to inhabit monitored mainstream spaces (e.g., skateboard parks, snowboard hills, and designated surf areas), subcultural theorists would point out how, through bodily movement and expression, subcultural groups can at least partially subvert these outside controls. An innovative skateboard trick, for example, is a free expression. Although this action might be only *symbolically* subversive, it represents at least a temporary escape or sense of empowerment through movement. In this instance, it is clear how, on the one hand, notions of subcultural resistance could benefit from an increased sensitivity to a Foucauldian depiction of surveillance (Best, 1997), while on the other, a Foucauldian reading of the disciplined sporting body could be informed by a more succinct understanding of how subcultures actually do 'win space' within ever-present social constraints. Both lines of enquiry must explore the enabling and constraining aspect of human co-existence.

In making this argument, we are not suggesting that subcultural theory does not acknowledge structural constraints (it manages this through notions of hegemony), or that Foucauldian theory does not account for resistance (it does, although resistance is not privileged or well-defined in Foucault's theory of power — Hall, 1996). We are indicating, however, that by integrating a well-developed model of subcultural resistance with Foucault's impressive portrayal of and perspective on the disciplined body, a compelling departure point for analysis is created. In this instance, we look to Pronger's (1998) work on the ways that sport can be a vehicle for resisting homophobia as a template for understanding subcultural resistance and the body.

Building on this suggestion for an integrated understanding of the ways that bodies and subcultures are oppressed by and resistant to *external forces* of domination, we consider here the integrative potential for work that focuses on how subcultural groups are characterised by their *self-imposed* subcultural rules, norms, and rituals (that often requires sacrifice, conformity and self-discipline). On the one hand, then, 'body-rules' imposed on subculture members (such as the play-through-pain ethic) can be understood from a symbolic interactionist perspective on sport subcultures that is sensitive to the ways that bodily sacrifices and rituals are often part of negotiating identity during one's career as a subcultural member (cf., Donnelly & Young, 1988). This interactionist position could also be contextualised in a Foucauldian theory of power that considers how these rules of self-control are part of a method/structure of oppression whereby the body is disciplined through the seemingly indirect "polymormous techniques of power" (Foucault, 1990: 11) that provide ever-present, undifferentiating controls of body expression and image (Cole, 1993; Theberge, 1991).

Consider also how the structuralist theory that underlies 'readings' of bricolage and homology in work on subcultural style is also replete with similar understandings of body modification in sport (Atkinson, 1999). For example, while subcultural theorists usually study the oppositional potential of specific body-related styles (e.g., postures, clothing, hairstyles, or tattoos), body analysts usefully point out the ways that the body has become a site of consumption, monitoring, and a symbol of oppression (and the ways in which subculture members are duped into desiring a particular 'look') (Featherstone, 1991). Although inevitable tensions exist about the most appropriate perspective for analysing body (sub)cultures, we argue that it is crucial to acknowledge how subcultural style, as it is articulated through the body, can be understood from these various positions, and then to privilege a particular 'reading' with reference to empirical data (such as interviews, participant observation, or media analysis findings).

Work on sport subcultures that focuses on the ways that risk/pain/injury is routinised, rationalised, and glorified (e.g., Young & White, 1995; Young, White, & McTeer, 1994) is also conducive to a conceptual integration. In this context, bodybuilding is an excellent example of a case study that has benefited from various conceptual treatments, although these treatments have been essentially unintegrated in the literature. Some work has examined the subculture of bodybuilders (e.g., Klein, 1993; Scott & Morgan, 1993) and the norms of steroid use and risk, while other studies have adopted a critical feminist perspective on the 'bigger-is-better' doctrine that guides segments of the subculture (White & Gillett, 1994). Still other work has explained how the exaltation of the 'cybernetic' body is consistent with postmodern trends toward the breaking down of barriers between technology and humanity (e.g., Cole, 1998; Rintala, 1995), and the ways that super-human (hyper-real) images of body-success are ever-present in mass-mediated body culture (e.g., MacNeill, 1998). Clearly, by organising and integrating various works on bodybuilding (and other similarly treated topics), a more comprehensive and responsible understanding could be developed.

Bourdieu's (1984) argument that people's preferences for certain leisure activities/experiences are reflections of their class positioning also has implications for the subculture and body literatures (see Chapter 10). On the one hand, Bourdieu's (1978, 1984) suggestion that leisure preferences or 'tastes' are embodied, and that the 'pleasure preferences' that attract individuals to certain leisure activities are intricately related to social positioning (i.e., social class) was a momentous recognition in the context of sport and body literature because it emphasised how bodily experience is somewhat determined. In the sociology of sport, work by Wilson and Sparks (1996) examined how Black and non-Black adolescent male basketball fans (what they refer to as 'sneaker cultures') evaluated the importance of athletic apparel (e.g., basketball shoes) as social and cultural symbols. Although not emphasised in Wilson and Sparks' (1996) study, this sort of work lends itself to an integrated analysis of the body and subculture because of its potential to examine how body displays/symbols are interpreted by and internalised in class, race, gender and age-defined subcultural communities/taste cultures.

The final suggestion concerns the integration of methodological approaches. Studies of subcultures, as noted previously, have generally adopted ethnographic methodologies in an attempt to gain rich, detailed understandings of subcultural groups (Prus, 1996). Those who study body culture have been more inclined to view the body as a 'text', and to interpret various changes in body presentation and body norms using semiotic analysis. Semiotic analysis is a technique that requires the researcher to explain the implicit and explicit meaning of any text (e.g., newspaper articles, television commercials, or in this case, (re)presentations of the body). In many ways, semiotic analysis and ethnographic research are inseparable in practice, since analyses of data gathered ethnographically inevitably require the researcher to interpret and piece together information about a social group. However, semiotic analyses of the body in the sociology of sport often fail to account for the actual interpretations that subculture members give to their own body representations/experiences (as opposed to the meanings that academic 'semioticians' give) (Hall, 1996). By the same token, much of the work that has usefully examined body culture using qualitative methods could also be enriched with complementary 'reading' of the body and body expression. Of course, not all research aims to, nor should aim to, use multiple methods. Nevertheless, and following Willis' (1978) argument for 'clustering' methods, we suggest that combining semiotic analysis and ethnographic inquiry in work on the body and subcultures could be a productive venture.

Conclusion

The literatures on sports subcultures and sports bodies demonstrate ambitious attempts to better understand social life through the study of sport practices. However, if researchers begin to pursue ways of combining the conceptual themes shared within the two streams of literatures, together they may stimulate growth in the sociology of sport and push researchers to consider both subcultures and the body in new and innovative ways. Ultimately, one of our goals as researchers in the sociology of sport is to build bridges within the discipline, while continuing to lobby for insightful connections between seemingly disparate substantive fields and agendas.

We conclude by re-emphasising the need to integrate concepts such as subculture and the body at this *historical juncture* — a time characterised by increasing global cultures and by postmodern movements. This call for integration is, in our opinion, both an optimistic and ambivalent stance, but in all cases, necessary. On the one hand, we find it encouraging that authors in the 1990s pushed the boundaries of the sociology of sport in a way that required more sophisticated approaches to the study of sport in various societies. Our argument for integrating subculture and body literatures is an attempt to advance this movement towards more well rounded, multidisciplinary research. On the other hand, researchers responsive to socio-cultural developments of the 1990s and beyond *are compelled to*, by virtue of the increasingly mass mediated and fragmented nature of the social world, consider more diverse (and at times, integrated) frameworks. Research on Internet culture is probably the best example of this connection. Not only is it *necessary* to consider how mainstream work on Internet subcultures (Porter, 1997) could be extended to include sport-related studies of sport fan (sub)cultures in 'chat rooms' or 'newsgroups' (Mitrano, 1999) or the use of '(fan)zines' by alternative sport groups, it is also important to examine how these cultural mutations have impacted our understanding of the positioning of (virtual) bodies within an increasing global sport media/marketing culture.

Moreover, and in addition to these substantive suggestions for studying cultural phenomena, a main goal of this chapter is to emphasise the need to be theoretically flexible and prepared for the continued development of sport subcultures and sporting bodies in the twenty-first century. While the conceptual tools reviewed here are a useful point of departure, these tools can be optimised only if sensitivity to contemporary developments in other relevant fields, and to the potential for conceptual integration within the sociology of sport, are maintained.

References

Albert, E. (1991). Riding the line: Competition and co-operation in the sport of bicycle racing. *Sociology of Sport Journal, 8,* 341–360.

Andrews, D. (1993). Desperately seeking Michel: Foucault's geneaology, the body, and critical sport sociology. *Sociology of Sport Journal, 10,* 148–167.

Atkinson, M. (2001). Miscreants, malcontents and minesis: Sociogenesis, psychogenesis, and the Canadian tattoo figuration. Unpublished doctoral dissertation, University of Calgary, Canada.

Atkinson, M. (1999). Is the body back in?: Examining the modified body in the sociology of sport. North American Sociology of Sport Annual Meetings, Cleveland, Ohio, 3–6 November.

Balogun, J. (1987). Body image before and after assessment of physical performance. *The Journal of Sports Medicine and Physical Fitness, 27,* 343–344.

Baudrillard, J. (1983). *Simulations.* New York: Semiotext(e).

Beal, B. (1995). Disqualifying the official: An exploration of social resistance through the subculture of skateboarding. *Sociology of Sport Journal, 12,* 252–267.

Beck, U. (1991). *Risk Society: Towards a New Modernity.* London, UK: Sage.

Bednarek, J. (1985). Pumping iron or pulling strings: Different ways of working out and getting involved in body-building. *International Review for the Sociology of Sport, 20,* 239–261.

Best, B. (1997). Retheorizing resistance. In: S. Redhead (ed.), *The Clubcultures Reader: Readings in Popular Cultural Studies* (pp. 18–35). Malden, MA: Blackwell Publishers.

Bordo, S. (1989). The body and the reproduction of femininity: A feminist appropriation of Foucault. In: S. Bordo and A. Jaggar (eds), *Gender/Body/Knowledge: Feminist Reconstructions of Being and Knowing* (pp. 13–33). New Brunswick, NJ: Rutgers University Press.

Bordo, S., & Jaggar, A. (1989). *Gender/Body/Knowledge: Female Reconstructions of Being and Knowing*. New Brunswick, NJ: Rutgers University Press.

Bourdieu, P. (1978). Sport and social class. *Social Science Information, 17*, 819–840.

Bourdieu, P. (1984). *Distinction: A Social Critique of the Judgement of Taste*. Cambridge, MA: Harvard University Press.

Bruce, T. (1998). Postmodernism and the possibilities for writing "vital" sport texts. In: G. Rail (ed.), *Sport and Postmodern Times* (pp. 3–19). Albany, New York: State University of New York Press.

Butler, J. (1989). *Gender Trouble: Feminism and the Subversion of Identity*. London, UK: Routledge.

Coakley, J., & Donnelly, P. (1999). *Inside Sports*. New York: Routledge.

Cohen, A. (1955). *Delinquent Boys: The Culture of the Gang*. New York: Free Press.

Cohen, P. (1972). Subcultural conflict and working-class community. *Working Papers in Cultural Studies, 2*, 5–52.

Cole, C. (1993). Resisting the canon: Feminist cultural studies, sport sociology and technologies of the body. *Journal of Sport and Social Issues, 17*, 77–97.

Cole, C. (1998). Addiction, exercise, and cyborgs: Technologies of deviant bodies. In: G. Rail (ed.), *Sport and Postmodern Times* (pp. 261–275). Albany, New York: SUNY.

Crosset, T., & Beal, B. (1995). The use of 'subculture' and 'subworld' in ethnographic works on sport: A discussion of definitional distinction. *Sociology of Sport Journal, 14*, 73–85.

Curry, T. (1991). Fraternal bonding in the locker room: A profeminist analysis of talk about competition and women. *Sociology of Sport Journal, 8*, 119–135.

Donnelly, P. (2000). Interpretive approaches to the sociology of sport. In: J. Coakley and E. Dunning (eds), *Handbook of Sports Studies* (pp. 77–92). London, UK: Sage.

Donnelly, P. (1980). *The Subculture and Public Image of Climbers*. Unpublished doctoral dissertation, University of Massachusetts, Amherst, MA.

Donnelly, P., & Young, K. (1988). The Construction and Confirmation of Identity in Sport Subcultures. *Sociology of Sport Journal, 5*, 223–240.

Elias, N. (1978) [1939]. *The Civilizing Process Volume 1: The Development of Manners*. New York: Pantheon Books.

Elias, N., & Dunning, E. (1986). *Quest for Excitement: Sport and Leisure in the Civilizing Process*. Oxford, UK: Basil Blackwell.

Faulkner, R. (1975). Coming of age in organizations: A comparative study of the career contingencies of musicians and hockey players. In: D. Ball and J. Loy (eds), *Sport and Social Order* (pp. 521–558). Reading, MA: Addison–Wesley.

Featherstone, M. (1991). The body in consumer culture. In: M. Featherstone, M. Hepworth and B. Turner (eds), *The Body* (pp. 157–195). London, UK: Sage.

Foley, D. (1990). The great American football ritual: Reproducing race, class, and gender inequality. *Sociology of Sport Journal, 7,* 111–135.

Foley, D. (1992). Making the strange familiar: Writing critical sports narratives. *Sociology of Sport Journal, 9,* 36–47.

Foucault, M. (1977). *Discipline and Punish: The Birth of the Prison.* London, UK: Penguin Books.

Foucault, M. (1988). Technologies of the self. In: L. Martin, H. Gutman and P. Hutton (eds), *Technologies of the Self: A Seminar with Michel Foucault.* London, UK: Tavistock.

Foucault, M. (1990). *The History of Sexuality, Volume 1: An Introduction.* New York: Vintage Books.

Frank, A. (1991). For a sociology of the body: An analytical review. In: M. Featherstone, M. Hepworth and B. Turner (eds), *The Body* (pp. 36–102). London, UK: Sage.

Geertz, C. (1973). *The Interpretation of Cultures.* New York: Basic Books.

Giddens, A. (1991). *Modernity and Self Identity.* Cambridge, UK: Polity Press.

Giulianotti, R. (1995). Football and the politics of carnival: An ethnographic study of Scottish fans in Sweden. *International Review for the Sociology of Sport, 30,* 191–224.

Goffman, E. (1959). *Presentation of Self in Everyday Life.* Garden City, New York: Doubleday.

Gramsci, A. (1971). *Selections from Prison Notebooks.* London, UK: Lawrence & Wishart.

Gruneau, R. (1988). Introduction: Notes on popular culture and political practice. In: R. Gruneau (ed.), *Popular Cultures and Political Practices* (pp. 11–32). Toronto, ON: Garamound Press.

Haerle, R. (1975). Career patterns and career contingencies of professional baseball players: An occupational analysis. In: D. Ball and J. Loy (eds), *Sport and Social Order* (pp. 457–519). Reading, MA: Addison–Wesley.

Hall, A. (1996). *Feminism and Sporting Bodies: Essays on Theory and Practice.* Champaign, IL: Human Kinetics.

Hall, S., & Jefferson, T. (1976). *Resistance Through Rituals: Youth Subcultures in Post-War Britain.* London, UK: Hutchison.

Haraway, D. (1985). A manifesto of cyborgs: Science, technology, and socialist–feminism in the 1980s. *Socialist Review, 80,* 65–107.

Haraway, D. (1991). *Simians, Cyborgs, and Women: The Reinvention of Nature.* London, UK: Free Association Books.

Hebdige, D. (1979). *Subculture: The Meaning of Style.* New York: Methuen & Company.

Heinemann, K. (1980). Sport and the sociology of the body. *International Review of Sport Sociology, 15,* 41–56.

Hoberman, J. (1992). *Mortal Engines: The Science of Performance and the Dehumanisation of Sport.* New York: Free Press.

Humphries, D. (1997). Shredheads go mainstream?: Snowboarding and alternative youth. *International Review for the Sociology of Sport, 32*, 147–160.

Humphries, D. (1998). *Boarders, Punks and Ravers: An Introduction to the History of Commercialized Rebellion.* Unpublished Masters thesis, University of Otago, Dunedin, New Zealand.

Ingham, A. (1975). Occupational subcultures in the work world of sport. In: D. Ball and J. Loy (eds), *Sport and Social Order* (pp. 333–389). Reading, MA: Addison–Wesley.

Klein, A. (1993). *Little Big Men: Bodybuilding Subculture and Gender Construction.* Albany, New York: State University of New York Press.

MacNeill, M. (1998). Sex, lies, and videotape: The political and cultural economies of celebrity fitness videos. In: G. Rail (ed.), *Sport and Postmodern Times* (pp. 163–184). Albany, New York: State University of New York Press.

Maguire, J. (1993). Bodies, sportscultures and societies: A critical review of some theories in the sociology of the body. *International Review for the Sociology of Sport, 28*, 33–52.

Maguire, J. (1999). *Global Sport: Identities, Societies, Civilisations.* Cambridge, UK: Polity Press.

McRobbie, A. (1977). *Working-Class Girls and the Culture of Femininity.* Unpublished Masters thesis, Centre for Contemporary Cultural Studies, University of Birmingham, UK.

McRobbie, A. (1987). Settling accounts with subcultures: A feminist critique. In: T. Bennett, G. Martin, C. Mercer and J. Woollacott (eds), *Culture, Ideology and Social Process* (pp. 111–123). London: B.T. Batsford Ltd.

McRobbie, A. (1993). Shut up and dance: Youth culture and changing modes of femininity. *Cultural Studies, 7*, 406–426.

McRobbie, A. (1994). *Postmoderism and Popular Culture.* London, UK: Routledge.

Merleau–Ponty, M. (1962). *The Phenomenology of Perception.* London, UK: Routledge & Kegan Paul.

Merton, R. (1938). Social structure and anomie. *American Sociological Review, 3*, 672–682.

Miller, L., & Penz, O. (1991). Talking bodies: Female bodybuilders colonize a male preserve. *Quest, 43*, 148–163.

Mitrano, J. 1999. The "sudden death" of hockey in Hartford: Sports fans and franchise relocation. *Sociology of Sport Journal, 16*, 134–154.

Muggleton, D. (1997). The Post-subculturalist. In: S. Redhead (ed.), *The Clubcultures Reader: An Introduction to Popular Cultural Studies* (pp. 186–203). Malden, MA: Blackwell.

Pearson, K. (1979). *The Surfing Subcultures of Australia and New Zealand.* St. Lucia: University of Queensland Press.

Polsky, N. (1969). *Hustlers, Beats, and Others.* New York: Anchor.

Porter, D. (1997). *Internet Culture.* New York: Routledge.

Pronger, B. (1998). Post-sport: Transgressing boundaries in physical culture. In:

G. Rail (ed.), *Sport and Postmodern Times* (pp. 277–298). Albany, New York: SUNY Press.

Prus, R. (1996). *Symbolic Interaction and Ethnographic Research: Intersubjectivity and the Study of Human Lived Experience*. Albany, New York: SUNY Press.

Rail, G., & Harvey, J. (1995). Body at work: Michel Foucault and the sociology of sport. *Sociology of Sport Journal, 12*, 164–179.

Redhead, S. (1990). *End of the Century Party: Youth and Pop Towards 2000*. New York: St. Martin's Press.

Redhead, S. (1997a). *Subcultures to Clubcultures: An Introduction to Popular Cultural Studies*. Malden, MA: Blackwell.

Redhead, S. (1997b). *The Clubcultures Reader: Readings in Popular Cultural Studies*. Malden, MA: Blackwell.

Reynolds, S. (1998). *Generation Ecstasy: Into the World of Techno and Rave Culture*. Toronto, ON: Little, Brown & Company.

Richardson, L. (2000). New Writing Practices in Qualitative Research. *Sociology of Sport Journal, 17*, 5–20.

Rintala, J. (1995). Sport and technology: Human questions in a world of machines. *Journal of Sport and Social Issues, 19*, 6–75.

Scott, M. (1968). *The Racing Game*. Chicago, IL: Aldine.

Scott, S., & Morgan, D. (1993). *Body Matters*. London, UK: The Falmer Press.

Shaw, C., & McKay, H. (1927). *Juvenile Delinquency and Urban Areas*. Chicago, IL: The University of Chicago Press.

Shilling, C. (1993). *The Body and Social Theory*. London, UK: Sage.

Stone, G. (1972). Wrestling: The great American passion play. In: E. Dunning (ed.), *Sport: Readings from a Sociological Perspective* (pp. 301–335). Toronto, ON: University of Toronto Press.

Sugden, J. (1987). The exploitation of disadvantage: The occupational subculture of the boxer. In: J. Horne, D. Jary and A. Tomlinson (eds), *Sport, Leisure, and Social Relations* (pp. 187–209). London, UK: Routledge & Kegan Paul.

Sutherland, E. (1947). *Principles of Criminology*, (3rd edition). Philadelphia: Lippincott.

Tanner, J. (1996). *Teenage Troubles: Youth and Deviance in Canada*. Toronto, ON: Nelson Canada.

Theberge, N. (1991). Reflections on the body in the sociology of sport. *Quest, 43*, 123–134.

Theberge, N. (1995). Gender, sport and the construction of community. *Sociology of Sport Journal, 12*, 389–402.

Turner, B. (1996). *The Body and Society*. London, UK: Sage.

Wacquant, L. (1995). Pugs at work: Body capital and bodily labour among professional boxers. *Body and Society, 1*, 65–93.

Weinberg, S., & Arond, H. (1952). The occupational culture of the boxer. *American Journal of Sociology, 57*, 460–469.

Wheaton, B., & Tomlinson, A. (1998). The changing gender order in sport?: The case of windsurfing subcultures. *Journal of Sport and Social Issues, 22*, 252–274.

White, P., & Gillett, J. (1994). Reading the muscular body: A critical decoding of advertisements in Flex magazine. *Sociology of Sport Journal, 11,* 18–39.

Williams, R. (1977). *Marxism and Literature.* Oxford, UK: University of Oxford Press.

Willis, P. (1977). *Learning to Labour: How Working Class Kids Get Working Class Jobs.* New York: Columbia University Press.

Willis, P. (1978). *Profane Culture.* London, UK: Routledge.

Willis, P. (1990). *Common Culture.* San Francisco, CA: Westview.

Wilson, B., & Sparks, R. (1996). 'It's gotta be the shoes': Youth, race and sneaker commercials. *Sociology of Sport Journal, 13,* 398–427.

Young, K. (1983). *Subculture of Rugby Players: A Form of Resistance and Incorporation.* Unpublished Masters thesis, McMaster University, Hamilton, Ontario.

Young, K., & White, P. (1995). Sport, physical danger, and injury: The experiences of elite women athletes. *Journal of Sport and Social Issues, 19,* 45–61.

Young, K., White, P., & McTeer, W. (1994). Body talk: Male athletes reflect on sport, injury and pain. *Sociology of Sport Journal, 11,* 175–194.

About the Editors and Contributors

David L. Andrews received his Ph.D from the University of Illinois, Champaign–Urbana, and is currently Associate Professor at the University of Maryland. He is an assistant editor of the *Journal of Sport and Social Issues*, and has published on a variety of topics related to the critical analysis of sport.

Michael Atkinson is an Assistant Professor of Sociology at the Memorial University of Newfoundland, where he teaches in the areas of sport, deviance, and criminology. His major research interests include the study of criminal violence in sport, sport-related forms of body modification and sports subcultures. He has published in the areas of sport and commercialisation, deviance in sport, and body modification cultures.

Becky Beal received her doctoral degree in Physical Education at the University of Northern Colorado (1992) and her Bachelor's degree in History from Pomona College (Claremont, California) (1985). She is currently Associate Professor in the Department of Sport Sciences at the University of the Pacific (Stockton, California). She teaches a variety of courses related to the sociology of sport, and her research interests include gender relations and alternative sports. She is an active member of the North American Society for the Sociology of Sport, and has served on the editorial board for the *Sociology of Sport Journal*.

Rob Beamish is Associate Dean in the Faculty of Arts and Science at Queen's University, Canada. His scholarly interests are in social theory, with a special emphasis on the development of Karl Marx's ideas, and in Sociology of Sport, with a primary focus on sport as work. Rob is also actively involved in the Canadian minor ice hockey system. His publications include *Q: What do you do for a living? A: I'm an athlete* (1988), *Marx, Method and the Division of Labour* (1992), and "The Making of the Manifesto Socialist Register" (1998).

Douglas Booth teaches courses in the history of sport and sports policy in the

School of Physical Education at the University of Otago, New Zealand. He is the Book Review Editor of *International Sports Studies*, and serves on several editorial boards, including the *International Journal of the History of Sport* and the *Journal of Sports History*. Douglas is the author of *The Race Game: Sport and Politics in South Africa* (1998) and a co-author, with Colin Tatz, of *One-Eyed: A View of Australian Sport* (2000).

Hart Cantelon is Associate Professor in the School of Physical and Health Education, Queen's University, Canada. In addition to his academic interests in the Sociology of Sport, Hart has coached Canadian inter-collegiate football and youth ice hockey for almost 25 years. His current research interests lie in the area of globalisation of sport.

Peter Donnelly is a Professor in the Faculty of Physical Education and Health at the University of Toronto, and Director of the Centre for Sport Policy Studies. He taught at schools in England before receiving his PhD in Sport Studies from the University of Massachusetts in 1980. Peter has served in various offices for professional organisations in the Sociology of Sport, including the Editorship of the *Sociology of Sport Journal* (1990–94), and was President of the North American Society for the Sociology of Sport (1999–2000). He co-edited *Sport and the Sociological Imagination* (with Nancy Theberge, 1999) and *Inside Sports* (with Jay Coakley, 1999). The second edition of his collection, *Taking Sport Seriously* was published in 2000.

Eric Dunning is a founding figure in the development of the Sociology of Sport. He has authored and edited several books in the area, most notably on sport and violence. These include *Barbarians, Gentlemen and Players: A Sociological Study of the Development of Rugby Football* (with Kenneth Sheard, 1979), *Quest for Excitement: Sport and Leisure in the Civilising Process* (with Norbert Elias, 1986), and *Sport Matters: Sociological Studies of Sport, Violence, and Civilisation* (1999). Eric is Professor Emeritus in Sociology, at the University of Leicester, and holds a Visiting Professorship at University College, Dublin.

Jeremy W. Howell received his Ph.D from the University of Illinois, Champaign–Urbana, and is currently Assistant Professor in the Sports and Fitness Management Graduate Program at the University of San Francisco. His research interests focus on the production, promotion and consumption of sports and fitness spectacles, goods and experiences. Jeremy has extensive health and fitness industry experience, and serves on the advisory boards of a number of Bay Area health, fitness and technology corporations. He is also on the editorial board of the *Journal of Sport and Social Issues*.

Alan G. Ingham obtained his Master's degree in Physical Education from Washington State University and his Ph.D in Sociology from the University of Massachusetts (1978). He has taught at the University of Washington (1974–1984) and is currently a Professor of Sport Studies at Miami University, Ohio. Alan has co-edited *Sport in Social Development* (with John Loy), and has published articles in journals such as the *Journal of Experimental and Social Psychology, Journal of Social History, Theory, Culture & Society, Sociology of Sport Journal*, the *International Review for the Sociology of Sport*, and *Quest*. From 1984 to 1988, he was the President of the International Committee for the Sociology of Sport (ICSS/ISSA).

Steven J. Jackson received his Ph.D from the University of Illinois, Champaign–Urbana, and is currently a Senior Lecturer in Sport and Leisure Studies in the School of Physical Education, University of Otago, New Zealand. Steve's sport-related research interests include globalisation, media, violence and advertising. He is a member of the editorial board of the *Sociology of Sport Journal* and co-author (with David Andrews) of two forthcoming books, *Sport Stars: Public Culture and Private Experience* and *Sport, Culture and Advertising: Identities, Commodities and the Politics of Representation*.

Joanne Kay received her Ph.D. in sociology of sport from Université de Montréal. Her dissertation examines the social signification of adventure sport from the perspective of the social theory of P. Bourdieu. Kay's teaching and research areas include gender, new sport culture, media and the corporate/sport complex. She is an elite level triathlete and has raced as a member of Canada's national team. She is also a freelance journalist whose features have appeared in Canadian newspapers such as *The National Post, The Montreal Gazette*, and *The Ottawa Citizen*.

Alan Klein is Professor of Sociology and Anthropology at Northeastern University. Alan has spent the past 20 years researching the culture and politics of sport, primarily Latin American baseball and the subculture of bodybuilding. He is the author of *Sugarball: The American Game, the Dominican Dream* (1991), *Little Big Men: Gender Construction and Bodybuilding Subculture* (1993), and *Baseball on the Border: A Tale of Two Laredos* (1997). His forthcoming book is entitled *Growing the Game: Globalisation and Baseball*.

Suzanne Laberge is a Professor in the Department of Kinesiology at the Université de Montréal where she teaches sociology of sport and physical activity. She has published on gender relations, doping in sport, extreme sport, and social theory in journals such as *Men and Masculinities, Sociologie et Sociétés, Sociology of Sport Journal*, and *Society and Leisure*. She first used Bourdieu's social theory in her Ph.D research in anthropology, and currently employs it critically in research relating to health practice, body culture, gender and social class.

John Loy is a founding figure in the development of the Sociology of Sport. His academic interests lie broadly within the socio-history of body culture and sport. John has published widely on a variety of sports-related issues, and has served on numerous executive and editorial boards in the field. He is presently Adjunct Professor in the Department of Anthropology and Sociology at the University of Rhode Island.

Joseph Maguire is Professor in the Sociology of Sport in the Department of Physical Education, Sports Science and Recreation Management at Loughborough University. He is President of the International Sociology of Sport Association. Joseph has served on a number of journals in the field and has published widely on topics such as national identity, sports labour migration, and globalisation. His single authored book is *Global Sport: Identities, Societies, Civilizations* (1999) and his latest book is *Sport Worlds: A Sociological Perspective* (2002) with co-authors Jarrie, G., Mansfield, L. and Bradley, J.

Louise Mansfield is a Senior Lecturer and teaches courses in the Sociology of Sport at Christ Church University College, Canterbury, UK. Her doctoral studies combine figurational sociology with feminism, and focus on active women and their embodied experiences of sport and exercise. Currently, her research involves life history, fieldwork and in-depth interviews.

Howard L. Nixon II is Professor and Chairperson in the Department of Sociology, Anthropology and Criminal Justice at Towson University in Maryland. Howard earned his doctorate in Sociology from the University of Pittsburgh. He has published a number of books and journal articles, primarily in the Sociology of Sport area. His major research interest over the past several years has been social and cultural aspects of pain and injury in sport.

Geneviève Rail teaches sociology of physical activity, the body and health at the University of Ottawa's School of Human Kinetics and Institute of Women's

Studies. Her research interests include gender and sexuality. She uses feminist cultural studies, post-structuralism, post-modernism and post-colonialism in her critique of institutions related to the body (health systems, sport, and the media). She has published in several journals, both in French and in English, and has edited an anthology entitled *Sport and Postmodern Times* (1998, SUNY Press).

Kimberly S. Schimmel is an Associate Professor in the Sociology of Sport at Kent State University. She has published on topics including professional sport franchise relocation, production–consumption relations in sport, and regime theory and sport and related urban development. She is co-editor of a forthcoming book, *Sport and Global Political Economy* (in press). Kim's current research focuses on 'fandom' in both local and global contexts.

Jennifer Smith Maguire was a doctoral fellow in Sociology at the Graduate Center of the City University of New York, and of the Social Sciences and Humanities Research Council of Canada. Her research examines how consumer body culture educates us in the duties of self-care and self-improvement. Through the lens of fitness, she discusses how a host of authorities make claims upon how we care for and improve upon our bodies and our selves.

Shona Thompson is currently teaching in the Departments of Sport and Exercise Science and Sociology at The University of Auckland. She is a New Zealander who has lived and studied in both Canada (BPE and MA, University of Alberta) and Australia, where she completed her Ph.D in Sociology and Women's Studies at Murdoch University. This research has been published in the book, *Mother's Taxi: Sport and Women's Labor* (1999).

Brian Wilson is an Assistant Professor in the socio-managerial area of the School of Human Kinetics at the University of British Columbia, Canada. His research has focused on topics such as the rave subculture, youth culture in recreation/ 'drop-in' centres, media portrayals of race and gender, and audience reactions to these portrayals. His current work on alternative media and social movements includes a study of the 'anti-jock' Internet-based youth movement.

Kevin Young is currently Senior Research Fellow in the Department of Physical Education, Sports Science and Recreation Management at Loughborough University UK; in 2003 he will be Associate Professor in the Department of Sociology at the University of Calgary, Canada. He has published on a variety of sports-related topics such as violence and subcultural identity, and is the co-editor (with Philip White) of *Sport and Gender in Canada* (1999). He has served on the editorial boards of *Sociology of Sport Journal, Avante*, and *Soccer and Society*, and on the executive board of the North American Society for the Sociology of Sport.

Author Index

Subject Index